Tories, Dons, and Rebels

Tories, Dons, and Rebels

The American Revolution in British West Florida

J. Barton Starr

Sponsored by the American Revolution
Bicentennial Commission of Florida

A University of Florida Book

The University Presses of Florida
Gainesville / 1976

Library of Congress Cataloging in Publication Data

Starr, Joseph Barton, 1945–
 Tories, dons, and rebels.

 "A University of Florida book."
 Bibliography: p.
 Includes index.
  1. West Florida—History—Revolution, 1775–1783.
 2. American loyalists—West Florida. I. Title.
 E263.F6S72   973.3'14   76–28953
 ISBN 0–8130–0543–4

TYPOGRAPHY BY CANON GRAPHICS
TALLAHASSEE, FLORIDA

PRINTED BY THE ROSE PRINTING COMPANY, INCORPORATED
TALLAHASSEE, FLORIDA

Preface

For many years the history of British West Florida was largely untold. In the mid-1940s, however, Cecil Johnson of the University of North Carolina wrote a number of articles which culminated in 1943 in the publication of *British West Florida, 1763–1783*. Although there were earlier works by Kathryn Abbey, Peter J. Hamilton, Wilbur H. Siebert, Clarence Carter, William Beer, John Caughey, and others, Johnson's *British West Florida* most clearly pointed the way toward more in-depth study of the area. Clinton N. Howard's *The British Development of West Florida, 1763–1769* was published in 1947 by the University of California Press. *Governor Johnstone and Trade in British West Florida, 1764–1767*, by John D. Born, was published in 1968. The only other book-length work on West Florida to date is Robert V. Haynes, *The Natchez District and the American Revolution* (1976). A number of other edited works dealing with British West Florida have appeared, such as Robert R. Rea and Milo Howard's *The Memoire Justificatif of the Chevalier Montault de Monberaut: Indian Diplomacy in British West Florida, 1763–1765*. In recent years numerous articles dealing with various phases of the history of British West Florida have also been written. The most prolific writer in the field at present is Robert R. Rea of Auburn University, with more than a dozen articles dealing with West Florida under British control. Articles occasionally appear by other authors such as John D. Born, Cecil Johnson, and Robin Fabel.

Most of the literature, including all of Robert Rea's articles, deals with such topics as the king's agents, military deserters, medicine, or the early development of West Florida as a British province. There is no totally adequate treatment of West Florida in the American Revolution. Cecil Johnson devotes only one brief chapter to it, and, other than a few articles dealing with specific events such as James Willing's raid, until recently the revolutionary period has been almost ignored. By far the best treatment of the Revolution in West Florida appeared in 1975: J. Leitch Wright, Jr., *Florida in the American Revolution*. James A. James, *Oliver Pollock* (1937), and John Walton Caughey, *Bernardo de Gálvez in Louisiana, 1776–1783* (1934), present pictures of the American Revolution from the viewpoints of an enterprising American and an active Spanish governor.

The reason for the lack of work on the American Revolution from the British point of view is simple. There is an almost overwhelming amount of material—both manuscript and published—which deals either directly or indirectly with British West Florida, the major source of information being the Colonial Office Papers in the Public Record Office in London. But a cursory glance at the Colonial Office Papers, the Sir Thomas Gage Collection, and the Sir Henry Clinton Collection at the William L. Clements Library indicates that the vast majority of available information deals with the much-researched (but far from exhausted) earlier period of development of West Florida as a British province.

West Florida was important in the American Revolution and the concomitant Anglo-Spanish war which broke out in 1779. In the American Revolution, West Florida was frequently considered in terms of navigation of the Mississippi River, Spanish aid to the rebellious colonies, and as a refuge for the harried loyalists. Throughout the Revolution there was almost constant debate between the British and their Spanish neighbors in Louisiana over use of the Mississippi River. Fundamental to the whole argument was whether the Americans—as rebellious subjects of Great Britain—were entitled to the privilege of navigating the Spanish-controlled portion of the river. From the outbreak of the Revolution, Americans sought—and very often obtained—assistance from the friendly Spanish officials of New

Orleans. The British in West Florida, of course, interpreted such aid to the "rebels" as a violation of "international law."

Established as a loyalist haven in 1775, the colony of British West Florida received refugees from all of the colonies in rebellion during and after the American Revolution. But the colony was loyal essentially by default; there was little pressure to decide allegiance until war with Spain made loyalty a foregone conclusion. In terms of an overall imperial war, West Florida was important as a diplomatic pawn before, during, and after the American Revolution. In a real sense, the loyalty of West Florida can be attributed to national pride against the neighboring Spanish "menace," for the semi-mediocre British period in West Florida was a respite from almost total mediocrity and mismanagement under Spanish control.

Throughout this work the spelling, capitalization, and punctuation in quotations have been modernized in order to allow for easier reading and comprehension.

I wish to extend my thanks to Professor J. Leitch Wright, Jr., for his critical assistance in preparing the manuscript. I am also indebted to Professor Robert R. Rea; Professor William S. Coker; Professor Robert Calhoon; Troy State University; and the staffs of the Library of Congress, William L. Clements Library, National Archives, Robert M. Strozier Library at The Florida State University, Public Archives of Canada, P. K. Yonge Library of Florida History at the University of Florida, New York Public Library, Alabama State Archives, Mississippi State Archives, Mobile Public Library, Archives of the Diocese of Mobile, and the John C. Pace Library of the University of West Florida. I also wish to express special appreciation to my wife, Rebekah, for her encouragement, critical assistance, and typing; too often she had to live with Peter Chester, James Willing, John Campbell, Elias Durnford, and many other obscure eighteenth-century men and women, along with her husband.

The Bicentennial Commission of Florida also provided financial support for the publication of this volume. Without its assistance this book would have been further delayed. I am deeply grateful for its generosity.

To many others too numerous to name who assisted in this work, my sincerest gratitude is due.

To Rebekah

Contents

1. "The Horrors of an Unknown Land"   1
2. "The Spirit of What Is There Called Liberty"   35
3. "The Late Rascally Transaction of Mr. Willing"   78
4. "To Prevent Any Surprize or Sudden Mischief"   122
5. "By Beat of Drum"   142
6. "The Lustre of the British Arms"   161
7. "We Are Now Tolerably Prepared"   175
8. "Vigor and Spirit to the Last"   193
9. "Conquered by Its Own Force"   216
10. "The Betrayed Loyalists of America" or Loyal
    by Default?   225
11. Conclusion   241
Appendix: Note on Loyalist Historiography   245
Bibliography   247
Index   263

1

"The Horrors of an Unknown Land"

The hollow beat of the drum and the flutter of regimental flags reflected the gloomy atmosphere that hung over the shell-pocked landscape like the humidity that precedes a thunderstorm on the Gulf Coast. At precisely 3:00 P.M., the British forces under the command of Major General John Campbell somberly marched across five hundred yards of earth that two days earlier had been the scene of agony and defeat. With the surrender of British flags and arms to the Spanish forces of General Bernardo de Gálvez, British West Florida ceased to exist, the victim of imperial war. The date was May 10, 1781.

The preceding eighteen years are a story of settlement, growth, bickering, intrigue, optimism, disillusionment, and defeat. British West Florida came into existence in 1763 at the end of the French and Indian War as a result of cessions by the Spanish and French governments to the victorious British. Spain ceded Florida to England in return for Havana, which the British had captured. A year earlier, France had provided West Florida with a formidable opponent on the Gulf of Mexico by ceding Louisiana to Spain.

Although the motivation of the English in taking Florida instead of retaining Cuba is not totally clear, ownership of West Florida, and particularly Pensacola, gave the British a port on the Gulf of Mexico which could be protected by British sea power. To the Spanish, Pensacola was just one more outpost to guard; to the British, Spanish West Florida, along with the

1

French grant east of the Mississippi River, represented control of almost half of the Gulf of Mexico.[1] The land cessions provided in the peace treaty "indicate the ascendancy in British colonial affairs of the imperialists, the group which held that the needs of the growing empire should receive paramount consideration even when they conflicted with the time-honored tenets of mercantilism."[2] Mercantile interests were not totally incompatible with those of the imperialists, however, as there were economic benefits to be gained from the new possessions. It was expected that West Florida would serve as a center for trade with the Spanish, in which British manufactured goods would be exchanged for Spanish bullion. The creation of this market and the establishment of political and military power in West Florida would deflect trade from New Orleans, thus hampering and perhaps even destroying the Spanish commercial influence at New Orleans.[3] The fact that most of the anticipated results were illusory does not detract from the original motivation.

As a result of the land cessions, the size of the British Empire increased significantly, as did problems of land policy. Word of Pontiac's rebellion reached England in late July or early August 1763, and the Board of Trade recommended the immediate issuance of a proclamation to prevent further settlements in Indian territory and to open East and West Florida for settlement. King George III approved the recommendation, with the provision that boundaries and matters pertaining to the Indian trade should be dealt with.[4] On October 7, 1763, the king issued the Proclamation of 1763, whose primary purpose was to soothe the feelings of the Indians by reserving lands exclusively for

1. Clinton N. Howard, "Alleged Spanish Grants in British West Florida," pp. 74–75.

2. Cecil S. Johnson, *British West Florida, 1763–1783*, pp. 1–2. Lawrence Henry Gipson also briefly discusses the early years of British West Florida in his monumental *The British Empire before the American Revolution*, 9:200–231.

3. Clarence E. Carter, "Some Aspects of British Administration in West Florida," p. 370.

4. Representation of the Board of Trade, August 5, 1763, in *Documents Relating to the Constitutional History of Canada, 1759–1791*, ed. Adam Shortt and Arthur G. Doughty, 1:151–53; Earl of Halifax to the Board of Trade, Sept. 15, 1763, ibid., pp. 153–55; Clarence E. Carter, "The Beginnings of British West Florida," p. 321.

their use. Secondarily, the proclamation was to provide a means of expansion that would be attractive to settlers and Indians alike. The British ministry hoped that the settlement of East Florida, West Florida, and Canada would relieve the pressure along the frontier line of settlement by providing the settlers with an alternative to the Indian territory now closed to settlement.

Following recommendations from the Board of Trade, the proclamation set the boundaries of West Florida: "The government of *West Florida*, bounded to the southward by the *Gulf of Mexico*, including all islands within six leagues of the coast from the river *Apalachicola* to the lake *Pontchartrain*; to the westward by the said lake, the lake *Maurepas*, and the river *Mississippi* which lies in the 31 degrees north latitude, to the river Apalachicola, or Chattahoochee; and to the eastward by the said river."[5] Newly appointed Governor George Johnstone's commission included the same boundaries as those set forth in the proclamation. The Board of Trade had had little accurate information about West Florida, and it had drawn the northern boundary at the thirty-first parallel, based on "Mitchell's Map of North America." It soon became apparent that this boundary was not sufficient; Governor Johnstone notified the Board of Trade that the established boundary did not include Mobile and several settlements on the Mississippi.[6] While the governor's information was incorrect and the boundary did in fact include Mobile, it excluded much of the surrounding territory and, in particular, much of the rich land on the Mississippi River. Consequently, the Board of Trade recommended to the king that West Florida "shall be bounded to the north by a line drawn from the mouth of the River Yazoo, where it unites with the Mississippi, due east to the River Apalachicola, by which we humbly conceive every material settlement depending upon West Florida will be comprehended within the limits of that government."[7] Accordingly, further orders were sent to John-

5. "By the King, a Proclamation. George, R.," pp. 36–37.

6. Commission of George Johnstone, West Florida Papers, Library of Congress (microfilm located at The Florida State University, reel 1), hereafter cited as West Florida Papers. Carter, "The Beginnings of British West Florida," p. 317; Johnson, *British West Florida*, p. 6.

7. Board of Trade to the king, Mar. 23, 1764, Colonial Office Group, Class 5, Piece 599, Public Record Office, hereafter cited as C.O. 5/599.

stone incorporating this change, which moved the boundary to approximately 32° 28′ north latitude.[8]

The Royal Proclamation of October 7, 1763, had set forth in general terms the colony's basic governmental structure, and the commission and instructions of Governor George Johnstone provided the structural details. The executive branch consisted of a governor, a lieutenant governor, and an appointed council. The legislature was a bicameral body with the lower house elected by the people and the council serving as the upper house. The basis of the judiciary was English common law, and the major officer was a crown-appointed chief justice. The government of West Florida was basically like that of any royal colony, with one major exception. Some eighteenth-century crown colonies were partially subsidized, but because West Florida was a thinly settled frontier region, Parliament totally financed the civil establishment with an annual grant ranging from £ 3,900 to £ 7,200.[9] This annual grant prevented much of the usual dissension over control of the purse that was prevalent in royal colonies, but did not preclude quarrels between the legislative and executive branches.

Approximately a year of military government passed before this form of civil government went into effect.[10] The British had wasted no time in taking over possession of West Florida: the Treaty of Paris had been signed on February 10, 1763, and by early August, Lieutenant Colonel Augustine Prevost and the Third Battalion of the Royal American Regiment of Foot arrived in Pensacola. Prevost met with Spanish Governor Diego Ortiz

8. Further Commission of George Johnstone, June 6, 1764, West Florida Papers, reel 1.

9. A copy of Johnstone's instructions is in C.O. 5/201. For a published copy of the commission and instructions, see James A. Padgett, ed., "Commission, Orders and Instructions Issued to George Johnstone, British Governor of West Florida, 1763–1767"; Cecil S. Johnson, "Pensacola in the British Period: Summary and Significance," pp. 264–65. The figures on the amounts of the civil establishment are taken from Johnson, British West Florida, p. 21. For a yearly breakdown of the civil establishment, see C.O. 5/571–98; the annual estimates are scattered throughout these volumes.

10. Clinton N. Howard, "The Interval of Military Government in West Florida." See also Clinton N. Howard, The British Development of West Florida, 1763–1769, pp. 11–19. Sending troops to West Florida as a permanent establishment was part of an overall policy change calling for a standing army in time of peace. For a discussion of this policy and the "Southern Brigade" or "Florida Brigade," see Charles L. Mowat, "The Southern Brigade: A Sidelight on the British Military Establishment in America, 1763–1775."

Parilla, who immediately surrendered possession of the town, acting on orders from the king of Spain. About a month later, the Spanish left Pensacola, taking with them 108 Christian Yamasee Indians.[11] In the meantime, on July 19 Major General William Keppel had ordered Major Robert Farmar to occupy the French post at Mobile, "which was [in 1763] really the entrepot of West Florida and the gateway to all the territory of the old southwest." Farmar (with the Twenty-second and Thirty-fourth regiments) took possession of Mobile and Fort Conde on October 20, 1763, and renamed the latter Fort Charlotte. There were 350 inhabitants in Mobile and 90 others in the district.[12]

On November 22, 1763, a force of thirty men of the Thirty-fourth Regiment under the command of Lieutenant Thomas Ford took possession of Fort Tombeckby, a post located about one hundred leagues north of Mobile on the Tombigbee River. Renamed Fort York, the post would have a checkered history as British troops twice occupied and abandoned it. Indians and traders continued to use the post throughout the British period, despite the fact that the fort soon fell into ruins. The British never occupied Fort Toulouse because of the difficulty involved in the supplying and reinforcing of it in the event of an Indian war.[13]

Various reports of military officers to their superiors recorded the first British reactions to West Florida. Colonel Augustine Prevost's opinion of Pensacola was mixed. While he faced a town whose buildings were in ruins and were slowly being reclaimed by the forest and surrounding swamps, he saw some

11. Clinton N. Howard, "The Military Occupation of British West Florida, 1763," pp. 182–83, 185. For a copy of Lieutenant Colonel Prevost's orders, see W[illiam] K[eppel] to Lt. Col. Prevost, July 3, 1763, C.O. 5/582. See also "Copy of the King of Spain's Instructions to the Governor of Florida to deliver up that Province to England," Apr. 18, 1763, C.O. 5/548. For a full discussion of the transfer of West Florida to the British, see Robert L. Gold, *Borderland Empires in Transition: The Triple-Nation Transfer of Florida*.

12. Howard, "Military Occupation," pp. 187, 193, 197. For a copy of Major Farmar's orders, see W[illiam] K[eppel] to Major Farmar, July 19, 1763, C.O. 5/582; "Report of the State of East and West Florida," in Lt. Col. James Robertson to Gen. Thomas Gage, Mar. 8, 1764, C.O. 5/83. Mobile served as the capital of West Florida during the period of military government.

13. For a full discussion of the history of the ill-fated Fort York, see Robert R. Rea, "The Trouble at Tombeckby"; Lt. Col. [James] Robertson to Gage, Mar. 8, 1764, C.O. 5/83. For a fuller discussion of Fort Toulouse, see Daniel H. Thomas, "Fort Toulouse: The French Outpost at the Alibamos on the Coosa," although this article deals almost exclusively with Fort Toulouse in the French period.

possibility of improvement for the future.[14] Major William Forbes of the Thirty-fifth Regiment complained of the bark huts which formed the principal dwellings in Pensacola.[15] Captain Philip Pittman was blunt: "When we took possession of Pensacola, in the latter end of the year 1763, it consisted of a fort and a few straggling houses; the fort was constructed of high stockades, enclosing in a very small space a house for the governor, and several miserable huts, built with pieces of bark, covered with the same materials, and most of them without floors; so that in the summer they were as hot as stoves, and the land engendered all sorts of vermin: in these wretched habitations the officers and soldiers dwelt."[16]

The situation which Major Robert Farmar found in Mobile was no better. The fort was in an advanced state of decay, and the people of the town claimed most of the land necessary for a military post.[17] Throughout the British period, reports from military officers, civil officers, and travelers were varied: some praised the beauties and promises of West Florida ("the emporium, as well as the most pleasant part of the New World"); some declared the province to be a barren swamp.[18]

From the moment the British landed in West Florida, complaints about the unhealthiness of the province were prevalent. Although in the long run West Florida was as healthy as the other southern English provinces, such was not the case in the first few years. Troops arriving in West Florida in late summer were not previously acclimatized, the high stockades enclosing the barracks prevented the free circulation of air, Pensacola and

14. Prevost to [Secretary of War], Sept. 7, 1763, C.O. 5/582.
15. Major William Forbes to [Secretary of War], Jan. 30, 1764, cited in Johnson, *British West Florida*, p. 9.
16. Philip Pittman, *The Present State of the European Settlements on the Missisippi [sic]*, ed. Frank Heywood Hodder, p. 25.
17. Robert Farmar to Earl of Egremont, Jan. 24, 1764; Farmar to Secretary of War, n.d.; Farmar to Secretary of War, Jan. 24, 1764, C.O. 5/582. See also "Report of the State of East and West Florida," in Lt. Col. James Robertson to Gage, Mar. 8, 1764, C.O. 5/83; Robert R. Rea, ed., "A New Letter from Mobile, 1763."
18. *Gentleman's Magazine* 35 (1765):77. Some of the best-known contemporary accounts are [Lord Adam Gordon], "Journal of an Officer Who Travelled in America and the West Indies in 1764 and 1765," in *Travels in the American Colonies*, ed. Newton D. Mereness, pp. 365–453; William Bartram, *Travels Through North and South Carolina, Georgia, East & West Florida*; Bernard Romans, *A Concise Natural History of East and West Florida*; Pittman, *Present State of the European Settlements on the Missisippi*.

Mobile were surrounded by swamps and stagnant water, and sanitary conditions were almost unknown. While Albert James Pickett in his *History of Alabama* blames the high mortality rate on "the English population [which] generally, lived too fast, converting day into night, and sporting their lives away in dissipation,"[19] and Peter J. Hamilton writes that the "excesses of the soldiers brought the place into unnecessary discredit on the score of health,"[20] the conditions and climate of West Florida were more at fault. As the British rebuilt the forts and towns, conditions improved, soldiers arrived during the late fall of the year to allow for the necessary acclimation period, and the mortality and sickness rate declined considerably. But in the first years, West Florida was truly a "grave-yard for Britons," the major diseases being yellow fever, malaria, dysentery, typhoid, and typhus. The Thirty-first Regiment landed in Pensacola in August 1765, and by September 14, "above 1/4 of the soldiers [were] dead (owing to their unhospitable situation in relation to barracks & other conveniences) and 1/5 of the inhabitants."[21]

Mobile was equally unhealthy. James Gray, surgeon of the Twenty-first Regiment, reported that all of the men were well when the troops landed in August 1765, but that in 1765 alone 171 men had died and 698 were sick with "Fevers & Agues, Putrid Fevers & Fluxes, Asthma's, and Scurvy." These figures do not include women and children who died or were sick during the same period. After January 1766, the number of sick and dead declined quickly as the soldiers became acclimated, conditions improved, and cool weather replaced the late summer heat. By November 1766, the regiment was recording no deaths.[22] Reports reached the home government as late as 1772,

19. Quoted in Robert R. Rea, "1763—The Forgotten Bicentennial: An Historiographic Commentary," p. 289.
20. Peter Joseph Hamilton, *Colonial Mobile*, pp. x–xi.
21. "Govr. Johnstone, Septr. 14th" [1765], C.O. 5/218; Robert R. Rea, " 'Graveyard for Britons,' West Florida, 1763–1781," p. 348.
22. James Gray (Surgeon) to Major James Chissolm, commanding officer of the Twenty-first Regiment at Mobile, enclosed in Chissolm's letter to Major General Harvey of Mar. 22, 1767, C.O. 5/167. One resident of West Florida reported that "There's not a more healthful town in all America" than Pensacola. He blamed Mobile for the sickness in Pensacola: "An ague is not known here, except it's brought from Mobile, which is more sickly." Jonathan Ogden, "Pensacola in 1770," pp. 7–13.

however, that Mobile "has been remarkably unhealthy ever since it was settled, insomuch that most of the settlers have removed to other parts of the country."[23]

Governor George Johnstone received his commission and instructions in the fall of 1763, but it was not until October 1764 that he arrived in West Florida. In the interim the military establishment was in complete control of the new province. One of the first problems facing the military after taking possession of the various posts in the province was the adjustment of the relations with the former inhabitants. Before the end of the period of military rule, 112 of the former residents (mainly French) who remained in West Florida had taken oaths of allegiance to the British government. Another problem facing the military regime was the necessity of forming at least a temporary Indian strategy. Because of Pontiac's War, which had spread over the Northwest but had not yet physically touched the South, the British continued to give presents and maintain trade as their basic Indian policy.[24]

It was also during this interval of military rule that the British conceived the idea of clearing the Iberville River in order to give themselves a passage from the Mississippi River to the Gulf of Mexico through the Iberville River, Lake Maurepas, and Lake Pontchartrain. This passage would allow free access to the British possessions on the Mississippi in time of peace or war by eliminating the journey up the Mississippi by way of Spanish-controlled New Orleans. The British poured much time, effort, and money into this project, but after about ten years of uncoordinated activity, the Iberville still was not

23. Gage to Hillsborough, Mar. 6, 1772, C.O. 5/89. For a full and interesting discussion of health and medicine in West Florida, see Rea, " 'Graveyard for Britons,' " and Laura D. S. Harrell, "Colonial Medical Practice in British West Florida, 1763–1781."

24. For a full discussion of this year of military rule, see Howard, "Military Government." The problem of the Indians during the British period in West Florida is almost inseparable from the problem of the Indians in the South as a whole. In this study the Indians will be discussed only as they relate to the development, progress, or results of the American Revolution in West Florida. The best overall summary of Indian diplomacy as it relates to the American Revolution is James H. O'Donnell III, *Southern Indians in the American Revolution*. Also important in understanding the Indians in West Florida are John Richard Alden, *John Stuart and the Southern Colonial Frontier . . . 1754–1775*, and Clarence E. Carter, "British Policy towards the American Indians in the South, 1763–1768."

navigable. The coming of the American Revolution, which occupied the attentions of the British ministry, finally precluded the attempt to open a channel.[25]

During the year of military rule in West Florida, the British occupied the colony, established the posts, made improvements (however poor and temporary), instituted a temporary Indian policy, and welcomed a large number of immigrants to the province. All the activities of this first year amounted, however, to little more than reactions to situations and problems which arose in the process of establishing a new colony. It remained for the coming civil government to make more lasting improvements and gains for the health, prosperity, and peace of the colony. Ultimately, success was achieved only in the matter of health, as efforts toward prosperity and peace (internally and externally) proved to be illusory.

George III appointed George Johnstone governor of West Florida on November 20, 1763. Opinions of Johnstone varied greatly. Charles Strachan, a Mobile merchant and fellow Scotsman, regarded Johnstone as "too hot" for West Florida,[26] while Colonel David Wedderburn described Johnstone as "the meek, moderate, patient, ill-treated Johnstone; and really I could not have believed, that any man, would have submitted so quietly, as he has done, to the treatment, he has met with."[27] More typically, Johnstone was seen as a "brawling Scot" of a "belligerent and overbearing manner" whose "bickerings with military officers and civilians kept the colony in turmoil until he left Pensacola in 1767."[28]

Johnstone was not ready to leave England until late summer 1764, when he finally set sail in the transport *Grampus*, loaded with Indian presents as well as his personal belongings. His

25. For a good discussion of the proposed channel, see Douglas Stewart Brown, "The Iberville Canal Project: Its Relation to Anglo-French Commercial Rivalry in the Mississippi Valley, 1763–1775." The most important single primary source for a discussion of this subject is the Sir Thomas Gage Papers, William L. Clements Library.

26. John D. Born, Jr., "Charles Strachan in Mobile: The Frontier Ordeal of a Scottish Factor, 1764–1768," p. 38. In the past, historians credited the Earl of Bute with recommending Johnstone's appointment to George III. The story is dispelled in Robin Fabel, "Governor George Johnstone" (Ph.D. diss.), pp. 17–18.

27. David Wedderburn to Alexander Wedderburn, Apr. 15, 1765, quoted in Robert R. Rea, "Outpost of Empire: David Wedderburn at Mobile," p. 222.

28. Johnson, *British West Florida*, p. 60; Born, "Charles Strachan in Mobile," p. 24; John Richard Alden, *The South in the Revolution, 1763–1789*, p. 121.

arrival at Pensacola on October 21 signaled the end of the
military regime and the beginning of civil government in West
Florida. Within ten days Johnstone had evaluated the province
which was his responsibility:[29] "It appears to me that the only
circumstances wanted to complete the prosperity of the colony
are first a sufficient force to command respect from the Indians
& secondly, some clear intelligent instructions to His Majesty's
ships for permitting the commerce of Spanish vessels who may
bring bullion or such other merchandizes as cannot interfere
with our commodities."[30]

A number of problems faced Johnstone upon his arrival. He
had first to establish civil government to replace military rule.
Mobile and Pensacola were in great need of repair, and he had
to devise some system for the distribution of town lots. It
seemed evident that many of the French of Louisiana, who were
unhappy about the transfer of Louisiana to Spain, would with
some encouragement come to the British side of the Mississippi. Finally, it was essential that Johnstone develop friendly
relations with the powerful tribes of Indians within the borders
of West Florida.

Johnstone approached these problems with his characteristic
energy and dispatch. After he appointed members of the council
and other provincial officials, the governor and council spent
much of their time hearing petitions and granting lands. Encouraging the French to move from Louisiana to British West
Florida was a scheme which demanded the attention of every
governor in West Florida during the British period,[31] for they
frequently received word "that half the inhabitants on the other
side would pass the Mississippi if there were an establishment
for their protection."[32]

29. Clinton N. Howard, "Governor Johnstone in West Florida," pp. 281–82.
For a detailed discussion of Johnstone's administration, see this work. See also
Clinton N. Howard, "Colonial Pensacola: The British Period"; Johnson, British
West Florida, pp. 24–60. While he left England on the Grampus, Johnstone
reported he changed ships en route and arrived on the Nautilus. Johnstone to
the Secretary, Sept. 3, Oct. 31, 1764, C.O. 5/574.

30. Johnstone to "the Secry" [Halifax], Oct. 31, 1764, C.O. 5/574. See also
Johnstone to John Pownal, Feb. 19, 1765, ibid.

31. Minutes of the Council, Nov. 24, Nov. 27, Dec. 12, 1764, Jan. 7, 1765,
C.O. 5/625, Records of the States of the United States of America, Library of
Congress in association with the University of North Carolina (microfilm located
at The Florida State University, West Florida, reel 1), hereafter cited as RSUS.

32. Johnstone to [?], Feb. 19, 1765, C.O. 5/218. While land distribution will

Governor Johnstone's commission and instructions authorized him, with the advice of the council, to summon an elected representative assembly when deemed necessary. Until such a body met, the governor and council were responsible for the necessary regulations for governing West Florida. A memorial requesting that he call an assembly was presented to Johnstone on February 7, 1766, by a fourteen-man grand jury. It concluded that an assembly "alone can give content to a free people, & remove those jealousies and difficulties ever attended on an imperfect form of government."[33] Johnstone presented this petition to the council, who advised that, because of the number of inhabitants necessary to form an assembly and the necessary property and other qualifications for its members, "such an establishment was as yet impracticable."[34]

Five months later some of the inhabitants of Mobile again petitioned for an assembly. The council decided that in view of the need for various laws and the doubtful legality of the governor's and council's authority to enforce penalties on their regulations, Johnstone should call for the election of an assembly. Consequently, he issued such a proclamation on August 18, 1766. Because of the limited population, the franchise was extended to all who owned a freehold. The call provided for the election of six representatives from Pensacola, six from Mobile, and two from newly established Campbell Town. The first assembly gathered on November 3, 1766, in Pensacola and, after some brief formalities, it quickly proceeded to regular legislative business. The activities of the assembly reflected the frontier nature and local needs of West Florida, for the laws which the legislature passed dealt with regulating slaves and indentured servants, cleaning the streets of Pensacola, restraining drunkenness, encouraging foreigners to settle in West Florida, granting duties to support government, and preventing masters of vessels from taking debtors from the colony. The assembly also sent an address to the Board of Trade reporting the condi-

---

be discussed more fully in relation to settlement later in this study, no effort will be made to go into the minutiae involved in land policy. For a discussion of land policy, see Howard, *British Development of West Florida*; Johnson, *British West Florida*, pp. 115–31.

33. "Memorial of the Grand Jury requesting the Governor to call an Assembly," Feb. 7, 1766, C.O. 5/574.

34. Minutes of the Council, Feb. 25, 1766, C.O. 5/625, RSUS, reel 1.

tions in West Florida and requesting assistance. On January 3, 1767, Johnstone prorogued the first assembly until February 23. Overall, Johnstone's relations with the assembly were fairly good, in contrast to his relations with other branches of government, particularly the military.[35]

Francis Parkman noted the proclivity of men in a wilderness to fight. British West Florida, as a frontier region, was no exception. The constructive achievements of Johnstone's administration are overshadowed by the constant bickering which took place between the civil and military branches of service. Disputes occurred over such trivial matters as whether or not the guns of the fort should be fired on St. Patrick's Day. Johnstone issued orders that the artillerymen were not to fire the weapons, but Arthur Neil of the provincial Board of Ordnance had the powder delivered, and Lieutenant Colonel Ralph Walsh had "the whole artillery of the garrison . . . discharged."[36] But the problem was broader than simply the tendency of men to quarrel in a frontier region. The civil-military dispute in West Florida was indicative of a larger dilemma. According to the Proclamation of 1763, the British wanted to encourage settlement in the four new colonies. In order to attract immigrants, West Florida had to offer military protection, but to compete with the older colonies, the remote province also had to have a civilian government. The home government was centralizing military command in North America and at the same time attempting to establish attractive civil government in the new colonies. The dilemma facing the British officials was how to coordinate the two goals. Unfortunately for the tranquillity of West Florida, there were no orders clearly indicating the division of authority between the civilian governor and the military commander in the province. This lack of clear-cut areas of authority and the distance between West Florida and New York or London meant that the power of the conflicting sides depended upon the

35. Proclamation of Governor Johnstone, Aug. 18, 1766, West Florida Papers, reel 1; Johnson, *British West Florida*, p. 46; Minutes of the Lower House of Assembly, Nov. 3, 1766–Jan. 3, 1767, West Florida Papers, reel 1; "The Humble Representation of the Council and Assembly for the Province of West Florida" to the Board of Trade, Nov. 22, 1766, C.O. 5/584. For a fuller discussion of the work of the first assembly, see Howard, *British Development of West Florida*, pp. 43–47.

36. Johnstone to John Boddington (Secretary of the Board of Ordnance in London), July 19, 1766, C.O. 5/584.

precedents they set. The effort to establish these precedents led to constant bickering over problems of basic importance as well as over matters of a trivial nature.[37]

From the beginning of Johnstone's administration, the civil government and the military were at odds over their respective jurisdictions. The disputes initially centered around the right of the governor to review cases which the judge advocate's court had ruled on during the interval of military rule. Johnstone claimed the right to review the cases, and the military denied that he had this right. This argument became more serious when it became a question of who had control of the troops, the governor or the ranking military officer, who derived his power from General Gage as commander-in-chief. In order to try to clear up the situation, in early 1765 the British ministry drew up guidelines respecting the division of powers:

His Majesty's intention is that according to his commissions granted for that purpose, the orders of his commander in chief, &, under him, of the brigadier generals commanding in the Northern & Southern Departments, in all military matters, shall be supreme, & must be obeyed by the troops, as such, in all the civil governments of America.

That in cases, where no specific orders have been given by the commander in chief, or by the brigadier generals commanding in the district, the civil governor in Council, & when no Council shall subsist, the civil governor may, for the benefit of his government, give orders of the marching of troops, the disposition of them, for making & marching detachments, escorts, & such purely military services, within his government, to the commanding officer of the troops, who is to give the proper orders for carrying the same into execution; provided they are not contradictory to, or incompatible with, any orders he may have received from the commander in chief, or the brigadier general of the district; & the commanding officer is, from time to time, duly to report, with all convenient expedition, to the commander in chief, or to the brigadier general such orders, which he shall have so received from the civil governor.

37. John Shy, *Toward Lexington: The Role of the British Army in the Coming of the American Revolution*, pp. 155–56.

That the civil governor of the province shall give the word in all places, where he shall be within his province, except when the commander in chief or brigadier general shall be in the same place.

That the return of the state & condition of the troops, magazines & fortifications shall be made to the governor, as well as to the commander in chief and brigadier general.

That the civil governor is not to interfere with the details of the military regimental duty and discipline, the reports concerning which are to be made to the commanding officer, who is to make his general report to the civil governor.

When the commander in chief, or brigadier general shall be present, all military orders are to be issued by them only.[38]

In attempting to reinforce the guidelines set forth by the ministry, Gage asserted that "His Majesty never did intend the governor should have supreme command." On the other hand, Johnstone's commission had stated that "We do hereby require and command all officers and ministers, civil and military and all other inhabitants of our said province to be obedient, aiding and assisting unto you the said George Johnstone in the execution of our commission and of the powers and authorities herein contained."[39] These overlapping instructions remained a source of contention throughout the Johnstone administration.

Johnstone's belligerent nature brought him into conflict with the military within two weeks of his arrival; while governor of West Florida he quarreled with virtually every military man in a commanding position. His initial skirmish was with Captain Robert Mackinen, a member of his council, followed in rapid succession by disputes with Major Robert Farmar, Captain Andrew Simpson, and Lieutenant Colonel Ralph Walsh. Johnstone did not save his wrath for the military alone, however. He also became embroiled in disputes with members of his own administration. He suspended Attorney General Edmund Rush Wegg and Chief Justice William Clifton and carried on a running battle with Lieutenant Governor Montfort Browne, all three

38. Secretary of War [Welbore Ellis] to Halifax, Feb. 7, 1765, C.O. 5/574. See also Shy, *Toward Lexington*, pp. 181–84.

39. Quoted in Carter, "The Beginnings of British West Florida," pp. 331–32.

of whom had sided with the military in the continuing struggle over prerogatives.[40] The problems of a newly established frontier government located primarily at two military posts called for a governor of tact and diplomacy—two qualities which Johnstone was lacking. Thus, the violent disputes which kept the province in a state of turmoil largely negated the achievements of Johnstone's aggressive administration.

General Gage perceived the need for a brigadier general in West Florida to give some order to the military and to quiet the troubles with Governor Johnstone, for the guidelines set forth by the Secretary of War on February 7, 1765, gave a brigadier an unchallengeable position: "When the commander in chief, or brigadier general shall be present, all military orders are to be issued by them only." After several unsuccessful attempts to fill the position, Gage appointed Colonel William Tayler, who was the commanding officer at St. Augustine, as acting brigadier. Tayler immediately moved his headquarters to Pensacola, where he remained until March 1767, when Colonel Frederick Haldimand succeeded him. Gage felt that Haldimand's presence would end the disputes in the civil government, but by the time Haldimand arrived, the major source of conflict—Governor Johnstone—was no longer in the province. Haldimand remained in West Florida until March 1773. Although he had one brief dispute with Governor Peter Chester over the giving out of the parole, overall relations between the civil and military were fairly good after Haldimand's arrival.[41]

40. Johnson, *British West Florida*, pp. 48–57; Howard, "Governor Johnstone in West Florida," pp. 283–300; Carter, "The Beginnings of British West Florida," pp. 332–35; Howard, *British Development of West Florida*, pp. 20–25. These disputes fill many pages of the correspondence in the Gage Papers and in C.O. 5/574–98.

41. Mowat, "The Southern Brigade," pp. 62–65. For Haldimand's evaluation of the poor condition of Pensacola, see Frederick Haldimand to Captain Ross of the 31st Regiment, Aug. 6, 1767, British Museum, Additional Manuscripts, 21726, photostatic copies, Library of Congress. Colonel Henry Boquet arrived in West Florida in August 1765, but died within thirteen days. Tayler's disgust with Johnstone is apparent in a letter he wrote to Gage on August 8, 1766: "If violence, indecency, want of candour, and misrepresentation of facts can produce harmony with His Majesty's troops and encourage the colony I think this will flourish" (Gage Papers). Mowat states: "In the British army 'brigadier general' was (and is) a temporary rank given to the officer commanding a brigade, a unit consisting of two or more regiments brigaded together. The rank thus stands between those of colonel and major general. Sometimes the simple term 'brigadier' is used." For a discussion of Haldimand's career in West

At various congresses in 1765, Johnstone had attempted to conciliate the Indians. Nevertheless, in 1766 troubles arose again as the Upper Creeks, under the leadership of The Mortar, accused the British of disregarding the boundary lines and of inciting the Choctaws to make war on them. Johnstone denied both charges and concluded that "to receive our presents, eat our provisions, use our powder and balls, and cut our throats, it is neither felt that you should do so, nor that we should permit it." Tensions continued to grow, until on October 3, 1766, the governor received word that the Creeks had murdered two more whites. Quickly summoned, a partial meeting of the council recommended that Johnstone request Brigadier General Tayler to erect defensive fortifications. The councilors also advised that "It is the opinion of the governor and Council, that after a due time is given for the traders to withdraw from the Creek nation, which time should be employed in proper preparations, that every hostile measure, permitted by the laws of nations, should be used against the Creek Indians, in return for the murders, depredations, and other breeches of the most solemn treaties, which they have recently committed against His Majesty's subjects."[42]

In view of the weak situation of West Florida and the fact that Tayler would not begin a war without orders from Gage, the councilors' decision, although later approved by the full council, was an ill-advised and warlike gesture. Johnstone planned to attack the Creeks with the help of the Chickasaws, Choctaws, and Cherokees, and he saw the situation as an opportunity to destroy the power of the Creeks. Gage, however, had just ended one Indian war and was not anxious to get into another. The Earl of Shelburne concurred with Gage: "Your opinion of the impropriety & inexpediency of an Indian war is certainly just, and accords entirely with His Majesty's sentiments who wishes that every means may be used to conciliate those tribes."[43] As a consequence of the governor's actions con-

---

Florida, see Robert R. Rea, "Brigadier Frederick Haldimand—The Florida Years."

42. "Proceeding of the Committee of Council for West Florida," Oct. 3, 1766, C.O. 5/584.

43. Earl of Shelburne to Gage, Feb. 19, 1767, C.O. 5/85; Johnson, British West Florida, pp. 59–60; Minutes of the Council, Nov. 6, 1766, C.O. 5/632, RSUS, reel 6; Howard, "Governor Johnstone," p. 301.

cerning the Indians and "on account of the spirit of disunion which has weakened and distracted the colony of Pensacola," Shelburne recalled Johnstone in February 1767, instructing him to turn over the government to Lieutenant Governor Montfort Browne immediately. Johnstone escaped this embarrassment, however, since he had left the colony January 9 on a six months' leave of absence. Hostilities did not break out in West Florida; the Indians gave satisfaction for the two murders, and Colonel Tayler worked to conciliate the Indians.[44]

Shelburne instructed Montfort Browne to stop the hostilities against the Indians, to make every effort to conciliate them, and "to change the policy in respect of them as quickly as a proper regard & appearance of consistency will allow, taking all possible care to make the Indians sensible that they owe their peace to His Majesty's clemency." Browne's orders also presented a good view of the ministry's ideas concerning Johnstone's administration: "The late animosities which have too much subsisted in West Florida between His Majesty's civil and military officers, & that want of harmony so necessary for the establishment of an infant colony, which has hitherto prevented its increase and cultivation, could not but be very displeasing to His Majesty. You will therefore be as careful to restore concord in your government, and to heal all internal differences as to conciliate the affections of the Indians."[45]

44. Shelburne to Johnstone, Feb. 19, 1767, C.O. 5/618. See also Shelburne to James Grant (governor of East Florida), Feb. 19, 1767, C.O. 5/548; Johnson, *British West Florida*, p. 60; Grant to Shelburne, Aug. 8, 1767, C.O. 5/548; Shelburne to Sir William Johnson, Feb. 19, 1767, in James Sullivan, *The Papers of Sir William Johnson*, 5:493. Fabel argues that Johnstone's removal was due to internal politics in England. While presenting a rather impressive array of support for his position, his argument is not conclusive (Fabel, "Governor George Johnstone," pp. 67–69). See also R. F. A. Fabel, "Governor George Johnstone of British West Florida," pp. 504–11. Upon his return to England, Johnstone was elected to Parliament, where he soon came to be regarded as an expert on American affairs. In 1778, he was appointed to the Carlisle Peace Commission. Congress soon forced him to resign from the commission after he took what they considered improper steps toward winning over an American commissioner. Upon his return to England, he again entered Parliament, where his influence over Lord Sandwich soon got him a promotion to commander-in-chief of a squadron off the coast of Portugal. The best complete study of Johnstone's career is Fabel, "Governor George Johnstone."
45. Shelburne to Lt. Gov. Montfort Browne, Feb. 19, 1767, C.O. 5/618. For a brief biographical sketch of Browne, see Johnson, *British West Florida*, pp. 61–62n.

Browne was only slightly more successful than Johnstone in maintaining peace within the province. Browne had arrived in West Florida in January 1766, bringing with him a group of forty-eight French Huguenots who settled Campbell Town.[46] He had quickly allied himself with the enemies of the governor, and although he had been appointed to the council, Browne had little to do with administering the affairs of government because of his disagreements with Johnstone. Thus, when he took control of the government of West Florida, he was almost totally unfamiliar with the routines of government. The presence of a strong party of Johnstone's friends, known as the "Scotch Party," led by council member Daniel Clark, multiplied his troubles. That Browne's appointment was only temporary, to end with the arrival of the newly appointed governor John Eliot, further weakened his position.[47]

Despite the fact that everything seemed to be working against him, Browne's first efforts were of a constructive nature. He was able to quiet the Indians, make efforts toward opening the trade with the Spanish, and make an inspection tour of the western part of the province. Some of Browne's major problems came in his relations with the assembly. According to Johnstone's prorogation, the assembly met on February 23, 1767.[48] In this meeting the delegates spent much of their time with regulations of a local nature, much as in the first session. Overall, the session

46. Despite government support, the township failed, to the extent that on October 19, 1768, the assembly passed a bill including Campbell Town as a part of the district of Pensacola. On December 18, 1770, James Bruce read a petition in which he mentioned the fact "that there are now remaining only one family in that whole township of the original settlers, the others having either died or left." Minutes of the Council, Dec. 18, 1770, C.O. 5/629, RSUS, reel 3; Minutes of the Lower House of Assembly, Oct. 19, 1768, West Florida Papers, reel 1. Sixty-one French Protestants left England with Browne, but thirteen either died or deserted before they landed at Pensacola. Minutes of the Council, Feb. 21, 1768, C.O. 5/526, RSUS, reel 1. The official correspondence is full of material on this group of immigrants. See particularly C.O. 5/574–75. See also *Journals of the Commissioners for Trade and Plantations, 1704–1782*, Nov. 21, 1763, July 2, 1765, Public Record Office. For a full discussion of Campbell Town, see J. Barton Starr, "Campbell Town: French Huguenots in British West Florida."

47. Johnson, *British West Florida*, p. 62. See also *Journals of the Commissioners for Trade and Plantations*, Sept. 2, 1765; Johnson, "Pensacola in the British Period," p. 273. Eliot was appointed governor early in 1767.

48. Minutes of the Lower House of Assembly, Feb. 23, 1767, West Florida Papers, reel 1. For a copy of Browne's report on his expedition up the Mississippi, see Browne to Lord Hillsborough, July 6, 1768, C.O. 5/577.

was an active one which did some good toward the development of the colony. Disputes between the assembly and the governor marred the session, however, as they charged one another with selfishness, inactivity, ineffectiveness, and illegal actions. Finally, Browne dissolved the assembly on June 6, 1767, charging that "much of your attention [is] taken up in unworthy attempts to throw reflections on my conduct and the opinion of His Majesty's Council by the most insolent and shameful resolutions that any assembly ever presented to a governor." There were two more sessions of the legislature before Governor Eliot arrived, and while Browne's relations with the Commons House improved, friction remained.[49]

John Eliot received his appointment as governor of West Florida in early 1767, not long after Johnstone's recall, but it was not until two years later that he arrived at Pensacola. In the spring of 1768, Eliot was at last making preparations to leave England. As one scholar has written, "He seemed loathe to come,"[50] but come he did. He landed at Pensacola on April 2, 1769, but did not take over the "administration of government" until the following day. Although Browne was in Mobile at the time of Eliot's arrival, he soon returned and requested an investigation by the governor and council of his accounts during his term as acting governor. Browne reported that the examination which had begun on April 27 had proceeded well for several days but was cut short when "on the second of May [Governor Eliot] hung himself in his study."[51] Eliot had met with the council the day after his arrival and was to meet with them seven times before his death. He had brought with him from the Privy Council instructions which disallowed the law used in electing the current assembly. He had, therefore, dissolved it and issued warrants for writs of election for a new assembly.

49. Minutes of the Lower House of Assembly, Apr. 3–June 6, 1767, C.O. 5/627, RSUS, reel 2. The house met Dec. 15, 1767, was prorogued on Jan. 11, 1768, until Feb. 20, and was dissolved on Oct. 21, 1768, upon expiration of the term for which the members were elected. On Jan. 25, 1769, a new assembly met, but it was prorogued on Feb. 2, until the time of the expected arrival of Governor John Eliot. See the respective dates in the Minutes of the Lower House of Assembly, West Florida Papers, reel 1.

50. Howard, "Colonial Pensacola," p. 256; Johnson, British West Florida, pp. 69, 103–4.

51. Browne to Hillsborough, May 13, 1769, C.O. 5/577; Johnson, British West Florida, p. 69; Eliot to Hillsborough, Apr. 3, 1769, C.O. 5/586.

Eliot, however, was dead and Browne had again resumed control of the government before the new legislature could convene.[52]

Browne informed the council on May 3, 1769, of Eliot's apparent suicide and reported that, as a consequence of Eliot's death, "the administration of government did devolve upon him agreeable to His Majesty's commission to him as Lieut. Governor and the commission to his late Excellency."[53] The colony was shocked at the death of the man who many apparently felt would quiet the internal dissensions of the colony. John Cambel, an engineer in Pensacola, lamented: "In less than a month after your departure, Governor Eliot arrived, whose presence revived our hopes, and filled us with expectations; but in a month after, exactly to an hour, he blasted them all, by hanging himself in his study. And in order to rivet our calamities upon us, his death is succeeded by the utmost state of anarchy and confusion, several have quit the province, and others are preparing to follow their example."[54]

A state of confusion did follow Eliot's death, as the supporters and enemies of Browne vied for power. A petition to the council from fifty-seven inhabitants of Pensacola, including several members of the assembly, stated, in part, "From the unhappy experience we have already had under his [Browne's] late administration, we retain the most disagreeable apprehensions from his past conduct and with horror behold his second approach." The petition concluded, "We cannot therefore from Mr. Browne's character, or abilities both of which are well known to your Honors, think him a fit person to govern this province." When the council refused to take any action on the petition, his opponents attempted to force Browne to write home resigning his position. This action also was to no avail. Fifty-three settlers drew up another petition, this one to the king, complaining of Browne's conduct.[55] The supporters of Browne were active also, as sixty-three of them begged Browne

52. Minutes of the Council, Apr. 3, 1769, C.O. 5/626, RSUS, reel 1; Howard, "Colonial Pensacola," pp. 260–61; Johnson, British West Florida, p. 105.

53. Minutes of the Council, May 3, 1769, C.O. 5/626, RSUS, reel 1.

54. John Cambel to Haldimand, June 9, 1769, British Museum, Additional MSS, 21729.

55. "Remonstrance to the Council from several Inhabitants of the Town of Pensacola," May 2, 1769, C.O. 5/577; "Petition of the Inhabitants of the Province of West Florida" to the king, May 12, 1769, C.O. 5/586.

to "accept, Sir, our thanks for the mildness and lenity of your past government and give us leave to assure your Honor, that you may always rely, on our best endeavours to assert and maintain the honor, and dignity, of His Majesty's crown and government and that we shall to the utmost of our power, preserve and promote unanimity and concord so essential to our own welfare, nay even to our very existence."[56]

In the midst of the confusion, Browne reassumed control of the government, the only constitutional step that he could have taken. Browne apparently made some effort to conciliate his not-so-loyal opposition, however. In the council, at the reading of the petition opposing Browne, the lieutenant governor announced that he planned to seek their advice in the future, particularly relating to financial matters.[57] This assertion must have been of little comfort to Browne's enemies. The same members (or men of the same beliefs) composed the council against which they had remonstrated earlier. Browne also took the opportunity to remove two members of the council who opposed him. With the antagonisms that existed, it is difficult to imagine that the assembly could have accomplished anything constructive, and Browne's second brief term as acting governor was one continuous argument.

When Browne asserted "that from the measures I have pursued, the spirit of party and dissension is almost at an end,"[58] he was correct, but for different reasons than he intended. Lord Hillsborough had written letters of recall to Browne which he had not yet received. On May 9, Elias Durnford had informed the council that, with the king's permission, he was going to England on a leave of absence. Browne apparently considered Durnford his friend and gave him a letter of defense to deliver. What Durnford reported as to the condition of the province is not known and may not have been of any consequence in the decision to remove Browne. But Hillsborough informed Browne on August 4, 1769, that after examining the minutes of the council which had investigated his financial matters, and after receiving a petition from the inhabitants of West Florida com-

56. "Letter from several of the Inhabitants of West Florida to Lt. Govr. Browne," n.d. [May 1769], C.O. 5/577.
57. Minutes of the Council, May 4, 1769, C.O. 5/626, RSUS, reel 1.
58. Browne to Hillsborough, Oct. 8, 1769, C.O. 5/577.

plaining of his conduct, "His Majesty has thought fit, upon a consideration of these papers, to revoke the commission by which you was [sic] appointed Lieutenant Governor of West Florida." Hillsborough also immediately suspended Browne from his seat on the council.[59]

When Durnford returned to Pensacola, he presented Browne with Hillsborough's letter of recall; he had also appointed Durnford lieutenant governor and ordered Browne to "deliver up to him His Majesty's commission & instructions to Governor Eliot, together with all other public papers in your possession, and His Majesty's Seals, & other regalia of government."[60] Although Durnford commanded respect throughout the province and received two addresses (one from twenty-eight people in Pensacola and one from twenty inhabitants of Mobile) congratulating him and expressing their joy at his appointment, internal peace in West Florida did not come until after Browne left the colony. Browne was humiliated at his recall and was angry at Durnford, whom he had considered his friend. Durnford charged that Browne was slow in turning over the public papers as instructed, and Browne felt that Durnford was attempting to keep him from getting papers necessary for a defense of his conduct. Durnford reinstated the two members of the council whom Browne had removed, and after examining Browne's financial records, the council accused Browne of sup-

59. Hillsborough to Browne, Aug. 4, 1769, C.O. 5/586. At present the best work available on Durnford's career is Robert Edward Gray, "Elias Durnford, 1739–1794: Engineer, Soldier, Administrator" (Master's thesis). For a brief but totally favorable sketch of Durnford's life, see Mary Durnford, *Family Recollections of Lieut. General Elias Walker Durnford*, pp. 8–28. An interesting anecdote of questionable validity concerns Durnford who was supposedly nicknamed the "Black Prince" because of his dark complexion from the Florida sun. "It was his custom when abroad to carry pistols loaded—but on one occasion being on a picnic one of the party intending to play him a trick, unloaded the pistols and replaced them where he was accustomed to keep them. In the course of the day, as the company were seated, taking refreshments, some species of tiger, probably the jaguar, suddenly sprang towards them—He instantly seized his pistol, and pulling the trigger was surprized to find it unloaded. With great presence of mind, he stood quite still and steadfastly fixed his eye on the animal which intimidated by his looks, presently retired." T. W. J. Conally, MSS, Royal Engineer Corps Library, Chatham, England. Mr. Douglas Marshall of the William L. Clements Library kindly furnished me with a copy of this story.

60. Hillsborough to Browne, Aug. 4, 1769, C.O. 5/586. It is not clear exactly when Durnford returned to Pensacola, but he presided at the council meeting of Dec. 29, 1769. Minutes of the Council, Dec. 29, 1769, C.O. 5/626, RSUS, reel 1.

plying his family and slaves with goods from the Indian presents. The situation reached its climax when Browne shot Evan Jones in a duel on Gage Hill. Browne was imprisoned when it appeared that Jones would die, and Chief Justice William Clifton refused to allow bail or issue a writ of habeas corpus. After a few days, Justice of the Peace Alexander Moore ordered Browne's release. Clifton took the matter to the council, but since Jones appeared to be recovering and the boat in which Browne was to sail was ready to leave, the council decided to let Browne depart. To hold Browne might be construed as an attempt to prevent him from defending himself, and Browne's removal from the province was necessary for the restoration of peace.[61]

After Browne sailed in mid-February on the *British King*, the remaining six months of Durnford's term as acting governor were quite peaceful. The major accomplishment of Durnford's brief administration was probably the passing of a law for the regulation of the Indian trade. The situation of the province had changed so much that a man in a regiment returning to Pensacola after being away for a brief period reported that "It is impossible for you to have an idea of the alterations that have taken place in this infant colony for the better since we left it. Beef is in the greatest plenty and sold at half a bit per pound. Venison and wild turkeys are sold much cheaper than in [St.] Augustine, and we have likewise mutton in great abundance. Society is much increased, civil and military disputes seem now to be at an end; in short everything has a different appearance, and a person formerly acquainted here would imagine they begin to revise the Golden Age."[62]

61. Address of the inhabitants of Pensacola to Elias Durnford, n.d. [endorsed Jan. 27, 1770], C.O. 5/587; another copy of this petition contains twenty-eight names, whereas the first one contains twenty-seven, Address of the inhabitants of Mobile to Durnford, n.d., ibid.; Johnson, *British West Florida*, pp. 72–73; Minutes of the Council, Feb. 13, 1770, C.O. 5/626, RSUS, reel 1. A copy of the bitter correspondence between Browne and Durnford is in C.O. 5/577. For a brief account of Browne's career after he left West Florida, see Johnson, *British West Florida*, pp. 61–62n. Evan Jones was a very active English merchant in New Orleans. He remained important in New Orleans life for many years after the British left West Florida. John G. Clark, *New Orleans, 1718–1812: An Economic History*, pp. 164–65.

62. "N." to Haldimand, Mar. 12, 1770, British Museum, Additional MSS, 21729; Howard, "Colonial Pensacola," pp. 266–67; Johnson, *British West Florida*, p. 73.

During the late 1760s, the military in West Florida under the direction of Brigadier General Frederick Haldimand had been able to remain aloof from the disputes that had plagued civil-military relations in the first four years of the colony's existence. Possession of the province was basically complete; the military was reduced to the role of a standing army ready for defense, its soldiers consigned to the drudgery of garrison duty. But in the summer, fall, and winter of 1768–69, the military once again occupied the forefront of attention in West Florida, and the colony was united in a common effort which transcended the constant bickering. In August 1768, Lieutenant Governor Browne received the following brief and disturbing dispatch from General Gage: "In consequence of orders which I have lately received, I transmit directions to Brigadier General Haldimand to withdraw the troops posted at the Natchez and Fort Bute: and to embark the two regiments in West Florida, except three companies which the Brigadier will leave at Pensacola and Mobile, and proceed with them to St. Augustine."[63]

The colony was stunned. Browne asserted on August 16 that "the distraction the province is in . . . may be easier conceived than expressed. The posts at Fort Bute and the Natchez are all calling in, so that the number of poor families that have spent their little fortunes in coming from other provinces and establishing themselves on the Mississippi must abandon their plantations and stores. The town of Pensacola which has amazingly increased these twelve months must of course be abandoned as the inhabitants will never think their persons and effects safe in the midst of such a number of savages. . . . The prospect before us is really melancholy."[64] Nine days later, Browne again lamented the loss of the troops, but, after having had time for sober contemplation of the troop withdrawal, he observed, "Pensacola, My Lord, I am not in the least apprehension about, but will not answer for Mobile nor the inhabitants of it."[65] Meanwhile, Browne had called the assembly together. All of the petty disputes that had plagued the province were forgotten as a united assembly and council prepared a memorial to Hills-

63. Gage to Browne, June 27, 1768, British Museum, Additional MSS, 21663. For a copy of Gage's instructions to Haldimand, see Gage to Haldimand, June 27, 1768, ibid.
64. Browne to Hillsborough, Aug. 16, 1768, C.O. 5/585.
65. Browne to Hillsborough, Aug. 25, 1768, ibid.

borough begging that he consider the case of West Florida and order enough troops to remain to protect the province. The council and assembly also sent a similar memorial to George III. Merchants in Liverpool and London were also greatly concerned about this withdrawal of troops from West Florida and drew up at least three petitions containing a total of eighty-nine signatures, protesting to Hillsborough the troop removal and urging a reversal of the decision to withdraw them.[66]

The orders which Haldimand had received from Gage were for immediate execution, however. For lack of transports, it was several months before all of the troops could withdraw, and Haldimand observed that it would be less difficult to embark three thousand men in Philadelphia than to move three hundred from Pensacola to St. Augustine. Finally, however, in August, September, and October, all of the troops, except the three companies that were to remain in West Florida, left for East Florida. Fort Bute was dismantled, "as there were no inhabitants of considerable property settled at Fort Bute as yet," and an Indian trader, John Bradley, took over the post at Natchez.[67]

The memorials of the inhabitants, council, and assembly of West Florida, and those of merchants in England, apparently had an effect. Admiral William Parry ordered two companies of artillery to Pensacola in early 1769 to help protect the

66. Memorial of the Council and Assembly of West Florida to Hillsborough, Aug. 24, 1768, Minutes of the Lower House of Assembly, Aug. 23–24, 1768, West Florida Papers, reel 1; Memorial of the Council and Assembly of West Florida to the king, Aug. 24, 1768, Minutes of the Lower House of Assembly, Aug. 24, 1768, ibid. Another petition from the inhabitants of West Florida to Browne and the council was also drawn up and signed by twenty-two residents of the colony. The date of this petition is uncertain, but it appears to have been written on Aug. 14, 1768, two days before Browne's first letter to Hillsborough (C.O. 5/86). "The memorial of the Merchants of Liverpool, in behalf of themselves and Others trading to West Florida" to Hillsborough, n.d., C.O. 5/585; "The Memorial of the Merchants [London] trading to West Florida in behalf of themselves and the Inhabitants of the said Province" to Hillsborough, Nov. 3, 1768, ibid.; "Memorial of the Merchants trading to West Florida, in behalf of themselves and the inhabitants of the said Province" to Hillsborough, n.d., C.O. 5/114. While these are three separate memorials, some of the signatures are duplicated.

67. Browne to Hillsborough, Dec. 1, 1768, C.O. 5/586; Browne to John Bradley and [?] Fairchild, Aug. 15, 1768, British Museum, Additional MSS, 21673; Mowat, "The Southern Brigade," p. 70; Gage to Hillsborough, Jan. 5, 1769, C.O. 5/87. Indians later forced Bradley to evacuate the post. See Minutes of the Council, Feb. 7, 1770, C.O. 5/626, RSUS, reel 1.

province from the Indians. He also forwarded with his strong
endorsement the petition of the assembly and council begging
for military aid. Hillsborough informed Governor Eliot on December 10, 1768, that the king had received the memorials and
had sent them on to Gage. He concluded, "I doubt not from the
manner in which my sentiment to him upon this occasion is
expressed, that he will give full consideration to every circumstance of danger and inconvenience stated to attend the
leaving of so inconsiderable a number of troops in West
Florida."[68] After a reevaluation of the situation in West Florida,
Lord Hillsborough decided that three companies were inadequate to protect West Florida, and he therefore ordered Gage
to place six companies in the colony.[69] By the time reinforcements finally sailed for Pensacola from St. Augustine in February 1770, the situation had changed again. Browne reported
on August 19, 1769, the arrival in Louisiana of the new
Spanish governor, Count Alexandro O'Reilly, accompanied
by 4,500 regular Spanish troops, 300 artillerymen, 600 free
Negroes and mulattoes, and 300 cannon. Referring to O'Reilly
as "the most experienced general in the Spanish service,"
Browne fretted that his arrival "with such a force cannot fail
of alarming the whole continent of America and this colony
more immediately."[70] Acting upon the king's orders "to
send to West Florida such a number of troops, and to put
the forts into such a state of defence, as I shall think sufficient to discourage or disappoint, any sudden attempt, to distress and break up our infant settlements," Gage ordered the
Sixteenth Regiment to sail from New York directly to Pensacola. He also ordered Haldimand to return to Pensacola to

68. Quoted in Johnson, British West Florida, pp. 67–68; Minutes of the
Lower House of Assembly, Feb. 2, 1769, West Florida Papers, reel 1.
69. Gage to Haldimand, Jan. 6, 1769, British Museum, Additional MSS,
21664. For Gage's evaluation of the situation in West Florida just prior to his
ordering reinforcements, see Gage to Hillsborough, Mar. 5, 1769, C.O. 5/87.
70. Browne to Gage, Aug. 19, 1769, C.O. 5/577; Haldimand to Gage, Feb. 10,
1770, British Museum, Additional MSS, 21664. For some reason, perhaps more
accurate information, Gage reported the arrival of 3,500 Spanish troops under
O'Reilly (Gage to Haldimand, Nov. 10, 1769, ibid.). Undoubtedly the size of the
Spanish force was intended to prevent another insurrection by the French
inhabitants of Louisiana. The British troops were sent despite Gage's conviction
that the best defense for West Florida "is Ships of War, to attack them before
they land" (Gage to Hillsborough, Mar. 5, 1769, C.O. 5/87). At this time Spain
and Great Britain were also involved in a dispute over the Falkland Islands.

direct the defense of the colony. Thus, West Florida was again protected by as large a force as it would have until after Willing's raid down the Mississippi in 1778. To show its appreciation, the council of West Florida sent an address to Hillsborough thanking him for the reinforcements. In reply, Hillsborough warned that it had been difficult to obtain the reinforcement, and that the province should not expect further additions, especially as the threat from Spanish forces had lessened.[71]

The brief moratorium in the internal dissensions of West Florida caused by the dismay over the removal of troops quickly ended. The remainder of Browne's administration and the beginning of Durnford's term were a continuation of the strife that had been an integral part of the colony's life since the British had arrived. The last six months of Durnford's administration were relatively tranquil.

When Peter Chester arrived in West Florida on August 10, 1770, Durnford's brief term as acting governor came to an end, and West Florida finally had a governor who would be in office for a relatively long period of time. In its brief seven-year history, West Florida had had one year of military rule, two governors, and two lieutenant governors. Governor Chester remained in office from August 11, 1770, until the surrender of the province to Spain in 1781. Such continuity, albeit from a man of mediocre talents, was a luxury to which West Florida was unaccustomed.[72] But the old conflicts remained. Facing

71. Gage to Haldimand, Feb. 26, 1770, British Museum, Additional MSS, 21664; Address of the council to Hillsborough, n.d. [endorsed, "In Lt. Govr. Durnford's . . . of 9th July 1770"], C.O. 5/587; Hillsborough to Peter Chester, Apr. 1, 1771, C.O. 5/588. The posts on the Mississippi River were not repossessed, however, until after Willing's raid. For a good discussion of the troop withdrawal, see Mowat, "The Southern Brigade," pp. 66–72.

72. Chester's instructions were dated Mar. 2, 1770, C.O. 5/203. Philip Livingston, Jr., of New York accompanied Chester to West Florida as his private secretary at a salary of £ 200 sterling per year. He was also to be deputy secretary of the province at £ 250 per year. Livingston, who became an important figure in West Florida throughout Chester's administration, felt that the prospects for him in West Florida were brighter than in New York. He asserted, "If the climate agrees with me I shall contrive & believe my plan will succeed to my wishes, if not I shall immediately return." Livingston to [?], May 4, 1770, Philip Livingston, Jr., Papers, 1:130, New York Public Library, hereafter cited as Livingston Papers. For a sketch of Chester's life, see Johnson, British West Florida, p. 76, and Eron Dunbar Rowland, ed., "Peter Chester, Third Governor of the Province of West Florida under British Dominion, 1770–1781," pp. 1–16.

Chester was the perennial problem of Indian relations. In the main, John Stuart had lost in authority over Indian relations what the six southern colonies had gained. Yet the regulation by law was nonexistent except in West Florida, and even there enforcement was lax. Chester's two congresses with the Indians in 1771 accomplished little, yet at the outbreak of the American Revolution, the necessity of obtaining Indian adherence would be obvious to the British and Americans alike.

Governor Chester's relations with the assembly were also not congenial, as he jealously guarded what he felt were the prerogatives of the governor and the crown. Such were the relations between the assembly and the royal governor that after dissolving the popular body in 1772 because of a dispute over election procedures, Chester did not call it together again until 1778, and this latter session was of no value, dealing mainly with matters he considered items of royal privilege. After the brief 1778 session, the assembly never met again, apparently due to the unwillingness of either the governor or the assembly to relinquish what they considered their vested privilege. In reality the reasons for not calling the legislature ran deeper. The revenue collected was of little use, and the laws passed were inadequate and, at best, poorly enforced. Also, since the colony operated from the parliamentary support fund, the legislature was not needed to supply revenue. The benefits to be derived from the meeting of a body with such a propensity to quarrel indeed must have been few, and as the beginnings of the American Revolution raged over the Atlantic colonies, to allow such a disenchanted and prerogative-seeking body to meet would have been an open invitation to revolution.

There is little else worthy of note in Chester's early administration. The dismissal and reinstatement of John Thomas, deputy Indian superintendent on the Mississippi River, dragged on for two years in 1772–73, and there were minor problems concerning the military under General Haldimand.[73] Soon after his arrival, Governor Chester had requested that Haldimand send troops to the posts on the Mississippi, but Haldimand refused

73. For materials on the John Thomas case, see C.O. 5/73, pp. 228–29, 578; Minutes of the Council, Apr. 2, 1772, C.O. 5/629, RSUS, reel 3; Book of Fiats (Pardons), West Florida Papers, reel 1; Letterbook of John Fitzpatrick, 1768–90, 1:132, New York Public Library.

because Gage had ordered him not to move troops to the western posts. However, relations between the governor and Haldimand were generally cordial as, in the main, each stayed within his own area of responsibility: Chester met with the Indians and argued with the assembly, while Haldimand directed the continuing construction of fortifications. During the summer of 1771, there was a brief eruption of the old civil-military dispute concerning an interpretation of the king's regulations as to who had the authority to "give the word" (the countersign) in the province. Haldimand also learned that Chester planned to build a governor's house within the garrison, but Haldimand claimed control of the fort. Constitutionally, Governor Chester had control of the fort at Pensacola, while Haldimand had authority only over the troops. At any rate, the dispute between Chester and Haldimand was brief and of little consequence. Haldimand left West Florida in March 1773 to serve as commander-in-chief while Gage was on a leave of absence in England. Haldimand never returned to West Florida, and the colony was without a brigadier until General John Campbell arrived in 1778 after Willing's raid.[74]

Land policies and settlement patterns in the colony, as well as political and military realities, influenced West Florida's role in the Revolution and the war with Spain. The Proclamation of 1763 was the first document to set forth regulations for the granting of land, and it dealt only with grants to soldiers who had served in the French and Indian War.[75] Governor Johnstone's instructions contained the next details concerning grants to individual settlers other than soldiers. Heads of families received one hundred acres plus fifty acres for a wife and each child, indentured servant, or slave; the governor granted the acreage on "headright" or "family right," on authority of royal mandamuses (Orders in Council), the Proclamation of 1763, or the royal instructions to the governor. A settler

74. Hillsborough to Gage, Jan. 11, 1772, abstracted in Peter J. Hamilton Papers, Alabama Department of Archives and History; Mowat, "The Southern Brigade," p. 75.

75. "By the King, A Proclamation," pp. 38–39. The amounts to be granted were as follows: field officer, 5,000 acres; captain, 3,000 acres; subaltern or staff officer, 2,000 acres; noncommissioned officer, 200 acres; private, 50 acres. For a full discussion of land policy, settlement, and expansion in West Florida, see Johnson, British West Florida, pp. 115–49.

could purchase up to one thousand additional acres. The crown exerted strict control over westward expansion as well as size of estates. The policy apparently was intended to put the quit-rent system on a paying basis, which the ministry felt would be accomplished by granting land in small tracts. To have granted large tracts of land would have been to create a quasi-feudal absentee class of landholders in direct contradiction to the policy of control of lands by the crown, from whom small farmers and the artisan class would hold their lands directly. Despite the regulations set forth in the Proclamation of 1763 and the royal instructions, various men at times skirted the land policy. For example, on authority of a royal mandamus, the Earl of Eglington received a grant for twenty thousand acres in West Florida. Grants such as these were rare, and even when the governor and council permitted them, they were not of the size to which speculators had become accustomed in the older established colonies.[76]

The speculation for lands in West Florida began even before the first troops arrived to take possession. A propaganda effort had encouraged settlers to come to the new province, but speculators had already rushed to purchase a number of estates from the Spanish and to have the titles confirmed by the British government. After a lengthy dispute, Governor Johnstone and the council disallowed most of these Spanish "sales" on the ground of invalid Spanish titles. Almost all of the speculators agreed to give up their claims in return for an adjustment granted them by the council.[77]

In the summer of 1773, Chester received from the Earl of

76. Johnson, British West Florida, pp. 117, 121; Howard, "Military Occupation," p. 182; Howard, "Alleged Spanish Grants," pp. 83–84; Robert L. Gold, "Politics and Property during the Transfer of Florida from Spanish to English Rule, 1763–1764," p. 24; Clinton N. Howard, "Early Settlers in British West Florida," p. 49; Minutes of the Council, Aug. 8, 1765, C.O. 5/625, RSUS, reel 1.

77. Clinton N. Howard, "Some Economic Aspects of British West Florida, 1763–1768," pp. 209–12; Gold, "Politics and Property," p. 25. Gold asserts that the British disallowance of the speculators' purchases was illegal, as the Treaty of Paris allowed the Spanish and French to sell their property. He concludes, "British national interests thus triumphed over international legality." For a discussion of the propaganda campaign, see Charles L. Mowat, "The First Campaign of Publicity for Florida"; Jeanette M. Long, "Immigration to British West Florida, 1763–1781" (Master's thesis). See also various descriptions and plans for settlement of West Florida in Earl of Shelburne Papers, 48:19–76, 113–23, 159–78, 263–90, 621–26; 50:127–56, William L. Clements Library.

Dartmouth a letter that was a portent of things to come: "I hope that pending the reference which has been made of this matter [the granting of lands on the Mississippi, Amite, and Iberville rivers] to His Majesty's consideration, no steps whatever have been taken by you to increase those improvident grants which were made by your predecessors in that part of the province." As a result of this letter, the council advised Chester that anyone who had taken out a warrant of survey prior to the arrival of the letter could be granted the lands applied for, but that in the future Chester should grant land only on family right and only to those "actually within the province."[78] Chester received a circular letter in October which instructed him not to issue any more warrants of survey until further orders, except as set forth for the veterans in the Proclamation of 1763. After reading this new instruction to the council, the governor noted that there were a large number of people who had come to West Florida expecting a grant on family right. With the advice of the council, Chester allowed all who had come to the colony but had not had time to obtain a grant of land to settle on any vacant lands they chose. This occupation would give them a prior claim when he could once again grant land.[79]

Governor Chester received new instructions from the king in the late summer of 1774. The provincial surveyor was to divide the land into tracts of not less than 100 or more than 1,000 acres, the governor was to set a price of no less than six pence per acre, and the highest bidder could purchase the lands. A stern warning accompanying the new regulations admonished Chester not to grant lands in any other manner whatsoever without the consent of the Privy Council, except in the case of the officers and soldiers provided for in the 1763 proclamation.[80] This new rule apparently never went into effect;

78. Minutes of the Council, Aug. 25, 1773, C.O. 5/630, RSUS, reel 4.
79. Minutes of the Council, Oct. 6, 1773, ibid.; Chester to Haldimand, Oct. 8, 1773, British Museum, Additional MSS, 21673.
80. "Copy of His Majesty's Instructions to the governors of Nova Scotia, New Hampshire, New York, Virginia, No. Carolina, South Carolina, Georgia, East Florida and West Florida, respecting the Granting of lands in those Provinces," Feb. 3, 1774, Great Britain, House of Lords (microfilm located at the Library of Congress, 1 reel); Minutes of the Council, Sept. 5, 1774, C.O. 5/634, RSUS, reel 7; Additional instructions to Peter Chester, Feb. 3, 1774, "Chalmers collection of documents relating to West Florida, 1763–1782," New York Public Library, hereafter cited as Chalmers Papers. In his discussion of the regulations govern-

West Florida proceeded essentially as if the ban on grants to all but military personnel were still in effect. In the period between the receipt of the new instructions and the arrival of the next order, the council issued only one warrant of survey for a grant, and that warrant was for a one-thousand-acre purchase in lieu of a warrant of survey issued in 1773. Apparently, these new regulations were too confining and were considered excessively expensive for West Florida. Chester, it appears, asked Dartmouth for some relief from the new regulations, for on June 9, 1775, the governor rejoiced that "It gives me great pleasure to find that His Majesty permits me to grant lands to those people who have made settlements, and improvements; and whose circumstances will not enable them to purchase, in which I shall be very careful not to exceed His Majesty's gracious intentions, but that it shall be attended with such restrictions as shall correspond with the spirit and intentions of the instructions."[81] The final instructions concerning land grants in West Florida came in July 1775, when the province became a loyalist haven for refugees fleeing from the colonies in rebellion against England. Thus, as a result of the American Revolution, the home government lifted the restriction on land grants a little less than a year after the instructions arrived in Pensacola.

A detailed perusal of the council minutes of West Florida discloses the progress of settlement of the colony. During the period 1765–66, the governor and council granted land mainly around Pensacola and Mobile, since poor roads and the resulting lack of communication, combined with sparsity of population and the threat from the Indians, encouraged settlement close to military garrisons. Only a few adventurous people moved out beyond the immediate area of the two towns.[82]

Two movements to expand the province began in late 1767. One of these migrations moved up the Tombigbee and Alabama rivers, the other toward the Mississippi, Natchez in particular.

ing land policy, Cecil Johnson omits this intermediate regulation of Feb. 3, 1774, an important step in the overall development of the land policy of West Florida.

81. Chester to Dartmouth, June 9, 1775, C.O. 5/592, Minutes of the Council, Mar. 4, 1775, C.O. 5/634, RSUS, reel 7.

82. Howard, "Economic Aspects," pp. 213–15. On the French inhabitants in the Mobile area, see "List of the French Inhabitants within the District of Mobile," Sept. 26, 1763, C.O. 5/83.

Some progress was made in settling West Florida during the first five years, but it was in the following years that the greatest influx of settlers occurred. The population swelled on the lands of the Mississippi, Iberville, Amite, and Comite rivers, on Lake Pontchartrain, Second Creek, St. Catharine's Creek, and, in general, in the entire western area of the province. Following the rivers which flowed into the area, settlers migrated to West Florida from virtually every colony. From the colony's beginning, the inhabitants and officials had talked about the rich lands in the western portion of the province. Governor Johnstone had noted the necessity of "establishments which must take place on the Mississippi before West Florida can ever become a colony of consequence," a sentiment expressed repeatedly throughout the period of British control of West Florida.[83]

Although growth of the western portion of the colony proceeded cautiously at first, by the end of the 1760s settlement was advancing rapidly as settlers came alone, in small groups of one or two families, and in large colonizing ventures.[84] The minutes of the council are replete with examples of all three classes of immigrants. Several of the large schemes were of ambitious proportions, such as those of General Phineas Lyman and the Company of Military Adventurers, Adam Chrystie, Colonel John Clarke, Elias Durnford, Daniel Huay and John McIntyre, and the Reverend Samuel Swayze. These men agreed to bring into the colony a certain number of settlers in exchange for lands and other considerations.[85] The greatest period of

83. Johnstone to Sir John Lindsay ["Commanding His Majesty's Ships at Pensacola"], Dec. 14, 1765, C.O. 5/574. See also Gage to Hillsborough, Apr. 24, 1770, C.O. 5/88; Gage to Haldimand, Oct. 31, 1770, British Museum, Additional MSS, 21664; Gage to Haldimand, Nov. 28, 1770, ibid.

84. Carter, "British Administration," pp. 370–71. Philip Livingston reported in late 1775 that "the banks of the Mississippi are settling very fast." Livingston to [his father?], Nov. 19, 1775, Livingston Papers, 1:150.

85. Memorial of Phineas Lyman, n.d. [1769?], C.O. 5/577; Minutes of the Council, June 13, 1774, Oct. 14, 1771, C.O. 5/629–30, RSUS, reels 3, 4; Haldimand to Gage, July 14, 1772, British Museum, Additional MSS, 21665; Deposition of Daniel Huay, Aug. 25, 1770, C.O. 5/578; John McIntyre to Chester, July 19, 1770, ibid.; Chester to Hillsborough, Sept. 26, 1770, ibid.; Minutes of the Council, Apr. 19, 1773, C.O. 5/630, RSUS, reel 4; Clarence Walworth Alvord, The Mississippi Valley in British Politics, 2:166–77. For a list of land grants through Feb. 24, 1769, see Howard, British Development of West Florida, pp. 50–101. For a list of land grants Aug. 10, 1770–Nov. 4, 1773, see "A State of All Grants of Land," C.O. 5/591.

immigration to the western regions was after the province became a loyalist haven for refugees. This large influx of people into the western regions of West Florida led to a movement to establish the area along the Mississippi as a separate colony, or at least to give the area some self-government in order to cope with the lawlessness which prevailed. Both of these movements came too late for serious consideration before war came to West Florida.[86]

In its first dozen years, the colony of West Florida had been possessed and settled. Disputes between the governor and the military commander were common, and the province was often in a state of turmoil and confusion. The role of the military was in a constant state of change as troops arrived and were withdrawn with little apparent forethought as to the effect on the colony. Although the province was a constant drain on the budget and of little immediate mercantilistic worth, it seemed to have great economic potential. Referred to as a "barren swamp" hardly worth the expense of constructing and maintaining its forts, it actually was (or could have been) very valuable for strategic purposes, though the colonists themselves cared little for the intricacies of diplomacy or the management of empires. Thus, West Florida approached the American Revolution in a state of unresolved contradictions.

86. Memorial of proprietors of land in West Florida to the Board of Trade, Feb. 11, 1779, C.O. 5/580; Memorial of proprietors of land in West Florida to Germain, n.d. [early 1779?], ibid. The official papers and correspondence of West Florida contain dozens of letters in which it is reported that efforts are being made to get the French to move from Spanish Louisiana to British West Florida. Every British governor, except Eliot, was highly concerned with this effort and did as much as was discreetly possible to encourage the desired migration. The home government was also interested in the possibilities presented by such migration, but it maintained an attitude of detached awareness. Despite the many efforts put into this scheme, it appears to have met with little success. For a discussion of everyday life in West Florida, see Robert R. Rea, "Pensacola under the British (1763–1781)," and J. Leitch Wright, Jr., *Florida in the American Revolution,* pp. 8–15.

2

"The Spirit of What Is There Called Liberty"

T he story of West Florida in the American Revolution and in the Anglo-Spanish war is not mainly one of high ideals but rather of self-interest. The Revolution was slow in coming to West Florida, and very little of the colony's history in the preceding decade was related to war's outbreak in that region. In actuality, the war in West Florida was a battle of defense for protection of life and property in which the inhabitants joined hands with the military only when directly threatened. As Clinton Howard observed, "the fact that the colony went to Spain after the Revolution is a matter of government, not peoples."[1] When the war was over, self-interest again prevailed, for primarily only the British officialdom left West Florida.

Neither the American Revolution nor the Anglo-Spanish war was the logical conclusion of a series of preliminary events within the colony. There was indeed friction between the Spanish of Louisiana and the British in West Florida during the years leading up to war, 1763–79, but when the Anglo-Spanish war broke over the Gulf Coast, it was the consequence of factors of international rivalry and not of the petty bickering between the neighboring provinces.

In the older established colonies, the disputes between the governor and assembly and the civil and military reached the point of civil strife, with a native "American" force struggling for native "American rights" against a royal authority centered

1. Howard, "Economic Aspects," p. 220.

3,000 miles away. In newly colonized West Florida, however, the disagreements were never elevated to such a plane. There is little evidence that the inhabitants of West Florida were particularly aware of events such as the Sugar Act, Colonial Currency Act, Townshend Acts, and the Coercive Acts—traditionally considered as causes of the American Revolution in the original thirteen colonies. The exception, however, was the Stamp Act, which West Florida openly opposed. In contrast, when news of the act reached neighboring East Florida, Governor James Grant reported that "the licentious spirit, which has appeared in most of His Majesty's American colonies, in opposition to an act of the British Parliament has not spread to East Florida."[2] Although there was not any open opposition to the act in East Florida, when Parliament repealed the law, "every inhabitant rejoice[d] at the repeal of it."[3]

British officials in West Florida quickly put the Stamp Act into operation late in 1765. Jacob Blackwell became distributor of stamps, with John Misdale his deputy. Seeking the advice of the council concerning the implementation of the Stamp Act, Governor George Johnstone asked whether grants and patents should be on stamped paper, and the body unanimously advised that the documents "ought to be on paper stamped as the said act prescribes in order to render them valid according to law."[4] Open but unorganized opposition soon arose in West Florida. Governor Johnstone reported on February 26, 1766, that "the minds of the lower class of inhabitants had . . . been much agitated for some time past, since the establishment of the Stamp Act." As royal governor, however, Johnstone felt that he had no choice but to enforce the law; indeed "the very nature of empire [demands] that every dependent part thereof must be

2. Gov. James Grant to Secretary of State, Apr. 26, 1766, C.O. 5/548. See also Starr, " 'The Spirit of What Is There Called Liberty': The Stamp Act in British West Florida," and Winfred B. Kerr, "The Stamp Act in the Floridas, 1765–1766," p. 463.

3. Grant to Secretary of State, Aug. 21, 1766, C.O. 5/548.

4. Oath of Jacob Blackwell in Blackwell to John Brettell, Oct. 23, 1765, Rockingham MSS, Sheffield City Library; Minutes of the Council, Feb. 25–26, 1766, C.O. 5/625, RSUS, reel 1. The only other mention of the Stamp Act in the council occurred Feb. 26, 1766, during debate concerning a land grant, and is too brief to be of value in understanding the operation of the law in West Florida. Transcripts of Blackwell's oath and several letters relating to the Stamp Act in the Rockingham MSS were graciously made available to me by Professor Robin Fabel of Auburn University.

obedient to the sovereign power wherever it is lodged. . . ." He complained that his insistence soon turned many of the inhabitants against him and "alienated much of that affection to my services, that the vulgar were accustomed to express on former occasions. . . ."[5] He believed that many of the colonists "who would willingly have gone to death in my service six months ago . . . would now as civilly put me to death for believing the legislature of Britain has some authority in West Florida. . . ."[6]

According to Johnstone the basic reason for the opposition in commerce-oriented West Florida was economic, and from the governor's explanation it appears that the inhabitants had some legitimate reasons to complain. He reported that the law fell "extremely hard" on West Florida because of the "infancy" of the colony and the trade restriction which deprived the settlers of an adequate supply of currency. The lack of powers of the governor and council and the absence of an assembly also prevented the colonial government from finding an adequate solution. In addition, the poverty of the colonists made it nearly impossible for them to pay even the normal fees connected with obtaining land, much less any further taxes of the nature of stamp duties. The provincial officers also felt the burden because of the necessity of printing new forms for their offices without any means of direct reimbursement. Asserting that the colony was in close contact with the other continental American colonies, the governor concluded, "the spirit of what is there called liberty begun [sic] to infuse itself here, and many arguments were handed about, to show why the act should not take place."[7]

It is not clear what were the "many arguments" to which Johnstone referred, but two of his letters contain evidence of three of the main contentions. The colonists argued that since no letter of commission had arrived for the stamp distributor, the act was not in force. Second, as Johnstone had not promulgated the Stamp Act in the colony, to act on a law not

5. Johnstone to John Pownal (Secretary to the Board of Trade), Feb. 26, 1766, C.O. 5/574.
6. Johnstone to Pownal, Apr. 1, 1766, C.O. 5/583.
7. Johnstone to Pownal, Apr. 1, 1766, C.O. 5/574. This is a different letter from that cited in footnote 6.

received was improper. Asserting that these arguments bordered "upon the metaphisical stretches of common sense," the governor countered that the requisite commission would arrive (as it had by late February) and that, just as the commission had come, he expected a copy of the Stamp Act to arrive soon. He contended, however, that even if the instituting of the law were irregular, a delay in executing the Stamp Act would void all business between the time of the passage of the act and its arrival. In order to prevent such an invalidation of business, an act of Parliament would be necessary to give sanction to the colony's actions in the interval between the passage and the arrival of the Stamp Act. In order to protect the colony, therefore, he felt himself obligated to enforce the law.[8] Because of lack of violent opposition and given his autocratic nature, it is not surprising that Governor Johnstone did not follow the practice of many of the other colonies of allowing business to continue and ships to clear the harbor with the notice that stamps were not available.

The third argument against the new act is far more intriguing, but, unfortunately, little is known beyond the mere statement of the premise. Johnstone reported that Attorney General Edmund Rush Wegg (whom the governor had earlier suspended during one of his frequent disputes) had done much to agitate the populace. Wegg argued that "no man can be bound to any government, unless his own consent is conveyed, either by himself or representative." While there is no further mention of this idea in the records of West Florida, it seems evident that at this point Wegg was thinking as some of his fellow "Americans" in the older colonies were, concerning "the spirit of what is there called liberty." It is equally clear that Governor Johnstone strongly disagreed with Wegg, asserting that such contentions "never had a foundation, either in experience or common sense."[9]

Despite the objections to the Stamp Act, some of which Johnstone considered "reasonable," the governor did his best to enforce the new law, thus exposing himself to a "torrent of abuse." Some of the inhabitants refused to take out grants for land even though they were completed, and masters of ships

8. Ibid.
9. Johnstone to Pownal, Feb. 26, 1766, ibid.

were afraid to leave the harbor "with such badges of slavery." In an effort to force acceptance of the Stamp Act, Johnstone notified the land petitioners that if they did not take out their grants, he would give the lands to somebody else. According to the governor, with one or two exceptions, this action "had the proper Effect."[10] There is nothing in Johnstone's report to indicate his actions concerning the shipmasters, but two intriguing letters from General Thomas Gage in New York suggest that there were delays in the arrival of letters from Pensacola, "arising I conclude from the difficulties about the Stamp Act, which has delayed the sailing of vessels."[11]

In spite of Johnstone's insistence that the law be executed, he was apparently reluctant to enforce it because of technicalities. He informed Blackwell on October 10, 1765, that "it appears to me that you cannot perform any office in this province without producing a publick authority for that purpose. . . ." On October 21, Blackwell forwarded to Johnstone a copy of the Stamp Act and a letter from John Brettell, secretary of the Stamp Office, which indicated that Blackwell had indeed been appointed distributor for West Florida. Two days later the governor administered the oath of office to Blackwell, still maintaining reservations: "but concerning which act of Parliament or the appointment of Mr. Blackwell I have not rec[eive]d any publick notification further than the sight of a letter from John Brettel[l] to Mr. Blackwell intimating that the Lords of the Treasury had appointed him the said Jacob Blackwell distributor of stamps but no such appointment is as yet arrived in West Florida." Despite his misgivings, for the reasons mentioned above, Johnstone felt he had an obligation to enforce the Stamp Act.[12]

Governor Johnstone's enemies in West Florida also used the occasion of the passage of the Stamp Act to attack him. He reported that there was a "class of gentlemen here" who displayed "decency and good behavior," but he excluded from the realm of the virtuous several prominent West Floridians—Chief Justice William Clifton, Attorney General Wegg, Ordnance

10. Johnstone to Pownal, Apr. 1, 1766, ibid.
11. Johnstone to Pownal, Feb. 26, 1766, ibid.
12. Johnstone to Blackwell, Oct. 10, 1765, Rockingham MSS, R31; Blackwell to Johnstone, Oct. 21, 1765, ibid.; Affidavit of George Johnstone, Oct. 23, 1765, in Blackwell to John Brettell, Oct. 23, 1765, ibid.

Storekeeper Arthur Neil, Acting King's Commissary Stephen Watts, Major Robert Farmar, and others.[13] The governor complained that these opponents and the "lower class" of people saw in his effort to enforce the laws of the British Empire an opportunity to attempt to discredit him. He lamented that "the renewed pretensions of the military, by which the populace perceived the ultimate power to restrain them was torn away from my hands" (a reference to the continuing feud between the governor and the military commander), along with action by civil officials, turned the people against him. Attorney General Wegg theorized on the power of government; the grand jury drew up an address calling for an elected assembly; Chief Justice Clifton opposed the governor and did "every thing in his power to destroy all order in the community"; and Lieutenant Governor Montfort Browne initiated a petition for Johnstone's removal. Despite the opposition, the governor assured the Board of Trade, "If vice, oppression, or folly, should generate like the polypus, I will still oppose them, certain, that in the end, they cannot stand the firmness of an upright heart." If this unctuousness did not satisfy the Lords Commissioners, Johnstone concluded, "I am so sincere a friend to real liberty, that what I wish the most, is, that in correcting the present abuses, the goddess may remain unsullied and unhurt."[14]

While violent opposition to the Stamp Act did not materialize in West Florida, the potential for such drastic measures was real, as evidenced by a sworn affidavit from Robert Collins on April 1, 1766. Collins learned from fellow Pensacolian Matthew Butler in the middle of March that "there was going to be a great revolution or rebellion in this said town [Pensacola] shortly." Collins asked Butler what he meant, and Butler "said that Mr. [James] Noble had told him, that they was [sic] drawing up the heads of a remonstrance . . . in order to depose his Excellency Governor Johnstone, and to put in Lieutenant Governor Browne." For this plan to work, the conspirators needed the assistance of the military under Lieutenant Colonel Ralph Walsh, and Walsh had agreed to help. Clifton apparently was the "Chief Projector" in the plot, but the leaders also included virtually all the prominent opponents of the governor. Collins

13. Johnstone to Pownal, Apr. 1, 1766, C.O. 5/574.
14. Johnstone to Pownal, Feb. 26, 1766, ibid.

informed the governor's secretary, Primrose Thompson, and Johnstone of the scheme, but the governor was confident that such a plan would be impossible to execute, since the military and the inhabitants would not join the disgruntled leaders. Collins testified that Johnstone told him that he would "let it [the plot] die."[15] Johnstone explained his actions as a matter of statesmanship. To pursue such plots based on jealousy generally encouraged their continuation and growth, and "the consequences of unraveling the plot must have proved fatal to many, and thrown us into great convulsions." He therefore decided to "imitate the example of Caesar, in not wishing to know the whole list of my enemies. . . ." Johnstone believed that time was the necessary cure for the agitation caused by the Stamp Act, and he was confident that, in spite of whatever Walsh might do, the military would not come to the assistance of the conspirators, and without the army's aid the plot could not be carried out.[16] It is possible that in presenting the affidavit of Collins—which does not specifically mention the Stamp Act —Johnstone was attempting to strengthen his position with the ministry by insinuating that the discontent in West Florida was a result of illegal opposition to a parliamentary statute rather than his personal obnoxiousness. There is no reason to believe that Montfort Browne would not have enforced the Stamp Act if he had succeeded to the governorship.

Even though Johnstone had indicated that the Stamp Act was particularly hard on the infant province of West Florida, he did not mean his remarks as a general evaluation for "opulent or established communities." Never doubting the legality of the Stamp Act, and asserting that "the subject of taxation and money is perhaps less understood, tho' in every man's mouth, than any other subject in politics," Johnstone felt that the stamp duties were the best system of taxation since they were self-enforcing and "fall on the vices of mankind." He was of the opinion that, had the tax been quietly introduced and the money collected placed in a treasury in America in order to prevent the further depletion of silver, the law would have been greatly beneficial to the colonies. The governor also felt that it was not too late for the duty to be of advantage for America, as

15. Affidavit of Robert Collins, Apr. 1, 1766, ibid.
16. Johnstone to Pownal, Apr. 1, 1766, ibid.

"the most beneficial acts . . . have always found the greatest resistance at first." In the manner of a truly paternalistic autocrat, he counseled, "one must do good to the people like administering phisic [sic] to a child."[17] Johnstone attributed the open resistance to the Stamp Act which occurred throughout the colonies to a single factor: "the power of the sword in case of resistance to lawful authority being taken from the chief executive magistrate." The military, "if such an institution is necessary in the extent of empire," must be under the control of the governor in order to check a rebellion before it begins.[18] Interestingly, eight years later, Johnstone labeled the Stamp Act "unnecessary and dangerous."[19]

While there was resistance to the duty in West Florida, there was no organized opposition. The newly arrived French- and English-born settlers apparently respected Parliamentary authority. The number of British troops (large in proportion to the population) presumably impressed on the inhabitants the futility of resistance. The colonists in the thirteen original colonies had first based their opposition to the Stamp Act on the inability to pay, but the opposition had moved to a fight for "no taxation without representation." In West Florida, the opposition never passed the initial stage. Despite Wegg's questioning of the authority of governments, opposition to the Stamp Act in West Florida was mainly a struggle to avoid the payment of any taxes. The duty was also the occasion to continue the internal disputes which constantly plagued the colony. To say that the Stamp Act was an initial step in the coming of war would confuse the desire to avoid taxation in West Florida with the complex, idealistic opposition concerning the nature of empire in the established colonies.[20]

For four years after the repeal of the Stamp Act in mid-1766, there was relative peace in West Florida. Petty bickering continued during the administrations of Johnstone and Lieutenant Governor Montfort Browne, but, overall, the main concern of the settlers was to attain some degree of prosperity. There was

17. Ibid.
18. Johnstone to Pownal, Apr. 1, 1766, C.O. 5/583.
19. Fabel, "Governor George Johnstone," p. 47.
20. Alden, The South in the Revolution, p. 98; Mark Mayo Boatner III, Encyclopedia of the American Revolution, p. 1051.

some English contraband trade and other minor points of friction with the Spanish, but, in the main, relations were fairly good between the English in West Florida and their Spanish neighbors. These amicable relations became strained almost to the breaking point in late 1770, however, over an external issue which involved neither West Florida nor Louisiana directly. The Spanish governor of Buenos Aires had dispossessed some British subjects of their homes in the Falkland Islands, and it seemed that unless the court of Spain disavowed the action, war was likely. The British government expected a peaceful settlement, but in case of war, felt "it would be better to attack, than to wait to be attacked in West Florida." General Gage therefore instructed Colonel Frederick Haldimand to make contingent plans and preparations for an attack on Spanish New Orleans.[21]

Although the dispute was distant from West Florida and it appeared that there would be an amicable settlement of the disagreement, West Florida nevertheless attempted to place itself in a posture of defense. At the time of the Falkland Islands crisis, there were only 474 soldiers in West Florida, including officers. Of this total, 51 were in Mobile, the remainder in Pensacola.[22] Despite the expenditure of a considerable sum of money, the fortifications in West Florida remained weak. Governor Chester evaluated the condition of Pensacola: "We are by our situation environed on all sides by the Spaniards, and exposed to their attacks from the Havana, La Vera Cruz, or New Orleans. Three or four ships in six or eight days sail from the Havana would in our present situation make a most easy conquest of us. Our greatest security will be a naval armament to cruise in the Bay [Gulf] of Mexico."[23]

The circumstances of the Spanish in Louisiana were no better. Alexandro O'Reilly—described by Lieutenant Governor Montfort Browne as "the most experienced general in the Spanish service"—had arrived in Louisiana in 1769 with 2,056 men, most of whom soon returned to Havana with O'Reilly. Only a small force of about 179 regular troops remained in New

21. Gage to Haldimand, Nov. 30, 1770, "Secret and Confidential," British Museum, Additional MSS, 21664.
22. Troop Return, Pensacola, Mar. 10, 1771, C.O. 5/578.
23. Chester to Hillsborough, Mar. 8, 1771, in Rowland, "Peter Chester," p. 34.

Orleans, and O'Reilly raised 13 militia companies, totaling 1,040 men, under native officers, to serve as the defending army of Louisiana. O'Reilly considered Louisiana useful and desirable for Spain, but he felt "that Louisiana does not merit defense in time of war, and that its fate will be determined in times of peace." He recommended, however, in light of the possibility of war over the Falkland Islands, that Governor Luis de Unzaga y Amezaga of Louisiana be vigilant concerning the actions of the British, and that an additional 100 men reinforce Louisiana.[24] Colonel Haldimand informed General Thomas Gage in February 1771 that the number of Spanish troops in Louisiana was increasing and that the Spanish were boasting that they were strong enough to take Pensacola. He confided that, in his estimation, they were actually apprehensive, since it would be easy for the British to capture Louisiana.[25]

With both West Florida and Louisiana weak and yet preparing for war, Lord Hillsborough warned that "there is but too much reason to apprehend that the matter in negotiation with the Court of Spain will have its issue in a speedy war, the success of which will depend upon the most vigorous exertion of every strength this kingdom is able to put forth." Consequently, he ordered Gage to mobilize an army for an attack on New Orleans upon the commencement of hostilities. Gage would personally command the expedition, and the admiral of the squadron at Jamaica would assist him in any way necessary. Less than a month later, however, Hillsborough reported that England and Spain had concluded a settlement of the dispute.[26]

Upon receiving Hillsborough's letter, Gage ordered Haldimand to stop preparations for the New Orleans campaign. Less than a month later, Gage assured Haldimand that even though the newspapers "talk of nothing but war," peace was restored. Haldimand, however, did not feel that peace would last long. Perhaps Hillsborough penned the best expression of

24. Antonio Bucareli y Ursua to Julian de Arriaga, July 7, 1769, in *Spain in the Mississippi Valley, 1765-1794*, ed. Lawrence Kinnaird, 1:87–88; Browne to Gage, Aug. 19, 1769, C.O. 5/577; John Walton Caughey, *Bernardo de Gálvez in Louisiana, 1776-1783*, p. 41; Alexandro O'Reilly to Marqués de Grimaldi, Sept. 30, 1770, in Kinnaird, *Spain in the Mississippi Valley*, 1:184–86.
25. Haldimand to Gage, Feb. 13, 1771, British Museum, Additional MSS, 21665.
26. Hillsborough to Gage, Jan. 2, 1771, C.O. 5/89. Hillsborough to Gage and all the governors in America, Jan. 22, 1771, C.O. 5/72.

the general sentiment concerning the probability of war or peace in a letter to Governor Chester: "There is not, I think, at present the most distant prospect of any disturbance to the public tranquillity; but at the same time I see with satisfaction the steps that are taken to fortify the harbour of Pensacola."[27] Thus England and Spain had avoided war, at least temporarily, and had removed the external circumstances that seemed destined to lead West Florida into conflict.

Although there was not a logical sequence of events leading toward rebellion in West Florida, the colony was by no means unaffected by the impending American Revolution. As early as 1768, both the American colonies and the British ministry were vying for the loyalty of West Florida. In response to the Massachusetts Circular Letter of February 11, 1768, denouncing "taxation without representation" and seeking concerted resistance against the Townshend Acts, Hillsborough sent a circular letter to all the governors in North America except Massachusetts Bay, East Florida, and Quebec. Hillsborough denounced the Massachusetts Circular Letter for "a most dangerous and factious tendency, calculated to inflame the minds of his good subjects in the colonies, to promote an unwarrantable combination, and to excite and encourage an open opposition to and denial of the authority of Parliament, and to subvert the true principles of the constitution." He instructed the governors (including Lieutenant Governor Browne) to use their influence "to defeat this flagitious attempt to disturb the public peace, by prevailing upon the Assembly of your province to take no notice of it, which will be treating it with the contempt it deserves."[28] West Florida took little notice of the Massachusetts Circular Letter or of Hillsborough's letter. The inhabitants actually were little aware of the disturbances occurring in the northern colonies, being more concerned with their own internal discord and problems of survival on the frontier.

The First Continental Congress resolved on October 21, 1774,

27. Hillsborough to Chester, July 3, 1771, C.O. 5/588; Gage to Haldimand, May 17, June 12, 1771, British Museum, Additional MSS, 21665; Haldimand to Gage, July 30, 1771, ibid.
28. Hillsborough to all the governors in America except Massachusetts Bay, East Florida, and Quebec, Apr. 21, 1768, C.O. 5/69. There is no evidence that the Massachusetts Circular Letter ever reached West Florida. For a discussion of this circular, see Merrill Jensen, The Founding of a Nation, pp. 250–64.

to send a letter to West Florida because the colony had not elected "deputies to represent them in this Congress." Congress appointed a three-member committee, Thomas Cushing, Richard Henry Lee, and John Dickinson, to draw up the letter. The next day, the committee presented its report, which the delegates approved. The letter to the inhabitants of West Florida reviewed the activities of the Congress and urged united action: "So rapidly violent and unjust has been the late conduct of the British administration against the colonies, that either a base and slavish submission, under the loss of their ancient, just and constitutional liberty, must quickly take place, or an adequate opposition be formed."[29] The committee addressed the letter to the speaker of the assembly; it was delivered to Attorney General Edmund Rush Wegg, who was the current speaker. Wegg took the letter to Governor Chester, who recommended silence. Nevertheless, inhabitants of the colony learned of the letter, and several demanded that it be shown to them. Wegg responded that he had given it to Chester. The governor reported that no one had asked him to present the letter and that he had never made the letter public, having "had great reasons to apprehend from the spirit and temper of many of the inhabitants, that the calling a House of Assembly could neither promote His Majesty's service, nor be productive of any advantage to the colony."[30]

The Continental Association which was effective December 1, 1774, had little impact on West Florida. Similarly, when, five months later, the Continental Congress unanimously adopted a resolution that "all exportations to Quebec, Nova Scotia, the Island of St. John's, Newfoundland, Georgia, except the Parish of St. John's, and to East and West Florida immediately cease,"[31] this measure had little effect upon West Florida. The Second Continental Congress met in May 1775, but again there were no delegates present from West Florida. A thorough search of the records of the province at this time indicates that West Florida was almost totally engrossed in its own problems and oblivious

29. Worthington C. Ford et al., eds., *Journals of the Continental Congress, 1774–1789*, 1:101–3; Henry Middleton (President of Congress) to the inhabitants of West Florida, Oct. 22, 1774, C.O. 5/595.
30. Chester to Germain, Nov. 24, 1778, C.O. 5/595.
31. Ford, *Journals*, 2:54.

to the developing revolution to the north. Lord George Germain sent instructions to West Florida in December 1775, prohibiting "all trade and intercourse with the several rebellious colonies in North America."[32] This prohibition also had little effect in the colony, for although there was some smuggling to the rebellious colonies, in the main there was little commercial intercourse with the Americans.

West Florida could not remain unaffected by the American Revolution after the influx of loyalists from the thirteen colonies in rebellion began. As early as May 1774, a West Floridian had suggested that if immigration to West Florida were "properly encouraged, [it] would greatly aid in purging and regulating the discontented colonies."[33] On July 5, 1775, the Earl of Dartmouth informed Chester of a ministerial decision concerning the loyalists that would leave an indelible impression upon West Florida in coming years:

> In the present situation, His Majesty wishes to afford every possible protection to such of his subjects in the colonies in rebellion, as shall be too weak to resist the violences of the times, and too loyal to concur in the measures of those who have avowed and supported that rebellion; and it is hoped that the colony under your government may not only prove a secure asylum to many such, but may also, under a proper encouragement, afford in part at least those supplies to the islands in the West Indies, which they cannot now procure from the other provinces.
>
> To this end, it is His Majesty's pleasure, . . . that gratuitous grants, exempt from quit rents for ten years should be made to any persons from the other colonies, who may be induced, under the circumstances I have stated to seek such an asylum in your government. . . .
>
> As it may possibly happen that some families, who may from the motives I have mentioned, retreat to your province from the other colonies, may arrive in a state of indigence, it is very much wished that you should make

32. Germain to the governors of the West Indian Islands, Nova Scotia, East and West Florida, Feb. 1, 1776, C.O. 5/77; Chester to Germain, June 28, 1776, C.O. 5/592. Germain enlarged upon these instructions in a letter on Feb. 26, 1776.
33. Lt. John Cambel to Dartmouth, May 1774, C.O. 5/592.

such a sparing use of the contingent fund, left to your
disposal, as to afford in such a case a reasonable succour
to such persons at the public expense; but it will be
proper, in every case of bounty and other encouragements,
to take great care, that the persons receiving the benefit, do
give good evidence of their real attachment to the constitution, and of their nonconcurrence in the rebellious proceedings in the other colonies.[34]

When Parliament granted the new appropriations for the civil
establishment for the period June 24, 1776–June 24, 1777, there
was an extra £1,000 added to the contingent fund to enable
Chester to give assistance to the loyalists who sought refuge in
West Florida.[35]

Chester informed the council on November 11, 1775, of the
arrival of the new instructions. On the same day, with the
advice of the council, he issued a proclamation establishing
West Florida as a sanctuary for loyalist refugees. He "notified
. . . all of His Majesty's good and faithful subjects who may be
induced . . . to seek a retreat in this province that the governor
of the said province will afford them every possible protection
and countenance in his power."[36] A brief perusal of the council
minutes indicates that Chester's proclamation had its desired
effect. The refugees were slow in coming at first, but by April
1776 loyalists were flocking to West Florida in large numbers.

When a refugee petitioned for land, the governor and council
administered the following affidavit: "A. B. maketh oath that he
came from the colony of ——— in order to avoid the troubles
then prevailing in that colony and to seek an asylum in West
Florida; that he is well attached to His Majesty's government
and disapproves of the present rebellion in the northern
colonies."[37] The council then considered the petitioner's claim
and granted land on "family right" (or "headright") as had been
the standard practice in West Florida. The head of the family

34. Dartmouth to Chester, July 5, 1775, C.O. 5/619. Dartmouth succeeded
Hillsborough as secretary of state.
35. William Knox to Chester, Mar. 5, 1777, C.O. 5/593. For a copy of the
estimate, see "Estimate of the Civil Establishment of . . . West Florida . . . from
. . . June 1776 to . . . June 1777," C.O. 5/600.
36. Minutes of the Council, Nov. 11, 1775, C.O. 5/634, RSUS, reel 7. Proclamation of Governor Peter Chester, Nov. 11, 1775, C.O. 5/592.
37. Minutes of the Council, Feb. 26, 1776, C.O. 5/634, RSUS, reel 7.

received one hundred acres for himself and fifty acres for his wife and each child, indentured servant, or slave. In addition, the council granted land as bounty, with the amount granted depending on the petitioner's former situation in the colony from which he fled and the degree to which his loyalty was the cause of his losses. Although each refugee took the loyalty oath, it is obvious from a survey of the petitions for land that some of the refugees were not really loyalists but merely neutrals who were tired of living in colonies torn by civil strife. Some came virtually penniless—a condition which they ascribed to their loyalty. Overall, however, the majority of the immigrants for whom records are available were wealthier than the earlier settlers of West Florida. Some brought slaves and white indentured servants with them. The land records reveal that 88 loyalists who applied for land brought between 674 and 908 slaves with them, an average of 7.66–10.32 per owner. The fact that the new settlers went almost exclusively to the western regions of the province where, in the main, the poorer class of immigrant had settled earlier made the difference in wealth more obvious.

The refugees in West Florida were a strange mixture. They came from every colony in revolt, as well as from several islands of the West Indies, but the southern colonies of South Carolina and Georgia furnished the largest number. Most of the refugees came overland or down the Mississippi River to West Florida, but many also came by ship from the more distant regions of the colonies. For some of the fleeing loyalists, West Florida was merely the first stop: Lieutenant Colonel John Robinson of the South Carolina Royalists, for example, fled overland through the Indian nations to Pensacola and then on to St. Augustine. Other settlers had intended to return to other colonies but stayed when the Revolution erupted, as was the case of John Glover and twenty others who obtained grants on January 6, 1776, on family right and bounty on the Amite and Comite rivers and Castang Bayou near Lake Pontchartrain. These men and their families and slaves had come to West Florida from New York in 1772 as contracted artificers employed for construction in West Florida. Their contract stipulated that upon completion of the work, they would return to New York at government expense. They had completed their work, but because of the rebellion in New York, they chose to stay in West Florida. Loyalists fled to West Florida from New York, Massachusetts Bay, Maryland, East Florida, Dominica, Connecticut, and Grenada. Larger numbers of refugees came from Virginia, Pennsylvania, St. Vincent, Georgia, South Carolina, and North Carolina.[38] The population of the western region of West Florida increased so rapidly that officials in Georgia and South Carolina urged the ministry to send troops to their respective provinces to prevent further loss of loyalists from their colonies: "Others who would be glad to assist the king's troops if they had an opportunity are preparing to go in great bodies to settle on the banks of the Mississippi River—whereby the rebels are growing stronger and the friends of government weaker every day."[39]

Although the noted botanist and traveler William Bartram made no mention of the American Revolution in a book about his tour of West Florida in 1778, the province was by then well aware of the Revolution and the influx of loyalists into the newly proclaimed sanctuary. West Florida was not yet involved in fighting with the Americans, and the war with Spain had not yet begun, but the officials in the colony felt keenly the possibility of such a war. In only one way were the inhabitants of West Florida seriously threatened in the first three years of war: ships leaving the province were subject to capture by American privateers. Chester reported to Germain in October 1776 that the rebels had commissioned three privateers in South Carolina, two at Charleston and one at Beaufort, and one at Savannah, Georgia; these would stop any ships going in or out of the Gulf of Mexico. In April 1775, the American privateer *Congress* captured the schooner *Thistle* in the Gulf of Mexico while the latter was on a voyage from Mobile. The American sloop *Pallas* attacked the schooner *Polly and Nancy*, commanded by John Davis of Mobile, bound for Jamaica, and captured the British

---

38. The source for this discussion of the loyalist migration to West Florida is the Minutes of the Council for the years 1775–80, found in RSUS. See Table 1, chap. 10. See also Louise Butler, "West Feliciana—A Glimpse of Its History," pp. 93–94; *Ontario Bureau of Archives, Second Report, 1904*, 2:800. Statistics will be provided as far as possible in chap. 10. There is not a good study of West Florida as a loyalist haven. Johnson, *British West Florida*, pp. 144–48, has a brief discussion of the subject.

39. William Campbell, James Wright, William Bull, and John Graham to Germain, Aug. 1777, C.O. 5/94.

schooner off the Dry Tortugas on January 24, 1777.[40] While evidence is scarce, captures of shipping from West Florida by American privateers undoubtedly continued throughout the war.

Beginning in early 1776 and throughout the American Revolution, there were constant "war scares" as West Floridians received reports of an impending attack. Germain was apprehensive for the safety of West Florida, "there being much ground to suspect that, the rebels in North America may early in the spring invade the province of West Florida by the channel of the Ohio and Mississippi Rivers, and may make some attempt upon Pensacola," and he ordered the commanding officer of the squadron at Jamaica to be particularly attentive to the colony. Two ships were to be kept off the coast of West Florida, and if the Americans made any attempt to attack the province, the first battalion of the Sixtieth Regiment stationed at Jamaica was to embark immediately for West Florida.[41] Following a warning from the Lords of the Admiralty that to send the two ships and then to move the requested battalion from Jamaica would leave the island exposed, Germain recalled his first command. He then ordered the placement of a small ship in Pensacola harbor and the procurement by Rear Admiral Clark Gayton of a small vessel to patrol Lakes Maurepas and Pontchartrain. Germain instructed Gayton to send as many vessels as possible to Pensacola, "for its relief and protection," if the rebels invaded West Florida.[42] Major Alexander Dickson wrote Chester in late February 1776 that in his opinion, open rebellion of the colonies and the fact that they had attacked Canada made it seem probable that the rebels would make

40. Chester to Germain, Oct. 26, 1776, C.O. 5/593; Deposition of Charles Roberts, Mar. 28, 1777, ibid.; Norris v. The Schooner *Polly and Nancy*, Aug. 14, 1778, The Revolutionary War Prize Cases: Records of the Court of Appeals in Cases of Capture, 1776–87, National Archives. One proposed expedition against West Florida never took place. On February 1, 1777, the Marine Committee of the Continental Congress ordered Capt. John Paul Jones on an expedition to capture the West Indian island of St. Kitts. He was then to sail to Pensacola to capture several British vessels and seize some cannon. Finally, he was to proceed to the Mississippi in order to capture British vessels coming down the river. The proposed expedition never materialized. Nathan Miller, *Sea of Glory: The Continental Navy Fights for Independence, 1775–1783*, pp. 225–26.

41. Germain to the Lords of the Admiralty, Jan. 6, 1776, C.O. 5/123.

42. Germain to the Lords of the Admiralty, Jan. 22, 1776, ibid.; see also Lords of the Admiralty to Germain, Jan. 11, 1776, ibid.

strenuous efforts to gain the loyalty of the southern Indians. In order to accomplish this goal, Dickson felt, the Americans would take steps to prevent the Indians from receiving arms, ammunition, and goods from West Florida. He advised that the small number of troops in the province should not be divided between Pensacola and Mobile, but should remain in one body. A few days later, Dickson appeared even more concerned about the situation of West Florida: "It is strongly reported, and most people here seem to think, we shall certainly be attacked in this province by way of Fort Pitt. Our numbers are at present so small, and those not all fit for service, with no place of strength to throw ourselves into, that should any attempt be made, we must certainly fall a sacrifice."[43] William Howe became commander-in-chief in April 1776, and he attempted to alleviate Dickson's concern: "I do not apprehend the rebels can make any attempt upon Pensacola." Howe also instructed Dickson not to spend any more money on fortifications without specific orders, except on those which were absolutely necessary.[44]

Despite all the earlier intelligence indicating the possibility of an attack on West Florida, it was not until the fall of 1776 that the first major "war scare" hit the province. First reports were vague and uncertain. Howe warned Indian Superintendent John Stuart on August 25 "that an attack is . . . meditated upon Mobile and Pensacola with 1500 men," and ordered Stuart to use every means possible to get the Indians to help in defense of West Florida. Stuart was to "appoint proper persons to accompany and lead the Indians."[45] Howe intended in this last order for Stuart to employ just a few men for leadership purposes to make the Indians more effective. Two days earlier, Stuart had proposed a similar but more ambitious plan: "I think it my duty to acquaint your Lordship that in the different

43. Dickson to Gage, Mar. 3, 1776, C.O. 5/93; Dickson to Chester, Feb. 26, 1776, in Minutes of the Council, Feb. 27, 1776, C.O. 5/634, RSUS, reel 7.

44. Gen. William Howe to Dickson, May 23, 1776, British Headquarters Papers, 190, Colonial Williamsburg, Inc. (microfilm, The Florida State University, reel 1), hereafter cited as BHP. This collection is also cited as the Sir Guy Carleton Papers or the Lord Dorchester Papers. These papers are calendared in Great Britain Historical Manuscripts Commission, *Report on American Manuscripts in the Royal Institution of Great Britain.* See also Gage to Chester, May 9, 1775, Gage Papers; Gage to Dickson, May 9, 1775, ibid.

45. Howe to Stuart, Aug. 25, 1776, BHP, 258, reel 1.

Indian nations within this district about four hundred good white men, traders and packhorsemen, might be embodied, who would be extremely useful in carrying on any service jointly with the Indians: The command of whom might, if approved by your Lordship be entrusted to my commissaries, deputies, and their assistants. Such a body of men perfectly acquainted with the manner and language of the Indians, as well as the roads and settlements and every circumstance in the neighbouring provinces, might, I conceive, be very useful and tend to prevent the disorders and excesses which bodies of Indians, not conducted by white men might probably commit."[46]

While the ministry did not adopt Stuart's scheme immediately, the plan had merit, and within five months Germain accepted the proposal. Chester reported on August 30, 1776, that he had received intelligence similar to that which Howe had communicated to Stuart. The governor asserted that if the report were true, " [the rebels] may with great facility come down the Ohio into the Mississippi and take possession of all the western parts of the colony as there are no posts or troops in that quarter to support the inhabitants who of themselves are not sufficiently strong to oppose any considerable force."[47] Major Dickson had no doubt that a detachment of rebels would come down the Ohio and Mississippi during the fall or winter of 1776–77. He questioned only the size of the force. He felt that if the body were of sufficient size, it would capture at least part of the province, as the colony "is in no state of defense."[48]

Governor Chester revealed a major threat to West Florida in early September when he brought to the council some correspondence from David Taitt (Indian commissary with the Creeks). This intelligence reported that the Americans had assembled 6,000 or 7,000 men on the Ohio River with the intention of attacking West Florida. The rebels had constructed a line of forts along the banks of the Ohio as low as the Cumberland River and had garrisoned each post with 1,000 to 2,000 men. Superintendent Stuart assured Chester that he could depend on the accuracy of this intelligence. It was Stuart's opinion that the

46. Stuart to Germain, Aug. 23, 1776, C.O. 5/229. Stuart's plan will be discussed in some detail later.
47. Chester to [Howe?], Aug. 30, 1776, BHP, 261, reel 2.
48. Dickson to Howe, Aug. 30, 1776, C.O. 5/94.

rebels intended for these troops to attack West Florida by way of the Ohio and Mississippi rivers and from there by way of Lakes Maurepas and Pontchartrain. If, however, the rebels brought cannon with them, Stuart felt that the Americans would probably try to capture what ships they could on the Mississippi and then sail to Pensacola.[49] The council advised that they deemed essential for the safety of the colony the completion of the fortifications which were under construction and the retention of the armed sloop *West Florida* in the harbor until some other armed vessel arrived. In order to expedite the construction of fortifications, the council requested that Lieutenant Colonel William Stiell (the commanding officer in West Florida) furnish troops to assist in constructing the defenses. Stiell replied that his troops were in a very poor state of health, but that he would do all he could. He also wondered "whether it would not be more conducive to the publick utility to teach the 60th Regiment the use of arms which they at present do not know than to employ them as laborers in the works." The council never answered his question, but simply advised that Stiell should furnish as many troops as possible "consistent with the good of the service."[50]

At a meeting of the council on September 7, 1776, the advisory body recommended that Fort Charlotte at Mobile be repaired to repel any invasion. The council feared that the loss of Mobile would cut off all communication with the Choctaws, Chickasaws, and all other western tribes. Such a loss would separate Pensacola from the western regions of the colony and cut off its supply of fresh provisions. The council also advised that Chester order the officers of the customs in Mobile not to give clearance to any ship bound for the Mississippi River. Chester requested that the navy prevent any ships from sailing to the Mississippi illegally "in order that these vessels may be prevented from giving intelligence or affording any assistance in transporting the rebel troops which may come against us through the channel of the Mississippi." Chester lifted this

49. Chester to [?], Sept. 14, 1776, C.O. 5/583. See also Vice Admiral Clark Gayton to Philip Stephens in the Admiralty Office, Nov. 16, 1776, C.O. 5/126.
50. Minutes of the Council, Sept. 4, 1776, C.O. 5/634, RSUS, reel 7. Three days later Chester explained why the Sixtieth Regiment was unacquainted with the use of arms when he observed that they were "raw recruits." Minutes of the Council, Sept. 7, 1776, ibid.

embargo less than a week later, after he received the legal opinion of Attorney General Wegg, Elihu Hall Bay, Chief Justice Clifton, and Philip Livingston (all four of whom were lawyers) that the present circumstances were not serious enough to warrant such an embargo, which the laws of England permitted only in time of war. The council also decided to write to John McGillivray, an influential Mobile merchant, concerning an offer he had made to raise 200 men to defend Mobile.[51] At the council meeting of November 5, Chester reported intelligence from John McIntosh, commissary among the Creek Indians, that a large American army had penetrated the Creek nation and had occasioned the sudden return of the Creek chiefs to their nation. In forwarding this correspondence to Chester, Stiell said that he thought the rebel force intended to attack Pensacola. In order to prevent a surprise attack, he recommended the establishment of a horse patrol between Pensacola and the ford of the Escambia River at a place called the "Old Spanish Cowpen." The council accepted this plan and engaged Francis Lewis and ten men to form such a patrol.[52]

Officials in London felt that the governor and inhabitants of West Florida were unnecessarily alarmed. Germain expressed his bewilderment at their panic: "I confess I do not see any sufficient ground for the alarm taken by you and the Council." He argued that he could "never imagine" the rebels would attack West Florida when the Indians were so strongly in the support of the British.[53] London officialdom was not alone in its conviction. Concerning the threatened rebel invasion, Captain Thomas Davey wrote from the British ships stationed in West Florida that "people in general think it very improbable, for my part I do not think they have the least reason to fear."[54]

Whatever the opinion of the people outside the province, in the fall of 1776 West Florida was in a state of frenzied anxiety. It is not surprising, therefore, that the council participated in a little "witch-hunting." The councilors examined charges against William Struthers that he was an officer in the rebel army.

51. Minutes of the Council, Sept. 7, 13, 1776, ibid.
52. Ibid., Nov. 5, 11, 1776.
53. Germain to Chester, July 7, 1777, C.O. 5/593. This date should probably be Feb. 7, 1777, instead of July 7.
54. Captain Thomas Davey to Gayton, Oct. 8, 1776, enclosed in Gayton to Stephens, Nov. 16, 1776, C.O. 5/126.

Struthers was a partner in the Mobile trading firm of McGillivray and Struthers. He asserted that he was loyal to England and that even the rebels had labeled him a "damned Tory." After examining the man who brought the charges against him, the council acquitted him upon his taking an oath of allegiance and posting a £1,000 bond that he would not leave West Florida without permission from the governor or commanding officer of the province.[55]

If tensions relaxed any in early 1777, the news that arrived in March must have put a quick end to any feeling of security. Chester received intelligence that the Americans had built three hundred boats at Long Island on the Holston River in eastern Tennessee and that each was capable of transporting twelve men and their provisions. His information indicated that the rebels planned to use these "large canoes," as John Stuart called them, for an attack on West Florida. The only disagreement involved whether the force would come down the Mississippi River or by a series of rivers down to the Tombigbee River to attack Mobile.[56] While the inhabitants of West Florida were once again fearful of an attack, officials not directly threatened by such an invasion were optimistic. Residents of East Florida felt that the Americans were more likely to invade their province than West Florida. Governor Patrick Tonyn said that he had made inquiry into the rumored plans of attack and could not even find rebels assembled in such a body as reported. Brigadier General Augustine Prevost, writing from East Florida, felt that the report of a planned invasion of West Florida was "entirely void and chimerical," especially since East Florida was "so much easier of access to an invasion from the rebels."[57]

Cooler heads outside West Florida were more nearly correct in believing that the rebels would not invade West Florida at this time. In the long run, however, they underestimated the ease of attacking West Florida and the value placed on the

55. Minutes of the Council, Nov. 8, Nov. 11, 1776, C.O. 5/634, RSUS, reel 7.
56. Chester to Germain, Mar. 10, 1777, quoted in George C. Osborn, "Relations with the Indians in West Florida during the Administration of Governor Peter Chester, 1770–1781," pp. 259–60. See also James Colbert to John Stuart, June 2, 1777, C.O. 5/558; Colbert to David Tait, June 1, 1777, ibid.; Stuart to Tonyn, July 21, 1777, ibid.
57. Tonyn to Stuart, Apr. 15, 1777, C.O. 5/558; Prevost to Stuart, June 14, 1777, C.O. 5/78; see also Prevost to Howe, June 14, 1777, BHP, 584, reel 2.

colony by the Americans. Charles Roberts, master of the schooner *Thistle* which an American privateer had captured, was a prisoner in Philadelphia during 1776 and 1777. He reported that in the summer of 1776, a body of rebel troops had been ready to leave Fort Pitt to attack West Florida, but that they were recalled to reinforce Washington.[58] Virginia and the Continental Congress were also planning attacks on West Florida, but these were not implemented until early 1778.

There was justification for the fear expressed by the officials and settlers of West Florida in light of subsequent events: the rebels drew up plans to invade West Florida, the Cherokee Indians made peace with the Americans, relations with the Spanish were tense, and the defenses of West Florida were still incomplete. Captain Thomas Lloyd of the sloop-of-war *Atalanta* requested in March 1777 that, as he had orders to take his ship into service immediately and as his crew was undermanned, the governor and council allow him to impress men from merchant ships to serve aboard the *Atalanta*. The council disapproved his request, but as there was a vagrancy act in the province, the magistrates agreed to aid in turning over to Captain Lloyd all vagrants and idle seamen.[59] There was a total of 806 troops in West Florida, 101 of whom were at Mobile and 31 at the Red Cliffs. Many were either sick or "raw recruits, unacquainted with the use of arms." The forts were in poor condition, and the batteries at the mouth of Pensacola harbor were "in such an unserviceable state, that it was supposed they would have fallen down with the firing of a few guns." Although he had ordered the engineer, Lieutenant Thomas Hutchins, not to spend any money on the fortifications, Chester reported that he had carried out such temporary emergency measures as he thought necessary for the security of the province.[60] General Howe was concerned about the quality of leadership in West Florida, and he requested permission from Germain to appoint a general to the province because "Governor Chester is not an officer of military talents or activity by

58. Deposition of Charles Roberts, Mar. 28, 1777, C.O. 5/593.
59. Minutes of the Council, Mar. 29, 1777, C.O. 5/634, RSUS, reel 7.
60. Chester to Howe, Nov. 21, 1776, BHP, 330, reel 2; "Return of His Majesty's Forces Stationed in the Province of West Florida—Pensacola 1st June 1777," C.O. 5/593.

any means sufficient for the service which may be carried on in that country." Germain disapproved Howe's requisition, and it was not until after Willing's raid in early 1778 that the commander-in-chief sent a brigadier general to West Florida.[61]

Relations between the civil government and military were cordial, but the troops in West Florida were inadequate for the defense of such a large and widespread area. Stiell boasted that "if even the provincial rabble has the temerity to penetrate our length they shall have a proper reception," but probably the only comfort to Howe and officials in London in the reports of the poor state of circumstances in West Florida was that "the spirit of the officers and men free us from any apprehension of insult."[62]

English officials were aware of these poor conditions, but they appeared unable or unwilling to send the necessary reinforcements. The ministry made an effort in early 1777 to strengthen West Florida without weakening any of the British military establishment. Howe ordered Stuart to form several companies of loyal refugees to be, with the Indians, an offensive force under Stuart's leadership. He was to supply the troops with arms, ammunition, and other necessities to make them "as serviceable as possible."[63] Stuart quickly organized four companies according to Howe's instructions. While these four corps, generally referred to as the Loyal Refugees, were not of major significance militarily and often caused more problems than they solved, they were important symbolically in that they were a group of fleeing loyalists who banded themselves together militarily to oppose American incursions. They were occasionally called upon by British officials to fight and patrol.[64]

61. Howe to Germain, July 7, 1777, C.O. 5/94.
62. Stiell to Howe, June 3, 1777, BHP, 561, reel 2.
63. Howe to Stuart, Jan. 13, 1777, ibid., 369, reel 2.
64. Stuart to Clinton, Nov. 22, 1778, Sir Henry Clinton Papers, William L. Clements Library, hereafter cited as Clinton Papers. The Loyal Refugees were apparently commanded by at least four separate captains, but returns are available for only two of the companies. While the number of men in each company varied, the two companies for which returns are available did not exceed one hundred men combined. In January 1778, Captain Richard Pearis' corps numbered 37 men including officers. A return for Captain Alexander Cameron's company on the same date listed forty-four men. "Return of a Troop of Light Horse Men of Loyal Refugees Commencing 1st January 1778 to 31st Inclusive Commanded by Richard Pearis," BHP, 907, reel 5; "Return of a Troop of Light Horse Men of Loyal Refugees Commencing 1st January 1778 to 31st Inclusive

While West Floridians were concerning themselves with threatened invasions from the rebellious Americans, relations between the British in West Florida and the Spanish in Louisiana progressively worsened. Friction between the two mother countries continued, and soon West Florida's major antagonist was Spanish Louisiana rather than the Americans. The rebels struck the first military blow with James Willing's excursion down the Mississippi in 1778, but the Spanish had already been aiding the Americans for over a year. A natural enmity existed between the rival mother countries: Britain had just defeated Spain in a war and had taken possession of part of her colonies. The Spanish also resented English efforts to encourage settlers to move from Louisiana to West Florida. The Indians were a major problem; each power accused the other of tampering with the Indians within its territory and of attempting to gain their affection. One of the most important sources of friction was the fact that neither the Spanish in Louisiana nor the British in West Florida considered as final the territorial settlements along the Mississippi River provided for in the peace of 1763. From the beginning, the English had felt—not completely accurately—that the province would never realize its full potential until New Orleans was part of West Florida. On the other hand, Spain wanted the Floridas back and wanted the English right of navigation of the Mississippi withdrawn. Since the Spanish in Louisiana and the British in West Florida (particularly on the Mississippi) produced many of the same goods, there was also a strong commercial rivalry between the two colonies.[65]

The friction between the two neighbors led naturally to distrust. Throughout the entire British period in West Florida, Spanish and British officials made constant efforts to seek intelligence about the strength and activities of each other. The British made good use of their merchants in New Orleans, traders and shipmasters on the Mississippi, and settlers on the

Commanded by Alexander Cameron," ibid., 906, reel 5. A copy of these two returns is also in Transcripts of the Manuscripts, Books, and Papers of the Commission of Enquiry into the Losses and Services of the American Loyalists . . . 1783–90, vol. 10, nos. 173, 174, New York Public Library, hereafter cited as American Loyalists Transcripts.

65. For a discussion of the Spanish attitude toward English commerce on the Mississippi, see Clark, New Orleans, pp. 158–204.

western edge of the colony. One Spanish official testified that
"there are some people in New Orleans who collect and write
to Pensacola all the news and information they can obtain
relative to anything about the government."[66] The best known
British spy escapade was Ensign Thomas Hutchins' mission to
New Orleans in 1773. Although he was ostensibly in town for
other reasons, Hutchins' real mission was to determine the
defenses of New Orleans and to give his opinion on the best
means of attack in case of war.[67] Spanish officials kept similar
watch on the British in West Florida; Governor Bernardo de
Gálvez sent two men, most notably Jacinto Panis, to Pensacola
to confer with Chester, but the men were actually on spy
missions.[68] The Spanish also garnered information from English
travelers and posted coastal patrols to report on naval movements. The distrust and suspicion which characterized relations
of British West Florida and Spanish Louisiana were not unwar-
ranted, since almost from the establishment of the colony, the
British in West Florida actually had plotted to gain possession
of New Orleans. In turn, the Spanish in Louisiana began aiding
the rebellious colonists early in the American Revolution and
continued to do so, ultimately entering the war as a non-ally.

The earliest aid given the Americans by the Spanish came in
the fall of 1776. With the British controlling the seas and cutting off the routes of supply for the rebellious colonies, the
Americans needed new centers of trade, and New Orleans was a
logical depot. It is not clear when the Americans first seriously
considered trying to obtain supplies from the Spanish at New

66. "Information and News," Oct. 13, 1777, Mississippi Provincial Archives,
Spanish Dominion, 1783–1820 (9 volumes of translations), 1:67, Mississippi
Department of Archives and History, hereafter cited as MPA,SD.

67. Gage to Ensign Thomas Hutchins, June 17, 1771, C.O. 5/579. Copies of
six different reports from Hutchins are located in vol. 140 in the Gage Papers.
For a good brief description of Hutchins' mission, see Joseph G. Tregle, Jr.,
"British Spy along the Mississippi: Thomas Hutchins and the Defenses of New
Orleans, 1773." The most nearly complete study of Hutchins is Anna Margaret
Quattrocchi, "Thomas Hutchins, 1730–1789" (Ph.D. diss.). See also Joseph G.
Tregle, Jr., introduction to Thomas Hutchins, An Historical Narrative and
Topographical Description of Louisiana, and West Florida, pp. v–xlvii.

68. For a discussion of the Spanish attempts to keep informed of British and
American activities throughout the colonies, see Kathryn T. Abbey, "Efforts of
Spain to Maintain Sources of Information in the British Colonies before 1779,"
and Robert L. Gold, "Governor Bernardo de Gálvez and Spanish Espionage in
Pensacola, 1777."

Orleans, but in October 1775 the British received intelligence that the Americans had a scheme whereby Spanish vessels carried powder, destined for use by the rebels, from Europe to New Orleans.[69] A force of Virginians under Captain George Gibson began a journey down the Mississippi in the summer of 1776, ostensibly to sell peltry to the Spanish. According to Chester, the party, consisting of eighteen men and one boy, came down the Ohio to Fort Pitt and from there, on July 19, began their journey down the Mississippi River. About the first of August, the rebels stopped at Walnut Hills (present-day Vicksburg), set up the American flag, and declared they were on their way to New Orleans with dispatches for the governor of Louisiana and the court of Spain. Sometime during the month of August, Gibson's small force arrived at New Orleans, where Governor Luis de Unzaga y Amezaga received him. That Unzaga even received the American was due to the influence of Oliver Pollock, an American merchant in New Orleans. Pollock had ingratiated himself with the Spanish during the administration of Governor O'Reilly, and his influence continued throughout the revolution as he became the "American agent" in New Orleans.[70]

When Unzaga met with Gibson, the American presented a letter from General Charles Lee, second-in-command of the Continental Army under Washington. Lee, writing for the Virginia Committee of Safety, stated that the colonies had ended all intercourse with the mother country after enduring oppression as long as possible. Because of the English naval blockade, the patriots were unable to get the supplies they needed. Thus, motives of both generosity and self-interest should convince the Spanish governor to give the necessary aid. The supplies which

69. "Intelligence. In a Letter from Sir Joseph Yorke. In Mr. Fraser's to JP of 25th Octr. 1775," Oct. 18, 1775, C.O. 5/138.
70. Chester to Howe, Nov. 21, 1776, BHP, 330, reel 2; John Stuart to Germain, Oct. 26, 1776, C.O. 5/78. For a discussion of the life and activities of Pollock, see James A. James, *Oliver Pollock: The Life and Times of an Unknown Patriot*. Pollock had received land grants in West Florida on Sept. 1 and Nov. 2, 1772 (see Minutes of the Council, C.O. 5/630, RSUS, reel 4), and was apparently a loyal English subject at that time. On Oct. 10, 1776, however, he wrote, "As I conceive myself too much interested in everything that concerns America (notwithstanding my present situation is remote from the scene of action) I eagerly embraced the opportunity of exerting my utmost endeavours for the glorious cause" (quoted in James, *Oliver Pollock*, p. 65).

Lee requested were "guns, blankets, and medicinal drugs, particularly quinine." To reinforce his position, Lee asserted that if Great Britain subjugated the colonies, all of the Spanish possessions in the West Indies and Mexico would be at her mercy. If, however, the colonies should defeat England with Spanish aid, Spain would have nothing to fear, as "the genius of the [American] people, their situation and their circumstances engage them by preference in agriculture and free trade, which are most suited to their interests and inclination."[71]

The cautious Unzaga hesitated; "I have kept the neutrality that I had proposed to myself."[72] The governor's actions, however, indicated that he felt it was to Spain's advantage to aid the Americans. He sold one hundred quintals of gunpowder to Gibson for 1,850 Spanish milled dollars. Unzaga reported that ten quintals of powder were of good quality, ten quintals of medium, and the remainder inferior. When Governor Chester reported on the matter, he said that he could not learn whether the powder came from public or private stores, but clearly the powder came from the Spanish "royal stores" in New Orleans.[73] Oliver Pollock declared that Unzaga's attitude had actually changed after Gibson's arrival with a copy of the Declaration of Independence. In a brief reply to Lee, the Spanish governor offered his services "for employment by you in accordance with your good pleasure and desire as well as for the advantage and benefit of those provinces." While not ready to agree, without approval from Madrid, to the systematic trade Lee suggested, Unzaga assured Lee of his "good will to please you, as can be testified by the ambassador [Pollock] of those provinces to whom I have granted the means that may expedite for him his purpose of succoring those provinces."[74]

Lieutenant William Linn and forty-three men began the trip back up the Mississippi on September 22, 1777, with three-fourths of the gunpowder. The bateau had a Spanish master,

71. General Charles Lee to the Governor of Louisiana [Luis de Unzaga y Amezaga], May 1776, Virginia Letters, 1776–78, Library of Congress.

72. Quoted in James, *Oliver Pollock*, p. 65.

73. Unzaga to Martín Navarro, Sept. 20, 1776, in Kinnaird, *Spain in the Mississippi Valley*, 1:234; Spanish loan to Virginia, signed by George Gibson, Sept. 21, 1776, ibid., 1:234–35; Chester to Howe, Nov. 21, 1776, BHP, 330, reel 2. A quintal is a metric unit of weight equal to 222.462 pounds.

74. Quoted in James, *Oliver Pollock*, pp. 65–66.

and the boat and her cargo were nominally Spanish, bound for trade with the Indians high up the Mississippi. The Spanish master also stated that he had hired the Americans on board the vessel to row the bateau up the river. Linn's force got to Fort Pitt and Wheeling just in time to prevent those posts from falling to the British and Indians.[75] While his force was returning to the refractory colonies, Gibson was imprisoned briefly by the Spanish to quiet suspicions. In October, however, Unzaga allowed Gibson to take passage on board a vessel bound for Philadelphia under the command of Captain George Ord. Under Spanish colors and with the avowed intention of procuring flour, the ship arrived at Philadelphia in November with the rest of the gunpowder and a message from Pollock to Robert Morris: "Permit me . . . to make tender of my hearty services, and to assure you that my conduct shall ever be such as to merit the confidence and approbation of the country to which I owe everything but my birth."[76]

Although Unzaga aided the rebels, he feared the idea of a large American force coming down the Mississippi to capture Mobile, Pensacola, and the English settlements along its banks. Gibson reported that such a force was already planning an expedition in the spring of 1777. At the same time, the Spanish in New Orleans feared an invasion from the British in West Florida. The defenses of New Orleans were inadequate, and the town was open to attack from both directions on the Mississippi. Given the choice, however, Unzaga preferred the American expedition, since it would eliminate Great Britain as a threat to the Spanish colonies without posing an immediate challenge to Spanish possessions. The Spanish government sent explicit instructions to the reluctant Spanish governor in December 1776, ordering him to assure the Americans that the Spanish court approved of their expedition down the Mississippi. It also instructed the governor to obtain from Havana whatever arms and provisions the Americans requested, but in

75. Chester to Howe, Nov. 21, 1776, BHP, 330, reel 2; James, *Oliver Pollock*, p. 69; Caughey, *Gálvez*, p. 87.

76. Quoted in James, *Oliver Pollock*, p. 70. See also E. Jenkins (Captain, 112th Regiment) to Germain, New Orleans, Nov. 1, 1776, C.O. 5/155; Deposition of Charles Roberts, Mar. 28, 1777, C.O. 5/593; Caughey, *Gálvez*, p. 87. According to Jenkins' letter to Germain, Gibson took 5,000 pounds of powder with him on board the ship.

order to maintain at least a cloak of neutrality, the Spanish
were to sell the goods to the Americans through private traders.
The court also instructed the governor of Cuba to send to New
Orleans whatever goods Unzaga requested.[77]

Although it was not the only point of contact with the
Spanish, New Orleans became quite important to the colonies
in rebellion, for the illegal commerce through the southern port
gave them another vital source of supply. The British were
aware of the value of the commerce, but they were at a loss for
action. Chester saw no way to prevent expeditions such as
Gibson's "unless we can obtain strict orders from the Court of
Spain to prevent their subjects from furnishing these supplies."
Such orders were not likely to be forthcoming.[78] Chester
realized that there was another aspect to the problem also, since
there were some British merchants in New Orleans who were
rumored to be willing to furnish supplies for the Americans.
Once again Chester was at a loss for action "unless all British
vessels concerned in suppressing the trade of that country, are
compelled to enter and discharge their cargoes at Pensacola and
the consignees give security that these goods be only disposed
of for the consumption of our inhabitants, and the Indians in
alliance with His Majesty."[79] Chester protested to Governor Unzaga about the cordialty which the Spanish had shown to Gibson and his company. By the time Chester received an answer
from New Orleans, however, the government had changed
hands, and Bernardo de Gálvez was governor. Following instructions from Madrid that the Americans were really Britons
and that "these same Americans will be admitted to the ports of
Spain although they present themselves with their own banner,
distinct from that of Britain," Gálvez engaged in double talk to
the effect that there was no way he could distinguish loyal
Britons from rebels.[80]

This letter was the beginning of the correspondence between

77. James, *Oliver Pollock*, pp. 67–69. For Unzaga's description of the Gibson
event, see Unzaga to José de Gálvez, Sept. 7, 1776. Miscellaneous Papers
Relating to Louisiana, 1740–1928, Library of Congress.

78. Chester to Howe, Nov. 21, 1776, BHP, 330, reel 2.

79. Chester to Germain, Dec. 26, 1776, C.O. 5/593.

80. Bernardo de Gálvez to Chester, Apr. 4, 1777, ibid. See also James A.
James, "Spanish Influence in the West during the American Revolution,"
p. 197.

Chester and the man who would be the main antagonist of the British in West Florida during the remainder of its history. Bernardo de Gálvez became governor of Louisiana on January 1, 1777. He was the nephew and "favorite protégé" of José de Gálvez, minister of the Indies and second in power only to King Carlos himself. A few months earlier, Bernardo de Gálvez had come to Louisiana to command the troops stationed there. He had a long, but mixed, service record behind him, having fought in Portugal and New Spain. Although he had had fifteen years of service, when he became governor of Louisiana he was only thirty years old. Combining the maturity of experience with the enthusiasm of youth, his personality and enlightened policies quickly made him a popular governor in the frontier province. He was a worthy opponent, and the British in West Florida held a high opinion of him. One member of the council confided that "in the event of a war between our crown and theirs [Spain] it's generally believed that it would take thousands [of troops] where hundreds only would have been necessary before his arrival to make a conquest of the island [New Orleans]."[81]

Throughout the years 1763–77, the British had carried on a lively trade with the Spanish on the Mississippi River. This trade grew especially large during Governor Unzaga's administration as he apparently closed his eyes to the smuggling. English ships sailed up and down the Mississippi selling goods to whoever would purchase them. These "floating stores" of the English generally carried better quality merchandise than the Spanish trade vessels and captured most of the business. One Spanish officer reported in 1776 that the commerce of Louisiana amounted to about $600,000 annually, but that only about $15,000 was in ships operating with royal permission.[82] When Gálvez arrived as governor, he was faced with the old problem

81. James Bruce to John Pownal, Oct. 16, 1777, C.O. 5/155. For a good survey of Gálvez' life, see Caughey's biography already cited. Gálvez' full name was Bernardo Vincente Polinar de Gálvez y Gallardo, conde de Gálvez. There is a great deal of confusion about Gálvez' age when he became governor. See Caughey, p. 68.

82. James, "Spanish Influence in the West," p. 194; Howard, "Economic Aspects," p. 208. For a brief and not very adequate treatment of commerce in West Florida, including a discussion of the contraband trade, see John D. Born, Jr., "British Trade in West Florida, 1763–1783" (Ph.D. diss.). See also Clark, New Orleans, pp. 158–204.

of contraband trade. The almost immediate arrival in New Orleans of regulations which allowed, in practice, almost free
trade with France and the French colonies alleviated the problem somewhat—but not as far as the British were concerned. At
first Gálvez continued Unzaga's policy of overlooking the contraband trade. English merchants in New Orleans later reported
that during these first few months they "were treated with the
greatest indulgence" and "every privilege we could wish for
was on the slightest application granted to us."[83]

Gálvez reversed his policy on the night of April 17, 1777,
when he ordered eleven ships seized for engaging in contraband
trade. According to one contemporary account, the British
moored some of the ships to the shore with planks or spars but
anchored a few of them in the river. Gálvez ordered the vessels
and merchandise (valued at about $70,000) seized and the
crews imprisoned. The next day he issued a proclamation: "We
command and order that the said British subjects do depart this
province in fifteen days at farthest from this day and we forbid
every citizen or inhabitant of this colony to receive into their
houses or habitations any stranger whatsoever without previously having obtained an express permission from the governor."[84]

The action which Gálvez took was legal, for the ships were
indisputably involved in contraband trade. The question is why
Gálvez acted when he did. According to his instructions, he
was to end the smuggling. The fact that he waited nearly four
months to act indicates that obedience to his orders was only

83. Merchants at New Orleans to Captain Lloyd, Apr. 26, 1777, in Minutes of
the Council, May 19, 1777, C.O. 5/634, RSUS, reel 7; Caughey, Gálvez, p. 70.
The English in West Florida had a surprising degree of insight into the relationship of the French to the problems which arose between the Spanish and
English over commerce. For example, see James Bruce to John Pownal, Oct. 16,
1777, C.O. 5/155: Bruce asserted that the Spanish encouraged French trade
because "it would appear that the French and Spanish courts had determined to
give as much countenance to the subjects of our rebellious colonies, as they
well could do without risking an open breach; and to prepare even against that
event in this corner . . ." (ibid.).

84. Proclamation of Gálvez, Apr. 18, 1777, in Minutes of the Council, May
19, 1777, C.O. 5/634, RSUS, reel 7; "An Account of the Interruption to Trade by
the Spaniards," n.d., BHP, 549, reel 2; Stiell to Howe, June 3, 1777, ibid., 561,
reel 2; Report of Alexander Dickson and John Stephenson to Chester, in
Minutes of the Council, Sept. 29, 1777, C.O. 5/635, RSUS, reel 8. A list of
the vessels seized and the price for which they were sold is in this report.

part of the motive for his action. The governor explained his actions in terms of retaliation for activities by the British armed vessel *West Florida*, which, under the command of Lieutenant George Burdon, had seized a small schooner and two canoes on Lake Pontchartrain for engaging in contraband trade. The Spanish vessels apparently had carried just a few barrels of tar, some wine, and tobacco obtained on the English side of the lake. Gálvez did not deny that their trade was illegal, but he felt that the returns from the small quantity of goods were so minute compared to the British profits on the Mississippi that such an action was "inconsiderate." The English were convinced that resentment of this seizure by Lieutenant Burdon was apparently the main motive for Gálvez' action: "It is certain that this violent measure of the Spanish governor at the time of profound peace with them has proceeded from some pique to individuals and not from his court for no vessel had arrived in the Mississippi from any port in Spain since the departure of our ships richly laden from the Mississippi to England; therefore if any such order had been given him prior to their departure, such order would have been carried into execution as they had rich cargoes on board, and were in a similar situation with the other vessels."[85]

Not long after the ship seizures by Gálvez, Captain Thomas Lloyd arrived in New Orleans in command of the British warship *Atalanta*. He politely protested Gálvez' action and called for an explanation. The governor replied by rebuking Lloyd for interfering with Spanish commerce on the Mississippi River in stopping and searching the French-owned *Margarita* and the Spanish *Marie*. Lloyd assured Gálvez that he had thought the ships were rebel vessels and that when he had discovered otherwise, he had detained them no longer. The correspondence between the two men dragged on for some time, the basic

85. "An Account of the Interruption to Trade by the Spaniards," BHP, 549, reel 2; George Burdon to Admiral Clark Gayton, May 14, 1777, Admiralty Office Group 1, Piece 240, University of Florida photostat, hereafter cited as Adm. 1/240; Stiell to Howe, June 3, 1777, BHP, 561, reel 2; Merchants at New Orleans to Captain Lloyd, Apr. 26, 1777, in Minutes of the Council, May 19, 1777, Sept. 29, 1777, C.O. 5/634–35, RSUS, reels 7, 8. Another contemporary stated that the Spanish vessels which were seized were carrying lumber they had cut on British lands. "Précis of Transactions on the Mississippi," n.d., Lord Sackville-Germain Papers, 1775–85, vol. 2, William L. Clements Library, hereafter cited as Sackville-Germain Papers.

arguments being Lloyd's assertion of the British right of free navigation of the Mississippi and Gálvez' reply conceding free navigation of the river but not contraband trade or moorage to Spanish lands. Gálvez also informed Lloyd that two of the vessels seized were American and not English.[86] While Gálvez boasted that "I received them with match in hand, not to allow any violence, and I believe that this precaution is what checked them," he was ill at ease. He had information that another British ship was coming to join Lloyd, and, fearing that the two vessels would almost be sufficient by themselves to capture New Orleans, he requested reinforcements. His fears ended, however, when on May 12 the *Atalanta* suddenly left New Orleans, heading down the Mississippi to investigate reports of an American privateer. Perhaps the main reason for Lloyd's departure was a letter he received from five British merchants in New Orleans. After recounting the events of the seizure of the British shipping and Gálvez' proclamation that the British subjects must leave Louisiana within fifteen days, the merchants reported that "the governor has relaxed from the severity we were threatened with and has consented to our staying with the usual privileges for the collection of our debts and settlement of our affairs and indeed in every other particular seems to be inclineable to put matters on their ancient footing." The merchants urged Lloyd to use "moderate measures for it is in the power of Mr. Gálvez to hurt the British merchants here far beyond the value of the vessels seized."[87]

86. The correspondence between Captain Lloyd and Gálvez concerning the seizure of the ships is in the Minutes of the Council, May 19, 1777, C.O. 5/634, RSUS, reel 7. Caughey, *Gálvez*, p. 75, cites the second edition of Charles Gayarré's *The History of Louisiana* (New Orleans, 1879), 3:107, to show that Gálvez secretly released the American vessels. The fourth edition (1903) of Gayarré's history does not note such a fact. Why the later edition does not contain this information is not known and, indeed, whether the American vessels were released or not is unclear. Caughey, *Gálvez*, p. 72, also refers to Lloyd's ship as the *Atlanta*, but all of the correspondence in the English records refers to it as the *Atalanta*. The American vessels were the brig *Steady Friend*, Joseph Calvert master, and the *Norton*, Captain Pickles of London master. According to Dickson and Stephenson's report, the two American ships were not released but were sold to Pollock. Minutes of the Council, Sept. 29, 1777, C.O. 5/635, RSUS, reel 8.

87. Merchants at New Orleans to Lloyd, Apr. 26, 1777, in Minutes of the Council, May 19, 1777, C.O. 5/634, RSUS, reel 7; Caughey, *Gálvez*, pp. 73–74. The merchants who signed the letter were Patrick Morgan, David Ross, John Campbell, William Struthers, and Robert Ross.

When the news of the seizures reached Pensacola, the British were alarmed and outraged at what they considered high-handed tactics by Gálvez. In mid-May the council reviewed all of the information and correspondence concerning the matter and recommended that two of its members go to New Orleans to investigate the seizures. Lieutenant Colonel Alexander Dickson and John Stephenson were chosen for the mission.[88] They did not arrive at New Orleans until early August. The arguments which they presented to Gálvez were the same as the ones used by Lloyd. They did not deny that the English were engaged in contraband trade. They questioned the right of the Spanish to seize the ships, declaring the action was illegal because, according to the treaty of 1763, the English had free navigation of the Mississippi. Their arguments did not persuade Gálvez and he was able to put the British on the defensive due to carelessness in the wording of their first letters. The correspondence between the British and Gálvez continued for about a month with no change, and the British representatives finally returned to Pensacola. The incident which apparently settled the matter came as a result of sickness in Pensacola. Gálvez sent 150 barrels of flour to help relieve the distress, and his generosity apparently had the desired effect. Interestingly, both sides received the approbation of their respective courts in the matter.[89]

Another source of friction developed at about the same time. When the British protested the hospitality Gálvez had shown to Captain Barry and the American frigate *Columbus*, Gálvez replied that the king had extended immunity to all American ships on the Mississippi. He added a stern warning: "Whoever fights on the river will incur the disapproval of my sovereign, and in consideration of my duty I would have to oppose to the extent of my power." The English had enough trouble already, and fearing further repercussions on the British merchants in New Orleans, they wisely chose not to harass American shipping on the Mississippi where the Spanish controlled both

88. Minutes of the Council, May 19, 1777, C.O. 5/634, RSUS, reel 7.
89. Much of the correspondence among Gálvez, Dickson, and Stephenson and the source from which this summary was drawn are located in MPA,SD, 1:82–113. Copies of these letters are also in Minutes of the Council, Sept. 29, 1777, C.O. 5/635, RSUS, reel 8.

banks.[90] It is clear the English considered the disputes in the early months of 1777 as serious: William Dunbar, a leading Mississippi planter, confided in his diary that "this morning [April 23, 1777] an express arrived from Manchac with the news of a Spanish war."[91]

Nor were the causes for strained relations at an end. Throughout the remainder of 1777, Gálvez carried on correspondence with the Americans with an aim toward assistance. In late summer Gálvez received a letter from Colonel George Morgan, who was the American commander at Fort Pitt and "Agent, under the Commissioners for Indian Affairs in the Middle Department." After reviewing the events of the American Revolution, in a highly biased appraisal, Morgan got to the heart of the matter: "If we could procure craft at New Orleans I think we might easily surprise Mobile and Pensacola, bring off the stores and destroy their works unless they are better guarded than I apprehend. I would gladly pay well to gain certain intelligence from thence and to have a plan of their fortifications with an account of their strength and what naval force they keep to guard their coast. If a thousand men would be sufficient and we could purchase or charter vessels at New Orleans at a short notice and procure cannon, it would be giving a blow in an unexpected quarter. But we can take no measure in this without the permission and concurrence of your Excellency. We have sufficient boats, provisions, etc. ready, but if this liberty cannot be obtained, we flatter ourselves we shall be indulged in a free trade from hence to New Orleans."[92] While it is not clear how Morgan planned to raise a thousand men, his scheme was one of the initial stages that culminated in Willing's raid less than a year later.

Gálvez' reply to Morgan's letter was a strange mixture of hesitation, insinuation, and promises of assistance. The gover-

90. Gálvez to Lloyd, May 12, 1777, BHP, reel 2. The Columbus was apparently the privateer Lloyd left New Orleans to investigate. As Gálvez' warning was dated the same day Lloyd left New Orleans, the message undoubtedly caught up with the Atalanta before Lloyd reached the Columbus.

91. Eron Dunbar Rowland, ed., Life, Letters and Papers of William Dunbar, p. 46.

92. Morgan to Gálvez, Apr. 22, 1777, George Morgan Papers, 1775–1822, Library of Congress; John Hancock to George Morgan, in Congress, Apr. 19, 1776, ibid., hereafter cited as George Morgan Papers; Max Savelle, George Morgan: Colony Builder, pp. 176–79.

nor had received a royal order instructing him to secretly encourage the Americans to attack the British posts in West Florida,[93] but he was reluctant to urge military action near the Spanish possessions he governed. Nevertheless, he assured Morgan that, although he could not give his consent to the American's request, "should anyone in the city engage in this trade, I will ignore it and pretend not to know about it." Gálvez urged that, in any future correspondence, Morgan use the utmost secrecy, for if the letters "should . . . be intercepted, they will not be understood." While pledging his services, Gálvez clearly did not encourage Morgan to make the proposed expedition.[94] Gálvez' explanation for his hesitancy was that he did not wish to be "the witness of a thousand hostilities and exposed to suffer them," and he feared "the excesses with which troops are apt to be managed in foreign countries."[95] The vessel that carried Gálvez' reply to Morgan was heavily laden with Spanish arms, ammunition, and provisions. Throughout this entire period, apparently, the British were ignorant of the correspondence between Morgan and Gálvez and of the small flotilla which carried the supplies back up the Mississippi.

A new correspondence opened between Gálvez and the Americans in the fall of 1777. Virginia Governor Patrick Henry wrote to acknowledge the aid Virginia had received from the Spanish and attempted to impress upon Gálvez the benefits that would accrue to the Spanish if they continued to give assistance. Spanish control of trade in the southern states, Henry argued, would deprive the British of naval stores. He also proposed that New Orleans become a free port and that the Americans open a post at the mouth of the Ohio "to facilitate the necessary correspondence between us," which, when combined with Spanish possession of the Floridas, would enable the Spanish to "enjoy a great part of the trade of our northern states." According to Gálvez' letter to Henry in October 1778, he had answered Henry's first letter, but all that has been found is a cover letter dated May 6, 1778, enclosing three other letters.[96] Three months after his first letter, on January 14,

93. Royal Order to Gálvez, Feb. 20, 1777, quoted in Caughey, *Gálvez*, pp. 90–91.
94. Gálvez to Morgan, Aug. 9, 1777, MPA,SD, 1:71.
95. Gálvez to José de Gálvez, June 2, 1777, quoted in Caughey, *Gálvez*, p. 91.
96. Patrick Henry to Gálvez, Oct. 20, 1777, in Kinnaird, *Spain in the Missis-*

1779. Henry again wrote Gálvez. Referring to the precariousness of sending messages by sea because of the prevalence of "British Cruizers," Henry informed Gálvez that he was sending Colonel David Rogers as a messenger down the Ohio and Mississippi rivers. After thanking Gálvez for his aid to "an infant state engaged in a formidable war," Henry dispensed with the formalities to present several items for Gálvez' consideration. The first point was "to consider whether the annexing West Florida to the American Confederation will not greatly distress the English West India settlements, and hinder the progress of their rivalship to Spain." He then reiterated his plan to construct a fort at the mouth of the Ohio. Finally, because of the heavy expenses incurred in fighting England, Henry requested that Gálvez send all the supplies he could with Colonel Rogers on his return trip and asked for a loan of 150,000 pistoles. The Virginian anticipated that Gálvez would ask what the Americans had to give in exchange for the goods and loan, and he declared that all Virginia could offer was "the gratitude of this free and independent country, the trade in any, or all of its valuable productions, and the friendship of its warlike inhabitants."[97] Rogers arrived in New Orleans in late September 1778, and on October 19, Gálvez replied to assure Henry that he did not feel that Spain would disapprove of the Americans taking West Florida and joining it to the American Confederation. While he approved of constructing a fort for a landing place and felt that it would be useful, he did not think that it would be possible to build such a post because of English and Indian opposition. In response to Henry's request for goods, Gálvez informed the American that Congress had instructed him to send all goods to their agent Pollock. Gálvez also ex-

sippi Valley, 1:241. Caughey, Gálvez, p. 92, gives the date of this letter as Oct. 24, and James, Oliver Pollock, p. 111, says the date is Oct. 18. See also Gálvez to Henry, Oct. 19, 1778, MPA,SD, 1:238; Gálvez to Henry, May 6, 1778, in Kinnaird, Spain in the Mississippi Valley, 1:272–73. According to this letter, Henry wrote letters to Gálvez dated Oct. 18 and Oct. 20, 1777.

97. Henry to Gálvez, Jan. 14, 1778, ibid., 1:248–50. For Gálvez' answer to this letter, see Miscellaneous Papers Relating to Louisiana, 1740–1928. A pistole was worth roughly $4.00. Juan de Miralles, Spanish agent to the Continental Congress, informed José de Gálvez on June 6, 1778, that Governor Henry had shown him his plans for conquering West Florida. Governor Henry told Miralles that he would present the plan to Congress shortly. Aileen Moore Topping, "Spanish Agents at the Continental Congress and Spanish-American Plans for the Conquest of East Florida," p. 4.

pressed regrets that he could not give the requested loan, as he had given all the money he could to Pollock. He assured the Virginian, however, that he would place the matter before his king. Rogers did not begin his return trip until the summer of 1779, when, with Gálvez' assistance, he went overland to St. Louis, where he received goods destined for Virginia which Pollock had sent up the river. On January 15, 1778, Patrick Henry had ordered George Rogers Clark to furnish fifty men and a "good officer" to meet Colonel Rogers on the Ohio. A little above the present site of Cincinnati, however, a band of Indians under the leadership of the loyalist Simon Girty attacked Rogers' force of about seventy men. They killed Rogers and all but thirteen of his men. Once again the British were unaware of the correspondence that was passing between the Spanish and the Americans. Although the Indians killed Colonel Rogers and took his captured papers to the British, the papers did not reach West Florida in time to be of any value to the province. By then, James Willing had already led his expedition down the Mississippi.[98]

British policy concerning the use of Indians in such raids is important to an understanding of their value in the war. When Great Britain gained control of West Florida, the southern Indians were under the control of John Stuart, Indian superintendent. Five years later, the ministry gave the assemblies of the southern colonies control of Indian affairs and reduced Stuart's position to that of overall supervisor of land adjustments. This method of regulation by individual colonies who jealously guarded their own Indian trade was not successful, as the officials did not enforce what few laws the assemblies passed. With the coming of the American Revolution, a change was necessary. General Howe informed Stuart on July 12, 1777, that he was going to write Brigadier General Prevost "requiring him to leave to your discretion the entire management of your department."[99] Thus, in a fourteen-year period, the management

98. Gálvez to Henry, Oct. 19, 1778, MPA,SD, 1:236–38; James, *Oliver Pollock*, pp. 188–89; Frederick Jackson Turner, ed., "George Rogers Clark and the Kaskaskia Campaign, 1777–1778," p. 494; Haldimand to Lt. Gov. Hughes, Nov. 30, 1779, British Museum, Additional Manuscripts, 21810. The copy of the letter from Gálvez to Henry, dated Oct. 19, 1778, in BHP, 1457, reel 6, has a note appended which indicates that it was not received until Nov. 24, 1779.

99. Howe to Stuart, July 12, 1777, BHP, 604, reel 2; Hillsborough to Sir

of Indian relations had gone full circle from Stuart to the colonies and back to Stuart.

Alexander McGillivray summarized in 1784 the guiding British principle in Indian relations: "Indians will attach themselves to and serve them best who supply their necessities."[100] After England gained control of West Florida, the Indians became almost totally dependent upon the British, since the English traders could best furnish their needs. Early in the American Revolution, the rebellious colonies and the Continental Congress appointed several men to serve as Indian superintendents in the southern colonies. The leader of this group of rebel Indian agents—and Stuart's chief antagonist—was George Galphin, who had recently been a British trader to the lower Creeks. The rebels were unable, however, to gain the loyalty of the Indians. They managed to establish an uneasy peace with the Cherokees as a result of military might, but they were never successful in drawing off any sizeable number of Indians from the British, who supplied their needs. The Indians also feared the land-hungry Americans. Thus, throughout the war, Great Britain retained the loyalty of a powerful body of "light infantry" despite American and Spanish efforts at alienation.[101]

The management of the Indians was, by 1777, back in the hands of John Stuart. His "influence with the southern Indians was great, and it was through his efforts that most remained British partisans during the revolution."[102] Maintaining the loyalty of the Indians was not simple, and it was also dangerous. Following rumors that Stuart had incited the Indians to attack the frontier settlements, the rebels forced the superintendent to flee from South Carolina to Savannah. Soon the Americans in Georgia compelled Stuart to leave Savannah, and, taking refuge

William Johnson and John Stuart, Apr. 15, 1768, C.O. 5/69; Carter, "British Policy towards the American Indians," p. 56; Gage to Hillsborough, Sept. 8, 1770, C.O. 5/88. For a full discussion of Indian policy in the South prior to the American Revolution, see Alden, *John Stuart*.

100. Alexander McGillivray to Arturo O'Neill, Jan. 1, 1784, in John Walton Caughey, ed., *McGillivray of the Creeks*, p. 65.

101. Ibid., p. 21; Alden, *The South in the Revolution*, p. 15; Stuart to Dartmouth, Dec. 17, 1775, C.O. 5/229; Stuart to Dartmouth, Oct. 25, 1775, ibid.; David Tait to Stuart, Aug. 1, 1775, C.O. 5/76; Wallace Brown, *The King's Friends*, p. 277.

102. Mark F. Boyd and José Navarro Latorre, "Spanish Interest in British Florida, and in the Progress of the American Revolution," p. 130.

on the schooner *St. John*, he went to St. Augustine. The South Carolina provincial congress "removed" Stuart from his position and informed him that his estate in South Carolina stood "as a security for the good behaviour of the Indians in the Southern Department." The insurgents later confiscated Stuart's property and placed his wife under house arrest.[103]

Stuart's Indian policy was simple in principle: keep the Indians loyal to the British—or at least neutral—and prevent indiscriminate Indian attacks. Indian neutrality apparently was not difficult to attain, since this concept was the natural inclination of the Indians. Stuart told the Indians that there was a dispute between the English and the people of America but asserted that it "cannot affect you." In return, the Lower Creek Indians expressed the sentiments of all the Indians in the South when they said that they were sorry that their white friends were having a disagreement, but that "we don't want to concern [ourselves] in the matter but leave you to settle the matter yourselves." One of Stuart's deputies confirmed these sentiments when he reported, "They were all very much pleased to hear that we was [sic] not asking them to go to war against the rebels which they were very much afraid of as nothing they want more than to sit neutrals."[104]

While Stuart was taking advantage of the Indian desire for neutrality, he was also making plans, with instructions from the ministry, for the offensive and defensive use of the Indians. Stuart was convinced that an offensive policy must be carefully controlled, and early in the war the home government began moving toward a more aggressive policy. Gage asserted, "We need not be tender of calling upon the savages, as the rebels have shown us the example by bringing as many Indians against us here [Boston] as they could collect."[105] Gage in-

103. Philip M. Hamer, "John Stuart's Indian Policy during the Early Months of the American Revolution," pp. 353–63. Stuart's wife escaped from South Carolina and arrived at St. Augustine in October 1777. Tonyn to Germain, Oct. 3, 1777, C.O. 5/558. See also Memorial to Sarah Stuart, n.d., C.O. 5/158.

104. Talk to the Creek Nation, Aug. 15, 1775, C.O. 5/76; Talk from Lower Creeks to John Stuart, Sept. 29, 1775, C.O. 5/77; David Holms and Thomas Scott to Stuart, Oct. 19, 1777, BHP, 706, reel 2. See also Lower Creek Nation to Stuart, Oct. 19, 1777, ibid.; The Head Warrior of the Cussitaw for the Lower Creek Nations to John Stuart, Mar. 23, 1776, C.O. 5/77.

105. Gage to Dartmouth, June 12, 1775, C.O. 5/92; Hamer, "John Stuart's Indian Policy," pp. 358–63.

structed Stuart that should the opportunity arise, the southern Indians should "take arms against His Majesty's enemies, and to distress them all in their power."[106] Stuart prepared to carry out these orders and informed Governor Chester and his own subordinates of his new orders. Writing to his deputy, Alexander Cameron, Stuart revealed his concept of the use of the southern Indians:

> I am now to acquaint you that I have received instructions to employ the Indians in my department to distress His Majesty's rebellious subjects by all practicable means, that government and the constitution may be re-established in the distracted provinces.
> Altho' I do not construe this instruction as an order to attack the frontier inhabitants of the province indiscriminately; by which means the innocent might suffer and the guilty escape, yet in consequence of it my duty requires that no time be lost in employing the Indians of the different nations to give all the assistance in their power to such of His Majesty's faithful subjects as may already have taken or shall hereafter take arms, to resist the lawless oppression of the rebels and their attempts to overturn the constitution and oppose His Majesty's authority.[107]

Although eager for revenge, Stuart was not for indiscriminate use of Indians, but rather the use of them in "any concerted plan" with organized troops of loyalist militia: "I am convinced that Indians by themselves will never perform any thing great but cooperating with troops conducted by able leaders may be made most usefull instruments to reestablish His Majesty's government and reduce the rebellious provinces."[108] Stuart intended to prevent indiscriminate slaughter as a matter of policy. Many of the "back-country" people were either friends of the British cause or were undecided. Traditionally opposed to the

---

106. Gage to Stuart, Sept. 12, 1775, C.O. 5/76.

107. Stuart to Alexander Cameron, Dec. 16, 1775, C.O. 5/77.

108. Stuart to Germain, Jan. 23, 1777, C.O. 5/78. Wright, *Florida in the American Revolution*, pp. 32–33. On April 10, Stuart held a conference with Chester and Lieutenant Colonel Stiell in which it was agreed that "incursions by small parties" of Indians would be of no value and would only serve to weaken the Indians. "Copy of a Conference with Govr. Chester and Lieutenant Colonel Stiell [with John Stuart]," Apr. 10, 1777, C.O. 5/94.

"low-country" people who were leading the rebellion, the back-country people feared the Indians even more. If Stuart turned the Indians loose upon them, they would join in a coalition with the rebellious colonists against a common enemy. Thus, Stuart's position was a matter of expediency as well as humanity.

It appears that, while the Indians did come to the aid of the British in West Florida on several occasions, their effect was merely to delay for a brief period a seemingly inevitable defeat. At the time of the American Revolution, both sides sought the loyalty of the Indians, but, in retrospect, their value to the British cause seems to have been questionable. The main advantage the British derived from retaining the affections of the Indians was that Great Britain did not have to concern itself with Indian attacks incited by the Spanish or the Americans.

Thus had West Florida come, by early 1778, to the eve of the outbreak of war in the colony. Nothing in the preceding decade had led directly to the American Revolution in West Florida. Physically untouched by the rebellion until 1776, the colony had in a negative way taken a position of loyalty, as there was little inclination to rebel. Rumors of impending attacks, concern over American trade down the Mississippi to New Orleans, and the influx of loyalist refugees characterized the early years of the revolution in West Florida.

In a period when most of the British colonies were involved in one war, West Florida was plagued with two distinct conflicts: the American Revolution and the war with Spain. West Florida's history in the Revolution is the story of Willing's raid, British troop movements, and Spanish-American trade on the Mississippi. In the Anglo-Spanish war, the colony's history encompasses Gálvez' expeditions against Baton Rouge, Mobile, and Pensacola, and Spanish aid to the Americans. In West Florida two distinct wars were inextricably interrelated in a confusion of contraband trade, ship seizures, Spanish aid to the Americans, and American plans aimed at capture of West Florida.

3

"The Late Rascally Transaction of Mr. Willing"

During 1778, the long-threatened invasion of West Florida occurred as the American Revolution finally reached the colony. It would be over a year before the Anglo-Spanish war broke out in the frontier province. Yet, events of 1778 contributed to the outbreak of that war when the Spanish sent a spy to Pensacola and assisted James Willing in his expedition down the Mississippi River. While it was a relatively minor event in the larger context of the American Revolution, Willing's raid led to important changes in West Florida. The neutral or pro-American settlers on the Mississippi River turned loyalist in sentiment as they deplored the tactics of the American captain. The British government also became more cognizant of the vulnerability of West Florida, and, consequently, Clinton ordered additional troops to the province and Governor Chester strengthened the defenses on the river. Spanish involvement with Willing's raid also incensed the inhabitants of West Florida and increased their animosity toward both the Americans and the Spanish.

Spain had instructed the Spanish officials at New Orleans and Havana to obtain all possible information concerning the civil conflict between the British colonies and the mother country. In accordance with the instructions, in mid-1777 Gálvez sent "a person in my confidence" to Pensacola under some pretense to gather what information he could. The spy apparently returned with a plan of the fortifications at Pensacola.[1] In early 1778, Jacinto Panis undertook at Gálvez' order a more extensive and important mission to West Florida. The professed reason for Panis' mission was to seek to secure Spain's rights as a neutral in the American Revolution. Gálvez explained to the Spanish Minister of the Indies, José de Gálvez, that the true purpose of the trip was to find out "if it is true that a reinforcement of troops and two frigates has arrived at that city (as I have been informed), their intentions, their actual force, and the news of what has occurred relative to the war between Great Britain and North America."[2]

Panis arrived at Mobile on March 2 to survey the condition of Fort Charlotte and the troops. He reached Pensacola a week later, where he observed "the fortifications in a primitive state." Upon arriving in Pensacola, Panis presented a letter to Governor Chester from Gálvez introducing Panis as one who "has my entire confidence and is authorized to treat with you in my name."[3] In separate letters of March 13, 16, and 22, Panis complained to Chester of English activities which Gálvez felt infringed upon Spanish rights. In the first note, Panis stated that Englishmen and Indians were attacking Spanish boats on the upper Mississippi. Chester evaded the issue by informing Panis that the area in question was under English control but was outside the boundaries of West Florida and therefore not under his jurisdiction. In addition, Colonel John Stuart had placed some Indians with a few white men on the Mississippi "to watch the movements of the rebels and to learn if they are making preparations to attack the province." Assuring Panis that the English had no intention of offending the Spanish, Chester hoped that Gálvez "will not scrutinize too closely these acts, which are necessary and prudent under the circumstances."

In answer to Panis' second letter, complaining of English

1. Abbey, "Efforts of Spain to Maintain Sources of Information," p. 57; Gálvez to José de Gálvez, July 10, 1777, MPA,SD, 1:62–63.

2. Gálvez to José de Gálvez, Mar. 11, 1778, quoted in Caughey, pp. 140–41. See also John Walton Caughey, "The Panis Mission to Pensacola, 1778." In 1780, Gálvez explained that Panis had been sent to Pensacola "to find out all about the place and, in case of a declaration of war, to form a judicious plan of attack." Gálvez to [Navarro?], [Summer 1780], MPA,SD, 1:380.

3. Gálvez to Chester, Feb. 20, 1778, MPA,SD, 1:180; Jacinto Panis to Gálvez, July 5, 1778, ibid., 1:218–19.

traders among the Spanish Indians, Chester took the offensive and accused the Spanish and Gálvez himself of alienating Indians under English control through several congresses. Chester did not deny that there were some English citizens among the Indians in Spanish territory, but he asked Panis to consider what kind of people they were. "These people are vandals and have for the greater part fled from punishment and justice to take shelter in regions of the north and . . . they live as savages and ferocious beasts. So it is natural that this kind of people are unruly."

The third charge against the English was that Lieutenant Burdon of the *West Florida* prevented Spanish subjects from fishing on Lakes Pontchartrain and Maurepas. Chester again sidestepped the issue, informing Panis that he had no control over the ships, since they were under orders directly from the admiral at Jamaica. He did, however, present the complaint to Burdon, who denied the charges. Panis also offered a proposal from Gálvez for the mutual exchange of runaway slaves, to which Chester agreed in part. This agreement, however, was never consummated or executed.[4]

Panis left Pensacola on April 9 to return to New Orleans. While the British apparently did not suspect that Panis was on a spying mission, they did not have complete confidence in him. The morning after Panis arrived in Mobile, he reported that "there arrived a messenger from Natchez with tidings of Willing's depredations."[5] John Stephenson, a Mobile merchant, observed that as a result of "the late rascally transaction of Mr. Willing," Panis had remained in West Florida longer than he intended. The inhabitants assumed that Panis knew of Willing's raid before he left New Orleans. Significantly, when Panis presented his report to Gálvez on July 5, he discussed only the fortifications, troops, and reactions to Willing's expedition. Nowhere in the letter did he discuss his negotiations with Chester.[6]

4. Chester to Panis, Apr. 7, 1778, ibid., 1:190–95. Chester answered all three of the notes from Panis in this letter. See also Gálvez to Chester, Feb. 20, 1778, ibid., 1:180. Most of the correspondence among Gálvez, Panis, and Chester may be found ibid., 1:179–95, 206–21.

5. Panis to Gálvez, n.d., quoted in Caughey, *Gálvez*, p. 142. See also p. 145.

6. John Stephenson to Patrick Morgan, Apr. 7, 1778, ibid., p. 142; Panis to Gálvez, July 5, 1778, MPA,SD, 1:218–21.

Willing's raid was the only military venture that the Americans made into British West Florida, and the results were mixed. The financial advantages which accrued to the Americans were not substantial, and the relatively neutral east bank of the Mississippi became anti-American. The idea for such an expedition was presented to the Continental Congress in mid-July 1777. Based on a plan which George Morgan presented to General Benedict Arnold, the Board of War recommended to Congress on July 19 that "an expedition be undertaken against Pensacola and Mobile in West Florida, to facilitate which, that Colonel George Morgan be sent to New Orleans with power to negotiate with the governor of that place, and endeavour to gain his interest and assistance in the business; and, that, one thousand men will be necessary for this service, and the command of the expedition be given to General [Edward] Hand."[7]

Congress postponed consideration of the report until July 24, then debated it for two days. While there was support for the measure, the opposition had some strong arguments: there was a lack of men and money; if the area were captured it could not be held; and it was too late for it to be undertaken in the coming fall and winter. Arthur Middleton of South Carolina presented the most telling argument: "It will draw the attention of the enemy to the southern states, and endanger them, particularly South Carolina."[8]

It was another South Carolinian, however, who argued most effectively against the report of the Board of War. Henry Laurens had not yet taken his seat in Congress when the Board of War first presented the report. He arrived in Philadelphia on July 21; the next day he took his seat in Congress and led the opposition to a "random scheme for a western enterprise." When Laurens arrived, Congress had received the proposal so well that "nothing remained to do . . . but to vote men and money." Laurens felt if the Americans could spare 1,000 troops, they would be of more value in Georgia or South Carolina. He also argued that the settlers in West Florida were loyalists, the project was too expensive, the climate along the Mississippi too unhealthy, and too little was known about the country in West

7. Ford, *Journals*, 8:566–67. See also Edmund C. Burnett, ed., *Letters of Members of the Continental Congress*, 2:421.
8. Charles Thompson, Notes of Debates, in Burnett, *Letters*, 2:421–22.

Florida. To hope for secrecy in an expedition that had been discussed in several colonies was naïve. Finally, "the governor of [New] Orleans would entertain no high estimation of our political forecast should we embark 1,200 men in dependence upon him at 1,000 miles distance for the very essentials of our expedition before treaty or even consultation." Even to consider seriously such a scheme, Laurens felt, indicated that "a great Assembly is in its dotage." Although Morgan did open a correspondence with Gálvez, there is no reference after July 25 (when the report was postponed) to the outcome of the proposal in Congress, and, the South Carolinian proudly boasted, "I delivered my sentiments and was successful. The question had scarcely an affirmative."[9]

Thus Congress dropped the matter until November 21, 1777, when the Commerce Committee instructed General Hand to outfit James Willing with men, a boat, arms, ammunition, and supplies. James Willing was the younger brother of Thomas Willing of the Philadelphia firm of Willing and Morris. He had arrived in West Florida in 1772 and had obtained a grant of 1,250 acres near Natchez and a town lot in Manchac. William Dunbar wrote in his diary that Willing was well known and had often been entertained in the homes of the gentlemen on the river where he "frequently indulged his natural propensity of getting drunk." Briefly a partner of Oliver Pollock at New Orleans, Willing was unsuccessful as a merchant because, Dunbar wrote, "he had by his folly squandered a fortune." The younger Willing returned to Philadelphia in 1777 and sought a commission for an expedition down the Mississippi "by which," Dunbar complained, "he might have an opportunity of demonstrating his gratitude to his old friends."[10] Apparently, when Congress failed to approve the report of the Board of War, the Commerce Committee on its own initiative and without the consent of Congress decided to send a small expedition and to

9. Henry Laurens to Lachlan McIntosh, Aug. 11, 1777, ibid., 2:443–44; Laurens to the President of South Carolina (John Rutledge), Aug. 12, 1777, ibid., 2:445–47. See also Laurens to John Lewis Gervais, Sept. 5, 1777, ibid., 2:477. The Morgan-Gálvez correspondence is discussed in chap. 2.

10. Commerce Committee to Edward Hand, Nov. 21, 1777, ibid., 2:565; Minutes of the Council, Aug. 4, Nov. 2, 1772, Sept. 23, 1773, C.O. 5/630, RSUS, reel 4; Rowland, William Dunbar, pp. 60–62; James, Oliver Pollock, pp. 118–19; John Walton Caughey, "Willing's Expedition down the Mississippi, 1778," p. 6.

commission Willing a captain in the American Navy. The instructions which the Commerce Committee gave to Willing have never been found, but they can be reconstructed fairly well from several sources. According to the orders to General Hand, Willing would carry dispatches to New Orleans. A letter dated the same day from the Commerce Committee to Pollock states that Willing would bring supplies back up the Mississippi and Ohio to Fort Pitt. Willing presented a memorial to Congress in October 1781 in which he asserted that the Commerce Committee had instructed him to go to Fort Pitt and there to equip, arm, and supply a boat and twenty-four men. Further, he was instructed to deliver dispatches to Gálvez and to Pollock, convoy supplies back up the river to Fort Pitt, and "capture whatever British property he might meet with in the said rivers." In a letter to Pollock on May 30, 1778, Willing again related that he was "ordered to make prize of all British property on the Mississippi River."[11]

Early in the Revolution, the British in West Florida had begun to receive rumors of a rebel expedition down the Mississippi River. The settlers in the western region of the province had good reason to worry, for, "should the rebels intend hostilities against this province . . . they may with great facility come down the Ohio into the Mississippi and take possession of all the western parts of the colony as there are no posts or troops in that quarter to support the inhabitants, who of themselves are not sufficiently strong to oppose any considerable force."[12] The rumors of an expected invasion continued throughout 1777, and early in 1778, officials in Pensacola received intelligence of an abortive expedition down the Mississippi against West Florida. A Frenchman who had deserted from the Americans and had escaped to New Orleans reported that the Americans had had forty-two bateaux with sixty-five men in each prepared to come down the river in the fall of 1777 but had waited too long and had been frozen in.[13]

11. Commerce Committee to Pollock, Nov. 21, 1777, Burnett, Letters, 2:565n; Memorial of James Willing, Oct. 29, 1781, ibid.; Caughey, "Willing's Expedition," p. 8; Willing to Pollock, May 30, 1778, in Kinnaird, Spain in the Mississippi Valley, 1:282.
12. Chester to Howe, Aug. 30, 1776, C.O. 5/94.
13. Hardy Perry to Farquhar Bethune, Feb. 4, 1778, C.O. 5/79. See also Perry to [Bethune?], Feb. 4, 1778, BHP, 920, reel 5.

In order to prevent a surprise attack down the Mississippi, John Stuart had instructed his deputies among the Choctaw Indians to stand watch on the river at Walnut Hills (present-day Vicksburg) at the confluence of the Mississippi and Yazoo rivers. It was apparently this force of Indians and white men about whom Panis had complained to Chester on his mission to Pensacola. The Indians kept watch, and Hardy Perry, one of the Indian agents among the Choctaws, was confident that "as for one batteau coming down, I do not think they will venture as they cannot but hear we are lying in wait for them."[14] When Willing began his excursion, the Indians had gone home and a party of about fifty more was coming to replace them. In this brief interval, Willing came down the Ohio and the Mississippi and captured Hardy Perry and Robert Welsh, the Indian conductors.[15] When Germain learned that there had been no Indians on the Mississippi to guard against such a surprise attack, he furiously criticized Stuart's department: "It was surely a most unpardonable negligence in the officers you had appointed to watch their motions upon that river, not only to have been without intelligence of their coming, but to have no parties of Indians at the landing places or even with themselves at the post you had ordered them to; for I cannot conceive it possible that after so large an expense incurred in the Indian department, parties could not have been engaged to succeed each other in keeping a constant watch upon the banks of the River, to give timely notice of the approach of the enemy, and of sufficient strength to defeat a much more formidable detachment than that which has been suffered to do so much mischief."[16]

Having received arms, ammunition, and supplies from General Hand at Fort Pitt, Captain James Willing left the post on January 10, 1778, in the armed boat *Rattletrap* with a force of about thirty volunteers. Although the British on the Ohio and the upper Mississippi were soon aware of Willing's expedition, no word of the enemy movement reached the inhabitants of West Florida. The British assumed that Willing's expedition

14. Perry to [Bethune?], Feb. 4, 1778, BHP, 920, reel 5.

15. Stuart to Germain, Mar. 5, 1778, C.O. 5/79; Stuart to Howe, Mar. 22, 1778, Clinton Papers.

16. Germain to Stuart, July 1, 1778, C.O. 5/79.

was aimed at the English posts on the Ohio, and Willing's force moved so swiftly down the rivers, it is unlikely news of his coming could have reached Natchez before him. On the trip down the Ohio and the Mississippi, Willing's forces increased to over a hundred men. The first landing of the Americans in West Florida occurred on February 18, 1778, at Walnut Hills. At 10:00 P.M. a party of about forty Americans under the command of Lieutenant Thomas McIntyre and someone named Hodder arrived at Walnut Hills in two small barges and surprised the Indian agents who were at the home of John Watkins. The rebels threatened to kill the four Indian agents (Robert Welsh, John Richmond Marshall, Henry Earnest, and John Earnest) but did not carry out the threat. They then asked Watkins if he was in English pay; he replied negatively. The rebels assured Watkins it was his good fortune, since the river was full of Americans coming to attack West Florida. Two hours later, after forcing Watkins to take the oath of neutrality and plundering his house, the insurgents left with their four prisoners. The next morning, Willing and the remaining sixty men passed Watkins' plantation, but only a small party of five went ashore. These men informed Watkins that they were an advance force for two thousand men who would follow in May, "that they were going to New Orleans, where they intended to try their prisoners and dispose of their plunder, and that all persons whom they should take employed in the Indian department or had been deserters from their service would be put to death without reserve." Watkins left Walnut Hills the next day and went to Pensacola.[17]

Anthony Hutchins reported that the rebels arrived at his plantation, which was just a short distance above Natchez, on February 17 or 18, but it is highly unlikely that his dates are

17. Caughey, "Willing's Expedition," pp. 8–9; "Substance of the intelligence received respecting the late transactions of the rebels in the River Mississippi," n.d., C.O. 5/129; Stuart to Germain, Mar. 5, 1778, C.O. 5/79; Minutes of the Council, Mar. 5, 1778, C.O. 5/635, RSUS, reel 8. A return of Willing's volunteers on Dec. 22, 1777, lists twenty-nine men in addition to Willing (Reuben Gold Thwaites and Louise Phelps Kellogg, eds., Frontier Defense on the Upper Ohio, 1777–1778, pp. 302–3). One of the members of the party of five men that landed at Watkins' plantation on Feb. 19 was Michael Noopock, a trader on the Mississippi. He and his goods had been captured by the Americans at Aux Arcs, and he had subsequently joined the Americans in hopes of regaining his possessions in New Orleans.

correct. The advance party did not even reach Watkins' house until 10:00 P.M. on the eighteenth. Allowing time for rebel forces to take prisoners, administer an oath of neutrality to Watkins, and plunder his house, not even the advance party could have arrived at Hutchins' plantation before February 19. The rebels took Hutchins prisoner and seized his property.[18] On Thursday evening, February 19, Willing's force arrived at Natchez. Early the next morning, Willing sent out small parties to make prisoners of the inhabitants. All of the settlers who would not come willingly were to be brought in by force. Apparently, these small groups told the settlers that Willing's force consisted of five hundred men and that two thousand men under Colonel Morgan were coming in the spring. The rebels captured all of the magistrates of the district and confiscated their property.[19] Willing made all of the inhabitants prisoners on parole, raised the flag of the United States, and claimed possession of the district for the United States.

On Saturday the inhabitants chose William Hiorn, Samuel Wells, Charles Percy, and Major Luke Collins to serve as "delegates" to treat with Willing. The delegates selected Isaac Johnson, Richard Ellis, and Joseph Thompson to serve as "associates" to aid them. The negotiators proposed an eight-point capitulation to Willing, which included releasing Robert Welsh, the Indian agent, sending a copy of the capitulation to Chester, and having Willing send a message to the Choctaws to prevent the Indians from attacking the settlers. The major points of the surrender were included in points one, two, and seven:

> That we will not in any wise take up arms against the United States of America or aid, abet or in any wise give assistance to the enemies of the said state.
> That our persons, slaves and property of whatkindsoever shall remain safe and unmolested during our neutrality.
> That the delegates and their associates do in and on behalf of the people take the following oath. That they will not take up arms or otherwise act to the prejudice of the

18. Anthony Hutchins to Germain, May 21, 1778, C.O. 5/594. See also John Q. Anderson, ed., "The Narrative of John Hutchins," p. 9.

19. Capitulation of the inhabitants of the Natchez district to Captain James Willing, Feb. 21, 1778, BHP, 960, reel 5; "Substance of the intelligence . . . ," n.d., C.O. 5/129.

United States nor in word or deed . . . treat with enemies but observe a strict neutrality.

The eighth point of the capitulation provided that one of the delegates would accompany Willing to New Orleans, but there is no indication of who actually went with him. Willing's response to the proposed articles was surprisingly generous: "Agreed to in the fullest extent in behalf of the United States of America (all public officers of the Crown of Great Britain who have property in this district excepted) those who have held commissions and have signed the oath of neutrality come within the above articles." Seemingly as an afterthought, Willing added, "the property of all British subjects who are not residenters also in this district excepted they being enemies of the said states."[20]

There is little to indicate that Willing committed depredations around Natchez. Indeed, most of the information concerning Willing's raid in the Natchez region reveals that he acted as a well-mannered and generous officer. Governor Chester attested indirectly to the humane treatment Willing accorded the Natchez settlers: "the settlers below the Natchez shared a different fate." There were a few exceptions to this good treatment. The most notable instance of plundering occurred at the plantation of Anthony Hutchins, where the rebels seized eighteen slaves and all his moveable property of any value. They also killed Alexander McIntosh's cattle and hogs and plundered his house. The ill treatment McIntosh received was apparently the result of an old feud between Willing and McIntosh, because Lieutenant McIntyre told McIntosh that "that damned scoundrel James Willing is come once more to pay you a visit," which McIntosh said was an allusion to his "former expressions about Willing." There was other minor plundering by the rebels: Joseph Dawes had one slave seized, and Henry Stuart lost four Negroes, four horses, and all his hogs. Willing's reputation changed rapidly, however, when he and his "body of banditti"

20. Capitulation of the inhabitants of the Natchez district to Captain James Willing, Feb. 21, 1778, BHP, 960, reel 5; Minutes of the Council, Mar. 17, 1778, C.O. 5/635, RSUS, reel 8. According to a petition for land by Robert Welsh, he was released by Willing as stipulated in the capitulation (Minutes of the Council, Nov. 17, 1778, ibid., reel 8).

left Natchez and began a raid of plundering and destruction in the sparsely settled regions.[21]

Between Natchez and Manchac the rebel forces pillaged and burned plantations, stole slaves, and forced the settlers to flee. The Mississippi was high, and movement down the river was rapid. Early in the morning of February 23, an advance party under Lieutenant McIntyre landed a little north of Manchac in a dense fog, attacked Manchac, and seized the *Rebecca*, a ship from London captained by John Cox. The small force also made the inhabitants of Manchac prisoners on parole. The main body of Willing's "army" soon followed "and laid waste to most of the settlements from Point Coupée to Manchac." Leaving a small force in Manchac, Willing's "banditti" continued to New Orleans, where they planned to sell their booty.[22]

The devastation of British property below Point Coupée was almost complete. Willing's forces burned houses, stole moveable property and slaves, shot livestock, destroyed indigo works, burned staves, and seized settlers. As one inhabitant observed, "They have cleared all the English side of the river of its inhabitants, and nothing [is] to be seen but destruction and desolation." The rebels also seized British property on the Spanish side of the Mississippi. The American policy of devastation was not totally indiscriminate. According to two British subjects, the rebels had a blacklist of the names of loyalists. They did not bother the friends of the American cause. Willing's men seized only half of the Negroes and property at one plantation, since they considered one of the partners a patriot.[23]

Volunteers from New Orleans also joined Willing's party on the lower Mississippi. One small force under Oliver Pollock's nephew, Thomas Pollock, engaged in raids and depredations.

21. Chester to [?], Mar. 25, 1778, C.O. 5/129; Minutes of the Council, Mar. 17, 1778, C.O. 5/635.

22. Chester to Germain, Mar. 25, 1778, C.O. 5/594; Stuart to Germain, Mar. 5, 1778, C.O. 5/79; Stuart to Howe, Mar. 22, 1778, Clinton Papers. Stuart stated that the advanced force reached Manchac on Feb. 24. See also Minutes of the Council, Mar. 5, 1778, C.O. 5/635, RSUS, reel 8.

23. Alexander Ross to Stuart, Mar. 5, 1778, BHP, 989, reel 5; Rowland, *William Dunbar*, pp. 60–62; [?] to John Cambel, Mar. 1, 1778, BHP, 968, reel 5; Caughey, "Willing's Expedition," pp. 11–12; Robert V. Haynes, "James Willing and the Planters of Natchez: The American Revolution Comes to the Southwest," pp. 8–9.

Another party left New Orleans under Captain Joseph Calvert and went down the river until it joined two canoes of rebels. The combined force then seized the *Neptune*, an English brig, about eleven leagues below New Orleans. Another British vessel escaped, but the rebels took the *Dispatch* near the mouth of the Mississippi. Its master was Captain James McCraight, and the vessel, loaded with fifty prime slaves and a hundred quarters of flour, was on its way from Jamaica to David Ross and Company on the Mississippi. McCraight, his crew, and his passengers disappeared, and the British justifiably suspected foul play.[24]

Up to this point, the Spanish had not been involved in Willing's raid, but after his arrival in New Orleans, the remainder of the story of Willing's invasion inextricably involves them. As Willing's force came down the Mississippi, English settlers fled with their moveable possessions and slaves into Spanish territory seeking sanctuary. Spanish officials gave the refugees protection and sought instructions from Gálvez as to the proper actions they should take. As a result, on March 3, 1778, Gálvez issued a proclamation which stated, in part, "Inhabitants entering Spanish territory shall have perfect freedom and liberty in so far as it accords with our law of neutrality, and without distinction, the sacred right of hospitality is extended to them."[25] Gálvez intended this proclamation to reaffirm Spanish neutrality and at the same time open Louisiana to English or American citizens "without distinction." Gálvez did not issue the proclamation for totally humanitarian reasons: "With this policy I hope to gain a great advantage for the king and for this province, first, because the property, such as jewelry, skins, etc., that they have brought into our territory shall not leave it without my permission and without a payment of duty upon it, and, second, because the Negroes they have brought and those that have escaped to our dominions or whose masters desire to return to Europe shall be sold to and bought by our inhabitants at not less than half their value."[26]

24. Chester to [Sir Peter Parker?], Mar. 25, 1778, C.O. 5/129; Caughey, "Willing's Expedition," p. 13; petition of David Ross and Company to Gálvez, Apr. 11, 1778 [?], C.O. 5/129. See also Joseph Calvert to Pollock, May 4, 1778, in Kinnaird, *Spain in the Mississippi Valley*, 1:271.

25. Edict of Gálvez, Mar. 3, 1778, MPA,SD, 1:175.

26. Gálvez to José de Gálvez, Mar. 11, 1778, ibid., 1:174.

The motivation behind the proclamation was of little concern to the Englishmen fleeing the Americans. Some of the English sought refuge out of fear for their lives. Such was the case with Henry Stuart, a person named Alexander, and Alexander Ross. Stuart "had a very narrow escape being obliged to fly in his shirt to the Spanish Fort at Manchac." The rebels offered a reward for Stuart to the corporal at Spanish Fort, but he refused the bribe. One witness reported that if the rebels caught Alexander he "was to have been cut into a hundred pieces" and that "Alexander Ross will be flayed alive if they catch him."[27] Most of the British fled from West Florida to escape with some of their property and their slaves. It is difficult to tell exactly how many West Floridians sought refuge in Spanish territory, but the number was apparently large. Some of those who fled even made the move a permanent one. The town of Gálveztown at the junction of the Amite and Iberville rivers was formed mainly of fleeing British inhabitants. Whatever Gálvez' motives, he gave "a friendly protection to all those that came to the Spanish territories."[28]

The British were not alone in being freely received in Louisiana. Gálvez, strongly influenced by Oliver Pollock, also cordially received the Americans. Pollock reported to Congress that "in February 1778, I received intelligence of Captain Willing's approach, and immediately I waited on his Excellency the governor and took every necessary arrangement with him."[29] The first of Willing's troops reached New Orleans on March 1 and asked Gálvez for permission to quarter themselves in Spanish territory. A Spanish report states that Gálvez at first refused the request (which seems inconsistent with the governor's pro-American sentiments), but he did, however, finally consent to the supplication of the Americans, "feeling

27. Alexander Ross to Stuart, Mar. 5, 1778, BHP, 989, reel 5; Donald Cambel to John Stuart, Mar. 5, 1778, C.O. 5/79; [?] to John Cambel, Mar. 1, 1778, BHP, 968, reel 5. The reward for Stuart was variously estimated, from $500 to $1,000. The Alexander referred to is probably Harry Alexander who had lands on the Mississippi, but it is possible that it was William or George Alexander.

28. Donald Cambel to Stuart, Mar. 5, 1778, BHP, 982, reel 5; [People of Manchac] to [Chester?], n.d. Adm. 1/241, University of Florida photostat. For a discussion of Gálveztown, see V. M. Scramuzza, "Gálveztown—A Spanish Settlement of Colonial Louisiana."

29. Pollock to the President of Congress, Sept. 18, 1782, quoted in Caughey, "Willing's Expedition," p. 15.

humanity demanded it, especially as the petitioning men held guns."[30] During the period of Willing's raid and residence in New Orleans, Gálvez talked loudly, but secretly he was quite apprehensive about the weakness of his forces and fortifications. He did not go through any such painful decision in allowing the Americans to quarter in New Orleans. His proclamation of March 3, 1778, had made it clear that both Americans and British would receive protection in Louisiana.

The friendly reception given to the Americans was of concern to the British, as they felt that Gálvez should treat the rebels as traitors. One British subject, while in prison on charges of "conspiring against the Spanish government," observed the freedom of the Americans in New Orleans: "The party of rebels under the command of . . . James Willing were permitted to have a public guard house in the said town, that they mounted guard and patrolled the streets, and the county round, recruited, exercised, and in every respect performed the function of soldiers, as publicly as the Spanish troops did. . . . Parties of rebels [were] fitted out from the said town of New Orleans, who went up the river and across Lake Pontchartrain, plundered the British subjects there of their Negroes, cattle, and other property which was brought to New Orleans, and by authority of the Spanish government, sold at public sale."[31]

It was the sale of British properties that particularly upset the inhabitants of West Florida. Although a Spaniard recorded that Gálvez refused to give the Americans permission to sell their booty, "he had no way of preventing them from disposing of it privately."[32] Gálvez noted that he intended "the sale of said Negroes shall be carried out with secrecy and I will be able to say that I was unaware of said sale. This is in order to forestall any complaints that may be made at the Court of London."[33] To hope for such secrecy in a city in which so many British subjects had taken refuge was absurd. Gálvez was soon besieged

30. "A general diary of happenings and events in the Province of Louisiana . . . ," n.d., MPA,SD, 1:123. There is nothing to identify who wrote this long diary (pp. 122–69), but the author apparently was a person of position, since he knew the story of Willing's raid from the inside; hereafter cited as "A general diary."
31. Deposition of Alexander Graydon, Apr. 16, 1779, C.O. 5/117.
32. "A general diary," MPA,SD, 1:124.
33. Gálvez to José de Gálvez, Mar. 11, 1778, ibid., 1:174.

with petitions from West Floridians who had suffered losses as a result of the rebel excursion. He had received at least fifteen memorials by March 15, complaining of the seizures made by Willing and particularly of the property he had taken in Spanish possessions or on the Mississippi while moored to Spanish shores. The prices paid for the booty that Willing sold through Oliver Pollock in New Orleans have been estimated from $15,000 to $1,500,000. The amount was certainly higher than the first figure and probably lower than the second, which is more likely the value of all the goods and property destroyed and sold. The value of the goods was also considerably higher than the amount for which they sold. Pollock's figure of the amount received for the goods is probably the most accurate. Stating that the total could have been much larger with a bigger raiding party, Pollock showed a return of $62,500 on the goods, not including the *Rebecca*, which the Americans had converted into an armed war vessel.[34]

Immediately upon receiving news of Willing's expedition and Gálvez' actions concerning the raid, the council advised Chester on March 2 to request that Captain William Garnier of the *Southampton* order a British ship to the Mississippi. The next day Garnier informed the advisory body that he had sent Captain John Fergusson of the sloop-of-war *Sylph* on the proposed mission. Fergusson's task was to sail to the Mississippi, "in order to intercept any of the British vessels which the rebels may have taken in that river, and to attempt to carry out to sea, to demand restitution from the governor of Louisiana, of all British property brought by the rebels into his colony, and

34. Caughey, "Willing's Expedition," p. 16; Kathryn T. Abbey, "Peter Chester's Defense of the Mississippi after the Willing Raid," p. 22. A mere seven loyalist claims after the Revolution show losses due to Willing's raid placed at £25,301 sterling: David Hodges (£1,000), James Bruce (£2,134), the widow of John Thomas (£13,754), Stephen Shakespear's wife (£1,000), Adam Chrystie (£2,500), Anthony Hutchins (£3,000), and John Blommart (£1,913). These claims are located in Audit Office 12/99, A.O. 12/100, and A.O. 13/2. Many other examples of individual losses appear throughout the primary materials dealing with West Florida: William Dutton, $7,040 (Affidavit of William Dutton, May 1, 1778, C.O. 5/79); William Ogilvie, £500 (Lydia Parrish, "Records of Some Southern Loyalists" [manuscript], p. 416, microfilm, The Florida State University; see also Depositions in Witness of William Ogilvie, n.d., A.O. 12/47); "Monsr. Rabico" [Rapicaut], $10,000–$12,000 ("Mr. Alexander McIntoshes information on the seizure of Monsr. Rabicos Batteau," Mar. 19, 1778, C.O. 5/79); William Dunbar, £200 (Rowland, *William Dunbar*, p. 62).

remonstrate against his giving them protection or furnishing them with supplies."[35] Fergusson arrived off New Orleans on March 14 and immediately opened a communication with Governor Gálvez. In a letter sent with an officer bearing a flag of truce, Fergusson stated, "Having information that your Excellency has received into your government, a body of armed men, enemies to my sovereign, and that you have suffered them from the Spanish territory, to commit depredations on this river, by forcibly seizing upon the vessels, property and persons of British subjects, in violation of the treaties of peace, the laws of nations, and the rights of men. I cannot help looking on such conduct on your part, as a tacit, if not an open declaration of war against the king my master."[36]

Gálvez informed Fergusson he could bring the *Sylph* to New Orleans without fear of insult, then answered his charges:

I do not know how you can take my mode of proceeding as a declaration of war, violation of the treaties of peace, laws of nations and rights of man; when at the same time I do not think, that I have taken a single step, which does not indicate a religious observation of the rights, which you accuse me of having violated. The assistance and protection which I have given to the subjects of His Britannic Majesty are in too great a number to be mentioned in this letter, if you inquire after them of the very people who received them. If I have received the Americans upon the territories which I command, it was out of regard of the same rights of men, which you say, I do not observe, and because in the present circumstances, I follow the example of the European courts, in whose seaports, the loyal Englishmen and the Americans are received indiscriminately, without it being looked upon by the Court of Great Britain, as a declaration of war.

You are at liberty to put what construction you please upon my way of proceeding; my ideas are certainly no others, than to remain neutral in the present war . . . and should you (persisting in your opinion of my way of acting) pretend to commit the least hostility from Manchac to

35. Minutes of the Council, Mar. 2, 1778, C.O. 5/635, RSUS, reel 8; Chester to Germain, Mar. 25, 1778, C.O. 5/594.
36. Captain John Fergusson to Gálvez, Mar. 14, 1778, C.O. 5/129. Copies of the Fergusson-Gálvez correspondence are in Minutes of the Council, Mar. 25, 1778, C.O. 5/635, RSUS, reel 8.

Balise, towards the subjects of my sovereign, or any one under his protection in this colony, you will find me as resolute to repress you by force of arms, as I am willing to preserve the friendship and good understanding of the two nations.[37]

The animated correspondence between Fergusson and Gálvez often dealt with trivia as well as the main issues. The petitions which the British subjects presented to Gálvez first set forth the basic points of conflict. The English disputed the legality of the rebel seizure of ships and goods on Spanish property, moored to Spanish lands, and on the Mississippi between Manchac and the Balise where both banks were Spanish. Contending that it was illegal for the Americans to carry captured goods into Spanish territory, the English also charged that it was improper for Gálvez to receive Willing into New Orleans and to allow him to sell the captured booty there.[38]

On the same date as his first letter to Gálvez, Fergusson complained of an insult offered to the *Sylph* by a small party of rebels under Lieutenant McIntyre, "who placed himself opposite to His Majesty's Ship under my command and made use of several threats and provoking speeches." Fergusson demanded "full and ample satisfaction . . . in order to prevent the fatal consequences, that may attend your giving more countenance to a lawless banditti, than you seem to do to His Britannic Majesty's servants and liege subjects." Although Gálvez considered Fergusson's complaint against McIntyre just, "it would be still more so, if one had not replied with harsh and offensive words to his simple hailing the ship, which were the motives of his insulting answer." The governor assured Fergusson that, despite the reason for the insult, he would require McIntyre to apologize "for his impudence" if Fergusson would send an officer to accept it. Fergusson refused to receive an apology and demanded that the Spanish turn McIntyre over to the British for punishment. Gálvez refused to surrender the American and asserted that McIntyre had given complete satisfaction. The governor also requested that the British not refer to anyone in Louisiana as "rebels," for while both Americans and English-

37. Gálvez to Fergusson, Mar. 14, 1778, C.O. 5/129.
38. Caughey, "Willing's Expedition," p. 17.

men were in Spanish territories, "they ought to forget that they are enemies, and that it is an immediate consequence, that where actions are prohibited, words should be the same." Fergusson assured Gálvez that he did not wish to insult him, but "I can find no word in my language so expressive as that of rebel." Finally, Gálvez made an insulting offer to Fergusson that he must have known the Englishman could not accept. While he did not expect the Americans to attack the *Sylph*, nevertheless Gálvez sent Fergusson a corporal and six grenadiers to guard the *Sylph*. Fergusson adamantly declined the offer, exclaiming that "I flatter myself I have sufficient force to defend the ship I have the honor to command." Five days later, Gálvez explained that he had not intended for the corporal's guard to defend the ship, but merely to avert hostilities by flying the "flag of a king which is respected by the Americans."[39]

Not all of the correspondence between Gálvez and Fergusson was of such a trivial nature. Gálvez did not see how Fergusson could view his actions as a declaration of war, since they were consistent with the conduct of European countries. Stating that he wished to remain neutral, Gálvez warned Fergusson against any hostile activity within the boundaries of Spanish territory. To Fergusson, Gálvez' actions were inconsistent with the policy he set forth to Captain Thomas Lloyd of the *Atalanta* in May 1777. Gálvez had declared that hostilities would not be permitted on the Mississippi. Now, Fergusson argued, by receiving the Americans, Gálvez had given his permission for the depredations which the rebels had committed. Concerning the European practice of admitting American ships into port, "the present point in dispute, is by no means parallel, as I look upon the River Mississippi, to be a common harbour to the ships of Great Britain and Spain." Consequently, Fergusson demanded restoration of all property seized by Willing "in violation of the privileges of the said River." If there were any property that did not come within that description, Fergusson suggested that it be deposited with the governor until the pleasure of the Spanish court was known.[40]

39. Fergusson to Gálvez, Mar. 14, 1778, C.O. 5/129; Gálvez to Fergusson, Mar. 15, 1778, ibid.; Fergusson to Gálvez, Mar. 15, 1778, ibid.; Gálvez to Fergusson, Mar. 20, 1778, ibid.
40. Fergusson to Gálvez, Mar. 15, 1778, ibid.

Three days later, on March 18, Gálvez assured Fergusson that he had misunderstood the letter to Captain Lloyd; Gálvez had meant only that he would not permit hostilities on the portion of the Mississippi in which Spain owned both banks—that is, from the Balise to Manchac. Consistent with this policy, Gálvez had already begun to release property that Willing's party had seized in that region. As to Fergusson's reasoning that uses of European ports and of the Mississippi were not parallel situations. Gálvez asserted, "I think it is [parallel] and a sound judgment does not depend upon ourselves." Fergusson received Gálvez' reply that he would restore the goods taken with regrets that the governor had not agreed to hold all other property until he received further orders from Spain. Fergusson was content now to let the matter of the propriety of Gálvez' receiving Willing rest with the courts of Great Britain and Spain. The captain could not let go without a parting shot on March 20: while European ports had allowed American vessels to come into their harbors, "they have never been permitted to land in arms . . . and from thence to commence hostilities against the liege subjects of His Britannic Majesty."[41] On the next day, March 21, Gálvez elaborated concerning the property seized outside of the Spanish territories: "I said that one part shall be returned to their owners, and the other follow the fate of war, you being at liberty to take them again, whenever you find them without the districts of my government, and I think this is the same as refusing your request of keeping them in trust."[42]

Fergusson issued a proclamation on March 23 to the loyal British subjects in Louisiana, informing them that Gálvez was returning the property seized between Manchac and the Balise, but, since Gálvez was still affording protection to Willing's party, Fergusson recommended that the loyal subjects leave Louisiana and place themselves under his protection. "Should you neglect this offer and blindly confide in the insidious professions of the enemies of your country," he concluded, "you must take upon yourselves the consequences."[43] While there is

41. Gálvez to Fergusson, Mar. 18, 1778, ibid.; Fergusson to Gálvez, Mar. 20, 1778, ibid.
42. Gálvez to Fergusson, Mar. 21, 1778, ibid.; see also Gálvez to Fergusson, Mar. 18, 1778, ibid.
43. Fergusson to the loyal British subjects in Louisiana, Mar. 23, 1778, Minutes of the Council, Apr. 25, 1778, C.O. 5/635, RSUS, reel 8.

evidence that many English settlers took advantage of Fergusson's offer of protection, some of the inhabitants refused
to board the *Sylph*. Fourteen British merchants in New Orleans
thanked Fergusson for his offer but were firm in their resolution
not to move. They argued that it would be "impracticable" for
those engaged in trade to settle their affairs in the short period
of time allotted, that the slaves of the plantations were scattered
and must be collected, and that the "inhospitable barren sands
of Pensacola" promised little except failure and starvation.
Driven from their homes on the Mississippi by a group of
"banditti" which could have been stopped by a small military
force, and faced with the alternatives in Pensacola, they chose
to stay in Louisiana until they could profitably settle their
affairs or return to their homes on the Mississippi.[44]

Fergusson issued a second proclamation on April 6 requiring
all English citizens to give him a list of the names and the
number of slaves they had lost. All the slaves not so claimed
would be put on shore so that the *Sylph* would not inadver-
tently depart with any Spanish or American slaves on board.
Fergusson had achieved at least a partial success: he had been
able to get the English property which Willing's plundering
parties had taken in Spanish territory returned to the British
subjects. The Spanish governor greatly assisted in Fergusson's
efforts—he was inflexible in his stand that Willing's men must
return all goods captured in Spanish territory or on the Mississippi bordered by Spanish lands. In a letter to Chester, Gálvez
reported that he had forced the return of all the property captured within Spanish borders, including Chester's slaves.
Gálvez was just as adamant in his stand that he would not "be
responsible for goods taken between Natchez and Manchac."[45]

While Fergusson was dealing with Gálvez, the British inhabitants in Pensacola were alarmed at reports that Willing's

44. The British merchants of New Orleans to Fergusson, Mar. 27, 1778, C.O.
5/129.

45. Gálvez to Chester, May 1, 1778, C.O. 5/594; Gálvez to Fergusson, Apr. 6,
1778, C.O. 5/129; proclamation by Fergusson, Apr. 6, 1778, Minutes of the
Council, Apr. 25, 1778, C.O. 5/635, RSUS, reel 8; Caughey, "Willing's Expedi-
tion," p. 21. A good, brief review of the correspondence between Gálvez and
Willing, and Gálvez' firm stand on the return of goods, is in Caughey, "Willing's
Expedition," pp. 21–23. Several of the letters between Willing and Gálvez are in
Kinnaird, *Spain in the Mississippi Valley*, 1:260–86.

party consisted of one hundred men instead of the twenty-five originally reported. Intelligence also arrived that the Americans had a larger body, variously estimated from 2,000 to 8,000, coming down the Mississippi in May. Consequently, the council advised Chester to request that Captain Joseph Nunn of the sloop *Hound* join the *Sylph* on the Mississippi River to guard against further rebel invasions. One of the vessels would also sail up the river to Manchac to remove any Americans who remained there and to prevent them from escaping up the Mississippi. Chester immediately sought Nunn's assistance, and the captain agreed to undertake the voyage as soon as he could procure a pilot for the Mississippi.[46]

The *Hound* arrived at New Orleans in early April. Nunn reported that "the headquarters of the rebels are now at Orleans from whence they make their plundering excursions both by land and water in so private a manner that it is not possible for the King's ships to prevent it. I most earnestly wish to know what your Excellency would recommend in such a situation. Do you think I should commence hostilities with Spain or would you have His Majesty's ships proceed up the river, where there is scarce a subject left and the most fertile parts of your province are laid waste. Manchac is totally stript and the bare walls of the houses remain as a monument of the cruel depredations that have been committed by a rebel banditti." Nunn also recommended that the governor and council prohibit all commerce to the Mississippi while the rebels were in possession of the area.[47]

The arrival of the *Hound* at New Orleans caused consternation. While outwardly he put on a show of confidence, Gálvez was extremely concerned with the weak state of Spanish defenses. With the arrival of Nunn's vessel and the report that a thirty-two-gun vessel was on its way up the Mississippi, Gálvez was convinced that "these two frigates can have no other object than this place, as they have no reason to go up to Manchac,

46. Rowland, *William Dunbar*, p. 60; Stiell to Lord Amherst, Mar. 28, 1778, War Office Group 34, Piece 110, University of Florida photostat, hereafter cited as W.O. 34/110; Stuart to Germain, Mar. 5, 1778, C.O. 5/79; Alexander Ross to Stuart, Mar. 5, 1778, BHP, 989, reel 5; Chester to Prevost, Mar. 21, 1778, BHP, 1030, reel 6; Minutes of the Council, Mar. 18, 1778, C.O. 5/635, RSUS, reel 8; Joseph Nunn to Sir Peter Parker, Mar. 19, 1778, C.O. 5/129.
47. Nunn to Chester, Apr. 14, 1778, C.O. 5/129.

Natchez, or the other English settlements, nor anything to gain, because there is nobody there."[48] Because of the presence of both American and English troops in New Orleans and the weakness of the defenses in Louisiana, on April 16 Gálvez required an oath of neutrality from the English subjects in New Orleans. According to a witness, the British living in New Orleans gathered at the government house at the time appointed for the oath to be administered. Upon presenting the oath to the British, Gálvez took out his watch and told them they had half an hour to decide whether or not to sign the document. The individuals who did not sign the neutrality pledge were to leave the Spanish territory by noon the next day. Gálvez also said that in order to preserve a strict neutrality, he would require the Americans to take the same oath. While a few Englishmen chose to leave New Orleans rather than take an oath of neutrality, apparently most of the British subscribed to the pledge as a matter of expediency. It seems clear also that those who signed the oath did not think the pledge prevented them from working against the Americans. The next day the Americans unanimously took the oath of neutrality.[49]

As soon as Captain Nunn received word of Gálvez' proclamation of April 16, he wrote an animated letter to the Spanish governor, in which he protested the requiring of an oath of neutrality from subjects of a country which was at peace with Spain. Nunn assured Gálvez that the British had no hostile intentions, but that if the navigation of the Mississippi was to be open to the British, protection was a necessity. Asserting that the governor had the means of removing the British war vessels simply by forcing the rebels who had committed the depreda-

48. Gálvez to Diego Josef Navarro, Apr. 14, 1778, in Kinnaird, *Spain in the Mississippi Valley*, 1:265.
49. "An oath the British subjects were compelled to make before the Spanish governor," Apr. 16, 1778, C.O. 5/129; Declaration of Stephen Shakespear, May 6, 1778, in Kinnaird, *Spain in the Mississippi Valley*, 1:275; "A general diary," MPA,SD, 1:124; Caughey, "Willing's Expedition," p. 25. Shakespear chose to leave New Orleans. Robert Ross and John Campbell, as two examples, chose to take the oath because "to leave the country at so short a warning was not to be done without drawing on ourselves utter ruin and involving our friends in Britain in the same ruin." They asserted, "As there was nothing in the oath regarding the Americans, we conceived that it was equally our duty as before to serve our country against the rebels" (Robert Ross and John Campbell to Fergusson, Prison of New Orleans, June 27, 1778, C.O. 5/117).

tions to leave the territory, Nunn concluded, "The recent depredations that have been committed on His Britannic Majesty's subjects by piratical parties fitted out from your province give me too much reason to apprehend hostile intentions on your part, if so, I could wish you would declare yourself openly."[50] Gálvez countered that he felt the oath was necessary to maintain peace in New Orleans while two enemies "which have an inveterate hatred against the other" were both in New Orleans. As to the charge that Gálvez had assisted the Americans, the governor replied spiritedly that Nunn's information was incorrect. While it is highly questionable that the oath of neutrality was of any real benefit to the Spanish, it did anger the British officials in West Florida and led them to distrust Gálvez even more.[51]

Only one other major incident arose between the Spanish and the British as a result of Willing's expedition. The West Florida had been sailing on Lakes Maurepas and Pontchartrain east of New Orleans and had received permission to pass the Spanish fort on the Bayou de San Juan without stopping each time. The commandant of the Spanish post stopped the West Florida on April 21, however, and detained it. Lieutenant George Burdon of the British vessel penned an angry and unsigned letter to Gálvez, demanding to know by what right the Spanish stopped an English vessel on the lakes. Burdon also asserted that, as a result of the stopping of the West Florida, "I will not suffer a boat to proceed across these lakes or anywhere I may be cruising." Gálvez was miffed about receiving an unsigned letter. He also refused to back down from his position; he sent fifteen men to reinforce the fort, and he ordered that the troops begin repairs on the fort at once, "since it was in a state of deterioration." Within a week, Burdon had seized two Spanish schooners on Lake Pontchartrain. Gálvez complained to Nunn about the seizures and demanded the return of the ships and compensation for losses to the owners. Nunn answered Gálvez that he could not reply to the charges because he did not know the full circumstances of the seizures. Even if he did have all the facts, Nunn explained, he still could do nothing, since

50. Nunn to Gálvez, Apr. 16, 1778, C.O. 5/129.
51. Gálvez to Nunn, Apr. 21, 1778, ibid.; Caughey, "Willing's Expedition," p. 25.

Burdon was not under his command. The *Hound* remained on the Mississippi River until early May, but succeeded in accomplishing little, other than taking British refugees on board for protection. The *Hound* and the *Sylph* left the Mississippi and arrived on May 8, 1778, at Pensacola.[52]

Throughout Willing's stay in New Orleans, Anglo-Spanish relations were strained almost to the breaking point. In correspondence between Governor Gálvez and Governor Chester, polite declarations of intention combined with veiled threats of retaliation. In one such letter Chester declared that "after such accumulated injuries, and after so many repeated demands made for restitution of the British property sold at New Orleans, should your Excellency still persevere in your refusal of redress, I should be warranted by the laws of nations to make reprisals, and to take and detain an equivalent in property of His Catholic Majesty's subjects, until complete satisfaction was given." Chester added that he would, for the present, restrain himself and not retaliate. Instead, he would present the case to the king, who would redress the grievances of the people of West Florida. The governor further warned Gálvez:

> Should this banditti again receive supplies in your dominions and pass over from thence to commit further depredations upon the inhabitants of this colony and afterwards retire to your province for a sanctuary to dispose of their plunder, I shall then after this formal notice, consider your giving countenance thereto, as an open violation of the treaties subsisting between our respective courts, and a breach of the law of nations. . . .
> And your Excellency may be assured, that altho' I have the most earnest desire to preserve the peace, that I will not suffer such enormities to be again committed, while I have it in my power to restrain and punish them.[53]

That hostilities did not break out between West Florida and Louisiana was due to a number of factors. Although he was in a weak position, the Spanish governor spoke with a confidence

52. "A general diary," MPA,SD, 1:136–41; Caughey, "Willing's Expedition," p. 25; Nunn to Gálvez, May 1, 1778, C.O. 5/129; Nunn to Sir Peter Parker, May 9, 1778, ibid.

53. Chester to Gálvez, May 28, 1778, British Museum, Additional Manuscripts, 24322.

that gave the British cause to avoid action. The tenuous Indian alliance with the British was in a state of confusion due to the American raid. Gálvez was in a commanding position, since he held the British property which the Americans had captured. The Spaniard had also made some friends among the English by releasing the majority of goods captured by Willing. Gálvez felt that "the excitement will die down in time, as there is nothing cold-blooded about it."[54] The major factor preventing hostile action was the disinclination of both parties to become embroiled in a war. Gálvez' position was weak, and, his threats to Gálvez to the contrary, Chester always added that he hoped they could avoid war. The entire British population on the Mississippi was in confusion, troop strength was weak, and fortifications were even weaker. Governor Chester was afraid to take any positive action which would involve an already war-plagued England with another enemy. His reluctance to act was practical, and the ministry disapproved of any action beyond threats: "altho' a most unjustifiable partiality and encouragement to His Majesty's rebellious subjects may easily be discovered in the Governor's [Gálvez] proceedings, yet there by no means appears . . . sufficient cause for taking so rash a step as that you meditated of seizing Spanish property, or committing any act of hostility against the King of Spain or his subjects." Germain therefore ordered Chester to do everything possible to prevent a rupture with the Spanish in Louisiana.[55]

Such restrictions did not apply to self-defense and offensive action against the rebels. When word of Willing's expedition reached Pensacola, the British officials began at once to take measures to counteract the American force. The initial reaction to the news of Willing's raid was fear. Jacinto Panis reported

54. Gálvez to José de Gálvez, May 17, 1778, MPA,SD, 1:197. See also Caughey, "Willing's Expedition," p. 26. The British seem to have feared that a Spanish war was in the offing, however. John Stephenson wrote an Irish friend in New Orleans on April 2: "I would like for you and all my friends living in that colony to leave as soon as possible, because a black cloud is forming above it, which will soon discharge its burden. I should regret that such a cloudburst would catch them" (Stephenson to "an Irish friend who had lived many years in the city of New Orleans," Apr. 2, 1778, MPA,SD, 1:228). Eight days later, Alexander Ross advised [?] Dumbandt ("an Englishman under the protection of Spain") to leave the area, "for I expect to see a different set-up on the Mississippi soon" (Ross to Dumbandt, Apr. 10, 1778, ibid., p. 229).

55. Germain to Chester, Aug. 5, 1778, C.O. 5/619.

that in Mobile "the commandant and leaders were frightened, thinking the Americans were about to attack them," and that a similar attitude prevailed in Pensacola.[56] The British officials in West Florida lost little time in acting to protect the colony. Panis arrived in Mobile on the night of March 2, 1778, and reported the alarmed state of the town. Earlier in the day, the council met with Governor Chester at Pensacola and requested that Captain Garnier of the *Southampton* send a ship to the Mississippi. As a result, Captain Fergusson and the *Sylph* went on the mission. The council also asked Captain Garnier to give whatever assistance he could to Lieutenant George Burdon and the *West Florida* on Lake Pontchartrain.[57]

The governor and council met again the next day and requested Lieutenant Colonel Stiell to detach an officer and twenty-five men to Burdon and the armed sloop *West Florida* on Lake Pontchartrain to defend the lakes and prevent further attacks on West Florida. Stiell agreed to send the requested reinforcement. Chester and the councilors also asked Colonel John Stuart to send a company of his Loyal Refugees to Lakes Maurepas and Pontchartrain and the Nitalbanie River "to protect the inhabitants or to assist them in bringing off themselves and their property as occasion may require." Stuart was present at the meeting and stated that he would send Captain Richard Pearis and twenty men on the mission. The council made arrangements for the sloop *Hillsborough* (John Mitchell, master) and the sloop *Florida* (Adam Chrystie, owner) to transport the troops, ammunition, and supplies to the lakes ("upon the faith of the Council that should either of their vessels be taken or lost they should be paid for by government"). The advisory body asked Adam Chrystie to accompany Pearis' company, which was to embark immediately, so that "the service upon which they were sent might be more effectually performed under the care of a magistrate of the district who was so well acquainted with the Country." Chrystie consented to go with the Loyal Refugees, having been instructed that "If you find their [the rebels'] numbers small and think it practicable with Captain Pearis, his rangers, and such other assistance as you can procure in the country to dispossess them, you will attack them

56. Panis to Gálvez, July 5, 1778, MPA,SD, 1:218–19.
57. Minutes of the Council, Mar. 2, 1778, C.O. 5/635, RSUS, reel 8.

and drive them from Manchac after which you will return here
with such prisoners as you may be able to take. If you find that
they have abandoned the place in that case you will also return
here endeavoring first to obtain the fullest information of all the
proceedings of the above party since they came into the province." In order to prevent any ambiguity concerning order of
command, the council appended a postscript: "You are not to
suffer any person or persons to embark on board your sloop or
the *Hillsborough* but such as will put themselves under your
command and obey your orders."[58]

There is no record of when Chrystie and Pearis' Loyal Refugees left Pensacola, but on March 5, Stuart recorded that
Pearis embarked with twenty-five men to aid the settlers on the
Amite and Nitalbanie rivers. When the force arrived at the
Nitalbanie, Chrystie set out at once to obtain what information
he could of the strength of the Americans at Manchac. He found
his own plantation and most of the others on the Amite River
"reduced to ashes." Surveying the situation of the rebels at
Manchac, Chrystie felt that a portion of the forces under Pearis
could surprise the Americans. After consulting with Captain
Pearis, Chrystie and a detachment of fifteen men under Lieutenant [George?] Pearis set out for Manchac. After a march of
eighteen miles over bad roads, the small force arrived at Manchac on March 14, just before daylight.[59] Quietly seizing the
rebel sentinel, the British attacked the guardhouse, where they
killed and wounded five Americans and took thirteen prisoners.
After a brief skirmish, the remainder of the rebels fled across
the Iberville River into Spanish territory. The only British casu-
alty was one man with a wounded arm. Considering their force
too weak to hold Manchac, Chrystie and Lieutenant Pearis
withdrew with their prisoners and booty. Rejoining Captain
Pearis, Chrystie and the Loyal Refugees sailed for Pensacola,
where they arrived safely and imprisoned their captives.[60] The

58. Minutes of the Council, Mar. 3, 1778, ibid.
59. Stuart to Germain, Mar. 5, Apr. 13, 1778, C.O. 5/79; "A general diary,"
MPA,SD, 1:125.
60. Stuart to Germain, Apr. 13, 1778, C.O. 5/79. There is some disagreement
among contemporaries concerning the casualties and prisoners. An Englishman
wrote from New Orleans that sixteen rebels were killed or wounded (Donald
Campbell to Stuart, Mar. 20, 1778, ibid.). A Spanish writer related that the
Loyal Refugees attacked Manchac, "killing two men and one woman, wounding
four or six persons, [and] capturing fourteen prisoners." This same source wrote

council thanked Adam Chrystie for his services and granted him three thousand acres of land as a reward. Germain shared the council sentiments: "It was some consolation, however, to me to find a check had been given to their depredations by the spirited enterprise of a few loyal subjects conducted by Mr. Chrystie and Lieutenant Pearis."[61]

This brief expedition to Manchac by Chrystie and Pearis' Loyal Refugees was just the beginning of British efforts to protect and regain the western regions of West Florida. The council, on March 5, 1778, requested Captain Garnier and the *Southampton* to remain in Pensacola until further information about the rebels rendered their presence unnecessary. Garnier informed the council that the party of Americans was so small that he felt West Florida had little to fear after the positive actions the colony had taken to protect itself. The *Southampton* drew seventeen feet of water and could not be of value to West Florida unless the rebels attacked Pensacola by sea. Unless Chester could present facts to indicate that the rebels contemplated an attack from deep water, the *Southampton* must return to Jamaica immediately. Chester could not supply the required information, and the *Southampton* weighed anchor.[62]

The governor presented to the council on March 10 a petition which sixteen residents of Mobile had written to their commanding officer, Lieutenant Colonel Alexander Dickson. It requested that Dickson use his influence to get reinforcements sent to Mobile. The council recommended "that every measure that can possibly be taken should be pursued for the immediate defense of the town and fort of Mobile." The council also asked Chester to consult with Stiell to see how many troops he could send to Mobile. Stiell said that he could not detach any troops from Pensacola, and the matter was dropped. At the same meeting of the advisory body, the governor and council decided to

---

that the English force left Manchac because Willing sent a detachment to recapture the town and thus "the royalists, knowing they were outnumbered, fled to the forests" ("A general diary," MPA,SD, 1:125). Stuart's report concerning the casualties is probably correct, as Pearis and Chrystie had returned to Pensacola by the time he wrote, and, consequently, he had had an opportunity to consult with the leaders themselves.

61. Germain to Stuart, July 1, 1778, C.O. 5/79. See also Minutes of the Council, Apr. 25, 1778, C.O. 5/635, RSUS, reel 8.

62. Minutes of the Council, Mar. 5, 1778, C.O. 5/635, RSUS, reel 8.

issue a proclamation that all the "strangers" in Pensacola take an oath of loyalty within five days of the date of publication. Anyone who arrived later would also take the same oath before a justice of the peace or any other officer of government within five days of his arrival, and would be required to state the colony from which he came and his motives for coming to West Florida. The proclamation apparently included the inhabitants of Mobile also, as one witness reported that the inhabitants there were sworn to allegiance.[63]

The council did not meet again for another week, but on March 17, Alexander McIntosh arrived from Natchez with a message from the inhabitants. Soon after Willing's party had left Natchez, the residents had decided to petition Chester and Stiell for a reinforcement of one hundred men. If the governor and commanding officer would send such a force to Natchez, the inhabitants agreed to break their neutrality and join the troops to defend themselves. They also requested a supply of ammunition. An interesting stipulation to the agreement was that the inhabitants declared "they would not break their neutrality to join any party of rangers and Indians that might be sent amongst them."[64] The next day, the governor and council asked Captain Joseph Nunn to sail to the Mississippi with the *Hound* to protect the province. They also applied to Captain Thomas Lloyd of the *Atalanta*, requesting that he remain in port at Pensacola until the council had received further intelligence of "the strength and designs of the enemy as may render that measure unnecessary." Lloyd replied that he would remain in Pensacola only until March 25; if the governor felt that he should stay longer, the request must be made at that time.

The *Atalanta* remained in Pensacola until mid-April in order to serve as a convoy for the British merchant vessels which sailed from West Florida. The council advised the governor to request that Lieutenant Colonel Stiell send one hundred men to reinforce the troops already dispatched to Lake Pontchartrain. Summoned to the meeting, Stiell stated that he could spare no men, and even if he could, they should go to Mobile first. He

63. Minutes of the Council, Mar. 10, 1778, ibid.; Stuart to Germain, Apr. 13, 1778, C.O. 5/79; Panis to Gálvez, July 5, 1778, MPA,SD, 1:219.
64. Stuart to Howe, Mar. 22, 1778, Clinton Papers. See also Minutes of the Council, Mar. 17, 1778, C.O. 5/635, RSUS, reel 8; Stuart to Germain, Apr. 13, 1778, C.O. 5/79.

asserted, however, that he would comply with orders from Chester to send the troops if the governor commanded him to do so. Chester informed the council that he did not feel that such orders would be wise, in view of Stiell's opinion concerning the necessity of keeping the troops in Pensacola. Consequently, the governor and council solicited Stuart to dispatch Alexander Cameron's company of Loyal Refugees to Natchez to assist the settlers. Cameron reported that he had only twenty men in Pensacola at present and that none of his officers was present for duty, so because of the lack of manpower, he could not comply with the request. Interestingly, Cameron (an Indian agent) stated his opinion that the Indians could not be relied upon to aid his company. Stuart offered to send Cameron's company to Natchez if Stiell would reinforce it to bring the strength to fifty men. Such a reinforcement was not forthcoming, and Stuart sent Cameron's Loyal Refugees to Mobile to reinforce the post (in response to that town's earlier petition).[65]

The council met again during the evening of March 18. Chester mentioned that John McGillivray of Mobile had volunteered to serve in raising men to act against Willing's force. The council thanked McGillivray for his "zeal and laudable exertions" and recommended "that he be appointed Lieutenant Colonel Commandant of a provincial corps to be forthwith raised by him and employed for the defense and protection of this province as His Majesty's service may require." The corps would have five captains (with McGillivray as one of them and as commandant and with Alexander McIntosh as "First Captain"), five lieutenants, five ensigns, ten sergeants, and two hundred and fifty rank and file. The pay for the officers would be the same as for regular troops, while the pay for the men would be the same as that received by Stuart's Loyal Refugees. At the close of the war, the veterans would also be entitled to the same land bounties as provided for all provincials. The colony would furnish provisions, arms, and ammunition. McIntosh received orders to go to Natchez immediately to raise troops there.[66]

65. Minutes of the Council, Mar. 18–19, 1778, C.O. 5/635, RSUS, reel 8; Lloyd to Parker, Mar. 26, 1778, C.O. 5/129; Stuart to Germain, Apr. 13, 1778, C.O. 5/79; Stuart to Howe, Mar. 22, 1778, Clinton Papers.

66. Minutes of the Council, Mar. 18, 1778, C.O. 5/635, RSUS, reel 8. See also Stuart to John McGillivray, Mar. 28, 1778, C.O. 5/79; Stuart to Germain, Apr. 13, 1778, ibid.

Chester explained his reasons for raising McGillivray's corps: "These provincial troops are intended for the protection of the Mississippi, and western parts of the province, or for such duty as His Majesty's service may require. Their pay no doubt is high, but their establishment is the same with that of Colonel Stuart's new[ly] raised corps—and it will be impossible to raise the men on less encouragement at present. These troops will, however, be still cheaper to government, than the expence of recruiting, and sending us new levies—besides they are inured to the climate, well acquainted with the woods, and are better qualified for the service they will be employed in than any new troops sent out from England."[67] Chester feared that despite the liberal encouragements given to induce men to join the provincial corps, McGillivray still would not be able to raise over one hundred men, and that even those would not agree to serve any longer than required for the expedition to Natchez.[68]

Before adjourning for the day, the governor and council also decided to require all the inhabitants of Pensacola and Mobile to appear before two justices of the peace to take an oath of allegiance, as well as to give a muster roll of themselves and an account of their arms and ammunition. The council also made a fruitless attempt to reinforce Lieutenant Burdon on Lake Pontchartrain with men from the condemned armed sloop *Florida*. The next day, March 19, the governor imposed an embargo preventing all shipping from leaving any ports in West Florida until further orders.[69]

While Chester and the council worked in Pensacola to protect the colony, the inhabitants of the invaded western region of West Florida were not idle. Anthony Hutchins, whom Willing had carried prisoner to New Orleans and put on parole there, maintained spies among the Americans. He spread disaffection among the rebel forces and, according to his own testimony, he "soon convinced [some of the rebels they] were doing wrong

67. Chester to Germain, Apr. 14, 1778, C.O. 5/594.
68. Chester to Germain, Mar. 25, 1778, ibid.
69. Minutes of the Council, Mar. 18–19, 1778, C.O. 5/635, RSUS, reel 8. Captain Joseph Nunn commanded the British ships in Pensacola at the time, and he stated that the officers of the *Florida* could not be transferred until the goods on board the condemned vessel had been taken over by a ship going to Jamaica. Also, Nunn asserted, "I think the force Lt. Burdon has is more than sufficient to repel any force he may have to oppose him."

and prevailed on them to endeavour to convince the rest of them." Hutchins also planned to capture Pollock, Willing, and McIntyre, offering rewards—to the disaffected rebels who would deliver them—of $1,000 for Pollock and $500 each for Willing and McIntyre. Two other British subjects who were in New Orleans under Spanish protection—John Campbell and Robert Ross—succeeded in stopping the flow of goods up the Mississippi River to the rebels. Alexander Graydon, a carpenter on the Mississippi, was captured by Willing and taken to New Orleans, where the Americans forced him to work for Pollock to earn his subsistence. While "under the disagreeable necessity" of working for the American, he learned of plans to send supplies up the Mississippi River. Graydon sent word of the proposed shipment to Ross and Campbell. Obtaining permission to go to Natchez, ostensibly to bring his apprentices to New Orleans, Graydon set out for the British town with verbal messages from Ross and Campbell to warn the residents to stop the rebel shipment. About twenty leagues above New Orleans, Graydon was taken prisoner again, either because he was riding a horse belonging to Ross or because of some indiscretion. The Spanish arrested Ross and Campbell on May 15, and Gálvez recalled the bateau which had set out on May 10, as he did not want to risk the capture of the vessel while it was under Spanish colors. The governor sent Graydon in chains to Havana, and Campbell and Ross remained in prison until they had paid a £ 300 fine for violation of their parole and a large sum as "compensation" for losses which the bateau suffered by returning to New Orleans.[70]

The efforts of the British on the Mississippi went beyond mere intrigue. While involved in his various forms of espionage, Anthony Hutchins received word that the rebels planned an expedition to Natchez "either totally to evacuate or to set up their standard, distress the friends of government, protect their

70. Anthony Hutchins to Germain, May 21, 1778, C.O. 5/594; Memorial of Robert Ross and John Campbell to the governor and council, Sept. 9, 1778, C.O. 5/177; Ross and Campbell to Fergusson, June 27, 1778, ibid.; Alexander Graydon's deposition concerning the case of Ross and Campbell, Apr. 16, 1779, ibid.; Deposition of Page Robertson concerning the case of Ross and Campbell, Sept. 24, 1778, ibid.; Ross and Campbell to Chester, Sept. 11, 1778, C.O. 5/595; Abbey, "Peter Chester's Defense," pp. 28–29; "A general diary," MPA,SD, 1:147–48; Haynes, "James Willing and the Planters of Natchez," pp. 29–31; Elizabeth Conover, "British West Florida's Mississippi Frontier during the American Revolution" (Master's thesis), pp. 92–95.

own friends, and take full possession of the country to the intent that the same might be legally ceded to the Spaniards as a compensation for certain services done to the rebels in North America." He felt that it was imperative to warn the inhabitants of Natchez of the approaching rebel force, for if the Americans succeeded, the British could not hold the allegiance of the Indians. His expenses paid by loyalist friends in New Orleans, Hutchins, in ill health, set out for Manchac, where he hoped to join with troops and Loyal Refugees to fight the rebels. He found no help at Manchac and, consequently, quickly left for Natchez.

Hutchins' efforts to defend Natchez met with one problem after another. When he arrived in the small wilderness outpost there were no troops, and the people still held to their oath of neutrality, despite their petition to Chester expressing a willingness to break the pledge. Hutchins reported that a few loyalists quickly and cheerfully took up arms with him, but that he met considerable opposition. He soon convinced the people that the rebels had broken the articles of the convention which they had signed at Natchez and that, consequently, the neutrality oath was no longer binding. As a result of this action, the size of Hutchins' force increased. He "became less polite" and demanded the attendance of the inhabitants in the name of the king, and threatened property seizures of those who refused to comply. According to Hutchins' account, many of the inhabitants tried to leave the area, and some did escape to the Spanish side of the river, but he was able to force all of them to return. In order to prevent escapes and to minimize the chance of the rebels receiving word of the British preparations, Hutchins had all of the boats, pirogues, and canoes destroyed except those he kept for use by his force. There was a shortage of ammunition, but he broke into a rebel storehouse which contained three hundred pounds of gunpowder. At this point the town seemed in a good state of defense, but then "an important person" who was a resident of Natchez returned from New Orleans and said that the Americans had not broken the capitulation and thus the neutrality pledge was still binding. Many of Hutchins' force left him, but most of them returned the next day when he sent for them. Once again, however, rebel sympathizers continued to undermine Hutchins' attempts to protect the colony until all who had any doubt of success had deserted, leaving Hutchins with about thirty men. This small force installed itself at White Cliffs, just below Natchez, and awaited the approach of the rebels.

The Americans set out from New Orleans in a bateau armed with five guns and carrying about thirty men. The small party was under the command of Reuben Harrison, who had been a settler in Natchez and had joined Willing. They proceeded up the Mississippi, intent on reminding the residents at Natchez of their oath of neutrality, unaware that Hutchins was waiting to receive them. About a league below White Cliffs, John Tally, a settler on the Mississippi, warned Harrison of the British force, and the American sent word to Hutchins that he entertained no hostile designs.[71] Hutchins urgently requested an immediate reinforcement from Farquhar Bethune on the morning of April 15, as the rebels were only four miles away. Upon receiving word of Willing's raid, Stuart had immediately sent Bethune to the Mississippi to gather all the Indians and traders he could and take them to Natchez for its defense. At the time of Hutchins' request for reinforcements, Bethune's party of 219 men (including Indians, traders, packhorsemen, and Captain Michael Jackson's company of Loyal Refugees) was apparently still eighteen miles from White Cliffs.[72]

There is no evidence that Bethune sent any reinforcements, but, in any case they could not have arrived in time. Fifteen minutes after Hutchins sent the request to Bethune, the rebel force appeared. Apparently Harrison felt that his message that he intended no hostilities had been persuasive, for he landed and had a brief discussion with Hutchins before realizing he was in a trap. One of Hutchins' supporters fired first and after a "very smart engagement" five of the rebels had been killed, three wounded, and the remainder taken prisoner. The British

71. Hutchins to Germain, May 21, 1778, C.O. 5/594; Caughey, "Willing's Expedition," p. 27. A Spanish writer stated that Harrison's party consisted of twenty-eight men ("A general diary," MPA,SD, 1:135). On February 11, 1778, Reuben Harrison had been granted three hundred acres of land on family right and as bounty (as a fleeing loyalist from Virginia) near Natchez (Minutes of the Council, Feb. 11, 1778, C.O. 5/635, RSUS, reel 8).

72. Hutchins to Farquhar Bethune, Apr. 15, 1778, C.O. 5/79; John Stuart to Charles Stuart, Mar. 2, 1778, ibid.; "Return of Indian Traders etc. . . . encamped at the White Clifts," Apr. 25, 1778, ibid.; Stuart to Germain, May 2, 1778, ibid. The "important person" may have been William Hiorn.

suffered only two minor casualties. Hutchins exulted that "their colors were soon torn down and now lie dejected at our feet, and those of His Britannic Majesty most splendidly appear in triumph."[73]

Gálvez complained to Captain Nunn about Hutchins' activities. He apparently felt that Hutchins' actions were a breach of his parole, and since the governor had been instrumental in obtaining the parole, he took the Englishman's violation of his freedom as a personal insult. Nunn informed Gálvez that "Colonel Hutchins is not under my directions, nor am I acquainted with the circumstances that might have induced him to take the steps which you complain of." Asserting that he disapproved of any violence against the subjects of Spain, Nunn observed that as Hutchins was recently "cruelly plundered" by the rebels, it was simply a matter of self-protection when Hutchins stopped Harrison's bateau.[74]

Bethune's force of over two hundred men arrived at White Cliffs on April 19, at which time Hutchins was expecting another attack from the Americans. The intelligence reporting the approach of a reinforcement of rebels proved false, and the combined forces settled down to the rebuilding of the fortifications at Natchez, particularly of Fort Panmure. Captain Michael Jackson's Loyal Refugees had only eleven men upon his arrival at White Cliffs with Bethune, but soon he had enlarged his force to thirty-five. John McGillivray arrived at Natchez on May 28 with provincials and Indians and took command of the district, and Natchez was safe against attack by a small force.[75]

73. Hutchins to Germain, May 21, 1778, C.O. 5/594; Hutchins to Bethune, Apr. 15, 1778, C.O. 5/79; Haynes, "James Willing and the Planters of Natchez," pp. 22–24. "A general diary," MPA,SD, 1:136, says that four rebels were killed, eight or ten wounded, and the rest captured.

74. Nunn to Gálvez, Apr. 23, 1778, C.O. 5/129; "A general diary," MPA,SD, 1:137; Caughey, "Willing's Expedition," p. 28. On May 21, 1778, the council voted its thanks to Hutchins for his actions against Harrison. The body recommended to Chester that Hutchins be appointed lieutenant colonel by brevet and a major in Lieutenant Colonel McGillivray's corps. When the militia was embodied in the Natchez district, Hutchins was to be in command. The governor and council also granted him 4,000 acres of land as a reward for his services (Minutes of the Council, May 21, 1778, C.O. 5/635, RSUS, reel 8).

75. Hutchins to Bethune, Apr. 15, 1778, C.O. 5/79; Bethune to Stuart, June 16, 1778, ibid.; "Return of Indian Traders," Apr. 25, 1778, ibid. See also Stuart to Germain, May 19, 1778, ibid.; Blommart to John McGillivray, Aug. 5, 1778, in Kinnaird, Spain in the Mississippi Valley, 1:301.

With Natchez fairly secure, the governor and council turned their attention to Manchac. The councilors met with Chester on Sunday morning, April 26, 1778, in the old council chambers inside the fort at Pensacola. This session was solely for consultation on the proper course of action which the colony should pursue. On Monday, decisions based on the deliberations of the previous day were made. First, the council recommended that Chester immediately call an assembly. The districts of Pensacola, Mobile, Manchac, and Natchez, and the town of Pensacola, were to have four representatives each, a total of twenty. The day the first news of Willing's raid reached Pensacola, March 2, the council had recommended that Chester call an assembly to deal with the "injury and devastation" which the Indians suffered as a result of the profuse introduction of rum into the Indian nations. The council had further advised, however, that the governor withhold the writs of election "until farther intelligence is received respecting the operations of the rebels in the western parts of this province."[76] As a result, the assembly did not meet until the fall of 1778.

At least two petitions had arrived in Pensacola from the British merchants and inhabitants on the Mississippi complaining of their distressed situation and urgently requesting assistance. "Encouraged as we were by His Majesty's royal proclamation to settle this province . . . and particularly of late invited to seek an asylum from the violences committed in the northern colonies we conceive we have a right to look to you for protection and we beg to know if it will be afforded us that we may return and cultivate our lands."[77] When the council convened on April 27, it unanimously recommended the establishment of a military post at Manchac. Lieutenant Colonel William Stiell was present at the meeting, and he agreed to send one captain, one lieutenant, one ensign, three sergeants, one drummer, and forty rank and file for the proposed garrison. Stiell also ordered the twenty-five men who had gone to reinforce Lieutenant Burdon on board the West Florida to take post

76. Minutes of the Council, Mar. 2, Apr. 27, 1778, C.O. 5/635, RSUS, reel 8.
77. "The Merchants [of the] British Settlement on the Mississippi to Governor Chester," [Apr. 1778?], C.O. 5/129. See also "Memorial of the Loyal British Inhabitants of the Mississippi" to Chester, n.d. [endorsed "In Gov. Chester's . . . of 7th May 1778"], C.O. 5/594.

at Manchac. Chester instructed McGillivray to detach from Natchez one hundred men, with proper officers, to go to Manchac with entrenching tools to set up outer trenches and prepare for the arrival of the British regulars. Stuart ordered Captain William McIntosh, whom he had just appointed to the command of a fourth company of Loyal Refugees, and his forty men to station themselves at Manchac.[78] The *Sylph* also received orders to sail to the new post, while the *Hound* remained at New Orleans. The council then unanimously adopted the following resolution: "Should the inhabitants of the Manchac district neglect to embrace the protection now offered to them but rather choose to continue under Spanish protection, the said post at Manchac after its having been established two months [shall be] withdrawn and the troops be sent to take post at the Natchez for the protection and security of the loyal inhabitants in that district." Chester also sought the advice of the council as to whether he should lift the embargo imposed on March 19, since the threat from Willing's party had diminished. Upon the council's recommendation, Chester lifted the prohibition on shipping.[79]

Three weeks after the first news of Willing's expedition reached Pensacola, Chester wrote Brigadier General Augustine Prevost, commanding officer at St. Augustine, Sir Peter Parker, admiral of the squadron at Jamaica, and Governor John Dalling, governor of Jamaica, requesting reinforcements of men and ships of war. Prevost informed Chester that he could not reduce his garrison "with propriety." Governor Dalling, however, sent 102 effectives from the first and third battalions of the Sixtieth Regiment, and Parker ordered the frigate *Active* (28 guns) and the armed schooner *Florida* (8 guns) to West Florida to join the *Hound* and *Sylph*, which would remain in the province. Parker also ordered the sloop-of-war *Stork* to West Florida upon its

78. Minutes of the Council, Apr. 27, 1778, C.O. 5/635, RSUS, reel 8; Stuart to Germain, May 2, 1778, C.O. 5/79. The troops under the command of Captain William Barker apparently arrived at Manchac in May 1778, because Barker wrote Gálvez on May 30 informing him that he was in command of a "considerable detachment" of troops sent from Pensacola to establish a post at Manchac "as a result of the plundering perpetrated by some miscreants, subjects in rebellion against His Britannic Majesty on the Mississippi River." Barker to Gálvez, May 30, 1778, in Kinnaird, *Spain in the Mississippi Valley*, 1:283.

79. Minutes of the Council, Apr. 27, 1778, C.O. 5/635, RSUS, reel 8.

return from a cruise. The council advised Chester to station the *Florida* in Mobile Bay until the *Stork* arrived. When the latter vessel reached Mobile, the *Florida* would depart for Lakes Maurepas and Pontchartrain to join the *West Florida*.[80]

In a discussion of Willing's raid, John Walton Caughey, a leading scholar, saw as "improbable" the reports which earlier writers had presented that Willing went above Mobile and agitated in favor of the rebel cause, stating that there was a lack of direct evidence to support such a contention. It is not clear if Caughey meant by this assertion that none of Willing's force went to the area of Mobile, but in the British records there are several references which show definitely that the Americans approached Mobile. An Englishman in New Orleans reported as early as March 20 that the rebels planned to carry out their depredations along the lakes and on to Mobile and Pensacola.[81] Two months later, the council recommended "that application be made to Colonel Stuart to send off two parties of rangers and Indians, one to the village and the other to Fish River in order to gain intelligence of a party of rebels who are said to be upon the Bay of Mobile." Chester informed the council two days later that he had received intelligence that a party of the Americans had sailed into Mobile Bay and captured a merchant brig—the *Chance*—laden with staves, and had apparently carried it to Ship Island. The council advised Chester to order the *Florida*, stationed at Mobile, to recover the brig and attempt to destroy the rebel vessels. The captain of the *Florida* lamented that he had only six hands fit for duty and that he could not go to sea until reinforced. Chester requested that Captain Williams of the *Active* lend the necessary number of men to the *Florida*. He also ordered a small force of regular troops on board the *Florida* to assist in her defense. The governor and council further appealed to Stuart to allow his sloop, the *Christianna*, to patrol

80. Chester to Prevost, Mar. 21, 1778, BHP, 1030, reel 6; Chester to [Sir Peter Parker?], Mar. 25, 1778, C.O. 5/129; Prevost to Chester, Apr. 20, 1778, BHP, 1116, reel 6; Minutes of the Council, May 26, 1778, C.O. 5/635, RSUS, reel 8. See also Parker to Philip Stephens, Apr. 19, 1778, C.O. 5/129; Chester to Germain, June 2, 1778, C.O. 5/594. Both of the last two letters cited report that Dalling sent three commissioned officers and one hundred rank and file to Pensacola.

81. Caughey, "Willing's Expedition," p. 34; Donald Campbell to Stuart, Mar. 20, 1778, C.O. 5/79.

between the lakes and Ship Island to keep open the vital communication. Chester also asked Stuart to embark a company of
Loyal Refugees on the *Christianna* to do duty on her.

The council minutes of May 29 reveal that Captain Williams
sent a reinforcement to the *Florida* and that a sergeant, a corporal, and eighteen rank and file boarded the schooner. Stuart
reported to the council that his sloop had Indian goods aboard,
and that, as soon as they were unloaded, he must have the
vessel repaired, as it was in extremely poor condition. As to the
request for Loyal Refugees, Stuart replied that he had ordered
them on service for the Indian department, but that if the
council procured a vessel, he would order part of Captain William McIntosh's company to embark on the service.[82] A week
later, the council recommended that the sloop *John and Peter*
(Charles Roberts, master) assist in recovering the merchant vessel and destroying the rebel bateaux. Again Chester had to
request reinforcements of seamen from the *Active* and troops
from Stiell. Captain Williams reported that he could spare only
twelve more men, and Stiell agreed to send the same size force
which had sailed on the *Florida*. Chester instructed the *John
and Peter* to depart for Mobile Bay to attempt to destroy the
rebel vessels and to guard the coast for no more than fourteen
days. The sloop would then convoy all British merchant vessels
coming east to the bar at Pensacola and return to Pensacola for
further orders.[83]

West Florida in the summer of 1778 was relatively free of any
excitement caused by the Americans in New Orleans. There
was a dispute at Natchez over who was in command of the
British forces there; Colonel David Rogers made his expedition
down the Mississippi River to New Orleans in late summer; the
British were strengthening their positions on the Mississippi;
but on the whole, the summer months were relatively quiet.
Nevertheless, it was during these hot and humid months that
Pollock and Gálvez grew more and more impatient with the
length of stay of the insubordinate Willing. Both men were

82. Minutes of the Council, May 26, 28–29, 1778, C.O. 5/635, RSUS, reel 8.
83. Minutes of the Council, June 6, 1778, ibid. Chester reported to Germain
on June 2, 1778, the action of the rebels near Mobile and the steps he had taken
(C.O. 5/594). See also "Précis of Transactions on the Mississippi," n.d.,
Sackville-Germain Papers, filed at the end of vol. 2.

anxious to see Willing leave Louisiana, and they drew up two plans to send the Americans back up the Mississippi. The British settlers on the river were aroused by this and they virtually closed the river to traffic. In August, Willing's men under Lieutenant Robert George received permission from Gálvez to return north by way of the Spanish settlements on the Mississippi on the condition that they "not attack any part of the British dominions, or their subjects or property" on the way.[84]

Willing did not accompany his men. He finally sailed from New Orleans on board the Morris on November 15, 1778. Several early writers report that the British captured Willing at Mobile and that he only narrowly escaped being hanged. Nothing in the British records indicates that such was the case, and it is difficult to imagine that Chester would not have mentioned it.[85] While there is nothing to indicate when, where, or how, it is clear that the British captured the Morris and Willing and took him to New York, "where he endured a long, a cruel, and expensive imprisonment." The British kept Willing on Long Island as a prisoner on parole, but after he responded to an insult from a British officer, they placed him in irons for three months in New York City. Congress directed the commissary general of prisoners on January 14, 1779, to supply Willing with £ 100 for subsistence while in prison in New York. One of Willing's sisters, whose husband was a British officer, interceded with Clinton in her brother's behalf; he allowed him to go to Philadelphia on parole until exchanged. After an abortive attempt to exchange him for Nicholas Ogden in July 1779, the British exchanged Willing on September 3, 1781, for a British officer by the name of Rogers.[86]

84. Robert George and Richard Harrison to Gálvez, Aug. 18, 1778, in Kinnaird, Spain in the Mississippi Valley, 1:303–4; George to Gálvez, Aug. 14, 1778, ibid., p. 303; Caughey, "Willing's Expedition," pp. 28–33.

85. Burnett, Letters, 2:565n; Caughey, "Willing's Expedition," p. 32; Thwaites and Kellogg, Frontier Defense, p. 192n; Hamilton, Colonial Mobile, p. 311. It is interesting to note that Pollock outfitted the vessel on which Willing left New Orleans and named it the Morris, obviously after Robert Morris, for whom he was an agent.

86. Haynes, "James Willing and the Planters of Natchez," p. 38; Burnett, Letters, 2:565n; Thwaites and Kellogg, Frontier Defense, pp. 192–93n; Ford, Journals, 13:65; Declaration of Don Francisco Vallé, July 8, 1782, in Kinnaird, Spain in the Mississippi Valley, 2:37; Declaration of Don Silbestre Labadia,

An analysis of "the late rascally transaction of Mr. Willing" must take into account the attitude of the British settlers on the Mississippi. As early as June 1777, there were two settlers on the Mississippi who believed that there were not five people in Natchez who were loyal to the king. When Chester requested reinforcements from Prevost, the brigadier general conjectured in reply that "the daring invasion of the rebels who have committed such depredations on the Mississippi give reason to suspect that if it had not been on a firm persuasion on their part of being joined by many of the inhabitants on that river, and the lukewarmness of the rest they would not have adventured on such an attempt."[87] An even more severe indictment of the settlers on the Mississippi came from William Dunbar, who confided to his diary that "one half of the inhabitants were in the American interest, which circumstance being well known to the loyal part of the people, was the means of tying up their hands and preventing their attempts to oppose the banditti."[88] Clearly, a sizeable portion of the British population on the Mississippi sympathized with the American cause. It is equally clear that a majority of the settlers were neutral in the matter, desiring mainly to be left alone in their pursuit of economic advancement. The number of people who took an active role in Willing's excursion on either side was small. Despite the various petitions pledging loyalty and seeking aid, the loyalist opposition was almost nonexistent until Chrystie and Pearis arrived at Manchac and Hutchins pleaded with, threatened, and cajoled the Natchez settlers to aid him in opposing Reuben Harrison's force. Similarly, the number of settlers who joined Willing was small. A survey of the primary materials relating to Willing's raid reveals the names of only seven men who joined the Americans. While obviously there must have been others, there is little reason to believe that the number exceeded a dozen.[89] Thus, while there were partisans on both the British

July 8, 1782, ibid., 2:38. Haynes states that the British wanted to exchange Willing for Col. John Connally.

87. Prevost to Chester, Apr. 20, 1778, BHP, 1116, reel 6; Robert McGillivray and Robert Welsh to Bethune, June 4, 1777, C.O. 5/78.

88. Rowland, *William Dunbar*, p. 62.

89. The seven men who joined Willing were James Elliot (later appointed a captain in the Continental Army and assistant geographer of the United States), Richard Harrison, Reuben Harrison, "Mr. [?] Francis," Jeremiah Routh, William

and American sides during Willing's expedition, the majority of the settlers were unwilling to take a stand until forced to do so.

In view of British concern about the treatment of loyalists by the colonies in rebellion, an interesting point crept into the consideration of the governor and council in May 1778. Anthony Hutchins requested instructions to guide him as to the proper disposition of captured rebel land, goods, and bills of credit. The council referred the matter to the attorney general, who ordered that the settlers holding such captured property make a list of everything seized and hold it until they received further orders. Chester sought instructions from Germain concerning the property, "whether to be sold for His Majesty's use, or whether the monies arising from the sale thereof, should not be applied in making some restitution to His Majesty's loyal subjects who have been sufferers by their late depredations."[90] The matter was never conclusively decided in West Florida, since Germain advised Chester in December 1778 that "with regard to the lands of such of the inhabitants of West Florida as have taken part with the rebels, I can at present give you no orders for disposing of them, but I should think you would be fully justified in allowing the loyal refugees from other provinces to occupy them until peace is restored or some other arrangement is made."[91]

The expedition under Willing's compelling but impulsive and insubordinate leadership was probably more detrimental than helpful to the rebellious colonies. From the beginning, writers have characterized the American excursion as one of cruelty and lacking in humanity. While elements of ill treatment were present, early scholars overemphasized this aspect of the raid, which did manage to interrupt briefly the flow of supplies from the Mississippi to Pensacola and the West Indies. Probably the most important result of Willing's raid was a change in attitude

Reid, and Francis Dolony. See Minutes of the Council, Mar. 10, 17–18, Apr. 25, 1778, C.O. 5/635, RSUS, reel 8; Chester to Germain, Apr. 14, 1778, C.O. 5/594; "A general diary," MPA,SD, 1:142; Ford, *Journals*, 13:291–92, 22:120. In a letter to Pollock, Richard Harrison wrote that he was in the service of the Continental Congress (Harrison to Pollock, July 7, 1778, in Kinnaird, *Spain in the Mississippi Valley*, 1:294). Conover, "British West Florida's Mississippi Frontier," p. 69, states that Joseph Calvert also joined the Americans.
    90. Chester to Germain, May 30, 1778, C.O. 5/594. See also Minutes of the Council, May 28, 1778, C.O. 5/635, RSUS, reel 8.
    91. Germain to Chester, Dec. 2, 1778, C.O. 5/594.

by the British on the Mississippi. Before the expedition, most of the residents were either neutral or pro-American in sentiment. After the plundering and devastation of the American raid, loyalist sentiment developed much more strongly. While many of the inhabitants must have agreed with William Dunbar that "twould be a prostitution of the name of Americans to honor them [Willing's party] with such an appelation,"[92] the depredations caused by an expedition sent down the Mississippi with a commission from Congress drove them to hold a firmer allegiance to the British crown, whose forces could protect them against such free-booting activities. Even the Americans were aware of this crystallization of loyalist sentiment. George Rogers Clark stated his opinion to the Spanish lieutenant governor at St. Louis that Willing's party had engaged in plunder and that although "Florida on the Mississippi might have been good subjects to the States if proper measures had been taken," such a result was now out of the question.[93]

This strengthening of loyalist sentiment was soon coupled with a sizeable troop reinforcement sent by Clinton to augment the defenses of West Florida. Chester had already begun reestablishing posts on the Mississippi. The huge drafts for supplies which Willing drew on Pollock also nearly totally destroyed Pollock's credit and, consequently, his usefulness to the American cause.

Thus the American optimism surrounding the beginning of Willing's expedition quickly turned to disillusionment as the stark reality of failure became obvious. An excursion aimed at attaching the western regions of West Florida to the American cause had had the reverse effect. Instead of maintaining the passage between New Orleans and the rebellious colonies, the expedition had resulted in the English virtually closing the Mississippi to non-English traffic. Clearly, Willing's raid was a failure to the American cause, as it led to a strengthened British position on the Mississippi, both in sentiment and in force of arms. In terms of its overall importance to the Revolution,

92. Rowland, *William Dunbar*, p. 63.
93. George Rogers Clark to Fernando de Leyba, Nov. 6, 1778, in Lawrence Kinnaird, ed., "Clark-Leyba Papers," p. 101; Caughey, "Willing's Expedition," p. 35. The French minister in Philadelphia, Conrad Alexandre Gérard, also doubted the wisdom of such an expedition led "by a young fool" (quoted in Conover, "British West Florida's Mississippi Frontier," p. 105).

however, the American expedition had little effect upon the rebellion, since the American advantages and losses were minimal, and as it only affected the British in the transferral of a body of regular troops, Waldeckers, and provincials from other posts.

4

"To Prevent Any Surprize or Sudden Mischief"

During the summer of 1778, British officials in West Florida continued to prepare for the province's defense in case of a large-scale American invasion or a war with Spain. The military worked on the fortifications and prepared to receive troop reinforcements that General Clinton was sending. At the same time, the people of West Florida elected representatives to meet in the assembly called by Governor Chester.

The election of an assembly in West Florida was authorized by the instructions issued to the governor, and the first session had met in November 1766. Following several stormy sessions in the Johnstone, Browne, and Chester administrations, Governor Chester had dissolved the assembly in 1772; it would not meet again until 1778. The council had recommended to Chester on March 2, 1778, that he convene an assembly to deal with the "injury and devastation" which the Indians suffered as a result of the profuse supply of rum for the Indian nations. The districts of Pensacola, Mobile, Manchac, and Natchez, and the town of Pensacola, were to have four representatives each, a total of twenty. On the same day as the council's recommendation, the first news of Willing's raid reached Pensacola, and the council advised that the governor withhold the writs of election until more news about the American raid was received. The governor in council decided on April 27 that an assembly should be convoked immediately; accordingly, writs of election were issued calling for the assembly to meet on June 6.[1]

After Governor Chester had prorogued the assembly several times because the writs of election for Manchac and Natchez had not arrived,[2] it finally met on October 1, 1778, and the delegates unanimously elected Adam Chrystie, of the District of Mobile, to be Speaker of the House. At this opening session, Governor Chester welcomed the delegates, and reported to the assembly that Parliament had passed an act establishing a peace commission which he hoped "may reestablish peace on the basis of equal freedom and mutual safety, and perpetuate a cordial and permanent union between the mother country and the colonies so essential to the welfare and prosperity of the whole British Empire."[3] Former West Florida Governor George Johnstone was a member of this peace commission.[4] Chester also informed the assembly that the king had learned of the Treaty of Amity and Commerce which France had signed with the colonies in revolt, and the English ambassador had been withdrawn from France. The king commanded the governor to be especially vigilant in order "to prevent any surprize or sudden mischief." Chester assured the assembly that he had received information also that the forces at Jamaica had been strengthened and would be available to aid West Florida and that he expected a considerable reinforcement in West Florida any day. It was still "highly proper," he continued, for the legislature to do everything possible for the defense of the colony. Among other measures, Chester urged the passage of an act to establish and regulate the militia, and he asked the assembly to consider further regulation of the Indian trade. Chester had received instructions to apply to the legislature to pro-

1. Minutes of the Council, Mar. 2, Apr. 27, 1778, C.O. 5/635, RSUS, reel 8.
2. Minutes of the Council, June 6, June 20, Sept. 10, 1778, ibid.
3. Minutes of the Upper House of Assembly, Oct. 1, 1778, C.O. 5/628, RSUS, reel 3; Minutes of the Lower House of Assembly, Oct. 1, 1778, ibid.
4. Minutes of the Upper House of Assembly, Oct. 1, 1778, ibid. Johnstone was soon forced to leave the commission because of improper tampering with the American delegates; the Continental Congress adopted a resolution which stated in part, "it is incompatible with the honor of Congress to hold any manner of correspondence or intercourse with the said Governor Johnstone, Esq., especially to negotiate with him upon affairs in which the cause of liberty is interested" (Ford, Journals, 11:770–74). For a complete discussion of Johnstone's role on the commission, see Fabel, "Governor George Johnstone," pp. 107–67.

vide for the subsistence of any rebel prisoners who might be brought into West Florida. The governor further requested that the assembly provide for the "due administration of justice" in the western regions of the colony and concluded his speech with an urgent plea for unanimity among the assembled delegates.[5]

The day after the legislature convened, the delegates wrote Chester, assuring him that they would do everything in their power to fulfill his requests. On the same day, the representatives also passed resolutions expressing the thanks of the colony to Captain John Fergusson, Captain Joseph Nunn, Anthony Hutchins, and Adam Chrystie for their efforts in protecting the colony from the depredations of James Willing's party of Americans. The organization of the assembly continued until October 8, when the delegates finally began to consider the matters for which Chester had called them together. Anthony Hutchins moved that the delegates appoint a committee to draft a bill "for establishing and regulating a militia" in the colony. The legislators concurred with Hutchins' motion and selected a committee consisting of Hutchins, Edmund Rush Wegg, John Miller, Arthur Strothers, and John [?] Bradley.[6] With this motion it appeared that the delegates were ready to get to the business at hand. Their work was interrupted for six days, however, and a note in the margin of the minutes of the Lower House explains: "The reason of no business being done in the House of Assembly from the 9th to the 15th of October was owing to a very melancholy cause. The severest hurricane ever felt or known in this part of the world, since West Florida has belonged to the crown of Great Britain, happened on the night of the 9th with such irresistable fury and violence as entirely to sweep away all the wharfs, stores and houses contiguous to the water side, with part of the front batteries of the garrison, besides destroying several houses and making a general havoc of the fences etc. in the town of Pensacola. All the ships and vessels in the harbour were either lost, or driven ashore, except His Majesty's Sloop of War the *Sylph*, which with difficulty rode out the gale. The great loss of property by this general

5. Minutes of the Upper House of Assembly, Oct. 1, 1778, C.O. 5/628, RSUS, reel 3.
6. Minutes of the Lower House of Assembly, Oct. 2–8, 1778, ibid.

calamity affected the whole community, and particularly some members of the Assembly, which prevented their attending the House, and therefore it was thought proper to put a stop to going on business till matters were a little settled, and all the members could with some degree of convenience attend."[7] Colonel William Stiell, the military commander, reported the effects of the storm on the fortifications: "The batteries facing the harbour, which had been constructed at a great expense are all ruined, and the provision magazine would have shared the same fate, but for a redoubt constructed in its front. The resistance made by it [the redoubt] before it was carried away, preserved that building [provisions magazine], the sea only reaching the foundation when the storm subsided." Relating with obvious relief that only seven lives had been lost in the storm, Stiell conjectured, "had the storm continued one hour longer, the whole town, inhabitants, and garrison, must have perished, as the sea broke in upon both flanks at the distance of a quarter of a mile, consequently would have surrounded us, and none could have escaped."[8]

The assembly reconvened on October 15 and immediately received a bill from Hutchins concerning the militia. It was read the first time and ordered to be read again four days later. However, through a series of postponements, consideration of the bill by the committee of the whole house, and recommitments to Hutchins' committee, the militia bill was considered seven more times without action before Chester adjourned the legislature.[9]

The 1778 session of the assembly did not accomplish anything constructive largely because of discord between the Lower House and the governor over Chester's failure to issue writs of election for the town of Mobile. The house instructed the committee on privileges and elections to investigate the representation of the town of Mobile. The committee reported that in previous assembly sessions, Mobile and Charlotte County (which included Mobile) had been allowed six or eight representatives, but that in the present session the town of Mobile

7. Minutes of the Lower House of Assembly, Oct. 9–14, 1778, ibid.
8. Stiell to Germain, Oct. 15, 1778, C.O. 5/595.
9. Minutes of the Lower House of Assembly, Oct. 15, 19, 23, 24, 27, 30, Nov. 3, 4, 1778, C.O. 5/628, RSUS, reel 3.

had no representation and Charlotte County had only four. Five days after the assembly reconvened following the hurricane, the House requested an explanation from Chester for his failure to issue writs of election for Mobile.[10] As Cecil Johnson correctly points out, "the reply of Chester, though sound enough from the legal standpoint, was not in a form calculated to allay discord and restore harmony."[11] The next day Chester spoke to the assembly, explaining his action. He began by reprimanding the delegates for devoting time to "matters of privileges" over which they had no control. The king alone judged the propriety of such matters, and he had delegated the same authority to the governor of West Florida. Paraphrasing his commission, Chester told the Lower House that the crown had given him authority to call an assembly "in such manner and form as hath been already used, *or as I in my discretion shall judge most proper.*" Consequently, he had called the assembly, allowing four members from each district (Pensacola, Mobile, Manchac, and Natchez) and four representatives from the capital of the colony. This legislature of twenty members was two larger than any previous session, and "this representation . . . had particularly in view the rising importance of the western parts of the colony, which had never hitherto been represented."[12]

Chester's reply to the assembly did not satisfy the delegates, and the Lower House passed a bill entitled "An Act for Establishing the Number of Representatives for the Different Towns and Districts or Shires in this Colony for Ascertaining the Rights of the Electors and the Duration of the Assemblies."[13] The next day the bill went for concurrence to the Upper House, where it was read for the first time. The Upper House postponed the second reading of the bill and appointed a committee to ask the governor why he had not issued the same number of writs of election for the town and district of Mobile as in the past. In reply, Chester sent a copy of the part of his commission that he had paraphrased in answering the same question for the Lower House.[14] The governor also explained that he deemed it

10. Minutes of the Lower House of Assembly, Oct. 8, 20, 1778, ibid.
11. Johnson, *British West Florida*, p. 109.
12. Minutes of the Lower House of Assembly, Oct. 21, 1778, C.O. 5/628, RSUS, reel 3.
13. Minutes of the Lower House of Assembly, Oct. 23, 1778, ibid.
14. Minutes of the Upper House of Assembly, Oct. 26–27, 1778, C.O. 5/633,

best not to give the town of Mobile representation because of its refusal in the last election to choose any delegates unless the indenture limited the term of service to one year.[15] At the request of the Upper House, Philip Livingston (Chester's secretary and a member of the Upper House) obtained an article of the governor's instructions which clearly supported Chester: "you do not upon any pretence whatsoever, give your assent to any law or laws to be passed in our province under your government by which the number of the Assembly shall be enlarged or diminished, the duration of it ascertained, the qualification of the Electors or the elected fixed or altered or by which any regulations shall be established with respect thereto, inconsistent with our instructions to you our governor, as prejudicial to that right or authority which you derive from us in virtue of our royal commission and instructions."[16] Upon the recommendation by Livingston, the Upper House rejected the bill as "inconsistent" with Chester's instructions from the crown.

The Commons House of the assembly was not yet ready to give up, however, and its members requested that the Upper House join them in an address to Chester asking him to issue writs of election for four representatives from the town of Mobile. In reply, the Upper House sent a committee to talk to the Lower House with instructions to tell that body that such a memorial would be "ineffectual," since Chester would send it to England for advice. The Upper House also instructed the committee to request that the Commons House "proceed to business for the general good of the colony at this critical conjuncture."[17]

After the failure of the attempt to regulate the representation in the legislature, the assembly met for six more days but accomplished nothing of consequence. Chester spoke to a joint session of the assembly on November 5, reviewing his reasons for calling the delegates together and declaring that he was sorry "that instead of attending to those important matters after

---

RSUS, reel 7. A copy of this seventeenth article of Chester's commission is in C.O. 5/595.

15. Quoted in Howard, "Colonial Pensacola," p. 394.

16. Ibid., pp. 394–95.

17. Minutes of the Upper House of Assembly, Oct. 27, 29–30, 1778, C.O. 5/633, RSUS, reel 7.

so long a delay, only one bill has passed your House [Lower House] and that a bill ascertaining the number of members and limiting the duration of the Assemblies; and I am equally sorry to find from a report lately entered upon your journals and from the general tenor thereof that you still have matters of privileges more in view than His Majesty's interest and the internal economy and defence of the colony." For these reasons he adjourned the assembly until September 1779, "at which time I flatter myself I shall meet you with minds more truly disposed to promote the interest of the province than you have evinced in the course of your late deliberations."[18]

Chester explained to Germain his actions in adjourning the assembly. After relating the brief history of the stormy session, Chester concluded, "As I consider that the calling of an Assembly in this province will be productive of no advantage to His Majesty's service during the continuance of the rebellion, I shall not meet the House again until peace is restored, unless I should receive your Lordship's commands signified for that purpose, or see a disposition prevail with them to promote His Majesty's service, and the real interest of the province."[19] As one scholar noted, "the West Florida Assembly, coming into existence as it did near the end of the colonial period, represented the summation of the colonial attitude toward legislative privilege which had developed during the preceding century and a half."[20] During the remaining three years of British control of West Florida, Chester did not summon another assembly. Yet, the province did not seem to suffer. The revenue collected was of little use, and the laws passed were inadequate or at best poorly enforced. Because of the parliamentary support fund, the legislature was not needed to supply money for operation of the colony. The benefits to be derived from the meeting of a body with such a propensity to quarrel were few indeed. The American Revolution was raging over the Atlantic colonies,

18. Minutes of the Upper House of Assembly, Nov. 5, 1778, C.O. 5/628, RSUS, reel 3. The assembly also presented its thanks to Lieutenant Colonel John McGillivray for his actions in opposing Willing's raid. Minutes of the Upper House of Assembly, Oct. 30, 1778, ibid.; Minutes of the Lower House of Assembly, Nov. 3, 1778, ibid.

19. Chester to Germain, Nov. 24, 1778, C.O. 5/595.

20. Johnson, British West Florida, p. 114.

and to allow such a disenchanted and prerogative-seeking body to meet would have been an open invitation to revolution.

In discussing the English inconsistency which in part led to the American Revolution, one English historian concluded that "English policy was always to allow the horse to be stolen, and then to make frantic efforts to lock the stable door when it was too late."[21] West Florida was a victim of this dilatory policy. Before Willing's raid, the policy makers in London paid little attention to the defense of West Florida; fewer than five hundred regulars were scattered around the province to guard it against Indians, "rebels," and the Spanish. After the American invasion, troops were hastily sent to the distant colony to protect it from American incursions. The men at Whitehall were planning for the future as well. While they were concerned about further rebel invasions, they were also preparing the colony's defenses in the event of war with Spain.

Willing's raid impressed upon the British officials the weak and defenseless state of West Florida. Despite the fact that naval and troop reinforcements had been sent to West Florida from Jamaica immediately after the American invasion, a much stronger reinforcement would be necessary to protect the infant colony. As early as March 21, 1778, the British government began taking steps toward sending such a force to West Florida. On that date, Sir Henry Clinton received secret orders from the king to send to the Floridas three thousand men, with the necessary supplies and arms. He was to split the men into two divisions, one to go to St. Augustine, the other to Pensacola. A general officer was to accompany the men to Pensacola, where he would take command of the British forces in West Florida.[22] Germain sent orders to West Florida on July 1, 1778, instructing the general officer on the steps he should take to prepare the defenses of the colony,[23] but over three months later, Clinton still had not ordered the reinforcements to Pensacola. He notified Germain that "the admiral having at length been able to

21. Hugh Edward Egerton, *The Causes and Character of the American Revolution*, pp. 25–26.
22. "Secret Instructions" to Clinton from the king, Mar. 21, 1778, Clinton Papers.
23. Germain to Clinton, July 1, 1778, ibid. The details of Germain's instructions to the general officer in West Florida will be discussed in detail later.

appoint a convoy, I shall in a few days have it in my power to
. . . send . . . 1,000 men to Pensacola, and 2,000 to St. Augustine.
For those garrisons I have employed foreign troops and provincials, whose loss to this army will not be so much felt."[24] It was
not until the end of the month (October 27) that Clinton finally
ordered Brigadier General John Campbell to proceed with the
troops under his control to Pensacola, where he would take
command of all the forces in the province.[25]

Apparently, the reinforcements finally left New York on October 31, for on that day one of the German soldiers wrote from
on board the transport *Crawford*, "Since the 20th of this month
we have been on the ship and this afternoon we finally sail.
Our destination, as many things allow us to surmise, will be
Pensacola. What a distance! How will one be able to find one's
way from there back to the Fatherland?"[26] The first stop of the
reinforcements after they left New York was Jamaica. The vessels became separated during the voyage; Campbell arrived at
Kingston, Jamaica, on November 30, 1778, after a voyage of four
weeks, while the last of the vessels arrived on December 2.
With Campbell at Jamaica on their way to Pensacola were 1,178
men—695 Waldeckers, 170 Pennsylvania Loyalists, and 313
Maryland Loyalists. Eight had deserted and 19 men had died
since the convoy had left New York.[27]

The stop in Jamaica was longer than planned due to the
necessity of repairing the ships and filling the stores of food
and water. While to some of the troops "everything [in Jamaica]
was a surprise to their eyes, a paradise on earth, which was
that much more beautiful after the long and hazardous sea

24. Clinton to Germain, Oct. 8, 1778, ibid.
25. Clinton to Brigadier General John Campbell, Oct. 27, 1778, BHP, 1491,
reel 7.
26. "On Board the Transport Crawford, October 31, 1778," in *Letters from
America 1776–1779; Being Letters of Brunswick, Hessian, and Waldeck Officers
with the British Armies during the Revolution*, translated by Ray Waldron Pet-
tengill, p. 205. See also Marion Dexter Learned, *Philipp Waldeck's Diary of the
American Revolution*, p. 87.
27. Campbell to Germain, Dec. 26, 1778, C.O. 5/236; Max von Eelking, *Die
Deutschen Hulfstruppen im Nordamerikanischen Befreiungskrieg, 1776 bis
1783*, p. 1; Learned, *Philipp Waldeck's Diary*, pp. 88–93; "State of a Detachment
of Troops under the Command of Brigr. Genl. Campbell, on their Passage from
New York for Pensacola in West Florida. Kingston [Jamaica] the 26th December
1778," C.O. 5/597. Waldeckers were German mercenary forces.

voyage,"[28] the hot and humid tropical island proved to be a graveyard for others. Lieutenant Colonel James Chalmers of the Maryland Loyalists reported numerous deaths from smallpox among his men. Though other troops suffered, the Maryland Loyalists were the hardest hit.[29]

While in Jamaica, Campbell endeavored to learn what he could about his destination, for he had been unable "to obtain any satisfactory information in regard to West Florida." "I must own," he lamented, "the idea I have thence been able to form, of the present situation of that colony is by no means pleasing." From the information he had received, it was apparent that West Florida "must be in very great distress": Willing's raid had caused the settlers to flee the most fertile lands in the province, supplies could no longer be obtained from New Orleans, and an embargo had been laid on provisions in Jamaica, cutting off one of the main sources of supply for West Florida. Campbell took aboard a sufficient quantity of provisions to insure that the troops would be supplied upon their arrival in Pensacola. Having learned that the troops in Pensacola did not receive a daily allowance of rum, a provision "to which the troops I carry with me . . . have been regularly accustomed," Campbell ordered 120 puncheons of rum shipped to West Florida to prevent "dissatisfaction and discontent, if not desertion or mutiny."[30]

The vessels transporting the reinforcements left Jamaica on

28. Eelking, *Die Deutschen Hulfstruppen*, p. 2; Learned, *Philipp Waldeck's Diary*, pp. 93–115.

29. *Ontario Bureau of Archives, Second Report, 1904*, 2:1164–66. Writing from Pensacola, General Campbell supported Chalmers' report when he wrote Clinton that "the small pox made its appearance among the Maryland Loyalists the very day we sailed from Jamaica, and still rages with violence" (Campbell to Clinton, Feb. 10, 1779, BHP, 1737, reel 7). The troop returns for the Maryland Loyalists indicate that when they left New York, the force had 320 men; by May 1, 1779, the corps had been reduced to 283 (Troop return, Kingston, Dec. 26, 1778, ibid.; "State of the Provincial Troops Under the Command of Major Genl. Campbell in West Florida . . . New York, 1st May 1779," C.O. 5/7). Hugh Mackay Gordon, deputy muster master general in West Florida, noted the sickness among the Maryland Loyalists when he wrote that they were not mustered until the end of February "owing to the number ill of the small pox. You will observe by the muster rolls enclosed this disorder carried off a great many which induced General Campbell to disperse one company" (Gordon to Edward Winslow, Mar. 20, 1779, Edward Winslow Papers, microfilm, Canadian Archives, Ottawa, reel 1).

30. Campbell to Germain, Dec. 26, 1778, C.O. 5/236. A puncheon is a large cask which varies in capacity but usually is 111.6 gallons.

December 31, 1778, and sailed for Pensacola. Land was seen on January 15, after a rough voyage, but the ships were unable to enter the harbor because of adverse winds. The vessels entered Pensacola Bay three days later, and on the nineteenth, orders were given to disembark. The two barracks were not completed, however, and not for another ten days did the troops finally set foot on the shores of West Florida.[31]

Despite the pleasure of being on land again, the initial reaction of the troops to their new post was unanimously negative. Philipp Waldeck, the chaplain of the Waldeckers, lamented that "now we are living at the outermost end of the great Gulf of Mexico, in West Florida, a desolate, uncultivated, waste, and here on the seacoast wholly unfruitful land. Wholly cut off from the world, we learn nothing that is going on in Europe, or in North America either. Before us is the Gulf of Mexico, behind us desert regions which are only now and then traversed by wandering hordes of wild Indians for purposes of hunting. For a full twelve miles around Pensacola not a place is seen of which one could say that a stalk of lettuce could grow on it, just nothing but white sand." Chaplain Waldeck particularly complained that the colony lacked a preacher, and that consequently there were children ten years old who had not been baptized.[32] Max Von Eelking described the Waldeckers' initial impression of the area immediately around Pensacola: "The sandy landscape was low and flat, and almost to the city limits was covered with oak and pine forests, in which Indians, wild animals such as bears, tigers, panthers, alligators and other monsters lived. The atmosphere was not one of comfort."[33]

The impressions of the Englishmen arriving in Pensacola were little different. Hugh Mackay Gordon, deputy muster master general and deputy inspector of provincials, complained of his "banishment" soon after his arrival: "You may easily conceive what a change coming from a pleasant, plentiful comp[any] into a most wretched one and I may say with safety I am now in the worst part of the world; nothing to be had but

    31. Learned, *Philipp Waldeck's Diary*, pp. 115–19; Eelking, *Die Deutschen Hulfstruppen*, p. 3.
    32. Pettengill, *Letters from America*, pp. 226–27. See also Learned, *Philipp Waldeck's Diary*, pp. 119–26.
    33. Eelking, *Die Deutschen Hulfstruppen*, p. 4.

lean beef and pork except poultry which is extravagantly dear and it is so damned hot fish stinks before it can be boiled. The only thing this pleasant place abounds in is a beautiful white sand which circulates freely."[34]

General John Campbell wrote most revealingly about West Florida. Expenses were high, provisions were scarce, the fortifications almost totally destroyed by the hurricane which hit Pensacola in October: "in short everything in a state of ruin and desolation." Conditions in Mobile were even worse and Campbell described Fort Charlotte and Mobile itself as "almost a scene of ruin and desolation. . . . To sum up, all the province of West Florida seems hitherto to have been attended to only by starts, after which every thing was again permitted to fall to ruin and decay."[35]

Campbell included an evaluation of the troops which he commanded. There were seven companies of the Sixteenth Regiment, which was composed of veterans, "almost worn out in the service," and German recruits. There were also eight companies of the Third and Fourth battalions of the Sixtieth Regiment, but these men were mainly "Germans, condemned criminals and other species of gaol birds." Campbell concluded that "the fidelity of all these except of the veterans of the 16th regiment is not to be depended upon."

The general described next the men he brought with him from New York. The largest number of these troops were Waldeckers, whom Campbell had "no objection to on account of military subordination" and whose commanding officer he respected. "But I must say," he continued, "that I think them totally unfit for active service, their appointments, their dress, their discipline, nay their very make and form of body disable them from acting with that rapidity and spirit wherewith it might probably be necessary to repel an invading enemy, and indeed must at all times render them improper troops for the woods and wilds of America." Campbell felt that as long as the Waldeckers were in garrison and well provisioned, they would be good troops—unless they succumbed to the temptation to desert to the Spanish, as many of the German troops in the Sixteenth and Sixtieth regiments had done.

34. Gordon to Edward Winslow, Mar. 20, 1779, Winslow Papers, reel 1.
35. Campbell to Clinton, Feb. 10, 1779, BHP, 1737, reel 7.

Finally, the new commanding officer described his troops as "most certainly the most unfit to be trusted in any post where there is the least temptation, or even from whence there is a facility to desert." Campbell shared the British officer's disdain for the provincial troops who served with the British army. The Pennsylvania and Maryland Loyalists arrived at Pensacola in "tatters and rags instead of uniforms," and Campbell described them (rather unjustly) as "composed of the greater part of Irish vagabonds (deserters from the rebels) who from natural fickleness and instability of their disposition, which has been confirmed by their late roaming way of life, would desert without any other temptation." According to reports Campbell had received, the Spanish governor in New Orleans provided an added temptation by offering free land, provisions, and money to deserters from the British.[36]

In addition to the regular troops already in West Florida and the force Campbell brought with him from New York, there were troops raised by Chester and Stuart in the colony. Soon after his arrival, Campbell received orders from Germain to put these two corps of provincial troops under his command and to "continue them on the footing of other provincials, if you shall think fit, or discharge them if you see no immediate service for them, which I hope will be the case."[37] Because of the lack of men, Campbell—with the concurrence of the governor—reduced the three companies raised by Chester to one company under Captain Francis Miller. Campbell planned to keep this one company as soldiers or bateau men, whichever proved most necessary. Miller's company contained only twenty-four rank and file, but Campbell hoped for augmentation by reducing the other two companies.[38] On August 23, 1779, the Board of Com-

36. Ibid. For a list of the officers of the Pennsylvania and Maryland Loyalists, see "List of Officers of the Established Provincial Corps of North America, [1778]," Clinton Papers. One of the ensigns in the Maryland Loyalists was William Augustus Bowles, who later played an important role in Florida history as "Director General" of the Creek nation. For a full discussion of Bowles, see J. Leitch Wright, Jr., *William Augustus Bowles, Director General of the Creek Nation*.

37. Germain to Campbell, Apr. 1, 1779, C.O. 5/597.

38. Campbell to Clinton, Apr. 7, 1779, BHP, 1897, reel 8; Campbell to Germain, Apr. 7, 1779, C.O. 5/597. The three independent companies had already been reduced to two companies by the governor in council in November 1778. Minutes of the Council, Nov. 9, 1778, C.O. 5/595; Chester to Germain, Nov. 27, 1779, ibid.

missioners for Executing the Office of Indian Affairs in West Florida discussed Germain's letter to Campbell in which Germain ordered the general either to put the Loyal Refugees (Stuart's forces) on an equal footing with provincials or to discharge them. The board decided to give the troops their choice. While records on the matter are meager, Campbell apparently disbanded the Loyal Refugees. He also requested that Clinton send a company of Negroes from Rhode Island to West Florida to help in the construction of fortifications.[39]

The justification for the reinforcements sent to West Florida under Campbell was the protection of the province from American (and perhaps Spanish) invasion. When Campbell arrived in Pensacola, there were orders awaiting him from Lord George Germain; he was to establish a "considerable post" on the Mississippi River for the protection of British trade, communications, and property in the western region of the colony. The site Germain viewed as most proper for the post was at "the entrance of the Mississippi into the Iberville at or near the place where Fort Bute stood." Germain left the exact location up to the discretion of Campbell and his engineers but ordered him, as soon as possible, to send the necessary troops, engineers, and matériel to construct a fortification capable of supporting and being defended by a garrison of three hundred men. Germain urged Campbell to use durable materials since the post would be permanent; experience had shown that fortifications built in West Florida of inferior material were a waste of money. The Secretary of State for American Colonies ordered Campbell to build floating batteries for the Mississippi, to be manned by troops from the garrison, to protect navigation of the river. Campbell's instructions also placed construction of new and adequate fortifications at Pensacola under his command. Germain admonished Campbell "to take every precaution to avoid

39. Minutes of the Board of Commissioners for Executing the Office of Indian Affairs in West Florida, Aug. 23, 1779, C.O. 5/81; Cameron to Campbell, June 30, 1780, BHP, 2850, reel 10 and C.O. 5/81; Cameron to Clinton, July 18, 1780, BHP, 2919, reel 10; George C. Osborn, "Major-General John Campbell in British West Florida," p. 319; Campbell to Clinton, Feb. 10, 1779, BHP, 1737, reel 7. See also Campbell to Germain, Mar. 22, 1779, C.O. 5/597. Germain approved Campbell's request for Negroes but did not order Clinton to send the requested force, and, apparently, the Negroes were never sent to West Florida (Germain to Campbell, June 24, 1779, C.O. 5/244).

disputes with, or giving occasion of offense to the subjects of Spain."[40]

The last part of Campbell's orders proved initially to be the easiest to carry out. Five days after he landed at Pensacola, the general informed Governor Bernardo de Gálvez in New Orleans of his arrival "with a body of troops, to repel the incursions, and protect the inhabitants of the province of West Florida from the insults and marauding depredations of the rebellious Americans." While most of the letter contained pleasantries and protocol, Campbell notified Gálvez that British troops would proceed up the Mississippi River and that he trusted the Spanish governor would allow his subjects to sell bateaux to a British commissary sent in advance to purchase the vessels. Gálvez agreed to let the British purchase whatever shipping they needed and permitted Campbell to send a commissary for that purpose.[41] These amicable relations lasted less than a year, for Spain soon joined the war against England.

The remainder of the orders to Campbell presented more difficulties. Campbell apprised Germain on March 22, 1779, that he was "under the necessity of accounting to your Lordship for the impossibility of executing them [his orders] with that promptness and dispatch that seem to be expected and required."[42] There were numerous reasons why the work on the Mississippi was not proceeding. Campbell did not like the location chosen by the home government because the land was inundated during the flood season; the surrounding land was so low that water became stagnant and caused the area to be "extremely sickly"; the Iberville River (which the home government felt could be used as a means of travel) was actually dry during part of the year; and his engineers informed him that it was likely that the course of the river would change and that the land planned for the fort would be carried away by the

40. Germain to the "Genl. Officer Commanding in West Florida," July 1, 1778, C.O. 5/594; Germain to Clinton, July 1, 1778, Clinton Papers; Clinton to Campbell, Oct. 27, 1778, BHP, 1491, reel 7. The Spanish in New Orleans knew the substance of Campbell's orders even before the British troops landed in Pensacola (Raymundo DuBreuil to Gálvez, Dec. 31, 1778, in Kinnaird, *Spain in the Mississippi Valley*, 1:322).

41. Campbell to Gálvez, Jan. 24, 1779, C.O. 5/597; Gálvez to Campbell, Feb. 4, 1779, ibid.

42. Campbell to Germain, Mar. 22, 1779, ibid.

river.[43] The British officials stood by their decision, however (in part because Clinton failed to confirm Campbell's assessment), and the British eventually constructed the fort at Manchac—a few miles south of Baton Rouge.

There were more serious problems than the site for the post. In his new situation Campbell found himself "without money or credit for contingent expenses; without vessels proper for the navigation, or even batteaux for the transporting to the Mississippi any number of troops or quantity of provisions adequate to the undertaking; without artificers wherewith to carry on works, whether by land or water; without any provision of materials to work upon, and without any prospect of their being procured by contract, or any otherwise but by the labor of the troops; without tools for accommodating the few artificers that could be found among the army; without engineers' stores; without even provisions (were every other difficulty removed) to justify sending many troops to the Mississippi."[44] Transportation within the colony was almost nonexistent except by water, and even that was not always to be counted upon. Except for some small paper notes that had been issued as money, the troops had not been paid since October 1778. The floating batteries for the Mississippi could not be built because there were no ship carpenters in the colony. Protection of the province was almost impossible until something was done to strengthen the fortifications in Pensacola and Mobile. As Campbell reported, almost everything needed to be rebuilt; the fortifications of both Pensacola and Mobile and their harbors were in a state of "ruin and desolation." It is little wonder that Campbell complained that "in short the sending of the troops seems to have been the only thing attended to, and everything else seems to have been neglected or forgot."[45]

To add to all of the confusion in West Florida, Indian superintendent John Stuart was in the final stages of a lingering illness and had not been able to carry on the duties of his office. Following his death, on March 21, 1779, Chester appointed a five-man commission to run the office of superinten-

43. Campbell to Clinton, Feb. 10, 1779, BHP, 1737, reel 7.
44. Campbell to Germain, Mar. 22, 1779, C.O. 5/597.
45. Campbell to Clinton, Feb. 10, 1779, ibid.; Osborn "Major-General John Campbell," p. 321.

dent until the ministry appointed a new man. When Campbell heard the names of the men Chester appointed and realized that the governor had omitted Charles Stuart, the deputy Indian superintendent, he withdrew his approval from the commission plan. Campbell then recommended that the king appoint William Ogilvy to take John Stuart's place.[46] The situation became even more muddled when Clinton appointed Alexander Cameron to act as superintendent of the Southern Department until he received further orders from the home government. Thus, through the spring and summer of 1779, Cameron and the commissioners attempted to function as separate authorities, neither recognizing the other. It was not until June 25, 1779, that Germain settled the confusion with the appointment of Alexander Cameron and Colonel Thomas Browne as Indian superintendents, each to have control of half of the Southern District. Communications were slow, and it was October before the news of the appointments reached Pensacola and some degree of order was restored.[47]

Confusion in the Indian department, weakness of the defenses, lack of quality and loyalty among his troops, lack of money or credit, inability to get provisions, building materials, and artificers, poor transportation, and the general overall deterioration of the settlements in West Florida were just a few of the problems which caused Campbell to complain to Germain: "In short, my Lord, I find myself in the most disagreeable, the most irksome, the most distressing of all situations to a soldier and a man of spirit; unable implicitly to fulfill the mandates of my sovereign, the duties of my station, or perform any immediate service to my country."[48] It is not surprising that Campbell confided his frustrations to Clinton in a "private" letter: "Permit me earnestly to solicit and entreat that your Excellency

46. Campbell to Clinton, Mar. 25, 1779, BHP, 1856, reel 8; Campbell to Germain, Apr. 7, 1779, C.O. 5/597; Campbell to Germain, Dec. 15, 1779, ibid. The five men appointed to the commission were Andrew Rainsford, John Mitchell, Robert Taitt, Alexander Macullagh, and David Helms (Circular Letter, Pensacola, Mar. 31, 1779, C.O. 5/80).
47. Clinton to Alexander Cameron, Apr. 29, 1779, BHP, 1955, reel 8; Germain to Cameron and Col. Thomas Browne, June 25, 1779, BHP, 2080, reel 8; O'Donnell, *Southern Indians in the American Revolution*, pp. 82–89. See also Germain to Clinton, June 25, 1779, C.O. 5/97. Browne had been the commander of a company of loyalist refugees in East Florida prior to his appointment.
48. Campbell to Germain, Mar. 22, 1779, C.O. 5/597.

will be pleased to release me from the command of West Florida as soon as you can conveniently, and beg as a particular favor, I may not be kept any length of time with a command I have so great an aversion to; give me leave to assure you sir, that I shall be very unhappy and discontented as long as I remain in this province. My spirits are almost exhausted with the difficulties and troubles that I have met with since my arrival at this place. I must own there is nothing I wish for so much as a relief from my present command, finding myself unable to undergo the fatigue and trouble of it, and indeed I must say (with great truth) insufficient for the variety of important business attending it. . . . I would not presume to trouble your Excellency with this request so early, if I was not perfectly convinced and satisfied that the fatigue etc. attending this command is more than my constitution can possibly bear. You cannot therefore bestow a greater favor upon me, than to recall me from West Florida."[49]

Conditions in West Florida apparently improved in the next few months, for Campbell apologized to Clinton for his earlier letter, which was "rather improper at this critical juncture." The general assured Clinton that he would "cheerfully remain" in Pensacola until Clinton could conveniently find a general officer to take his place; at the same time "I would be sorry," Campbell continued, "if any officer is ordered to come here against his inclination on my account." While Campbell still felt that his present position was "a troublesome command" and one which he feared would be of little credit to him, his health (which had been poor since his arrival) had improved, and he desired that Clinton "will not be unmindful of me, for it is my most sincere and earnest wish to merit the continuance of your kind friendly notice and countenance."[50] In the two months since the letter requesting his recall, the general had become accustomed to and better acquainted with the province he was sent to command, and, from the tone of his letters, apparently the colony was not as foreboding as he had assumed. Construction of the post at Manchac was proceeding with the use of cypress logs and clay. Work on the fortifications at Pensacola continued, and Campbell had plans to rebuild the

49. Campbell to Clinton, Mar. 10, 1779, BHP, 1815, reel 7.
50. Campbell to Clinton, May 10, 1779, BHP, 1989, reel 8.

officers' barracks, which were literally "falling to pieces." The annual fleet from England, loaded with supplies, had arrived in early April and had given a psychological boost to the new troops, who had felt they were forgotten in the outermost part of the British American empire. Upon rereading his first letter to Clinton, Campbell must have felt that his letter was improper and that he had seemed ungrateful for the recognition extended to him by the command. More persuasive than this sense of guilt, however, was his fear that such intemperate correspondence would lead the commander-in-chief to overlook him for future commands.

While the conditions in West Florida had improved by the latter part of the spring of 1779, there were still many problems. Although work had begun on the fortifications at Manchac, Pensacola, and Mobile, the construction would proceed slowly until more carpenters could be obtained to assist the overworked men. When the annual fleet arrived, there was only a three and one-half months' supply of flour for the garrison instead of a year's supply of provisions since one of the vessels had been destroyed in Jamaica. While the troops could obtain cattle from ranchers in the colony, the only substitute for flour was a small amount of Indian corn. Campbell requested assistance, but he had little hope that aid would be forthcoming.[51]

Perhaps the problem which gave Campbell the greatest concern was his lack of troops. He requested in May that Clinton send one regiment of British regulars to Pensacola to replace the Sixteenth Regiment, which was composed of men "worn out in the service." Any remaining men in the Sixteenth Regiment fit for duty Campbell wished to draft into the Sixtieth Regiment. With added men, Campbell concluded, "I . . . am confident I shall be able to repel any descent that may be attempted against this province, whereas at present I have no troops under my command that I can consider actually fit for active service nor indeed any that I can with safety trust at the frontier posts, which is a very disagreeable circumstance."[52]

51. Campbell to Germain, Apr. 7, May 10, 1779; Osborn, "Major-General John Campbell," p. 324.
52. Campbell to Clinton, May 10, 1779, BHP, 1989, reel 8. As of May 1, 1779, there were a total of 87 officers and 1,880 rank and file under Campbell's command in West Florida ("State of His Majesty's Forces Stationed in the Province of

In a little over a month, Spain would have declared war on Great Britain and West Florida would be at war with her western neighbor. This was the contingency for which Germain sent Campbell and his men to West Florida; all other problems paled in comparison. Despite the year of preparation between Willing's raid and the advent of war, West Florida was caught unprepared. The amount of work that needed to be done was simply beyond the means supplied by the home government.

West Florida under the Command of Major Genl. Campbell . . . 1st May 1779," C.O. 5/97).

5

"By Beat of Drum"

There was great activity in West Florida during the summer and fall of 1779 as the province became engaged in a life and death struggle with its Spanish neighbor. Spain, on June 21, 1779, declared war against England with the goal in America being the recovery of the Floridas. Five days earlier, the Marquis D'Almadavar had issued a manifesto explaining the Spanish grievances, including a charge that the English had incited the Choctaws, Cherokees, and Chickasaws "against the innocent inhabitants of Louisiana."[1]

Four days after the Spanish declaration of war, Lord George Germain instructed Campbell in the role West Florida was to play in the war. "In the consideration of the measures most proper to be adopted for making an impression upon the dominions of Spain, an attack upon New Orleans presented itself as an object of great importance, and to be executed with the force already prepared in West Florida." Conceding that the British forces in the colony might be fewer than desired, British intelligence showed the Spanish forces in New Orleans "greatly

1. Spanish Manifesto, June 16, 1779, BHP, 2057, reel 8. The date of the Spanish declaration of war is open to debate. Caughey, *Gálvez*, p. 149, and Osborn, "Major-General John Campbell," p. 325, give the date of the declaration as June 21. In a letter from Germain to Campbell, dated June 25, 1779, Germain states that he is enclosing a circular dated June 17 containing information about the Spanish declaration of hostilities (C.O. 5/7). J. Horace Nunemaker, "Louisiana Anticipates Spain's Recognition of the Independence of the United States," p. 762, states that there are at least seven different dates set forth as the date of the declaration of war.

inferior, and the inhabitants generally indisposed to the Spanish government." Thus, the home government felt that if regulars, militia, and Indians immediately undertook an expedition, Campbell could succeed in taking New Orleans if Spanish reinforcements did not arrive. Germain ordered Campbell to consider the recommendation and, if he thought it was possible to reduce New Orleans, to make immediate preparations toward that end. Those preparations were to include a request that Sir Peter Parker send as many vessels as possible from Jamaica in order to stop any communication with New Orleans, to protect West Florida, and to transport the expedition to New Orleans. Campbell was to raise as large a force as possible without leaving Pensacola open to attack by pirates and to use as many Indians in the expedition as the superintendents could supply. In order to pay the expense of such an expedition, Germain authorized Campbell to draw on the Lords Commissioners of the Treasury. In the event he succeeded at New Orleans, Campbell was directed by Germain to distribute the troops as he thought proper, to stop construction of the fort at Manchac, and to repair the fortifications at New Orleans.[2]

In his book *Loyalists and Redcoats: A Study in British Revolutionary Policy*, Paul H. Smith pointed out that "the ultimate effect of the Spanish entry was . . . to move the focus of the war southward."[3] While Smith was referring mainly to the British attention to Georgia and the Carolinas, there is no doubt that the English also watched West Florida more closely. Germain informed Governor Dalling of Jamaica of the outbreak of war with Spain and of the decision to use some of the naval squadron stationed at Jamaica to aid in the proposed attack on New Orleans.[4] The secretary of state notified Clinton that he had not followed the usual procedure of sending orders to Campbell through the commander-in-chief because time was so

2. Germain to Campbell, June 25, 1779, C.O. 5/7. Apparently upon request, on June 19, 1779, former Governor George Johnstone, in a private letter written to Germain, "put upon paper some measures which I think expedient to be adopted in case yet an attack on New Orleans sh[oul]d be determined upon." There is nothing to indicate that his views were even noted, much less followed. Johnstone to [Germain?], June 19, 1779, William Knox Papers, William L. Clements Library, hereafter cited as Knox Papers.
    3. Page 123.
    4. Germain to Dalling, June 17, 1779, Clinton Papers.

short. The Earl of Cornwallis and Admiral Marriot Arbuthnot set sail to reinforce hard-pressed Jamaica in the fall of 1779, "the first and grand object . . . understood to be the safety of Jamaica, the next the protection of Pensacola. The reduction of New Orleans was to be held in view, and undertaken as events might render advisable. Should Pensacola not appear to be immediately threatened, his Lordship will only reinforce it."[5] Clinton ordered Cornwallis "if possible to lay hold of New Orleans which would indisputably give us the Mississippi and all the southern Indians."[6]

Although England and Spain had declared war in June, Campbell did not receive word of the commencement of hostilities until September 8. Three days later, Campbell assured Clinton that a surprise attack on New Orleans was almost impossible because of "apparent insurmountable difficulties." Campbell was referring to the insufficiency of ships-of-war and naval transports capable of carrying five hundred men and supplies; a scarcity of field artillery and a total lack of entrenching tools; and above all, the poor condition of the troops under his command because of desertions and sickness. Campbell had "no confidence in their steadiness, fidelity, and attachment." He reported that 372 noncommissioned officers and enlisted men under his command were sick, and the amount of illness was increasing. Campbell concluded his letter with apparent resignation to his fate as commander of the forces in West Florida: "Notwithstanding all these discouraging views, your excellency may rest assured, that if found anyway practicable, I shall not be wanting in my endeavors to fulfill His Majesty's expectations, for the alternative undoubtedly is, whether we are to abandon the Mississippi, or get possession of New Orleans, as it will be impossible from what I conceive at present to maintain troops in that quarter while the Spaniards are entirely masters of the water communication, which they must be as long as

5. Clinton to Germain, Sept. 26, 1779, ibid.; Germain to Clinton, June 25, 1779, ibid. See also Smith, Loyalists and Redcoats, p. 112.
6. Clinton to Cornwallis, Sept. 23, 1779, Clinton Papers. Before Clinton received word that Spain had declared war on England, he told Germain, "Unless the Spaniards declare against us, I think the province of West Florida will be in perfect security, if a frigate or two can be spared for the protection of the port of Pensacola, the defenses of which were abolished last October by a violent tempest" (Clinton to Germain, Aug. 21, 1779, ibid.).

they retain that island, and to resign to them that part of this province bordering on the Mississippi, would be making them masters of the part of West Florida of the most real intrinsic value."[7]

Despite his pessimistic evaluation of the situation in West Florida and his doubt that a successful expedition could be undertaken against New Orleans, Campbell immediately began preparations to defend the colony and attack New Orleans. On the day that he received news of war, he informed Lieutenant Colonel Alexander Dickson, commander of the British forces at Manchac, of the outbreak of hostilities and ordered him to keep the information secret and to prepare the defenses at Manchac. Campbell's orders to Dickson contained instructions for defense, but Dickson was already involved in an active resistance against the Spanish.[8]

Campbell informed Governor Chester of the war and requested that the governor and council place an embargo on all vessels in Pensacola and Mobile in order to prevent information about the war from reaching New Orleans. The next day Chester met with the council, who advised the governor to issue a proclamation laying such an embargo on Mobile, Pensacola, and any other place where a vessel might weigh anchor, and subsequently to inform the Spanish of the outbreak of hostilities.[9] Campbell also ordered the "forcible possession" of all vessels capable of transporting troops.[10] Campbell asked Chester to detain the packet boat *Carteret*, a "strong well armed ship," in

7. Campbell to Clinton, Sept. 11, 1779, BHP, 2281, reel 9; Le Montais to Parker, Dec. 20, 1779, Adm. 1/242, University of Florida photostat; Learned, *Philipp Waldeck's Diary*, pp. 126–27. For a discussion of desertion, see Robert R. Rea, "Military Deserters from British West Florida."

8. James Campbell to Lt. Col. Alexander Dickson, Sept. 9, 1779, C.O. 5/598. James Campbell was General Campbell's secretary, and he penned these orders to Dickson upon instructions from the commander.

9. Campbell to Chester, Sept. 9, 1779, BHP, 2267, reel 9; Minutes of the Council, Sept. 10, 1779, C.O. 5/635, RSUS, reel 8. During this meeting Chester informed the council that he had just received a letter from Germain, dated June 17, informing him of the war with Spain. Undoubtedly, this was the circular letter bearing the June 17 date that Germain sent out.

10. James Campbell to Captain Le Montais, Sept. 10, 1779, BHP, 2275, reel 9. The same day, Le Montais wrote James Campbell that he had received word from Sir Peter Parker in Jamaica that he could not send any aid until the threat from D'Estaing's fleet was over (Le Montais to James Campbell, Sept. 10, 1779, BHP, 2276, reel 9).

Pensacola harbor for protection until reinforcements arrived, and its detention was so ordered.[11]

Concerned for the defense of West Florida and the necessity of arming all men capable of bearing arms, Campbell proposed that Chester declare martial law for not less than six months due to the lack of a militia law in the colony.[12] The council was evenly divided on the proposal; military men favored martial law, civilians opposed it. On the advice of the chief justice, who thought that the measure was unconstitutional, Chester declared that he would not proclaim martial law. The council advised Chester to issue a proclamation commanding all of the inhabitants of the colony to go to specified locations to declare their allegiance and to enroll as a militia "in case of actual invasion in defense of their country or otherwise as circumstances may require."[13]

Campbell also decided to issue a proclamation, since he felt that Chester's proclamation, the lack of militia laws or martial law, and the resolution of the inhabitants "not to quit their houses and only to act in defense of their own respective properties" demanded firm action by the military. It is not clear from the records, but possibly this proclamation calling for the citizens to enroll themselves in militia units is the one Chester issued. In a letter to Clinton, Campbell asserted that he was going to present the proclamation to the governor and council first, but that he was determined to issue the proclamation with or without the council's concurrence. Campbell's letter to Clinton and Chester's proclamation were both dated Septem-

11. Campbell to Chester, Sept. 14, 1779, C.O. 5/598; Minutes of the Council, Sept. 14, 1779, C.O. 5/598. In this letter Campbell cleared up one confusing point when he asked that the embargo not include vessels in the king's service—a request with which the council concurred.

12. Campbell to Chester, Sept. 10, 1779, BHP, 2277, reel 9. Campbell also requested that Chester issue orders that no gunpowder belonging to merchants or private individuals be delivered to them until he determined the needs of the garrison.

13. Minutes of the Council, Sept. 11, 1779, C.O. 5/595. Two months later, Chester wrote Germain that many of the inhabitants of West Florida had formed themselves into volunteer units as a result of his proclamation of Sept. 11. He went on to assert that, had martial law been declared, such a development would not have occurred, "as I was well assured, that it would have driven one half of them [the inhabitants] out of the country, and have thrown the remainder in the utmost confusion." Since they were now enrolled in militia units, however, "they are ready and willing to march to any part of the province, and to defend it to the utmost of their power" (Chester to Germain, Nov. 15, 1779, C.O. 5/595).

ber 11, 1779. The commander dated his proposed proclamation September 12, perhaps to allow the governor and council time to consider the edict before it was published. If the governor and council concurred, possibly they issued the proclamation the same day.[14] At any rate, a proclamation was issued: one by Chester, and perhaps another one by Campbell.

The British commander had little faith that the proclamation would have the desired effect, since he found "the inhabitants in general, self-interested and without public spirit, whose minds are only attached to gain and their private concerns; in short nothing can be had from them, even on this emergency, but at an enormous extravagant price, and personal service on general principles of national defense is too generous and exalted for their conceptions."[15] Campbell's evaluation was not altogether correct; forty-nine of the "principal inhabitants" petitioned the governor and council on September 10 for permission "to form ourselves into a temporary militia in these times of imminent danger." The governor and council sanctioned the request.[16] A month later, fifty-eight inhabitants along the Tombigbee River sent a petition to the council pointing out the weakness of their situation, seeking permission to build a fort, and requesting authorization to form a company of men to scout between their settlements and the Choctaw Indians (who, they feared, would join the Spanish) in order to give warning of an attack. The council granted their requests.[17]

Since the receipt of the Spanish declaration of war, Campbell had been active in preparing West Florida's defenses and planning an attack on New Orleans. He was ready to embark on an expedition to New Orleans with five armed vessels, two armed flatboats, five hundred men, supplies, and gifts for the Indians, when he received news of Colonel Dickson's surrender to

14. Campbell to Clinton, Sept. 11, 1779, BHP, 2281, reel 9.
15. Campbell to Germain, Sept. 14, 1779, C.O. 5/597. Campbell noted two exceptions to his overall indictment of West Florida inhabitants: Adam Chrystie and Doctor James Dallas. Copies of Campbell's proposed proclamation are in BHP, 9843, reel 27, and Minutes of the Council, Sept. 14, 1779, C.O. 5/635, RSUS, reel 8.
16. Minutes of the Council, Sept. 10, 1779, C.O. 5/635, RSUS, reel 8. The following day, the council recorded in the minutes that in case of invasion, all of the militia companies were to be put under the command of General Campbell (Minutes of the Council, Sept. 11, 1779, ibid.).
17. Minutes of the Council, Oct. 21, 1779, ibid., reel 8.

Gálvez at Baton Rouge. The capitulation forced Campbell to begin preparing a defense.[18] After Gálvez set out against the English at Manchac, he encountered an officer carrying a message from Pensacola to Manchac. The Englishman destroyed his message, but Gálvez speculated it contained plans for an attack. Apparently the message was Campbell's letter to Dickson informing him of the outbreak of war and describing actions to be taken.[19]

While Campbell did not receive news of war with Spain until early September, Gálvez learned of the commencement of hostilities much sooner. The Minister of the Indies sent notification to Gálvez on May 18 that Spain would declare war against England in the near future, and in that event he was to make himself "master of all the establishments which they [the British] have on the Mississippi and particularly Mobile and Pensacola."[20] This message reached Havana on July 17, and Diego Josef Navarro (governor and captain-general of Cuba) immediately forwarded the letter to Gálvez. The order did not arrive in Louisiana until August, however. Gálvez apprised the home government on August 17 that he had received the message and that he had already begun preparations; "within three days I shall set out with a number of troops, militia, and Negroes to attack Manchac. I shall always continue if God gives more fortune against Baton Rouge and Natchez."[21] The message

18. Campbell to Germain, Dec. 15, 1779, C.O. 5/597. See also Campbell to Clinton, Nov. 7, 1779, C.O. 5/99; Campbell to Clinton, Nov. 7, 1779, BHP, 2416, reel 9; "Mr. Gordon to Messrs. Thompson and Campbell, Merchants at Jamaica," Nov. 18, 1779, BHP, 2433, reel 9. Sir John Fortescue has written that the success of an attack on New Orleans depended on "rapidity of movement," but that "such was Germain's mismanagement that the news of the rupture with Spain did not reach Campbell until September" (A History of the British Army, 3:302). While there is little question that Germain made mistakes in the conduct of the American war, this specific charge of Fortescue does not hold up. Within a very few days of the Spanish declaration of war on England, Germain sent the Carteret packet boat to West Florida on a voyage which took it two months and fifteen days to reach Pensacola—a relatively short time for the trip. Germain also sent orders directly to Campbell rather than going through Clinton (the normal practice) in order to save time.

19. Gálvez to Diego Josef Navarro, Oct. 16, 1779, MPA,SD, 1:310–11.

20. Gálvez to José de Gálvez, Aug. 17, 1779, Adm. 1/241, University of Florida photostat. The Spanish had earlier planned to attack St. Augustine first but changed their minds when the U.S. apparently agreed to capture it and relinquish it to Spain. Topping, "Spanish Agents at the Continental Congress," p. 8.

21. Gálvez to José de Gálvez, Aug. 17, 1779, Adm. 1/486; Francisco Collell to Gálvez, Aug. 27, 1779, MPA,SD, 1:264; Nunemaker, "Louisiana Anticipates," pp.

to prepare for war and news of the actual declaration of war reached New Orleans about the same time.

Gálvez was aware that relations were strained between the English and the Spanish, and he was almost prepared to set out on an expedition against the English when news of the outbreak of war arrived in New Orleans. The reinforcements of Waldeckers that Campbell had sent to Dickson at Manchac also made Gálvez suspicious. Although he assured Dickson that he was "greatly pleased to know that these suspicious movements on the part of the English are not against us,"[22] Gálvez was not convinced that the troop movements were designed to protect West Florida from American incursions. He felt that the reinforcements were intended to strengthen the British forces on the Mississippi "in order to be in a better position to attack us at the first advice of a rupture."[23] The Spanish had intercepted two letters from English settlers to William Hiorn at Natchez. Elias Durnford warned Hiorn to be "ready for an expedition against New Orleans in which it is possible that we shall be engaged shortly." William Johnstone informed Hiorn that preparations were being made for an expedition against the "Dons of New Orleans." He continued, "Thank God that we are all firm and relishing the opportunity to strike a blow against the Dons."[24]

The Minister of the Indies sent instructions to Navarro on August 29, 1779, concerning the expeditions against the English possessions in West Florida. He warned, in part, that "to await help from Spain will endanger the success of the undertaking. Celerity is essential. Delay may lose us the chance to win."[25] Procrastination was not in the nature of the governor of

762–63. The best discussion of the roles of Gálvez and Louisiana in Spain's recognition of U.S. independence is in this article. See also Mortimer H. Favrot, "Colonial Forts of Louisiana"; Scramuzza, "Gálveztown," pp. 581–93; Caughey, Gálvez, p. 149.

22. Gálvez to Dickson, Aug. 28, 1779, MPA,SD, 1:289. See also Caughey, Gálvez, p. 149.

23. Gálvez to José de Gálvez, July 3, 1779, in Kinnaird, Spain in the Mississippi Valley, 1:345.

24. Both of these letters are quoted in Caughey, Gálvez, pp. 149–50. Caughey states that the letters were written to William Horn. While the English documents are not consistent in the spelling of his name, he is generally referred to as William Hiorn.

25. José de Gálvez to Diego Josef Navarro and Juan Bautista Bonet, Aug. 29, 1779, MPA,SD, 1:335.

Louisiana. Two days before José de Gálvez even sent orders to Navarro, the ambitious governor of Louisiana had begun an expedition against the English. Governor Gálvez had called a *junta de guerra* on July 13 and had presented the critical state of Louisiana, reviewed the size of the British forces on the Mississippi (which he estimated at "800 veteran troops"), stated the size of the Spanish forces as 600 men (including 150 too ill to be counted as effective), and sought the recommendations of the council of war. The council advised that the defense of New Orleans should be the chief consideration. Gálvez, nevertheless, decided the best defense for Louisiana was a quick strike at the nearest enemy stronghold before the British could unite their superior but scattered forces for an attack against New Orleans.[26]

Gálvez continued with preparations, and by mid-August he was prepared enough for the expedition to set August 22 as the date for departure. On the eighteenth, however, a violent hurricane hit New Orleans. It plunged the Spanish at New Orleans into great confusion as "the earth overflowed and everything on the river was under water, as were my plans . . . and hopes." Discouraged but not defeated, Gálvez quickly reorganized the defenses of New Orleans and again began preparations for an expedition. He was still determined to "seek the enemy at his own forts and settlements, for I knew full well that, if I did not go after them, they would come after me."[27]

Up until the time of the hurricane, Gálvez had kept all of his preparations secret. He had not told the people that war had been declared, that he had been appointed governor of Louisiana (he had been acting governor), and that he was preparing to attack the British. Now he felt the time was right to seek the sympathy and aid of the Spanish subjects in Louisiana. Gálvez called the people together on August 20, "talked with them in a pathetic manner about the unhappy situation in the colony," told them about the declaration of war, and agreed to take the office of governor only if the people would promise to

26. Caughey, *Gálvez*, pp. 150–51. For a full discussion of the Spanish preparations for an attack against Manchac and the Spanish efforts on the Mississippi, see ibid., pp. 149–70. See also Gálvez to José de Gálvez, Oct. 16, 1779, MPA,SD, 1:325–26. One member of the council of war, Lt. Col. Estevan Miró, disagreed.

27. Gálvez to José de Gálvez, Oct. 16, 1779, MPA,SD, 1:326. The British settlements escaped the hurricane.

support him and aid him—an assurance he received from the assembled crowd. It was at this meeting that Gálvez recognized the independence of the thirteen colonies in revolt. While the Spanish governor did not mention it in his description of the event, Campbell related that the Spanish recognized the independence of the states "by beat of drum."[28]

His preparations completed, Gálvez and his force set out for Manchac on the morning of August 27, 1779. His army consisted of 170 veteran soldiers, 330 recruits recently arrived from Mexico and the Canary Islands, 20 carabineers, 60 militiamen, and 80 free blacks and mulattoes. There were seven American volunteers and Oliver Pollock (who served as Gálvez' aide-de-camp). On the march to Manchac, 600 more men and 160 Indians joined the expedition, bringing the total force to 1,427 men. During the thirty-five-league trek to Manchac (a distance they covered in eleven days), the poorly equipped army had to march through thick woods with very poor trails. Sickness and the rapid march to Manchac reduced Gálvez' effective force by one-third.[29]

While making preparations and beginning his campaign, Gálvez had attempted to prevent news of the Spanish declaration of war from reaching the British. Without explanation, he arrested Farquhar Bethune (British Indian agent), who had come to Bayou St. John on business. William Dunbar went to New Orleans during the month of August to sell some staves; upon his arrival he was made a prisoner until Gálvez had captured Baton Rouge and returned to New Orleans.[30]

28. Ibid., 1:327; Campbell to Germain, Sept. 14, 1779, C.O. 5/597; Campbell to Clinton, Sept. 14, 1779, C.O. 5/99; Campbell to Germain, Dec. 15, 1779, C.O. 5/597. See also Eelking, Die Deutschen Hulfstruppen, pp. 7–8. Spain did not officially recognize the independence of the U.S. until Feb. 22, 1783 (Nunemaker, "Louisiana Anticipates," p. 768).

29. Gálvez to José de Gálvez, Oct. 16, 1779, MPA,SD, 1:328. Campbell reported to the home government that the Spanish force consisted of 2,600 men: 1,700–1,800 regulars and militia, 350 Indians, and the remainder Negroes ("200 of whom were armed"). Campbell to Germain, Dec. 15, 1779, C.O. 5/597; Campbell to Clinton, Dec. 15, 1779, C.O. 5/99. There is no reason to doubt that Gálvez' own report was accurate and that Campbell's was based on incorrect intelligence.

30. Caughey, Gálvez, p. 154; Rowland, William Dunbar, pp. 69–70. The actions of the Spanish probably surprised Dunbar, since there had been no indication that war with Spain was imminent. Indeed, in December of the preceding year, Dunbar wrote in his diary, "we received intelligence of an alliance between Great Britain and Spain which was confirmed by Govr. Gálvez, which is an

Gálvez wanted communication between the western part of West Florida and Pensacola and Mobile cut off. One of the most certain ways of achieving this objective was to gain control of Lakes Maurepas and Pontchartrain. William Pickles, in command of the American privateer *Morris* (formerly the *Rebecca* which Willing had captured at Manchac), captured the *West Florida* on Lake Pontchartrain in late September. The *West Florida* had been controlling the lakes for two years, and its removal opened the lakes for the Spanish. Pickles landed part of his men on the north shore of Pontchartrain and obtained from the settlers an oath of allegiance to the United States. Later he transported 122 Indians across the lake to New Orleans, and "on the Mobile coast" the next day he captured a British vessel which had thirteen Negroes valued at $2,600 on board.[31]

At Gálveztown, the Spanish captured four vessels which had taken supplies and ammunition to Manchac. In addition, on the Mississippi they seized a ship with three hundred barrels of provisions and a large quantity of rum destined for Manchac. The Spaniards also captured three more vessels on the lakes. A force of fourteen Creoles captured one of these vessels, which was carrying a contingent of fifty-five Waldeckers and ten or twelve sailors to Manchac.[32] Colonel Carlos Grand Pré seized two small British outposts on Thompson's Creek and the Amite River. Dickson destroyed a shipload of provisions on the Amite in order to prevent it falling into Spanish hands.[33]

Gálvez had marched his force to Manchac by September 6; there he expected to engage the British. Dickson, however, had received intelligence that the Spanish were approaching and

incident very much to be desired by the inhabitants on this river" (ibid., p. 66). An account of the capture of the *West Florida* is in Gerrald Savage ("late mastersmate of *West Florida*") to Le Montais, Oct. 24, 1779, Adm. 1/242, University of Florida photostat.

31. Caughey, *Gálvez*, pp. 159–60; Ford, *Journals*, 17:600, 18:492, 1130–31; Gálvez to José de Gálvez, Oct. 16, 1779, MPA,SD, 1:330.

32. Campbell to Clinton, Sept. 14, 1779, BHP, 2289, reel 9; Campbell to Germain, Sept. 14, 1779, C.O. 5/597; Campbell to Germain, Dec. 15, 1779, ibid.; Caughey, *Gálvez*, p. 161. Campbell states that there were 55 Waldeckers, Caughey says 56, and Eelking reports 54: Campbell to Germain, Sept. 14, 1779, C.O. 5/597; Caughey, *Gálvez*, p. 161; Eelking, *Die Deutschen Hulfstruppen*, p. 8.

33. Butler, "West Feliciana," p. 94; Caughey, *Gálvez*, p. 159; Gálvez to José de Gálvez, Oct. 16, 1779, MPA,SD, 1:330; Campbell to Germain, Sept. 14, 1779, C.O. 5/597.

had moved the main body of his force. General Gage had asserted as early as 1766 that the British should never have fortified the outposts on the Mississippi because of the poor communications[34] and when Dickson arrived at Manchac in 1779, his opinion was no different: "I am certain from my own knowledge of the country that the Spaniards can at any time with a sergeants' party cut off our communication with any post you can possibly erect in these parts."[35] Dickson had also obtained the opinion of the assistant engineer for West Florida that the proposed location was too dangerous for the post.[36] Therefore, when he received word that the rebels were preparing an invasion down the Mississippi River, Dickson had felt he must take some action, since "the situation of Manchac was unanimously condemned and the fort there considered as indefensible against cannon." He had decided to build a new fortification at Baton Rouge on the lands of Stephen Watts and Samuel Flowers.[37] Thus, with the Spanish forces approaching, Dickson and a council of war decided to move the troops, artillery, and stores from Manchac to the redoubt at Baton Rouge, since it "was in pretty good forwardness." When Gálvez arrived at Manchac, most of the garrison had been moved to Baton Rouge. Dickson had left a small force at a position he considered untenable as a delaying action to give the troops at Baton Rouge more time to prepare for the battle. He had a total

34. Gage to Tayler, Aug. 11, 1766, British Museum, Additional MSS, 21662. Eight months later Gage remarked that "it would be no easy matter to support these forts [Natchez and Ft. Bute] in case of a rupture with the Spaniards; on which account it might be best to abandon them on the approach of a rupture with that nation" (Gage to Shelburne, Apr. 3, 1767, C.O. 5/85).

35. Dickson to Campbell, Mar. 12, 1779, BHP, 1820, reel 7.

36. J. J. Graham to Dickson, Mar. 19, 1779, BHP, 1845, reel 7. After Willing's raid, Captain William Barker, in command of the troops at Manchac, had assured Colonel John McGillivray that in case the Americans attacked Manchac again, "we will do the most we can as there is no retreat" (Barker to McGillivray, Sept. 12, 1778, in Kinnaird, Spain in the Mississippi Valley, 1:307).

37. "Lieutt. Col. Dickson's Reasons for removing to Baton Rouge & Mr. Graham Asst. Engineer's Certificate," Sept. 22, 1779, C.O. 5/99. See also Stephen Watts to Dickson, Mar. 16, 1779, C.O. 5/597. Watts and Samuel Flowers were loyalist partners who left Pennsylvania and arrived in West Florida in January 1775. They brought their families and 64 slaves with them; as a result, the council granted 3,150 acres of land to Watts. The council postponed Flowers' petition for 1,750 acres family right and bounty until he proved his family right. There is no indication he was ever granted the land, although it is possible that he did receive it (Minutes of the Council, Sept. 16, Oct. 1, 1777, C.O. 5/634, RSUS, reel 8).

of 457 men, not including officers, under his command at Manchac, Baton Rouge, and Natchez.[38]

The Spanish militia assaulted Manchac on the morning of September 7 and carried the post easily. One officer and five men managed to escape "in the imperfect light of a breaking day," but one British soldier was killed and two officers and eighteen enlisted men were made prisoner. This skirmish initiated the Spanish militia to warfare; they served well and were encouraged by their success.[39] Having captured Manchac, Gálvez decided to allow time for his troops "who were falling sick" to recover from the march from New Orleans. After six days, the Spanish force left Manchac for Baton Rouge—about fifteen miles away—and took five prisoners of an advance guard on the way. Although the British redoubt at Baton Rouge had been under construction only since July 30, it was stronger than the untenable post at Manchac because it was on higher ground in a clearing and had a superior command of the Mississippi. The redoubt was constructed of earthen ramparts and surrounded by a ditch eighteen feet wide and nine feet deep. Inside the ditch there was an earthen wall, and surrounding the dry moat was a circle of chevaux de frise. Dickson had ordered some houses surrounding the redoubt torn down in order to prevent the Spanish from using them as shelter or cover. The armament of the redoubt was thirteen cannon. While Gálvez reported that the force inside the redoubt consisted of 400 regulars and 150 settlers and armed Negroes, the number of troops was actually much smaller. Dickson had fewer than 500 men under his command in the entire western portion of West Florida.[40]

38. "Lieutt. Col. Dickson's Reasons," Sept. 22, 1779, C.O. 5/99; Caughey, *Gálvez*, p. 155; Campbell to Germain, Sept. 14, 1779, C.O. 5/597.

39. Gálvez to José de Gálvez, Oct. 16, 1779, MPA,SD, 1:329. According to a British return of prisoners, two officers and twenty-one enlisted men were captured at Manchac. "Return of the Different Detachments of His Majesty's Troops Prisoners at New Orleans and the Posts Where Taken," Oct. 19, 1779, BHP, 2374, reel 9, hereafter cited as "Return of Prisoners." See also Caughey, *Gálvez*, p. 155.

40. Gálvez to José de Gálvez, Oct. 16, 1779, MPA,SD, 1:329; Caughey, *Gálvez*, p. 155; Campbell to Germain, Sept. 14, 1779, C.O. 5/597; "Examination in the Demand of Stephen Watts," Mar. 30, 1789, A.O. 12/72; "Examination on the Demand of Stephen Watts," Mar. 30, 1789, A.O. 13/10. A *cheval de frise* is "a portable obstacle . . . formed of large beams traversed by pointed spikes" (Boatner, *Encyclopedia of the American Revolution*, p. 226). The dearth of

When Gálvez arrived at Baton Rouge, Dickson's force was already drawn up inside the redoubt, and the governor decided it would not be possible to take the redoubt by assault unless the artillery first opened a breach in the walls. He felt that, as most of his army was militia, a hard-fought battle or a defeat "would throw the colony into mourning." A direct assault was therefore out of the question until completion of the emplacement of the artillery and commencement of the bombardment. The first problem was to get the artillery in place, so Gálvez planned decoy tactics. On the night of September 20, he sent a force of militia, Negroes, and Indians into a grove of trees close to the redoubt. While some of the men chopped down trees and threw up breastworks, the others fired on the redoubt as if they were protecting the laborers. All night long the British wore themselves out returning the fire—without wounding a single Spaniard. Meanwhile, the Spanish placed their cannon unobserved in a garden on the other side of the redoubt.

The next morning the British discovered their mistake, but it was too late. The Spanish were well entrenched, and at 5:45 A.M. the newly placed Spanish batteries opened fire against the English. The Spanish cannons were so effective that "not withstanding the English served their cannon well and with spirit," the British soon proposed a truce. Gálvez recorded that it was 3:30 in the afternoon when the British asked for a truce, but Dickson reported the bombardment continued for only three hours.[41] Gálvez refused to grant a truce and insisted that the

---

British records concerning the actual events at Baton Rouge forces the historian to rely on the Spanish records, and particularly Gálvez' account, for the details of the siege. According to a British account, the redoubt contained only four four-pounders (H. M. Gordon to Edward Winslow, Dec. 7, 1779, Winslow Papers, reel 1).

41. Gálvez to José de Gálvez, Oct. 16, 1779, MPA,SD, 1:329–30; "Lieutt. Col. Dickson's Reasons," Sept. 22, 1779, C.O. 5/99. An interesting anecdote of questionable authenticity is a report that Dickson was eating breakfast when the Spanish bombardment began. The first cannonball came through the wall of the building where he was eating. Dickson kicked the cannonball and remarked that if the Spanish were using cannon of that caliber, then resistance was useless and the fort would soon be battered into submission (J. St. Clair Favrot, "Baton Rouge, the Historic Capital of Louisiana," p. 614). The Spanish did have cannon of considerably larger caliber than the British, according to Caughey (Gálvez, p. 156), Hugh Mackay Gordon (Gordon to Edward Winslow, Dec. 7, 1779, Winslow Papers, reel 1), and a report of a Spanish official in New Orleans, Don Joseph Valiere (Jac Nachbin, ed., "Spain's Report of the War with the British in Louisiana," p. 472).

redoubt surrender and that Fort Panmure at Natchez be included in the capitulation. Gálvez gave the British twenty-four hours to bury their dead. Dickson refused to tell Gálvez how many casualties there were, but British records indicate four killed and two wounded. In accordance with the Articles of Capitulation, Dickson and his men (350 total) marched 500 yards out of the redoubt bearing arms, with drums beating and colors flying. They then surrendered their arms and the colors of the Sixteenth Regiment and became prisoners of war. Gálvez allowed the enlisted settlers and the Negroes whom he had captured to return home—because of the generous "heart of my sovereign" and because "it would have been impossible to guard them anyway."[42]

Gálvez sent a captain and fifty men to take possession of Fort Panmure at Natchez as provided for in the terms of the capitulation. The British had repaired and strengthened Fort Panmure after Willing's raid, and it was in good condition. Gálvez was relieved that Dickson had agreed to give up Natchez, since the strengthened fort would have been difficult to take.[43] If Isaac Johnstone's feelings can be taken as representative, the Natchez residents were disgusted at Dickson's surrender of Fort Panmure "to obtain tolerable terms" for himself. When the Spanish arrived to take possession of Natchez, Johnstone was "struck dumb to think of this place being thought so little of as to be trifled away to obtain terms." He wrote sarcastically that "in the mighty battle between Governor Gálvez and Colonel Dickson the Spaniards only lost one man and some say not one, the English about twenty-five and the commanding officer wounded in his head by his *tea table*. Picture to yourself the countenancy of those who were waiting with pleasure for the Americans to come down the river, at the sight of the fifty Spaniards landing; tears in their eyes, sorrow, rage, and distraction in every feature

42. Gálvez to José de Gálvez, Oct. 16, 1779, MPA,SD, 1:330–31; Return of Prisoners, Oct. 19, 1779, BHP, 2374, reel 9; "Return of Prisoners with the Spaniards & of the Killed and Wounded at Baton Rouge &c.," Oct. 1779, C.O. 5/99. Thirty men later died of wounds while they were prisoners (Albert W. Haarmann, "The Spanish Conquest of British West Florida, 1779–1781," p. 113). Copies of the Articles of Capitulation are in C.O. 5/99; C.O. 5/595; and BHP, 2312, reel 9.
43. Gálvez to José de Gálvez, Oct. 16, 1779, MPA,SD, 1:330; Campbell to Clinton, Feb. 10, 1779, BHP, 1737, reel 7.

of their faces. There surely never was a set of people more divided before nor never more unanimous to fight the Spaniards: to be thus thrown away without suffering us to fight for one of the finest countries in the world! The Spaniards might take Manchac but they could not take the Natchez so easy. Soldiers fight for [money?] but planters fight for their families and properties, the love of liberty and those precious laws we have hitherto enjoyed." Johnstone went on to state that when the British surrendered the fort, "there never was seen such dejection in almost every face."[44] On the day the Spanish arrived to take possession of Natchez, however, fifty-nine inhabitants of the settlement extended to Dickson their "most sincere thanks for your generous and disinterested attention to our welfare in the capitulation of Baton Rouge."[45] Resigned to their situation, the British settlers submitted peacefully to Spanish control. The inhabitants of Baton Rouge were grateful to Dickson and his men for their efforts to defeat the Spanish and they expressed their thanks.[46] After Captain Anthony Forster handed over Natchez to the Spanish, the British had eight months to decide whether to sell their properties and leave Natchez or to become Spanish subjects.[47]

Under Gálvez' leadership, the Spanish had captured three forts, eight vessels, and 484 British and Waldeck soldiers. These figures do not include the militia and Negroes whom the Spanish released or the crews of the captured ships. The Spaniards were also masters of 430 leagues of the "best land along the Mississippi." Gálvez' conquests secured New Orleans; the Spanish no longer had to worry about attacks from the

44. Isaac Johnstone to Anthony Hutchins, Oct. 5,1779, C.O. 5/595. While the original documents identify the author of this letter as Isaac Johnstone, it was probably the Isaac Johnson who had served earlier as an associate delegate (see p. 86). The garrison from Natchez arrived at New Orleans in mid-October (Nachbin, "Spain's Report of the War," p. 477).
45. "Address of the Inhabitants of Natchez to Lt. Col. Dickson," Oct. 4, 1779, C.O. 5/99.
46. "Harry Alexander for and in the name of all the inhabitants of the settlement [of Baton Rouge] to Lt. Col. Dickson," Sept. 21, 1779, ibid.
47. Minutes of the Council, Oct. 25, 1779, C.O. 5/595. This information was gathered from testimony by John Anderson, who had just arrived in Pensacola from Natchez. See also Caughey, Gálvez, pp. 157–59, for the efforts of Oliver Pollock to convince the settlers of Natchez that it was to their benefit to surrender without a fight.

British subjects on the Mississippi. According to Gálvez' account, the Spanish had one killed and two wounded.

The English prisoners had the freedom of New Orleans and did not violate their paroles. While several of the officers received paroles to go to England or to Pensacola (with the stipulation they would not serve against Spain or her allies until they were exchanged), most of the English prisoners (including the Waldeckers) remained in New Orleans for several months before being sent to Vera Cruz and then to Havana.[48] According to Dickson, the prisoners were "treated with the greatest generosity and attention, not only by the officers but even the Spanish soldiers seem to take pleasure in being civil and kind to the prisoners in general."[49]

When news of Gálvez' movements had first reached Pensacola, the English commander had redoubled preparations to attack New Orleans or to aid Dickson directly. But just as Campbell's force was ready to embark, word reached Pensacola that Dickson had surrendered to the Spanish.[50] Confusion reigned in Pensacola, for Campbell felt the message might be a trick by Gálvez to pull the British forces away from Pensacola so that the West Florida capital would be defenseless. The chaplain of the Waldeckers described the chaotic situation: "The general was in such a confusing and embarrassing situation that he did not know which way to turn. Should he embark or stay on land? Is this not a damned country, where the greater part of the army corps has been taken prisoner for five weeks, and where a stretch of land of 1200 miles has been

48. Gálvez to José de Gálvez, Oct. 16, 1779, MPA,SD, 1:331; Return of Prisoners, Oct. 19, 1779, BHP, 2374, reel 9; Caughey, *Gálvez*, p. 162. The prisoners were carried to Vera Cruz on the *Nuestra Señora del Carmen*, and on Aug. 26, 1780, they were sent on to Havana on the *El Cayman* (Martín de Mayorga to José de Gálvez, Oct. 4, 1780, in Kinnaird, *Spain in the Mississippi Valley*, 1:386).
49. Dickson to Campbell, Oct. 20, 1779, C.O. 5/99. See also Learned, *Philipp Waldeck's Diary*, p. 137. Lt. [?] Wilson of the Artillery, who was captured at Baton Rouge, arrived in Plymouth, England, on July 30, 1780 (Delague [?] to [?]. Endorsed "In Mr. Stephen's to Mr. Knox of 4th Augt. 1780," C.O. 5/131). By Sept. 29, 1781, Dickson was on his way back to England. Clinton wrote a letter of introduction for him on that date, stating he was returning (Clinton to Germain, Sept. 29, 1781, Clinton Papers).
50. Campbell to Germain, Sept. 14, 1779, C.O. 5/597; Campbell to Clinton, Sept. 14, 1779, BHP, 2289, reel 9; Campbell to Clinton, Nov. 7, 1779, C.O. 5/99.

taken without the commander-general knowing it?"[51] Soon a second message reached Pensacola confirming the capitulation of the western portion of the colony, and Campbell stopped preparing for attack and began to plan for defense.[52]

When Campbell informed British officials about the capitulation of Dickson's forces, he referred to the men as "the select and chosen troops of this province."[53] These are the same men Campbell had described earlier as veterans "almost worn out in the service," "condemned criminals and other species of gaol birds," and men "totally unfit for active service." He attempted to explain why the British forces on the Mississippi had been surprised and defeated. The Isle of Orleans controlled communication by water; the western part of the colony was separated from Pensacola and Mobile by the Choctaw Indians, whose attachment to the British was uncertain; the Spanish had more and better equipped forces than the English; Governor Chester had persevered "cold, phlegmatick and indifferent in his conduct and would not proceed one tittle beyond the strict and most limited construction of the law to save West Florida"; and, contrary to what the foreign office believed, the inhabitants of Louisiana were not "generally indisposed to the Spanish government." On this last point Campbell expanded his argument: "The Spanish sway was some time ago hateful to their French subjects, but since that time cajoling and lenient methods of managing them have been adopted, in which their present governor in particular has been very successful."[54]

Germain confessed that he "did not imagine all our posts there, with so considerable a number of men, as I see by the list of prisoners were present to defend them, would have been so easily and speedily subdued." In spite of his surprise, Germain admonished Campbell that "the safety . . . of what remains to

51. Eelking, Die Deutschen Hulfstruppen, p. 10.

52. Campbell to Clinton, Nov. 7, 1779, C.O. 5/99; Caughey, Gálvez, p. 171. Apparently the first definite word to reach Pensacola of the surrender of Baton Rouge, Manchac, and Natchez came on October 20 (Learned, Philipp Waldeck's Diary, p. 131).

53. Campbell to Tonyn, Nov. 3, 1779, C.O. 5/559; Campbell to Lt. Col. Fuser, Nov. 3, 1779, C.O. 5/183 and BHP, 2403, reel 9. Governor Chester referred to the troops who surrendered as "the flower of the Army in West Florida," but he had not earlier spoken of them derogatorily (Chester to Tonyn, Nov. 7, 1779, C.O. 5/559 and BHP, 2417, reel 9).

54. Campbell to Germain, Dec. 15, 1779, C.O. 5/597.

His Majesty of West Florida is now the chief object to be attended to."[55]

The fall of the entire Mississippi region shocked both military and civilian residents of Pensacola and Mobile. Gálvez threatened to bring the rest of West Florida under the control of Spanish arms. The British efforts to prevent the expansion of Spanish dominance in West Florida filled the remaining years of the American Revolution and Anglo-Spanish war. Gálvez turned his attention next to Mobile, where Lieutenant Governor Elias Durnford was hastily directing defense preparations.

55. Germain to Campbell, Apr. 4, 1780, C.O. 5/244.

6

"The Lustre of the British Arms"

With the western area of West Florida in the hands of the Spanish, Gálvez was now free to attack Mobile and Pensacola. Lord George Germain, aware of the danger to the two areas, ordered the general to prepare the defenses of Pensacola and Mobile until he was sent sufficient forces to allow him to take the offensive. Germain was confident that the English land and naval forces in Jamaica and the Leeward Islands would give the Spanish "full employment, in defending their own possessions," and Campbell would have only Gálvez' Louisiana forces about which to worry. Since Spain considered Pensacola "an object of great estimation," however, Germain warned Campbell to be on his guard against a surprise attack, but, if an attack came, to put up a "vigorous defense" until aid could arrive from Jamaica. The home government also urged careful attention to the management of Indian affairs in order to assure their loyalty, or at least their neutrality.[1]

Campbell had already taken steps for the defense of what remained of West Florida. He had formed "two troops of light dragoons . . . to protect the frontier inhabitants from marauding parties." These he placed under the command of Adam Chrystie.[2] Because of the small number of troops available in

1. Germain to Campbell, Apr. 4, 1780, C.O. 5/244.
2. Campbell to Clinton, Feb. 10, 1779, C.O. 5/99 and BHP, 2565, reel 9; memorial of Adam Chrystie, Nov. 3, 1783, C.O. 5/598; Alexander Innes to John Andre, Apr. 14, 1780, Clinton Papers. These dragoons were the West Florida Royal Foresters.

the Pennsylvania and Maryland Loyalists, on December 26, 1779, Campbell combined the two units into the United Corps of Pennsylvania and Maryland Loyalists, under the command of Lieutenant Colonel William Allen of the Pennsylvania Loyalists. A year later, Campbell received orders from Clinton to separate them again because of "the injury which the Lieutenant Colonels Commandant and other officers . . . would sustain by the annihilation of one of those corps."[3]

Campbell hoped that a meeting with the Indians planned for March 15 at Mobile would bring about better relations with the Choctaws. The commander realized the necessity of cultivating lands around Pensacola in order to assure the town of ample provisions. He was also aware that West Florida could expect no help from the Royal Navy in Pensacola since at present there was only "one crazy, condemned, unserviceable sloop, that can never go out of the harbour."[4]

Two months after failing to get the governor and council to agree to a proclamation of martial law, Campbell urged Chester to call a meeting of the General Assembly in order to pass a militia law. The general was confident that the legislature could pass such a law in a "very few days" since "the bill . . . [was] already prepared." Chester refused to call a meeting of the assembly, however, since he had called one in 1778 for that purpose. The governor argued that the militia bill had been as badly needed in 1778, yet the assembly had dealt only with "matters of privilege." Now the loss of the Mississippi area prevented the gathering of a quorum.[5] Germain reprimanded Chester for refusing to call an assembly even after several of the members of the body had informed the governor that they wished to pass a militia law. As to the governor's argument concerning a quorum, the secretary saw no reason why the members of the assembly from the captured western lands could not properly attend the meeting since a new election was not

3. General Orders, Issued at Pensacola by Campbell, Dec. 26, 1779, Clinton Papers and BHP, 2501, reel 9; Clinton to Campbell, Oct. 21, 1780, ibid., 3079, reel 11. See also Campbell to Clinton, Feb. 15, 1780, ibid., 9901, reel 27; Campbell to Clinton, May 13, 1780, ibid., 2736, reel 10; Campbell to Clinton, Feb. 10, 1780, C.O. 5/99.
4. Campbell to Clinton, Feb. 10, 1780, C.O. 5/99.
5. Campbell to Clinton, Nov. 7, 1779, ibid.; Campbell to Chester, Nov. 6, 1779, C.O. 5/595; Chester to Campbell, Nov. 8, 1779, ibid.

needed. Chester confessed that he did not know how the secretary had news that several members of the assembly wished to pass a militia law when he had not personally received such pledges. He assured Germain that had he received such promises, he would have called the legislature together. Since he had not, and since the dissatisfied faction which formed the 1778 session would dominate any new session, he was certain that "no essential business could have been transacted."[6]

At Campbell's request, on November 12 the governor, with the advice of the council, removed the embargo on shipping, which had been instituted when news of the Spanish war arrived but was no longer needed. Early in December the packet boat *Carteret*, which had been on a cruise, returned to the mouth of Pensacola harbor, fired two guns, and then crowded sail and left. While Chester was at a loss to explain this unusual behavior, the master of the vessel later explained that he saw some masts in Pensacola Bay (the supply ship *Earl of Bathurst*) and assumed that, since he did not expect the arrival of any British vessels, the Spanish had captured Pensacola. Germain roundly denounced the "reprehensible" behavior of the master of the vessel.[7]

Concerned about the safety of Mobile and Pensacola, Germain requested on February 23, 1780, that Sir Peter Parker and Governor Dalling provide all the assistance possible to West Florida and aid Campbell in an attack on New Orleans if the general felt such an attempt was feasible.[8]

6. Germain to Chester, Apr. 5, 1780, C.O. 5/595; Chester to Germain, Aug. 7, 1780, ibid. Germain replied that he wished Chester had put the people to the test by calling an assembly, but since West Florida was now reduced to Pensacola, the calling of an assembly would have been ridiculous (Germain to Chester, Jan. 13, 1781, C.O. 5/596).

7. Minutes of the Council, Nov. 12, 1779, C.O. 5/635, RSUS, reel 8; Campbell to Germain, Sept. 14, 1779, C.O. 5/597; Chester to Germain, Dec. 10, 1779, ibid.; Germain to Campbell, Apr. 4, 1780, C.O. 5/244; Campbell to Germain, Dec. 15, 1779, C.O. 5/597. The *Carteret* carried one officer, two sergeants, twenty-five rank and file, and "the best pilot in this place" with it when it departed (ibid.). Chaplain Waldeck reported that the wife of one of the Marylanders on the packet had traveled to England, the West Indies, and Pensacola in order to be with her husband. He sympathized that "after such a far and difficult trip this good woman failed to accomplish her mission in the end" (Learned, *Philipp Waldeck's Diary*, p. 137).

8. Germain to the Lords of the Admiralty, Feb. 23, 1780, C.O. 5/263; Germain to Dalling, Mar. 1, 1780, ibid., and Germain Papers, vol. 12.

British intelligence was unable to determine whether Pensacola or Mobile was regarded by Spain as the most likely target. General Campbell felt that the Spanish would attack Pensacola first. Alexander Cameron believed that "we have the greatest reason to apprehend that the Spaniards, flushed with their success to the westward, will soon attempt Mobile and the reduction of that contiguous country."[9] Campbell was convinced that even if the Spanish attacked Mobile first, "their main object must be Pensacola." An attack on Mobile, he argued, would simply be a step toward their ultimate goal in West Florida—Pensacola.[10]

There was disagreement among the Spaniards themselves as to which town would be most appropriate for their next campaign. Instructions from the crown had placed Gálvez at the head of the expedition against the British in West Florida, but there were men at Havana who felt themselves better suited to lead such an expedition and gain the glory such a victory would bring. Consequently, various civil and military leaders opposed Gálvez' plans. Diego Josef Navarro, captain-general of Cuba, wanted a naval attack against Pensacola, which he felt could be easily brought to a successful conclusion.[11] Gálvez argued that the attack should be against Mobile. To take Mobile would be to cut off a source of supply for Pensacola: "Mobile does not need Pensacola, but Pensacola could hardly exist without Mobile, for from there must come the means and provisions." These provisions, in turn, would be available for the Spanish at Mobile. The seizure of Mobile would give the Spanish control of all the Indians to the west of the town and deny their assistance to the British during the attack on Pensacola. Finally, Gálvez argued, if his force attacked Pensacola first and was not successful, "it would be impossible to take Mobile."[12] As a result of the disagreement over objectives, the

9. Cameron to Clinton, Dec. 20, 1779, C.O. 5/81. A copy of this letter, located in BHP, 2479, reel 9, gives the date as December 15, 1779.

10. Campbell to Clinton, Feb. 12, 1780, C.O. 5/99.

11. José de Gálvez to Navarro and Bonet, Aug. 29, 1779, MPA,SD, 1:336. A copy of this letter with a different translation is in Kinnaird, *Spain in the Mississippi Valley*, 1:355–57. [Gálvez] to [José de Gálvez], n.d. [Summer, 1780?], MPA,SD, 1:382; Haarmann, "The Spanish Conquest," p. 115; Caughey, *Gálvez*, p. 173.

12. Gálvez to Navarro, Oct. 16, 1779, MPA,SD, 1:316.

necessary troops, ships, artillery, and supplies were not sent to Gálvez. The governor decided, however, to go ahead with plans to launch an attack on Mobile, because the seizure of that port would protect Louisiana and the newly captured lands along the Mississippi and make it easier to prepare a campaign against Pensacola.

In the meantime, the British in West Florida prepared for the expected Spanish invasion. Even after Gálvez' arrival at Mobile, Campbell observed that "whether their putting into Mobile Bay be a feint, with a view to draw our force from this quarter, or that their real design is to attack that place first, time must determine."[13] Campbell had previously considered sending several armed vessels to Mobile Bay to protect the town from attack from the west, but he had decided against such a move because of the vital need for sea protection in Pensacola.[14]

The state of Mobile's defenses was critical. The fortifications were weak; supplies of provisions, ordnance stores, and artillery were needed; and a reinforcement of troops was requisite if the British were to make an adequate defense. Mobile was located on the west bank of Mobile Bay and the Mobile River. The bay was approximately thirty miles long and six miles wide with good anchorage but with a shallow bar at the entrance. Situated on a rising bank, the town extended about a half mile back on a level plain above the river, and about a mile in length along the bank. When the naturalist William Bartram made a tour of West Florida early in the Revolution, he described Mobile as "chiefly in ruins."

Fort Charlotte was near the bay at the lower end of the town.[15] In 1717, the French had used locally made brick and oyster shell lime to build the fort in the form of a square with four bastions and thirty-eight crenels for artillery. It measured three hundred feet between the bastions. When the British took over Mobile in 1763, Fort Charlotte was in an advanced state of decay. The British made various efforts to improve the fortress but with little success, mainly due to a lack of funds and artificers. Twice in 1770 Durnford proposed that the fort be

13. Campbell to Clinton, Feb. 12, 1780, C.O. 5/99.
14. Campbell to Germain, Dec. 15, 1779, C.O. 5/597; Durnford to Campbell, Dec. 15, 1779, quoted in Durnford, Family Recollections, p. 16.
15. Bartram, Travels, p. 256; Haarmann, "The Spanish Conquest," p. 115.

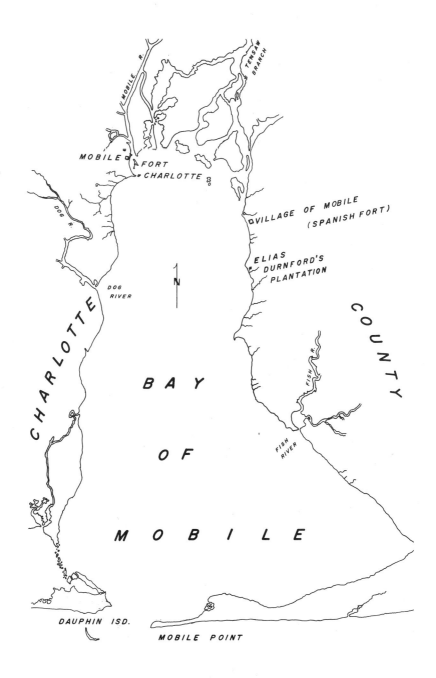

Mobile, 1768. Based on a map by George Gauld, 1768. Original in the British Museum. Drawn by Rex A. James, Jr.

dismantled and the materials used for barracks or facing batteries, since the expense of repairing it exceeded its value.[16] Seven years later, Sir William Howe referred to Mobile as "the weak side of West Florida." Jacinto Panis made his intelligence journey to Mobile and Pensacola in 1778, and he referred to the former as "badly fortified and exposed." The fortress "threatened ruin," the artillery was "almost dismounted," and the ditches were "choked up" in some places. When Campbell arrived in West Florida seven months later, there was no improvement in the conditions at Mobile. He reported the fort and barracks as *almost a scene of ruin and desolation.*"[17] Subsequently, Campbell ordered Durnford to Mobile to supervise the strengthening of Fort Charlotte. Civilian laborers in Mobile demanded a prohibitive two dollars a day, so Durnford had to put the garrison and slaves to work on the repairs. He supervised the restoration of the walls of the fort, the replacement of rotten artillery platforms, temporary improvements to the stockade, and necessary renovation of the barracks.

Fort Charlotte required a garrison of three hundred men to defend it, yet Durnford reported in December 1779 that the fort had a garrison of "eighty sick, or at best convalescent men."[18] It is not clear how many men Durnford had under his command at Mobile, but after the surrender of Fort Charlotte, he related that he had 304 men, including regulars, inhabitants, and slaves.[19] *Burke's Annual Register for 1780* stated that there were 284 men present, which in the main coincides with Gálvez' account of 284 prisoners taken.[20] An official British return of prisoners showing 428 men taken prisoner at Mobile undoubt-

16. Jacinto Panis to Gálvez, July 5, 1778, MPA,SD, 1:218; Haarmann, "The Spanish Conquest," p. 115; Gage to Hillsborough, July 7, 1770, C.O. 5/88; Gage to Haldimand, Aug. 28, 1770, British Museum, Additional MSS, 21664.

17. Howe to Germain, Apr. 4, 1777, C.O. 5/236; Panis to Gálvez, July 5, 1778, MPA,SD, 1:218; Campbell to Clinton, Feb. 10, 1779, C.O. 5/597.

18. Durnford to Campbell, Dec. 15, 1779, quoted in Durnford, *Family Recollections*, p. 16; Gray, "Elias Durnford," p. 65.

19. William Beer, "The Surrender of Fort Charlotte, Mobile, 1780," p. 699. See also Durnford, *Family Recollections*, p. 20.

20. Quoted in Durnford, *Family Recollections*, p. 19; "Journal of Don Bernardo de Gálvez . . . against Pensacola and Mobile . . . ," Mar. 20, 1780, in John Almon, ed., *The Remembrancer; or, Impartial Repository of Public Events. For the Year 1780*, part 2, p. 99, hereafter cited as the "Journal of Gálvez." Apparently about fifty-one of Durnford's men were armed Negroes.

edly includes more than the men captured at Fort Charlotte. Apparently Durnford had about 300 men under his command at Fort Charlotte, only a "small part" of whom were regulars.[21]

Gálvez' force embarked at New Orleans on January 11, 1780, for the campaign against Mobile. His troops consisted of 274 regulars, 323 white militiamen, 107 free blacks and mulattoes, 24 slaves, and 26 Americans, a total of 754 men. His fleet had twelve vessels: one merchantman frigate, one packet boat, four settees, two brigs, the frigate Volante, the galliot Valenzuela, the brig Gálvez, and the brig Kaulican.[22] The shallow mouth of the Mississippi, adverse winds, and a hurricane delayed the expedition, but on February 9, Gálvez' scattered fleet (some of whom had sailed as far east as the Perdido River) regrouped off the bar at Mobile Bay. Because of stormy weather and the absence of a competent pilot, it was two days before the small flotilla could enter the harbor. During these days, seven of the Spanish vessels ran aground, but the sailors refloated all but the Volante, which the Spanish finally abandoned. On the night of February 9, the Valenzuela engaged the British ship Brownhall (on its way to Mobile with presents for the Indians), and during the fighting both vessels ran aground. The Brownhall was captured. Five ships from Havana arrived on the twentieth, with 1,412 men and equipment and supplies.[23]

When the Spanish vessels first appeared off the bar at Mobile Bay, Durnford informed Campbell of the situation, but Campbell still was unsure whether or not this action was a ruse to draw him from Pensacola. He judged correctly, however, "that the fate of West Florida is suspended in the balance."[24] Word reached Pensacola that five Spanish vessels had run aground and were lost with about 750 men on board. It was also reported that these losses caused the Spanish to become discour-

21. Campbell to Clinton, Sept. 18, 1780, BHP, 9883, reel 27; "Return of Prisoners with the Spaniards of the Corps in West Florida . . . ," May 1, 1780, C.O. 5/99.

22. Caughey, Gálvez, pp. 174–77; Donald E. Everett, "Free Persons of Color in Colonial Louisiana," p. 42; "Journal of Gálvez," p. 91. The Americans did not arrive at Mobile until after the fort had surrendered (ibid., p. 99).

23. Caughey, Gálvez, pp. 175–76; Campbell to Clinton, Feb. 12, 1780, C.O. 5/99; Campbell to Germain, Feb. 10, 1780, C.O. 5/597; Navarro to Martín de Mayorga, Feb. 7, 1780, in Kinnaird, Spain in the Mississippi Valley, 1:369.

24. Campbell to Germain, Feb. 12, 1780, C.O. 5/597; Campbell to Clinton, Feb. 10, 1780, C.O. 5/99; Gray, "Elias Durnford," p. 65.

aged and withdraw, and that Mobile apparently no longer needed any assistance.[25]

The Spanish had not withdrawn, and they soon moved to Dog River, just nine miles below Mobile. For the next two days they continued their move to the camp on Dog River, while the British were busy making their fortifications more tenable. The *Valenzuela* approached Fort Charlotte on February 26, seeking a good landing place for troops. She fired on the fort, but the English did not return the fire. The Spanish crossed Dog River on the twenty-eighth and came within two miles of Fort Charlotte. Again the *Valenzuela* fired on the fort, but the British cannon did not reply. The British finally opened fire on February 29 when a reconnaissance party of four companies came within range of the fort, but the Spanish withdrew without any casualties. On the same day, the *Valenzuela* again approached the fortress and fired a few rounds. This time the English cannon replied with some shot through its rigging. The Spanish informed Durnford later that the shot had merely hit the vessel, but Durnford was certain that the *Valenzuela* was "well mauled" by the three nine-pounders.[26]

Gálvez informed Durnford that he had almost two thousand men under his command and that he knew Durnford had only about one hundred soldiers and some sailors. The Spanish commander called upon Durnford to surrender immediately or to suffer the "extremities of war."[27] Colonel Francisco Bouligny, who carried the letter, was an old friend of Durnford, and the two men, although national enemies now, shared dinner and drank "a cheerful glass to the health of our kings and friends." During the course of their conversation, Bouligny stated that the reports of shipwrecks were correct, but he would not admit that the Spanish had lost any men. He also told Durnford that the Spanish force consisted of about 2,500 men, but the lieutenant governor had received word that morning from a trusted Indian

25. Chester to Tonyn, Feb. 18, 1780, BHP, 2583, reel 9; Durnford, *Family Recollections*, p. 18.

26. Durnford to Campbell, Mar. 2, 1780, C.O. 5/99 and C.O. 5/597; "Journal of Gálvez," pp. 94–95; Caughey, *Gálvez*, p. 177; Gray, "Elias Durnford," p. 67.

27. Gálvez to Durnford, Mar. 1, 1780, BHP, 2601, reel 9. "Journal of Gálvez," p. 95, presents a slightly different version of this letter. The letter from the BHP is probably more accurate, however, as it is a copy of the original letter in French.

that a large number of the Spanish force were Negroes and mulattoes, and that the Spanish had no cannon. Durnford admitted that the Spanish force was superior in number to the British garrison, although he claimed that the latter was "much beyond your Excellency's conception." Durnford declared that his love for his king and country and his own honor "direct my heart to refuse surrendering this fort, until I am put under the necessity of doing it by conviction that resistance is in vain."[28]

Immediately after Bouligny's departure, Durnford assembled his small garrison and read Gálvez' demand for surrender. Durnford then told the men that if any man was afraid to remain, the gate would be opened for him. His statement "had the wished for effect, as not a man moved." He then read his answer to Gálvez, and the men "all joined in three cheers, and then went to our necessary work like good men." After the men had returned to their work, Captain Charles Walker and his twenty-eight dragoons of the West Florida Royal Foresters arrived at Fort Charlotte, as did Captain Huberd Rees and three canoes of militia. The arrival of these men lifted morale within the fortress, and a small party of fifty to sixty men went out on a patrol. Soon confronting a superior Spanish force, the British decided to retreat rather than lose men in an unimportant skirmish.[29]

For the next four days (March 2–5), the Spanish and the British occupied themselves in improving their positions. Durnford sent a dozen bottles of wine, an equal number of chickens and loaves of bread, and one lamb to Gálvez on March 5, along with provisions for British prisoners. Gálvez, in turn, sent Durnford a case of Bordeaux wine, a case of Spanish wine, citrons, oranges, tea biscuits, corn cakes, and a box of Havana cigars, with his assurance that the prisoners were being well treated. Gálvez apologized for bringing military matters into such pleasantries, but he felt he must offer a "small reproach" to Durnford for burning sections of Mobile: "Fortresses are constructed solely to defend towns, but you are commencing to destroy the

28. Durnford to Gálvez, Mar. 1, 1780, C.O. 5/99; Durnford to Campbell, Mar. 2, 1780, ibid.

29. Durnford to Campbell, Mar. 2, 1780, ibid.; memorial of Adam Chrystie, Nov. 3, 1783, C.O. 5/598; "Journal of Gálvez," p. 96; "Account from Pensacola," Sept. 30, 1780, BHP, 9984, reel 27. The Spanish did capture Charles Stuart on this patrol ("Journal of Gálvez," p. 96).

town in favor of a fortress incapable of defense." He offered not to construct any batteries behind houses if Durnford would stop burning them down. Durnford replied that he too regretted having to destory houses near the fort, but that the defense of Fort Charlotte was his chief aim, and the most effective defense called for the destruction of houses around the fortress.[30] It was not the first time that the British in West Florida had followed incendiary policy; Dickson had destroyed several houses on the plantation of Watts and Flowers at Baton Rouge. When Gálvez began a siege of Pensacola some months later, Campbell would follow a similar course of action.

When Durnford's letter containing Gálvez' summons for the surrender reached the commanding general on March 3, Campbell was at last convinced that the Spanish intended to attack Mobile. He had already learned of the arrival of the Spanish at Mobile, but it was not until March 5 that he acted to aid the town. He had promised Durnford aid whenever the Spanish invested Mobile. This assurance afforded Durnford "consolation," and he prepared to defend Fort Charlotte "to the last extremity." Durnford's strategy was based on the conviction that he had merely to hold Mobile until aid arrived from Pensacola. Gálvez, however, planned to reduce Mobile before reinforcements arrived.[31] Quick action by Campbell upon hearing of the Spanish arrival at Mobile could possibly have prevented a successful campaign by the Spaniards, but such alacrity was lacking in the capital of West Florida.

Belatedly, Campbell decided to march a relief column to Mobile. The reinforcements, consisting of 413 regulars and militia and 105 Indians carrying one 5½-inch howitzer and two three-pounder field pieces, left Pensacola in two divisions on March 5 and 6 under the command of Campbell. His aim was to march to Tensa (thirty miles north of Mobile), build rafts, and float down the Tensa River about three miles, navigate a small creek over to the Mobile River and float down the Mobile River to Fort Charlotte without the Spanish detecting his force. Heavy rains turned the roads into a quagmire and made the swollen Perdido River difficult to cross—four regulars drowned in the

30. Caughey, *Gálvez*, pp. 178–79; Gray, "Elias Durnford," pp. 70–71.
31. Durnford to Campbell, Mar. 2, 1780, C.O. 5/597; Caughey, *Gálvez*, pp. 179–80.

attempt. The relief force finally reached Tensa on March 10, where the men began construction and collection of rafts, canoes, and any other craft capable of transporting troops. Campbell sent out a reconnaissance party to make sure that the Spanish were not blocking his passage. Before his scouting party returned, however, the firing between the Spanish and Fort Charlotte had stopped. Fearing the worst, Campbell decided not to move his troops until he had determined Mobile's fate.[32]

While the British force had been trekking to Tensa, the Spanish had been busy completing their emplacements. Gálvez made a short speech on the evening of March 9 to raise the morale of the two hundred armed men and three hundred laborers he was sending out to open a trench for the battery within two hundred yards of the fort. They quickly set up a shoulder of fagots to hide the battery and continued the work. At dawn, 150 armed men and 150 laborers relieved the first party of men. The British had not detected the Spanish workmen at night, but on the morning of the tenth they discovered the new Spanish work and trained an effective fire of cannonball, grapeshot, muskets, and carbines on the Spaniards. At eleven o'clock Gálvez ordered his troops to retire from the trench, since six men were dead and five wounded. He intended to send his men back to work at night under cover of darkness, but a rainstorm prevented further work.

Two patrols reported to Gálvez on the eleventh that the English had a force of four hundred to six hundred men at Tensa, and Gálvez increased his guard as a precaution against surprise. That night the Spaniards completed the work on the new battery, so that at ten o'clock on the morning of March 12, eight eighteen-pounders and one twenty-four-pounder opened fire on Fort Charlotte. All day both sides continued the fire. The Spanish attack dismounted two cannon (which were quickly

32. Campbell to Clinton, Mar. 24, 1780, C.O. 5/99. In addition to the regulars, militia, and Indians in his force, Campbell mentioned that the "whole number of our volunteers" was also in the expedition. While there is nothing to indicate clearly who these men were or how many there were, presumably Campbell was referring to Patrick Strachan's company of thirty-eight West Florida Royal Foresters. Most of the information contained in Max Von Eelking's account of this expedition is incorrect (*Die Deutschen Hulfstruppen*, p. 11).

replaced) and battered the walls, opening two large breaches. The British cannon replied vigorously despite the hunger and fatigue from which the garrison was suffering. At the end of the day, the British fire had dislocated one Spanish cannon and had killed one Spaniard and wounded three. The artillerymen remained at their weapons until they ran out of suitable ammunition: the arsenal contained both cannon and ammunition but not of the same caliber. Durnford finally hoisted the white flag of truce at sunset. Gálvez agreed to the cessation of hostilities until eleven o'clock the next day, on the condition that nobody would leave the fort and that the fort would not receive reinforcements from Campbell.

Durnford proposed terms for a capitulation on March 13, terms which Gálvez felt were "inadmissible." Reminding Durnford of his precarious position, particularly that there were breaches in the wall large enough for troops to enter, Gálvez gave the British commander four hours to come to terms.[33] Realizing that his position was no longer tenable, Durnford agreed to the articles of capitulation, which he and Gálvez then signed. The surrender was virtually identical to the one at Baton Rouge, according the troops the honors of war. The one major difference was that the civilians who had taken up arms would be treated as prisoners of war and not released as they had been at Baton Rouge.[34] The British had had one man killed and eleven wounded (two of whom later died). The Spanish had had eight killed and twelve wounded.[35] At ten o'clock Tuesday morning, March 14, Durnford's force marched out of Fort Charlotte, and the Spanish took possession and raised their national flag. Durnford described the scene to Campbell: "It is my misfortune to inform you that this morning my small, but brave garrison, marched down the breach and surrendered themselves prisoners of war to General Bernardo de Gálvez's superior arms. His generosity is well known to you. . . . I

33. "Journal of Gálvez," pp. 97–98; Caughey, *Gálvez*, p. 181; Gray, "Elias Durnford," pp. 72–74. Gálvez reported that there were both cannon and ammunition of usable caliber in the arsenal of Fort Charlotte ("Journal of Gálvez," p. 99).
34. Articles of Capitulation, Mar. 13, 1780, C.O. 5/99. On March 17, eighty English civilians took an oath of loyalty to Spain (Caughey, *Gálvez*, p. 183). "Journal of Gálvez," p. 99, states the number was fifty.
35. Haarmann, "The Spanish Conquest," p. 119; "Journal of Gálvez," p. 101.

assure, Sir, that no man of the garrison hath stained the lustre of the British arms."[36]

Campbell's scouting parties informed him that there was a white flag over the walls of Fort Charlotte and that, on the morning of the fourteenth, the Spanish had hoisted their colors. Consequently, on March 15, Campbell's force set out for Pensacola, where they arrived on March 18–19. During the expedition, four men drowned and three men deserted, but Campbell did not consider the expedition a total loss since "from the ardent desire and eagerness of both officers and men to come to action with the enemy, I portend flattering presages of their future conduct in case of occasion."[37] When he left Tensa, Campbell ordered Patrick Strachan's company of West Florida Royal Foresters to stay behind to give protection to the British settlers in the region and to drive the cattle in the area to Pensacola. Two days after Campbell left the region, a Spanish force surprised Strachan and his men and took them prisoner.[38]

One Spaniard who was present at the siege of Mobile did not believe their victory was of consequence. "The conquest of Mobile is to us of little importance, so that we may say that all we have done has been to endure much fatigue and put the king to much fruitless expense."[39] With the capitulation of Mobile, however, British West Florida was reduced to the district of Pensacola. Mobile could no longer serve as a source of supply for Pensacola, and all effective communication was cut off to the west. The British control of the western Indians was in doubt; the Choctaws began turning against the British, and the loyalty of the Chickasaws was questionable. The "outpost of the plaza of Pensacola"[40] had joined Manchac, Baton Rouge, and Natchez in the fold of conquered territory. Only Pensacola remained British.

36. Durnford to Campbell, Mar. 14, 1780, C.O. 5/99.

37. Campbell to Germain, Mar. 24, 1780, ibid.

38. Ibid.; memorial of Adam Chrystie, Nov. 3, 1783, C.O. 5/598. It is not clear how many men the Spanish captured. Campbell stated that Strachan and sixteen men surrendered, while Chrystie reported the number as thirty-seven. Gálvez reported capturing a captain and twenty militiamen ("Journal of Gálvez," p. 99).

39. Gaspar Francisco to Gabriel Montenego, June 16, 1780, Clinton Papers.

40. José de Gálvez to Gálvez, June 22, 1780, quoted in Caughey, Gálvez, p. 186.

7

"We Are Now Tolerably Prepared"

The Spaniards were so elated with their success [in Mobile],"
William Ogilvie reported, "that . . . they have been threatening
to visit Pensacola, and making sure of adding it to their
conquests."[1] In the months between the fall of Fort Charlotte and
the investment of Pensacola, residents of the capital frequently
expressed similar sentiments. Thus, when Spanish vessels appeared off the bar at Pensacola Bay, Campbell advised Germain
that "the fate of Pensacola will probably be determined before
this can reach your Lordship."[2]

Gálvez had intended to lead an expedition against Pensacola
immediately after Fort Charlotte's surrender. A swift campaign
against Pensacola would take advantage of confusion in the town
following Campbell's unsuccessful attempt to reinforce Mobile
and would not allow time for the British to receive reinforcements or improve their fortifications. However, Gálvez' forces
needed strengthening and naval protection; 2,065 men were
ready to sail for Mobile from Havana on February 15, 1780.
When Navarro received information that British reinforcements
were on their way to Pensacola from Jamaica, the Cuban captain
general ordered his troops to disembark. Less than a month later,
on March 7, a Spanish fleet sailed to assist in the Pensacola

1. William Ogilvie to "Mr. Shaw," May 9, 1780, C.O. 5/81.
2. Campbell to Germain, Mar. 28, 1780, C.O. 5/597 and BHP, 2659, reel 10;
Campbell to Thomas Browne, Mar. 27, 1780, C.O. 5/81; Stiell to Lord Amherst,
Mar. 28, 1780, W.O. 34/124, University of Florida photostat.

campaign, but it returned to Havana on May 21 because the commander did not feel that his vessels could silence the forts guarding the entrance to Pensacola harbor. Gálvez then sent one of his engineers to explore the road from Mobile to Pensacola to determine whether his men could carry cannon overland against Pensacola. The officer returned and assured the governor that such a campaign was not possible.[3]

Gálvez received intelligence on April 11 that eleven British ships had reinforced Pensacola. Less than a month later he called a junta de guerra to discuss the problems which faced the Spanish forces. He sought the council's advice as to whether a surprise attack should be launched against Pensacola or whether the entire campaign should be abandoned: "All those present agreed that we were very much exposed, and the council judged it best now to dissolve the expedition." Accordingly, the majority of the Spanish forces soon departed Mobile and returned to Havana and New Orleans. Gálvez left a garrison under the command of José de Ezpeleta at Mobile.[4]

Campbell reported in mid-May 1780 that, contrary to his expectations, "Pensacola remains still unattacked." He attributed the Spanish delay to the "seasonable arrival of a naval reinforcement from Jamaica, which the enemy has fortunately estimated higher and of greater force than it really merited; and also to the dread he [the Spaniard] has conceived of a large body of Indians collected at this place."[5] The fleet which arrived from Jamaica on April 9 consisted of the sloops-of-war Hound and Port Royal and nine merchant vessels. On May 14 the man-of-war Mentor arrived in Pensacola Bay. Even though all but three of the British vessels were merchantmen, the Spanish apparently thought they were mainly armed warships.[6]

While the Spanish fear of the naval reinforcements in Pensacola was a result of poor intelligence, their fear of the English

3. [Gálvez] to [José de Gálvez?], [Summer, 1780?], MPA,SD, 1:394; Caughey, Gálvez, pp. 187–88. The letter cited is a detailed account of the problems Gálvez encountered in trying to outfit an expedition against Pensacola.

4. [Gálvez] to [José de Gálvez?], [Summer, 1780?], MPA,SD, 1:392, 394–95; Caughey, Gálvez, p. 191.

5. Campbell to Germain, May 15, 1780, C.O. 5/597; Campbell to Clinton, May 13, 1780, BHP, 2736, reel 10.

6. Captain James McNamara [of the Hound] to Philip Stephens, Aug. 6, 1780, C.O. 5/131; Campbell to Clinton, May 15, 1780, BHP, 2736, reel 10; Captain Robert Deans to Stephens, Aug. 3, 1780, C.O. 5/131.

use of the Indians was not illusory. During the siege of Fort
Charlotte, Charles Stuart had ordered Indian agent Farquhar
Bethune to march Choctaw Indians to the defense of Mobile;
although Bethune quickly gathered six hundred Indians, the fortress fell before they could arrive. Two hundred of the Indians
went on to Pensacola, while the remainder returned home.
Gálvez hoped that when Fort Charlotte fell to the Spanish the
Indians would aid the new masters of Mobile. But he was disap-
pointed, and as a result he wrote Campbell requesting that
neither side employ Indians, "to shelter us from the horrible
censure of inhumanity." Campbell rejected Gálvez' proposal as
"insulting and injurious to reason and common sense." There
were about 1,100 Indians (including women and children) in
Pensacola in mid-May of 1780, and Campbell asserted that the
Spanish fear of the savages was one of the reasons they had
abandoned their plans to attack.[7] Indian agent Alexander Cameron shared this opinion: "Our being still possessed of this place
[Pensacola] is entirely owing to the great number of Indians that
speedily repaired hither to our assistance."[8]

While Cameron overstated the case, the Indians would indeed
play an important role in the battle of Pensacola. Campbell
realized that the Indians could be important as allies even
though they were "a mercenary race . . . the slaves of the highest
bidder without gratitude or affection."[9] Campbell's view of Indian relations was bluntly described by Cameron: "He does not
understand anything of Indians or their affairs. He thinks they
are to be used like slaves or a people void of natural sense. He
will not be prevailed upon that presents are necessary or that
Indians have a right to demand any unless he calls them upon
actual service."[10] The 1,100 natives maintained by the British
Indian department at Pensacola in May 1780 had declined by the
following February to 788 Choctaw, Chickasaw, Alabama, and

7. Cameron to Clinton, July 18, 1780, BHP, 2919, reel 10; Gálvez to Campbell, Apr. 9, 1780, C.O. 5/597 and BHP, 2681, reel 10; Campbell to Gálvez, Apr.
20, 1780, BHP, 2692, reel 10; Campbell to Clinton, May 13, 1780, BHP, 2736,
reel 10; Campbell to Germain, May 15, 1780, C.O. 5/597.
8. Cameron to Clinton, July 18, 1780, BHP, 2919, reel 10.
9. Campbell to Germain, Dec. 15, 1779, quoted in Osborn, "Relations with
the Indians," p. 267. After the battle of Pensacola, Gálvez observed that the best
defense of Pensacola had been the Indians (Caughey, Gálvez, p. 213).
10. Cameron to Germain, Oct. 31, 1780, C.O. 5/82.

Creek Indians. When Pensacola capitulated, the number had dropped to between 400 and 500. While the number of Indians became progressively smaller, the British maintained these Indians at great expense, even to the point of causing a shortage of food among the troops and inhabitants of Pensacola.[11]

Campbell's indecisive direction of the Indian allies kept the Indian department in turmoil. For example, Campbell sent orders to Alexander McGillivray on November 22, 1780, to assemble as many Creek Indians as he could and march them to Pensacola to protect that place, so "that it may once more be recorded in the annals of Great Britain that Pensacola was again a second time preserved (within the space of twelve months) from falling a conquest to Spain by the courage and magnanimity of our Indian friends."[12] The Indians had gathered and were ready to march when Campbell's secretary informed McGillivray on December 8 that the general had learned that a hurricane had dispersed the Spanish fleet and that the Indians were no longer needed. A month later, Campbell again ordered McGillivray to collect the Indians and come to Pensacola, as he had received news that the Spanish had undertaken another expedition. Over a thousand Indians were on their way to Pensacola when the general's secretary again notified McGillivray that the services of the Indians were not required, since a naval reinforcement for Pensacola would sail from Jamaica in five days (February 15). Some of the Indians returned to their hunting grounds, but about a thousand of them set out to the north and waged war against the rebels at Long Island, Watauga, Holstein, and in the Ohio country. Not long after the Indians had dispersed, the Spanish

11. "Return of Choctaw, Chickasaw, Alabamas and Creek Indians Remaining at Pensacola the 1st February 1781," ibid.; Cameron to [Germain?], May 27, 1781, ibid.; Campbell to Clinton, Apr. 9, 1781, BHP, 9913, reel 27; Osborn, "Relations with the Indians," p. 272. An example of the cost involved is clearly seen in a report by Cameron on expenses incurred in the western district of the Southern Department from April 4 to June 30, 1780. For that three-month period alone, the expenses came to £ 5057.7.9–1/4 ("Account of Extra Expenses Incurred by Alexander Cameron . . . 4th April to the 30th June 1780," BHP, 9868, reel 27). The chaplain of the Waldeck troops wrote that for a brief period the troops had only bread and water for breakfast, water at dinner, and a pipe of tobacco and more water for supper. He also reported that sausages cost $7.00, tobacco $4.00 a pound, coffee $1.00 a pound, and brandy 8 shillings a pint (Max Von Eelking, The German Allied Troops in the North American War of Independence, 1776–1783, pp. 222–23).

12. Campbell to McGillivray, Nov. 22, 1780, C.O. 5/82.

fleet appeared off the bar at Pensacola, and Campbell sent an urgent message for the Indians to come to the aid of the town. This time, however, the Indians were too scattered to be gathered in any force. The commissaries did manage to collect a small body of Indians, but they arrived in Pensacola too late "to render any essential service."[13]

By his irresolute policy, Campbell thus negated much of the value of his Indian allies. Maintenance of the Indians at Pensacola was expensive, and Campbell did not wish to bear the expense unless the Indians could be of real service. One author has argued that "General Campbell's hoard of Indian allies had proved more of a liability than an asset."[14] Clearly the Indians were a financial burden, but they performed essential services as scouts and in conjunction with regulars and militia. At best they were useful allies; at worst, a liability. The most nearly accurate evaluation that can be made is that they helped to "delay the fall" of Pensacola.[15]

Despite the Spanish decision to postpone attacking Pensacola, the situation in the capital remained confused. Campbell, however, wrote cheerfully to Clinton on July 22, 1780, that despite the earlier uncertainty concerning a Spanish expedition, he could report now that the Spanish had decided to postpone their attack on Pensacola until the fall of the year. Campbell begged Clinton for reinforcements that he might defend Pensacola and perhaps even undertake an expedition against New Orleans. Cornwallis had captured Charleston, and Campbell thought he now had a better chance of receiving additional men. Cornwallis

13. Browne to [Germain?], Aug. 9, 1781, ibid.; James Campbell to McGillivray, Dec. 8, 1780, Jan. 12, Feb. 10, 1781, ibid.

14. Osborn, "Relations with the Indians," p. 272.

15. Caughey, McGillivray of the Creeks, p. 16. One additional note about the Indian department concerns the efforts of Cameron to raise a "troop or two of horse, to act with the Indians of my department upon every occasion." Since Stuart's Loyal Refugees had been disbanded, Campbell had found it necessary to create the West Florida Royal Foresters. Cameron proposed to Campbell the raising of a corps in his Indian department to work with the Indians or independently. He was confident he could raise at least fifty men from the areas captured by the Spanish, "as they are already perfectly sick of the Spanish tyranny" (Cameron to Campbell, June 30, 1780, C.O. 5/81 and BHP, 2850, reel 10). Campbell rejected Cameron's proposal as an "unwarrantable and unnecessary expense to government" (Campbell to Cameron, July 1, 1780, C.O. 5/81 and BHP, 2869, reel 10). See also Cameron to Clinton, July 18, 1780, BHP, 2919, reel 10.

reported in mid-July, however, that "the relative situation of this place [Charleston], the state of the naval affairs here, and the present condition of the province render it utterly impossible for me to give assistance."[16] Thus, while the West Florida situation had improved, affairs were still critical. Construction of fortifications continued through the summer. Campbell quickly expended his funds for paying the workers, and, consequently, defense preparations stopped except for work being done by the troops. The already high desertion rate increased. Campbell reported in mid-July that nine provincials and six regulars had absconded and fourteen more men had been arrested for plotting to escape.[17]

At this critical point, conflicts between the military and civilian population and between the governor and dissatisfied residents of West Florida continued unabated. An animated dispute had arisen in late 1778 between the governor and members of the assembly, led by the speaker, Adam Chrystie. While this disagreement—with accompanying petitions, charges, and defenses sent to the home government—was originally over the lack of representation of the town of Mobile in the assembly, it soon spread to charges against Chester for demanding exorbitant fees, dealing irresolutely with Willing's raid, and granting lands to men in open rebellion against England. So bitter was this controversy that it continued without interruption from late 1778 until 1782, a year after the capitulation of Pensacola.[18]

Relations between the military and the civilian population

16. Cornwallis to Clinton, July 14, 1780, Clinton Papers and C.O. 5/100; Campbell to Clinton, May 18, 1780, BHP, 2746, reel 10; Campbell to Clinton, July 22, 1780, C.O. 5/100.

17. Osborn, "Major-General John Campbell," p. 335; Campbell to Clinton, July 12, 1780, BHP, 9869, reel 27. A postscript noted that seven more provincials had just fled. A note in a return of Waldeckers states that ninety of the mercenaries deserted between June 25, 1780, and June 24, 1782 ("Waldeck Troops," June 25, 1780–June 24, 1782, BHP, 9992, reel 27).

18. The papers on this dispute are voluminous. Most of them are in C.O. 5/580, C.O. 5/595, and Chalmers Papers in the New York Public Library. See also Johnson, British West Florida, pp. 213–14; Howard, "Colonial Pensacola," pp. 396–97. The complaints about Chester's handling of Willing's raid began early. In mid-May 1778, a new resident to West Florida reported, "Our governor gets much blame from the inhabitants, and I believe not without great reason to let such a small party of 100 men disturb the settlements after frequent applications was [sic] made to him." William Wilton to Joseph Frederick Wallet Desbarres, May 16, 1778, Joseph Frederick Wallet Desbarres Papers, Public Archives of Canada.

were no better. Friction arose from inadequate definitions of the jurisdiction of the respective governmental branches in West Florida. Chester followed instructions he had received in 1776: "There can be no doubt that in all cases of sudden and great emergency, whether the danger arises from the invasion of a foreign enemy or domestic insurrection, it is the duty of the king's governor to employ every means in his power to repel the attack; and to that end he is to call for the assistance of every person who bears a commission or receives pay from His Majesty; and all officers both civil and military are bound to obey the governor's orders and he becomes responsible for those he gives."[19] Once Campbell, a general officer, arrived in West Florida, the situation changed. The American commander-in-chief explained that "no governor (as such) can have any command over the king's troops in his government whilst an officer is present with them of superior rank to a colonel."[20] Campbell explained his position in the dispute to Secretary of State Germain, but, unfortunately, the matter was never cleared up by the home government.

Campbell had little respect for either the civil government or the civilians of West Florida. He complained that his efforts to assure the cooperation of the inhabitants of Pensacola with the troops in case of attack "produced nothing but plausible resolves of Council. . . . In short . . . there is no civil authority in this province, only what is sufficient from the nature of the constitution to prevent the establishment of military."[21] When the Council of Pensacola requested in February 1780 the construction of a stockaded place for protection of the women and children in case of attack, Campbell responded to their requisition: "I can only say (that in my opinion) the inhabitants of Pensacola (were they animated with public spirit and would strenuously exert themselves for the protection of their families and for the defense of their liberty and property like brave men) might in a very short space of time render this very town the best asylum and protection for their wives and families. . . . But if they remain supine and inactive with the enemy almost in view and trust to petitions and remonstrances against grievances and *appre-*

19. Germain to Chester, May 27, 1776, C.O. 5/592.
20. Clinton to Campbell, Oct. 21, 1780, BHP, 3079, reel 11.
21. Campbell to Germain, Jan. 15, 1781, C.O. 5/597.

hensions that exist *only in idea* they will justly be despised by the brave, and their misfortunes (should any befall them) be unlamented by friend or foe."[22] Campbell refused the request for a stockaded area, and the council, feeling that Campbell's letter "appears to contain a number of severe aspersions upon the inhabitants of this town," appointed a committee to inquire whether "there are any grounds for the innuendoes contained therein." Predictably, this committee reported that "it appears to us that the said inhabitants are and always have been animated with public spirit, loyalty, and zeal for their king and country." Such a response by the committee was a direct rebuke of Campbell's charges and obviously did nothing to smooth relations between the commander and the inhabitants.[23]

A party of forty to fifty Indians attacked a patrol of ten West Florida Royal Foresters in late June 1780 at their camp on the Mobile road about twenty miles from Pensacola. While there is nothing to indicate that the Spanish inspired the raid, Campbell immediately sent some light infantry, Royal Foresters, and thirty Choctaws after the raiding party. Unable to catch up with the Indians, they soon returned home. Indians under the leadership of an officer and six men of the Royal Foresters attacked a Spanish post on the east side of Mobile in early November. The Spanish met the attack with fire from two four-pounders, which threw the Indians into confusion. The Royal Foresters and a Mr. Pitchlin (a trader sent by Cameron to help direct the Indians) quickly mounted their horses and left. The Indians advanced to the entrenchments, set fire to a few houses, killed several Spaniards, and scalped four. They retreated, however, after their initial thrust.[24]

22. Minutes of the Council, Feb. 17, 25, 1780, C.O. 5/635, RSUS, reel 8.
23. Ibid. The council later decided the best place for the women and children in case of attack was David Helms' plantation "up the Bay of Pensacola" (Minutes of the Council, Mar. 3, 1780, ibid.).
24. Cameron to Browne, June 25, 1780, C.O. 5/81; Cameron to Germain, Nov. 30, 1780, C.O. 5/82. In the time between these two incidents, some Choctaw Indians murdered a Spanish sergeant and two of his men who were escorting a British sergeant with a flag of truce from Mobile part of the way back to Pensacola. Campbell refers to this event as "an unfortunate accident . . . that Spain may possibly represent to the prejudice of Great Britain." Upon Campbell's orders, Cameron reprimanded the Choctaws for this action. Campbell to Clinton, Sept. 18, 1780, C.O. 5/101 and BHP, 9883, reel 27; Cameron to Campbell, Aug. 29, 1780, C.O. 5/101.

Both of these skirmishes were merely a prelude. After the Spanish had captured Mobile, Gálvez had built a post on the east side of Mobile Bay, known as the Village of Mobile or Spanish Fort. His purpose was to prevent a surprise attack on Mobile from Pensacola. Campbell, tired of waiting for the Spanish to attack, decided to take the initiative without waiting for reinforcements. He ordered Colonel Johann Ludwig Wilhelm Von Hanxleden, with 60 men of his Waldeck Regiment, 100 men of the Sixtieth Regiment, 11 Royal Foresters, 200 to 250 Pennsylvania and Maryland Loyalists, and 420 Indian allies, to seize the Village of Mobile on Sunday morning, January 7. The colonel waited until Sunday morning in order to allow the *Mentor* to arrive in Mobile Bay to prevent the Spanish crossing the bay to aid the Village of Mobile. At dawn on the seventh, Von Hanxleden attacked the 150-man force at the Spanish post with bayonets. British forces penetrated the Spanish works before the surprised defenders recovered and managed to repel the attack in bitter hand-to-hand combat. Colonel Von Hanxleden was killed early in the fighting; after his death, confusion prevailed among the attackers. The Spanish killed one other German officer (Lieutenant Sterling) and wounded another. Lieutenant James Gordon of the Sixtieth Regiment was also killed. As a result of these casualties, the command fell to Captain Philip B. Key of the provincials, who "judged it prudent to order a retreat." The Indians remained hidden during the assault and fired at every Spaniard they could see. Cameron explained that they did not join the attack because of confusion following Von Hanxleden's death. A prearranged signal was never given, and the Indians consequently did not attack but rather kept up a steady fire even after the rest of the troops had withdrawn. The British made a hasty retreat to Pensacola, where a dispute arose over blame for the defeat. Four days after the disaster, Campbell evaluated the battle: "This expedition I can now venture to say entirely miscarried from Colonel . . . Hanxleden's early fate." At the same time, the general praised the officers—Waldeck, regular, and provincial—for their bravery, as they "did everything that zeal and honor could dictate for the success of His Majesty's arms."[25] The Spaniards at the Village of Mobile had

25. Campbell to Germain, Jan. 11, 1781, C.O. 5/597; Campbell to Clinton, Jan. 5, 1781, BHP, 9899, reel 27; Campbell to Clinton, Jan. 7, 1781, BHP, 9900, reel

saved Mobile at a cost of fourteen killed and twenty-three wounded. The British had had fifteen killed (including Von Hanxleden, Sterling, and Gordon) and twenty-three wounded.[26]

Campbell had arrived in West Florida early in 1779. After almost sixteen years of British rule, the fortifications of the "arrogant step-father of the Gulf of Mexico" were still "in a primitive state."[27] What defenses the English had built had been destroyed by the hurricane which hit Pensacola in October 1778, and Campbell reported "a state of ruin and desolation."[28] He had hoped to strengthen the defenses of West Florida in order to repel any attack, but little work of any consequence had been done in Pensacola by December 1779. In that month Campbell informed Germain: "In my plan of defense of this place I have thought it necessary to erect a work on Gage Hill." Campbell's reasons behind his decision to build the new fortification were sound. The garrison fortress, located on a large plaza in the center of Pensacola, was a stockade fort, closely surrounded by houses of the town, and too large for the number of men the British had to defend it. In addition, Gage Hill was about 1,200 yards north of the plaza, and the general correctly observed that once an enemy took possession of Gage Hill with cannon and mortar, the town of Pensacola would no longer be tenable. Campbell asserted that a work constructed on the hill would be "the citadel of Pensacola." Should the Spanish gain possession of the plaza and town of Pensacola, they could not hold it while the British were in possession of Gage Hill.[29]

Gage Hill was three hundred yards wide and extended northwestward, rising twenty-two feet in nine hundred yards.

27; Campbell to Clinton, Feb. 15, 1781, BHP, 9901, reel 27; Cameron to Germain, Feb. 10, 1781, C.O. 5/82; Caughey, Gálvez, pp. 194–95; Eelking, Die Deutschen Hulfstruppen, pp. 15–16; Wright, Bowles, p. 14; Haarmann, "The Spanish Conquest," pp. 120–21; William H. Jenkins, "Alabama Forts, 1700–1838," p. 170. Among the provincials who participated in the attack—but as an Indian ally and not a provincial—was William Augustus Bowles.

26. Caughey, Gálvez, p. 195; "Return of the Killed and Wounded at the Village opposite Mobile—the 7th January 1781," C.O. 5/597.

27. Jacinto Panis to Gálvez, July 5, 1778, MPA,SD, 1:219; Panis to Gálvez, Aug. 16, 1779, ibid., 1:305. See also Germain to Chester, July 1, 1778, C.O. 5/594.

28. Campbell to Clinton, Feb. 10, 1779, BHP, 1737, reel 7.

29. Campbell to Germain, Dec. 15, 1779, C.O. 5/597 and BHP, 2480, reel 9.

The work Campbell ordered built on the southeast end of Gage Hill was named Fort George. It was a double stockade of wood and sand, square with salient angles at the corners, with a hornwork which descended to the south to two blockhouses on the road from Pensacola to Mobile. Fort George defended Pensacola, but should enemy forces possess the higher northwest end of Gage Hill, they would dominate Fort George. The higher ground, however, was too far away from the town to afford it any defense.[30]

Campbell reported to Clinton in March 1780 that, in order to protect Fort George, he had ordered the construction of a redoubt on the northwest end of the hill. This double stockade of wood and sand, known as the Queen's Redoubt, was a circular battery facing low ground to the west with parapets flanking to the north and south. About three hundred yards south of the Queen's Redoubt was a smaller redoubt, known as the Prince of Wales, which maintained communication between the Queen's Redoubt and Fort George. By May 1780 Campbell felt that "we are now tolerably prepared for their [the Spanish] reception, the body of Fort George being the same as finished." His men had also completed the Queen's Redoubt, but construction of the Prince of Wales' Redoubt had not yet begun, and the making of the glacis, stockading the ditch, and a number of other minor matters remained before Fort George would be "in a thorough finished state."[31]

Campbell reported in late October 1780 that construction had begun on fortifications at the Red Cliffs at the entrance to Pensacola Bay. The defenses of this fort, constructed of fascines and sand, faced inland toward Tartar Point. There were no fortifications on the sea side, since nature furnished the protection in the form of a "precipice." Campbell initially intended the fort merely to prevent the enemy from possessing the point from which they could harass or "entirely drive off" ships stationed in Pensacola Bay for defense of the town. He believed that in time a battery might be placed on the sea side, but at

30. Stanley Faye, "British and Spanish Fortifications of Pensacola, 1781–1821," pp. 278–79, 282; Haarmann, "The Spanish Conquest," p. 122.
31. Campbell to Germain, May 15, 1780, C.O. 5/597; Campbell to Clinton, Mar. 24, 1780, C.O. 5/99; Faye, "British and Spanish Fortifications," pp. 279, 282; Haarmann, "The Spanish Conquest," p. 122.

present no heavy cannon could be spared from other defenses. The general named the post the "Royal Navy Redoubt," because seamen were doing most of the construction and the navy would garrison and defend the new fort.[32]

By the end of November, Campbell had changed his mind as to the usefulness of the Royal Navy Redoubt. Because of its "apparent importance," he decided that it would be wise to place a strong battery facing the sea as well as having a defense toward Tartar Point. He ordered Waldeck Major Friedrich Pentzell with fifty rank and file (not including sergeants and commissioned officers) to garrison the Royal Navy Redoubt. In addition, upon the appearance of the enemy, a sufficient number of sailors would join the garrison to man the guns. Four days earlier the commanding officer had ordered all of the thirty-two-pounders at Fort George removed to the Red Cliffs. Campbell felt that these five large cannon, along with the six smaller ones in the redoubt, "will prove such an obstruction to the enemy's designs as they were not prepared to expect, or meet with at this place."[33]

Across the entrance of the harbor from the Royal Navy Redoubt was the western tip of Santa Rosa Island. Campbell was convinced that a battery at this location, plus the fortification at the Red Cliffs and one fifty-gun or forty-four-gun ship in the bay

32. Campbell to Germain, Oct. 31, 1780, C.O. 5/597. Chaplain Philipp Waldeck frequently referred to the construction of Fort George and the outlying redoubts in his diary. He reported frantic efforts to complete the fortifications: the soldiers were "becoming so exhausted that it is a wonder that they are not overcome by their fatigue." With only salted meat and a pound of bread for rations, the soldiers worked from morning until night with a break from noon to one o'clock. On February 26, he noted that "as soon as the soldiers come off watch they go to work and from work to picket. . . . It can't be changed, however. The work on the fort must continue at all costs." Philosophically, he concluded, "as soon as Fort George is finished it will be placed in an action stand so I hope with confident knowledge that we gain laurels on this sandhill that will nevertheless be colored with the blood of many brave men, but where have the crowns of victory been won without danger?" Even in the midst of the work and confusion, however, the residents of West Florida did not neglect the social amenities. Waldeck reports attending a party on the evening of February 16 (Learned, Philipp Waldeck's Diary, pp. 138–45).

33. Campbell to Germain, Nov. 26, 1780, C.O. 5/597; Eelking, Die Deutschen Hulfstruppen, pp. 14–15. At the time of the surrender of the Royal Navy Redoubt, there were 139 men in the fortification ("General Return of the Garrison of the Royal Navy Redoubt When delivered up to the Arms the 11th May 1781," C.O. 5/597).

to meet any vessels that got past the two batteries, would make it nearly impossible to enter the bay: "the attempt would be madness without first reducing one of the works on the Red Cliffs or Rose Island." When the Spanish landed on the island, however, they found only a few dismounted cannon and a burned stockade. Campbell lamented to Clinton in early January 1781 that he could not establish a battery on the island because there were not enough tools in Pensacola to carry on construction in two places at the same time, and the troops were already working on the Royal Navy Redoubt, Fort George, the Queen's Redoubt, and the Prince of Wales' Redoubt. He had no cannon to mount in a redoubt on Santa Rosa Island, and there was a shortage of men, artificers, and laborers.[34]

Campbell received a subscription of £900 from the inhabitants of Pensacola for the construction of a redoubt at each end of town. These two additional redoubts would form a triangle with Fort George, and, along with the swamp that nearly surrounded Pensacola, they would afford protection to the town. The redoubt at the east end of the town would also be in a position to fire on any vessel that brought its cannon to bear on Fort George. It is not clear whether the redoubt on the west end of town was ever constructed, but the residents of Pensacola built the post on the east end of the town.[35]

The first line of defense, however, was not land fortifications. The Royal Navy served as the major bulwark of defense, for two or three well-armed vessels could block the entrance of the bay. Germain had instructed the vice-admiral at Jamaica to support West Florida in the event of a war with Spain, and Clinton asserted that "a sufficient naval force . . . alone can secure the place."[36] Governor Chester declared in the fall of 1780 that "nothing in all human probability can prevent our downfall, unless Admiral Sir Peter Parker should luckily send down a fleet to intercept the Spanish squadron, or some ships of force

34. Campbell to Clinton, Jan. 5, 1781, BHP, 9899, reel 27; Faye, "British and Spanish Fortifications," p. 278.
35. Campbell to Germain, Dec. 15, 1779, C.O. 5/597; Minutes of the Council, Mar. 3, 1780, C.O. 5/635, RSUS, reel 8. For the parliamentary debates over the expense of building fortifications in West Florida, see Thomas C. Hansard, *The Parliamentary History of England from the Earliest Period to the Year 1803*, 22:292–93, 297–300.
36. Clinton to Germain, Mar. 16, 1781, C.O. 5/101.

to defend the entrance of our harbor before they approach it."[37]

The sloops-of-war *Hound* and *Port Royal* arrived at Pensacola with nine merchant vessels on April 9, 1780, and the man-of-war *Mentor* arrived May 14. The *Port Royal* had orders to remain in Pensacola, but Parker had instructed the *Hound* to escort to England what trade vessels might be ready to sail. Finding that the sloop-of-war *Stork* (the only warship already in Pensacola) had been condemned and sunk, leaving Pensacola without any naval defense, Captain James McNamara of the *Hound* waived his orders and, apparently at the request of the governor in council, imposed an embargo on all the merchantmen in the harbor. McNamara then ordered the ordnance ship *Earl of Bathurst* rearmed with thirty guns and requested the merchantmen with guns to go to the entrance of the harbor "to make the best show and defense we possibly could, should the harbor be attacked."[38] According to intelligence Campbell received from two Spanish deserters, the Spanish thought the *Earl of Bathurst* was a fifty-gun ship and the *Port Royal* a forty-four-gun ship, and that the merchantmen were frigates and sloops-of-war. They recognized the *Hound* from earlier encounters. This poor intelligence was in part responsible for the Spanish delay in attacking Pensacola. This small fleet remained at the entrance of the harbor from April 11 until June 2, then returned up the bay to Pensacola.[39]

Throughout the summer and fall and into the winter of 1780–81, the embargo remained in effect. At least five more vessels arrived during that period. The provision ships *Ann and Elizabeth* and *Love and Unity's Increase*, the transport *Jane*, the sloop *Diligence*, and the ship of the line *Phoenix* all entered the harbor during the last six months of 1780. Chester requested on

37. Chester to Germain, Nov. 24, 1780, C.O. 5/596.
38. McNamara to Stephens, Aug. 6, 1780, C.O. 5/131; Minutes of the Council, July 19, 1780, Feb. 21, 1781, C.O. 5/596; Campbell to Germain, Dec. 15, 1779, C.O. 5/597; Campbell to Clinton, May 15, 1780, BHP, 2736, reel 10; Capt. Robert Deans to Stephens, Aug. 3, 1780, C.O. 5/131; Le Montais, McNamara, and Lt. T. Kelley to masters of the merchant ships, Apr. 14, 1780, C.O. 5/596. On its way to Pensacola the *Mentor* captured three Spanish vessels and carried them as prizes to Pensacola. Parker to Stephens, Sept. 5, 1780, Adm. 1/242, University of Florida photostat.
39. Campbell to Germain, May 15, 1780, C.O. 5/597; Campbell to Clinton, May 13, 1780, BHP, 2736, reel 10; McNamara to Stephens, Aug. 6, 1780, C.O. 5/131.

August 11 that the masters of the merchantmen be prepared to join the ships of war at the entrance of the harbor upon a given signal. Captain Robert Deans of the *Mentor* (senior naval officer in Pensacola) finally lifted the embargo in February 1781 and ordered the *Hound* to convoy the eleven merchant vessels to England. The small fleet left Pensacola on February 25, 1781, leaving in the harbor to defend Pensacola only the *Port Royal* with eighteen guns and the *Mentor* with twenty guns.[40]

Sir Peter Parker, however, was making arrangements for reinforcements to go to Pensacola. The sloop *Childers* sailed from Jamaica and arrived in Pensacola in early March; the *Ulysses* left on March 11 with part of Major [?] Odell's two hundred volunteers on board; and a few days later the ordnance ship *Dutton* and the *Resource* sailed, the latter transporting the remainder of Odell's corps. Of all these vessels, only the *Childers* was at Pensacola on March 9 when the Spanish fleet appeared off the bar. That same night, the *Childers* got safely by the Spanish fleet and sailed for Jamaica.[41] Twenty days later the

40. Campbell to Germain, Sept. 18, 1780, BHP, 9883, reel 27; Chester to masters of the merchant ships in Pensacola harbor, Aug. 11, 1780, C.O. 5/596; McNamara to Parker, Mar. 7, 1781, C.O. 5/132; William Laird Clowes et al., *The Royal Navy*, 4:111, "Mentor's Logg Book Commencing 9th March 1780," manuscript, John C. Pace Library; Campbell reported that the *Mentor* was copper sheathed and mounted eighteen twelve-pounders and six four-pounders. Campbell to Clinton, May 15, 1780, BHP, 2736, reel 10.

41. Parker to Stephens, Sept. 5, 1780, Adm. 1/242, University of Florida photostat; Parker to Stephens, March 16, 1781, C.O. 5/132; Parker to Stephens, Apr. 27, 1781, ibid.; "Mentor's Logg Book," Mar. 7, 10, 11, 1781; Campbell to Clinton, Apr. 9, 1781, BHP, 9913, reel 27; James A. Padgett, ed., "Bernardo de Gálvez's Siege of Pensacola in 1781 (as Related in Robert Farmar's Journal)," p. 315, hereafter cited as "Robert Farmar's Journal." This source is a journal of the siege of Pensacola from the British point of view, supposedly written by Robert Farmar, one of the original settlers of West Florida. The journal first appeared in printed form in the *Historical Magazine and Notes and Queries* 4 (1860):166–72, edited by Buckingham Smith. All of my references will be to the copy in the *Louisiana Historical Quarterly*. The editor of this copy states that it is impossible to fix the exact date of Farmar's death, but that he remained a resident of West Florida until the end of the British period. He cites as proof the fact that some of the entries in the journal are dated as late as July 12, 1781 (pp. 313–14). What the editor fails to do is to question whether Farmar was really the author of the journal. An entry in the minutes of the Assembly of West Florida, dated Oct. 8, 1778, C.O. 5/628, RSUS, reel 3, states: "That Robert Farmar Esquire, who was elected to serve for the district of Mobile in the present Assembly, is since dead." Clearly Farmar died between the time of the election and the meeting of the assembly in October 1778, and, therefore, he could not possibly have been the author of a journal written in 1781. There is

Childers met the *Resource* and *Dutton*, which were on their way to Pensacola. Upon hearing that the Spanish had attacked Pensacola, the two vessels returned to Jamaica. The *Childers* arrived first, and Parker immediately sent it back out with orders for the *Resource* to take the troops off the *Dutton* (about two hundred men) and proceed with them to Pensacola and endeavor to enter the harbor. The *Childers* then escorted the *Dutton* back to Jamaica. In the meantime, the *Ulysses* had arrived off Santa Rosa Island at the end of March, only to find the Spanish in possession of the harbor. Captain John Thomas reported that he was waiting on the *Dutton* "that I may be able to put the remaining part of your orders into execution."[42] Apparently both the *Ulysses* and the *Resource* sailed back to Jamaica, for no reinforcements reached Pensacola.

Because no naval or troop reinforcements reached Pensacola after the Spanish arrived in March 1781, the fate of West Florida rested in the hands of the polyglot force already in the province. A return of the troops on January 1, 1781, reported 282 regulars, 310 Waldeckers and artillery, 273 Pennsylvania and Maryland Loyalists, and 41 West Florida Royal Foresters—a total of 906 men (including 54 officers) present and fit for duty in the province.[43] The regulars included seven companies of the Sixteenth Regiment and eight companies of the Sixtieth Regiment. In addition to these 906 men, there were a number of others involved in the defense of Pensacola. Without question, the largest group of defenders other than the military was the Indians. An exact count is not possible, but apparently there were four hundred to five hundred Indians in the British service at the time of Pensacola's capitulation. Much of the fighting outside Fort George and the redoubts was done by the Indians. Negroes, most of whom were slaves of the inhabitants, also participated in the defense of the town. An accurate count

no conclusive evidence on who did write the journal. It may have been written by Campbell as notes to refresh his memory later, or by James Campbell —General Campbell's secretary—or by any other person present at the siege. The journal may have been written by Major Farmar's son, Robert Farmar, who was probably present at the siege, but there is no evidence to confirm this assumption. The original has apparently been lost.

42. John Thomas to Parker, Mar. 26, 1781, C.O. 5/132; Parker to Stephens, Apr. 27, 1781, ibid.

43. Troop Return, May 1, 1781, Clinton Papers and C.O. 5/102. The Royal Foresters were under the command of Adam Chrystie.

is impossible, but there were at least fifty present: "Robert Farmar's Journal" refers to that number of Negroes supporting an advance party of Maryland Loyalists on March 30.[44]

While it is not known to what degree the inhabitants of Pensacola participated in the defense of the town, at least some of them helped to defend their homes and property. A report of a committee of the council presented in March 1780 included a list of the names of the civilian population. This document listed a total of 130 heads of family, but the committee reported that only 107 were capable of bearing arms. Of these, 40 were "immediately employed in the military department and king's works by General Campbell." The remaining men were enrolled in two companies of volunteers who "are ready and willing to exert themselves in defense of their country and property when circumstances may require their services."[45] A year later Campbell informed Clinton that a number of refugees from the Mississippi and Mobile had come to Pensacola and that, in order to keep them in the province, he was organizing the West Florida Royal Volunteers to employ these men and other inhabitants as necessity required for the defense of Pensacola. While there is no indication that he ever formed the Royal Volunteers, men capable of bearing arms did come to Pensacola.[46] The number of inhabitants involved in the defense of Pensacola can safely be placed at about a hundred.

After the siege had begun and it had become obvious that the officers and men aboard the *Port Royal* and *Mentor* would be of more value inside the fortifications than aboard their small vessels, the seamen augmented the garrison. Some were already at the Royal Navy Redoubt. A Spanish prisoner return listed 7 officers and 239 sailors. Taking into account the 30 killed and the 3 deserters not included in the return, 279 seamen were involved in the defense of Pensacola.[47]

44. "Robert Farmar's Journal," p. 318. See also Bernardo de Gálvez, "Diary of the Operations against Pensacola," p. 75. A copy of this diary is in N. Orwin Rush, *The Battle of Pensacola*.

45. Minutes of the Council, Mar. 3, 1780, C.O. 5/635, RSUS, reel 8; "A List of the Names of the Inhabitants of the Town of Pensacola in the Civil Line taken the ——Febry 1780," ibid.

46. Campbell to Clinton, Feb. 15, 1781, BHP, 9901, reel 27.

47. Albert W. Haarmann, "The Siege of Pensacola: An Order of Battle," p. 197; Campbell to Germain, May 12, 1781, quoted in Almon, *The Remembrancer. For the Year 1781*, part 2, p. 282. This Spanish prisoner

Thus, the best estimate of defenders lists 906 regulars, Waldeckers, Royal Artillery, Pennsylvania and Maryland Loyalists, and West Florida Royal Foresters, 400 to 500 Indians, at least 50 Negroes, 100 civilian inhabitants, and 279 seamen. The total force defending Pensacola was between 1,735 and 1,835 men. As to the quality of the troops, Campbell lamented to Clinton: "Your excellency must be sensible from your own knowledge and my repeated representations that the troops I have under my command are not only a few in number, but are likewise such, that the soldier whose reputation depends upon them, must be looked upon by the thinking and considerate of his profession [as] on the verge and summit of the precipice of misfortune; however, I hope to be able to perform what can reasonably be expected from me in the circumstances in which I am situated."[48] This letter can be considered a continuation of Campbell's long series of complaints or as an apologia for failure in advance of the event, but after the capitulation of his command, Campbell had nothing but praise for his troops for "their attention to order, discipline, and alertness."[49] Generally speaking, the defenders gave a good account of themselves throughout the two-month siege.

For over a year both the civilian and military population of Pensacola had awaited the Spanish attack and feverishly prepared for the expected visit. They had constructed new fortifications and improved older ones, gathered supplies, and appealed for reinforcements. When the occasion demanded, the mixed force of defenders worked together to present a show of strength to deter the Spaniard. The heterogeneous force of defenders was finally called upon to man its wood and sand fortifications to defend lives, homes, and property against an overwhelming enemy. Without reinforcements, the prospects were grim.

---

return lists a total of 1,113 regulars, sailors, and militiamen. Considering the battle casualties and desertions, the figure appears high. This return, however, undoubtedly includes sick and wounded and others not fit for duty who are not included in the British return of effectives.

48. Campbell to Clinton, Sept. 18, 1780, C.O. 5/101.
49. Campbell to Clinton, May 12, 1781, BHP, 9918, reel 27.

8

"Vigor and Spirit to the Last"

After more than a year of preparations, the British in Pensacola finally believed a successful resistance possible: "We have plenty of provisions, our fortifications are in good order, we despise our enemy but not so far as to forget our duty, and were it not for desertion, every circumstance would be in our favor."[1] While the West Floridians feverishly prepared to resist a Spanish attack, General Gálvez furthered preparations for a campaign against the only remaining British post in West Florida.

Unsuccessful in his attempts to obtain reinforcements by correspondence with Captain General Navarro, Gálvez went to Havana to gain support. He arrived in Cuba on August 2, 1780, and nine days later a junta de guerra decided that Gálvez should lead a force against Pensacola. The junta provided Gálvez with 3,800 men and three months' supplies. By the time the expedition sailed on October 16, Gálvez had 3,829 men and 164 officers under his command, with six months' provisions;

---

1. Campbell to Clinton, Apr. 9, 1781, BHP, 9913, reel 27. But Campbell concluded his appraisal pessimistically: "We must undoubtedly fall unless we are relieved." The British had received so many provisions in the past few months that in September 1780 Campbell complained that they had more provisions than they had room to store them (Campbell to Clinton, Sept. 18, 1780, quoted in Rush, *Battle of Pensacola*, p. 22). As an example of desertions in West Florida, in September 1781, there were enough German deserters in West Florida for the Spanish to form a forty-man company of them in Pensacola alone. Martín Navarro to José de Gálvez, Sept. 10, 1781, quoted in Kinnaird, *Spain in the Mississippi Valley*, 1:435.

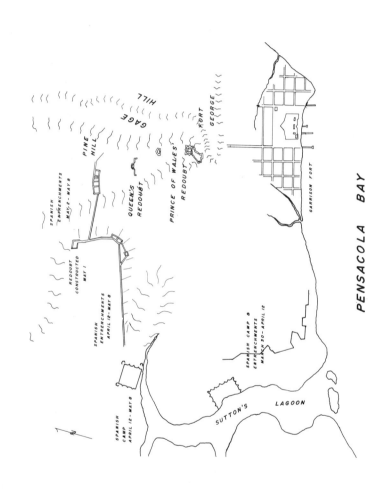

PENSACOLA BAY

Pensacola Bay, 1781. Based on maps by Henry Heldring, 1781. Originals in the William
L. Clements Library, Ann Arbor, Michigan. Drawn by Rex A. James, Jr.

all were transported and convoyed by a fleet of seven warships, five frigates, one packet boat, one brig, one armed lugger, and forty-nine transports. Gálvez' third attempt on Pensacola was doomed to failure, however. Two days out of port, the fleet hit a hurricane which lasted for five days. Eventually all but one of the vessels made it back to Havana, but again Pensacola had been spared.[2]

Despite his misfortune, Gálvez refused to give up his goal of reducing Pensacola. The junta decided unanimously to help Gálvez again, but this time granted considerably less aid. On February 13, 1781, after more than two months of preparations, Gálvez boarded the *San Ramón*. The next day the troops embarked. Once again it appeared that nature might intervene; Gálvez and his men sat aboard the vessels for two weeks before favorable winds finally allowed them to depart. Gálvez commanded 1,315 men, the frigate *Santa Clara* (thirty-six guns), the *Chambequin* (twenty guns), the packet boat *San Pio* (eighteen guns), the warship *San Ramón* (seventy-four guns), the frigate *Santa Cecilia* (thirty-six guns), and enough transports to carry the men (apparently twenty-five to twenty-seven vessels).[3] The voyage was uneventful until the morning of March 4 when the Spanish sighted the British merchantmen convoyed by the *Hound*, which had left Pensacola on February 25. Part of the Spanish fleet gave chase until nightfall, and then, unsuccessful in bringing the *Hound* to battle, they rejoined their fleet.[4]

The major aim of the junta in placing over 1,300 men and the fleet under Gálvez' command was to enable the general to reinforce the mainland. Gálvez, however, had no intention of simply reinforcing the Spanish posts in Louisiana and West

2. Caughey, *Gálvez*, pp. 192–93. See also "Report of Sundry occurrences at Havana from 6th November 1780 to my departure on the 7th January 1781," C.O. 5/560. Some material in this chapter is taken from Caughey's excellent chapter on the siege of Pensacola. Caughey, however, used Spanish sources almost exclusively. I will attempt here to tell the story from the British point of view, integrating information from both Spanish and English sources.

3. Caughey, *Gálvez*, pp. 195–99; Gálvez, "Diary," pp. 46–47; Campbell to Clinton, Apr. 9, 1781, BHP, 9913, reel 27, reported thirty vessels in the Spanish fleet; "Robert Farmar's Journal," p. 315, listed thirty-two ships in the squadron. Gálvez was given full authority over the navy as well as the army in order to prevent friction and ineffectiveness caused by a divided command.

4. Gálvez, "Diary," p. 48; McNamara to Parker, Mar. 7, 1781, C.O. 5/132; William Dickson to [?], May 1, 1781, C.O. 5/144; Capt. John Douglas to Stephens, Apr. 20, 1781, C.O. 5/132.

Florida. He sent Capt. Maximiliano Maxent to New Orleans on February 1 with orders for the troops there to prepare for an expedition against Pensacola. Prior to his departure from Havana, Gálvez notified the Louisiana forces to join his convoy at Pensacola. After he was at sea, Gálvez sent Sublieutenant Miguel de Herrera to Mobile with orders for Ezpoleta to march overland to Pensacola with as many men as he could bring.[5]

On the morning of March 9, the British *Mentor* fired seven shots to inform Pensacola that the Spanish fleet had arrived off Santa Rosa Island. The same night, with Gálvez leading the way, the Spanish disembarked on the island "with some misgivings, but without the least opposition." All of the troops had landed by three o'clock in the morning. In the meantime, the first landing party had begun the march to the western tip of the island (known to the Spanish as Siguenza Point). At 5:30 A.M. they arrived at the point and were amazed to find "only three dismounted cannons and a partly demolished breastwork of fascines" instead of a fortification.[6] The British were unaware that the Spanish troops had landed; the next morning nine men from the *Port Royal* landed on the island to tend the cattle and were quickly captured by the Spanish light infantry. The men aboard the *Port Royal* and the *Mentor* and in the Royal Navy Redoubt observed the Spanish capture and immediately opened fire on the enemy troops, but did not inflict any casualties.[7]

5. Gálvez, "Diary," pp. 47–48. On March 5 the brig *Gálveztown*, which had left Havana on March 2, joined the fleet.

6. Ibid., pp. 48–49; Eelking, *Die Deutschen Hulfstruppen*, p. 16. Jacinto Panis recommended to Gálvez that the Spanish troops land on the Perdido River and march overland to take the fortifications on the Red Cliffs, to allow the vessels to enter the harbor without facing a crossfire between that position and Santa Rosa Island. Gálvez concurred in the reasoning but felt it would be easier to take Santa Rosa Island. This decision by Gálvez proved highly beneficial to the Spanish. Panis to Gálvez, Apr. 29, 1779, in Kinnaird, *Spain in the Mississippi Valley*, 1:337–38.

7. "Robert Farmar's Journal," p. 315; Gálvez, "Diary," p. 49. The diary states that the Spanish took seven prisoners. One contemporary reported that the *Mentor* brought in a Spanish schooner on March 10 which had "on board baggage and stores for a Spanish lord, who was well fortified against the deprivations incident to travel in the American wilderness." On board the vessel were 20,000 thalers in cash, silver, wines, kitchen utensils, and other goods that evidently belonged to Gálvez (Eelking, *Die Deutschen Hulfstruppen*, p. 17). It is possible that such a capture took place, but it was not by the *Mentor*. The logbook of Captain Robert Deans of the *Mentor* does not mention this seizure and it is unlikely that such a prize would go unmentioned ("*Mentor's* Logg Book").

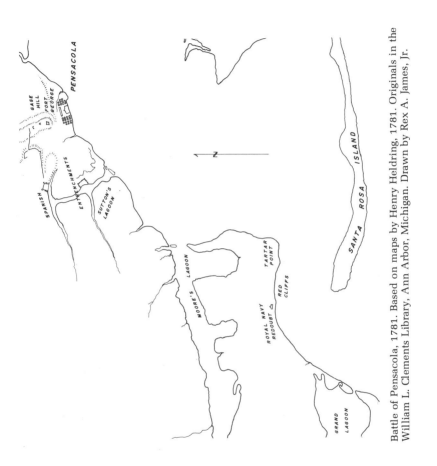

Battle of Pensacola, 1781. Based on maps by Henry Heldring, 1781. Originals in the William L. Clements Library, Ann Arbor, Michigan. Drawn by Rex A. James, Jr.

On the afternoon of March 10, Gálvez ordered two twenty-four-pounders, two eight-pounders, and four four-pounders erected in a battery facing Pensacola to keep the *Port Royal* and *Mentor* from bombarding the Spanish camp. The next day the new Spanish battery forced the two British vessels to withdraw.[8]

The Spanish fleet, led by Gálvez (aboard the *San Ramón* "in order to be in this operation and pass through the risk"), made its first attempt to enter the harbor on the afternoon of the eleventh. The *San Ramón* struck ground, however, and, after quickly freeing herself, came about and returned to her former anchorage followed by the rest of the fleet. The Spanish army on Santa Rosa Island was now in a dangerous situation. If a storm arose, the ships would have to put to sea to keep from being run aground, thus leaving Gálvez and his men without supplies or provisions and at the mercy of the English. In order to forestall such a possibility, Gálvez ordered supplies unloaded onto the island and tried unsuccessfully to get the navy to attempt again to enter the harbor—this time with smaller ships at the head of the convoy. These efforts occupied the next six days, and there was no contact between the opposing forces.[9]

Three Spanish galleys sounded the channel on the evening of the seventeenth in preparation for entrance of part of the fleet the next day. Although Gálvez was in command of the navy as well as the army, Captain José Calbo de Irozabal was responsible for the safety of the fleet. He refused to risk his vessels because of insufficient knowledge of the channel, lack of pilots, and the enemy battery on the Red Cliffs. Gálvez, however, had command of the four Louisiana vessels: two armed launches, the sloop *Valenzuela*, and the brig *Gálveztown*. Comprehending that unless the fleet soon entered the harbor the expedition would collapse, Gálvez resolved to do so with these vessels "in the conviction that this last resort would stimulate the others to follow him."[10]

8. "Robert Farmar's Journal," p. 315. Eelking, *Die Deutschen Hulfstruppen*, p. 17, states that the *Mentor* withdrew after being hit twenty-eight times by twenty-four-pounders. See also "*Mentor's* Logg Book," Mar. 17, 1780.

9. Gálvez, "Diary," p. 49; Caughey, *Gálvez*, pp. 201–2. See also Joseph Allen, *Memoir of the Life and Services of Admiral Sir William Hargood*, pp. 27–28. Hargood was a lieutenant aboard the *Port Royal*.

10. Gálvez, "Diary," p. 52; Caughey, *Gálvez*, p. 202.

At 2:30 on the afternoon of March 18, Gálvez ran up a "broad penant" and fired a fifteen-gun salute to signal that the commander was aboard the *Gálveztown*. The small fleet of four vessels then entered the harbor. The Royal Navy Redoubt maintained a steady fire which managed only to pierce the sails and shrouds. Amidst "the extraordinary applause of the army," Gálvez' tiny squadron anchored under the protection of the battery on Santa Rosa Island. After witnessing Gálvez' successful entry of the harbor, the captains of the fleet urged the entrance of the remainder of the vessels. Calbo again refused, however, having received no detailed plans of the channel. At 2:00 P.M. on the nineteenth the Spanish fleet—except for the *San Ramón*—entered the channel. During the hour it took the fleet to gain the bay, the Royal Navy Redoubt maintained "a well-kept up fire" from the battery on the cliffs. The bombardment inflicted only slight damage, however, and the Spanish suffered no casualties. Gálvez directed the vessels from his gig during the entire operation.[11]

While Gálvez landed his army and attempted to get his fleet into the harbor, the British watched and continued to strengthen their fortifications. Captain [Alexander?] Stevens arrived in Pensacola March 20, in charge of a party of Indians who had attacked a small Spanish boat with a crew of eleven men the previous day. The Indians had killed ten of the men and had taken the eleventh prisoner to Pensacola. At five o'clock on that afternoon, Campbell received under flag of truce a letter from Gálvez warning "that none of the ships or buildings of the King and private parties be destroyed, burned or torn down under pain of being treated with utmost rigor." Refusing to be intimidated, Campbell felt that "the threats of the enemy who assail us are not considered under any other aspect than as an artifice or stratagem of war, which he makes use of to further his own

---

11. Campbell to Clinton, Apr. 9, 1781, BHP, 9913, reel 27; Gálvez, "Diary," p. 52; "Robert Farmar's Journal," p. 316; Caughey, *Gálvez*, p. 203. After the fleet had entered the harbor, Calbo and his fleet of warships set sail for Havana (Caughey, *Gálvez*, p. 204). Spanish naval officers later investigated the ineffectiveness of the guns on the Royal Navy Redoubt and reported that the battery was too far away from the channel (1,533 yards) and at too high an elevation to allow for accurate marksmanship. They reported also that a battery on Siguenza Point would have prevented Spanish access into Pensacola Bay (Caughey, *Gálvez*, p. 213).

purpose." At 8:00 P.M. the British retired to the Royal Navy Redoubt after setting fire to the blockhouse on Tartar Point as a signal to Pensacola that the Spanish were attempting to land there. Actually, up until this time the enemy had made no such effort, although earlier in the afternoon Gálvez and a few men in a boat had examined the area as a possible landing place. The British at Tartar Point apparently concluded from their movements that a landing was imminent.[12]

At 10:00 A.M. on the twenty-first, Campbell sent Colonel Dickson and aide-de-camp Hugh Mackay Gordon to Gálvez under a flag of truce, bearing messages from himself and Governor Chester. Campbell's letter conceded that the garrison fort in the town of Pensacola could not be defended except through the total ruin of the town and its civilian inhabitants. With "humanity dictating the preservation of the innocent individual . . . from the cruelties and devastations of war," Campbell informed Gálvez that he had abandoned the post in Pensacola and planned to defend the town from Fort George and its various redoubts. He proposed that the town not be "occupied or used by either party, whether for annoyance or attack, preservation or defence, accommodation or conveniency; but shall remain an asylum to the sick, the infirm, the women and children to dwell therein." Should Gálvez choose not to accede to the proposal, Campbell asserted that he would be forced to destroy the town to prevent the Spanish using it, "and should I be drove [sic] to this cruel necessity, your excellency alone must be answerable both before God and man for the calamities and distresses attendant on this deed."[13] Gálvez was ill; he sent Dickson to inform Campbell of his opinion on the matter with a promise that he would reply in writing the next day. There is no record of Gálvez' opinion, but at 9:00 P.M. he witnessed the burning of two additional buildings on Tartar Point. Incensed, he casti-

12. Gálvez, "Diary," p. 53; "Robert Farmar's Journal," p. 316.
13. Campbell to Gálvez, Mar. 21, 1781, BHP, 9922, reel 27. All of the correspondence between Campbell and Gálvez concerning this proposal is in C.O. 5/597 and Gálvez, "Diary," pp. 54–57. Dickson was on parole in Pensacola along with six other officers. On March 23, they came out of Pensacola to surrender to Gálvez, "agreeable to their promise given and faith pledged." The officers were Dickson, Captain Alberti, Captain Miller, Lieutenant Bard, Quartermaster Lowe, Dr. Grant, and William Whissel, armorer of the ordnance. Their families, slaves, and three servants entered the Spanish camp, in addition to the officers (Caughey, Gálvez, p. 206).

gated Campbell for insulting the Spanish by ordering the fire at a time when the British general had sent proposals to spare the houses and people. He declared that "the word humanity . . . is little known in your heart" and that as a result of the British perfidy he would "look on the burning of Pensacola with as much indifference as to see afterwards its cruel incendiaries perish on its ashes. . . . May God preserve you many years."[14] Campbell responded that Gálvez' "imperious style" had made him "resolve more than ever to oppose the ambitious undertaking Spain has placed under your command." Concerning the fire on the Red Cliffs, he argued that the officer in charge was merely doing his duty to deprive his enemy of any protection without molesting women, children, or private property. As far as "the observations more immediately connected with me are concerned, as I believe them unmerited, I despise them."[15]

Governor Chester proposed to parole Spanish prisoners on provision that they not serve against Great Britain or her allies. He also informed Gálvez that the women and children would remain in their homes in Pensacola, trusting "that they [the Spanish] shall not increase the misfortunes of these non-combatants, their families and goods." To this plea for protection, Gálvez responded, "if, as is natural, the fate of these [the women and children] interests you, treat with General Campbell, for all depends on the good or bad conduct he observes."[16]

While this bickering continued, Gálvez began receiving reinforcements which would permit him to begin the actual siege. Ezpeleta arrived from Mobile on March 22 with 905 men, and during the same afternoon the *San Pio* and three other small vessels, which Calbo had sent to the Perdido River to ferry Ezpeleta's men across the river, entered Pensacola Bay. The guns on the Red Cliffs blazed away but did no damage to the small flotilla.[17] At 9:00 the next morning the Spanish sighted a fleet bringing reinforcements from New Orleans, and

14. Gálvez to Campbell, Mar. 22, 1781, BHP, 9922, reel 27; "Robert Farmar's Journal," p. 316.
    15. Campbell to Gálvez, Mar. 22, 1781, quoted in Gálvez, "Diary," pp. 57–58.
    16. Chester to Gálvez, Mar. 21, 1781, ibid., p. 55; Gálvez to Chester, Mar. 22, 1781, ibid., p. 57.
    17. Gálvez, "Diary," p. 56; "Robert Farmar's Journal," p. 316; Caughey, *Gálvez*, p. 206; Campbell to Clinton, Apr. 9, 1781, BHP, 9913, reel 27. Campbell estimated the force from Mobile at five hundred.

at 4:00 P.M. sixteen Spanish vessels crossed the bar into Pensacola Bay. Once again the cannon of the Royal Navy Redoubt kept up a steady but inaccurate fire, doing minor damage to the rigging. There were 1,637 men on the vessels: 1,400 regulars, 4 artillerymen, 25 American volunteers, 11 carabineers, 32 militiamen, 90 free mulattoes and blacks, and 75 slaves.[18] Gálvez now had 3,857 men under his command, and he could begin the attack in earnest. Campbell realized that Gálvez had only been awaiting this reinforcement to begin the attack, and in the early evening the British regulars evacuated Pensacola and took their positions in the redoubts—the Sixteenth Regiment in the Queen's Redoubt and the Sixtieth Regiment in the Prince of Wales' Redoubt.[19]

On the afternoon of March 24, all of Gálvez' troops—except two hundred Spaniards who were left to occupy Santa Rosa Island—crossed Pensacola Bay to the first of several camps. There the Spanish found themselves much more exposed to attack, mainly by the Indians, who ambushed Spanish soldiers who had gone beyond their lines on the morning of the twenty-fifth, wounding several, apparently killing two, and seizing twenty-three horses. For the next six days the Spanish explored the bay near Pensacola, seeking a proper place for a landing to establish their final camp close by Pensacola.

Chester sent John Stephenson (a member of the council) on March 27 to meet with Gálvez and discuss once again the safety of the women and children in Pensacola. Gálvez provisionally consented to a "mutual observation of certain articles referring

18. "Report of Troops Used in the Pensacola Expedition," Feb. 28, 1781, in Kinnaird, *Spain in the Mississippi Valley*, 1:421–22. Gálvez, "Diary," p. 58, indicates that 1,400 men arrived, but it is probable this is just a count of regulars. General Campbell reported the number of reinforcements as 1,338 "effective regular troops." There were sixty-four officers in the Spanish reinforcements, and since the British did not count officers as effectives in troop returns, Campbell's report contained a difference of only two men (Campbell to Clinton, Apr. 9, 1781, BHP, 9913, reel 27). Gálvez promised the Negro and mulatto slaves who fought at Pensacola several degrees of compensation. If seriously wounded, they would be freed and receive 100 pesos. If only slightly wounded, they would receive 100 pesos and the right to purchase freedom for 400 pesos. As usual, promises made to the slaves were not fulfilled. In 1785, seven of the Negroes wounded at Pensacola received 80 pesos from the Intendant Martín Navarro. All other slaves taking part in the siege of Pensacola received 8 pesos (Everett, "Free Persons of Color," pp. 42–43).

19. "Robert Farmar's Journal," p. 317.

to the security of the town of Pensacola," but when at noon on
the twenty-eighth Spanish prisoners who had escaped from the
British reported that they had been "ill-treated," the Spanish
general became enraged and sent Stephenson back to Chester,
"refusing to agree to any proposition."

The Spanish transports had arrived at a location between
Moore's Lagoon and Sutton's Lagoon by the twenty-sixth, and
the British sent out a detachment of 100 men under Captain
Byrd and 250 Indians under Cameron to meet them. Two days
later the combined British and Indian force attacked the
Spanish camp, but "with more noise than advantage." Four of
the Indians were wounded, and a few Spanish were killed and
wounded also. The Indians apparently attacked the enemy force
again at about midnight but were no more successful than they
had been earlier. Throughout the early part of the battle for
Pensacola, the Indians continued harassing attacks which ham-
pered the work of the Spanish.[20]

Gálvez prepared on March 29 to move his army across
Sutton's Lagoon closer to Fort George. The heaviest fighting up
to this point in the campaign occurred the following day. At
10:00 A.M. the Spanish column forced Captain Patrick Kennedy
and a party of Maryland Loyalists to abandon an advanced post.
Gálvez continued his movement unopposed and arrived on the
east bank of Sutton's Lagoon, where he posted sentinels and
ordered his men to begin entrenching the camp. Kennedy's
loyalists restationed themselves in Neil's Meadows—about a
mile and a quarter from Fort George and opposite the lines the
Spanish would later put up. At 2:00 P.M. a party of Indians
joined the loyalists, and together they attacked the outermost
Spanish lines. The loyalists and Indians maintained a heavy
fire for three hours after Captain Johnstone of the Royal Artillery arrived with two field pieces and one howitzer, fifty Negroes, and twenty-five men of the Sixtieth Regiment under
Lieutenant Meggs.

Gálvez, "seeing that the troops engaged were surrounded on
all sides by a class of enemies whose real advantage consists in
never coming out from the cover of the woods," sent in light
infantry and two field pieces, forcing Johnstone to withdraw

20. Ibid., pp. 317–18; Campbell to Clinton, Apr. 9, 1781, BHP, 9913, reel 27;
Gálvez, "Diary," pp. 58–60.

with his artillery.The Spanish occupied the ground, and Gálvez placed eight cannon on the lines to use against the British should they attack again during the night. Casualties were light: the British reported that the Indians brought in "1 head and a number of scalps," while Spanish records indicate "several killed and wounded." The Spanish lost three officers killed and fared somewhat worse than the Indians and British. The attackers lost one Indian killed and two Indians and one Negro slightly wounded.[21]

For the next two weeks the campaign proceeded slowly as the Spanish spent most of their time in reconnoitering the small hills northwest of Fort George and the redoubts, and moving troops into new positions. The British watched anxiously as the Spaniards moved from Sutton's Lagoon on April 2 and 3. Seventeen British deserters entered the enemy camp during this two-week period. The sailors from the *Port Royal* and *Mentor* had abandoned their vessels on March 23 and joined the defenders inside the fort. Captain Deans did not want the *Mentor* captured and, therefore, ordered his ship to an inland river where, upon the approach of the Spanish, it was burned. On April 3, the Spanish seized the *Port Royal*—which had about a hundred Spanish prisoners on board—and three other small vessels that were in the harbor. Chester sent Stephenson to Gálvez once again on the ninth to inform him that the small force of British troops in Pensacola was there to protect the inhabitants from the Indians. The same day, Chester advised the Spanish general that he had paroled eleven Spanish prisoners.[22]

The Spanish moved closer to the English on April 12. At first the British did nothing, and the Spanish began entrenching their position, just northwest of Gage Hill, placing several field pieces, and constructing a redoubt. At one o'clock the British opened fire against the new position, and three hours later the West Florida Royal Foresters (under the command of Lieutenant Joseph Pinhorn) and some Indians attempted to dislodge the Spanish.

21. "Robert Farmar's Journal," p. 318; Gálvez, "Diary," pp. 60–61; Campbell to Clinton, Apr. 9, 1781, BHP, 9913, reel 27; "Mentor's Logg Book," Mar. 23–Apr. 4, 1781.
22. Gálvez, "Diary," pp. 61–64; "Robert Farmar's Journal," pp. 318–19; Campbell to Clinton, Apr. 9, 1781, BHP, 9913, reel 27; Clowes, The Royal Navy, 4:111.

Lieutenant Pinhorn was shot in the head at the beginning of the skirmish, and the small force soon withdrew after discovering that Spanish cannon supported the enemy position. During this sally, Gálvez had gone to one of the advanced batteries to survey the situation, and a bullet went through his left hand and into his abdomen. Ezpeleta took over the command as Gálvez retired to have his wounds tended. (Within ten days Gálvez was back in active command.) While the Spanish drove the attackers from the field, they had one killed and nine wounded, including Gálvez. The British lost Lieutenant Pinhorn, and several Indians were wounded.[23]

The Spanish continued to improve their position during the next week, and the British waited. A violent thunderstorm which damaged British fortifications hit Pensacola on the fourteenth. The rain did even greater damage to the Spanish; their ammunition got wet, most of the tents collapsed (including the hospital tent), and part of their entrenchments washed away. Since they had no ammunition, Ezpeleta ordered the Spanish to use their bayonets in case of a British attack. Had the British been aware of the Spanish predicament, they probably could have successfully attacked the enemy position. But the rainstorm resulted in nothing more than discomfort for both sides.[24]

The British spotted a fleet outside Pensacola Bay on April 19, but their hopes for reinforcements from Jamaica were dashed when they received word that the fleet was fifteen ships-of-the-line, three frigates, and four tenders—all Spanish and French.[25] Spanish officials at Havana, fearing that the English were reinforcing Pensacola, had resolved to send some additional aid to Gálvez: twenty-three vessels under the command of Chief-of-Squadron Josef Solano and 1,600 Spanish soldiers under Field Marshal Juan Manuel de Cagigal. Several of the vessels were French, commanded by the Marquis de Montelle, and this fleet carried 725 French soldiers. The ten-day voyage to Pensacola had been uneventful, except that on April 16 the frigate *Unicorno* had given chase to a British vessel. The Spanish

23. "Robert Farmar's Journal," pp. 319–20; Gálvez, "Diary," pp. 64–65; Campbell to Clinton, May 12, 1781, BHP, 9918, reel 27. The Queen's Redoubt fired some grapeshot which killed one Waldeck sentry and wounded a sergeant.
24. "Robert Farmar's Journal," p. 320; Gálvez, "Diary," pp. 65–66.
25. Campbell to Clinton, May 12, 1781, BHP, 9918, reel 27.

learned later that the vessel had been the *Ulysses*, which had captured the *Unicorno* and taken it to Jamaica, thus cutting the fleet to twenty-two vessels.[26] The fleet crossed the bar at Pensacola on the twentieth and twenty-first under a sustained but ineffectual fire from the Royal Navy Redoubt. The next two days the troops disembarked: 1,600 Spanish regulars, 725 French regulars, and 1,504 seamen. With the 3,857 men Gálvez had at the beginning of the campaign, these reinforcements brought the total strength of the Spanish army to 7,686 men, compared to fewer than 2,000 defenders of Pensacola (including Indians).[27] Gálvez realized that the only way to take Pensacola without large losses was by siege, and he continued to perfect plans for the investment of the British defenses.

The British, at about noon on the twenty-second of April, observed a small reconnaissance party (including Cagigal, Gálvez, the quartermaster general, and the commandant of the artillery) on a hill near the Queen's Redoubt. The redoubt's guns opened fire on the enemy, and, with one man wounded, the Spanish withdrew. The British sent out a force of Indians, local inhabitants ("Robert Farmar's Journal" calls them "crackers"), provincials, and part of the Sixtieth Regiment to pursue the Spanish, but the enemy had retreated to its camp.

Campbell's aide-de-camp, Gordon, brought him a document, which an inhabitant had found on the twenty-second, containing a sketch of the Spanish lines and their plan of attack. The plans indicated that Gálvez intended to make seizure of the Queen's Redoubt his major objective. Accordingly, on April 23, Campbell sent forty men of the Sixtieth Regiment under Captain

26. Francisco de Miranda, "Miranda's Diary of the Siege of Pensacola, 1781," pp. 164–72, 193, hereafter cited as "Miranda's Diary." Several of the Spanish vessels were the ships that had been under the command of Calbo in the initial expedition but had returned to Havana with Calbo.

27. "Miranda's Diary," pp. 175–76; Gálvez, "Diary," p. 67. Miranda (p. 176) stated that the total Spanish and French strength was 7,803 effectives, but using the figures he gives, his math is incorrect. Solano offered the sailors (both artillery and crews) to Gálvez "in order that they might share in the glory of this conquest" (Gálvez, "Diary," p. 67). An English report listed the total opposing troops at 9,100 land force and 14,380 seamen—an unquestionably high figure ("Combined force of France & Spain at the reduction of Pensacola," n.d., Florida Miscellaneous, 1525–1821, Library of Congress, hereafter cited as Florida Miscellaneous, 1525–1821). See also "Surrender of Pensacola," May 10, 1781, Frederick Mackenzie Papers, William L. Clements Library, hereafter cited as Mackenzie Papers, and Haarmann, "The Siege of Pensacola," pp. 193–96.

Byrd, along with one hundred Indians, out about three hundred yards in front of the redoubt. At the same time, he ordered an abatis constructed to prevent, or at least hinder, an assault. Early the next morning, when the Spanish went out to survey a point northwest of the advanced redoubt where they intended to establish two batteries, the British troops and Indians attacked them. Although the Spanish reinforced the reconnaissance party and maintained their position, the attack cost them seventeen wounded and interrupted their work.[28]

For the rest of April this pattern of action continued. The Spanish opened trenches extending their lines to the northwest, while British regulars, provincials, and Indians sallied out from the fortifications in an attempt to halt the movement of the Spanish lines. The British killed thirteen Spaniards and wounded twenty-eight in skirmishes and from cannonade from the advanced redoubt, but they were unable to halt the construction of the trenches and did nothing more than annoy the attackers—thus prolonging the siege. The combined Spanish and French forces had completed their entrenchment by May 1, establishing a redoubt at the northwestern end and mounting cannon and mortars.[29] The English and Spanish bombarded each other heavily from the first to the third of May without inflicting many casualties. For example, on the third the Spanish fired 534 shot and 186 shells at the English but only killed one man and wounded two. Having completed the trenches northwest of Gage Hill, the Spanish began digging trenches eastward from the new lines to a hill in front of the Queen's Redoubt—a movement the British did not discover until the night of May 2. The following evening, Campbell ordered an attack of regulars and Indians against the Spanish works on Pine Hill, a mound about six hundred yards in front of the advanced redoubt. The force sallied forth without being detected by the Spanish, but the regulars and Indians became separated, and Campbell consequently recalled the troops.[30]

28. "Robert Farmar's Journal," pp. 321–22; "Miranda's Diary," pp. 176–77; Gálvez, "Diary," p. 68.

29. "Miranda's Diary," pp. 177–84; Gálvez, "Diary," pp. 68–71; "Robert Farmar's Journal," pp. 322–24; Campbell to Clinton, May 12, 1781, BHP, 9918, reel 27.

30. Campbell to Clinton, May 7, 1781, quoted in Rush, Battle of Pensacola, p. 99; Campbell to Clinton, May 12, 1781, BHP, 9918, reel 27; "Robert Farmar's

The next morning Campbell saw that during the night the Spanish forces had completed their entrenchments to Pine Hill and constructed a small redoubt, but had not yet had time to mount cannon. Hoping to take advantage of the lack of cannon and "observing that the enemy were so extremely cautious of exposing themselves that they could not possibly keep a good look-out," Campbell decided to attack the incomplete advanced Spanish works in hopes of surprising them. The day began as usual with an exchange of cannon fire, but at about one o'clock the British fire intensified greatly. At the same time, 120 Pennsylvania and Maryland Loyalists under Major John McDonald, and 80 Waldeckers under Lieutenant Colonel Albrecht DeHorn, sallied out of the advanced redoubt. A Spanish naval captain, Andrés Tacon, observed this movement and reported it to his superior officer, Pablo Figuerola, who chose to ignore the intelligence. The Spanish, under cover of their entrenchments, had stacked their arms and were eating lunch and "believed themselves as safe and out of risk as in the *plaza mayor* of Madrid."[31]

The two hundred loyalists and Germans advanced rapidly and launched a vigorous and effective bayonet attack against the unprepared Spanish force. They captured the small advanced redoubt and continued to the Spanish lines and redoubt on Pine Hill. The attackers soon returned to the small redoubt, where they spiked five cannon, set fire to the fascines and the trenches, and then retired to the Queen's Redoubt. Gálvez sent reinforcements under Ezpeleta, but by the time they had arrived, the loyalists and Waldeckers had already withdrawn. The Spanish had twenty killed (including two officers) and seventeen wounded (including one officer who was captured and later died). The British also captured three officers and one

Journal," p. 324; Gálvez, "Diary," pp. 71–72; "Miranda's Diary," pp. 184–85. Campbell had complained on December 15, 1779, of a lack of ordnance stores, and in his description of the defense of Pensacola he made occasional reference to this deficiency (Campbell to Germain, Dec. 15, 1779, C.O. 5/597; Campbell to Clinton, Dec. 15, 1779, BHP, 2480, reel 9). The author of "Robert Farmar's Journal" also made occasional reference to this shortage of ordnance stores when he described the British picking up shot and shell which the Spanish had fired "some of which we returned [to] the Don" (p. 324).

31. "Miranda's Diary," p. 185; Campbell to Clinton, May 12, 1781, BHP, 9918, reel 27; Campbell to Germain, May 7, 1781, quoted in Rush, *Battle of Pensacola*, p. 99.

private. The attackers had only a sergeant killed and a private wounded.[32]

The Spanish quickly repaired the damage, and for the next three days extended their trenches another 150 yards to within 500 yards of the Queen's Redoubt. The Spanish constructed two batteries along this line to play on the advanced redoubt. While the Spanish continued to expand their lines, the British maintained a bombardment all along the Spanish front, inflicting some casualties and annoying the Spanish laborers. The Spanish returned the fire upon the advanced redoubt, which by May 7 was "already in a shattered condition." The shelling damaged the Queen's Redoubt, but nightly repairs maintained it as a tenable fortification.[33]

Gálvez sent seven hundred grenadiers and light infantry against the Queen's Redoubt in the early morning hours of May 7, while another force made a diversion to keep Fort George occupied. Because of a lack of coordination, however, Gálvez called off the attack before the engagement began. One of the Spanish officers, Francisco de Miranda (better known for his efforts in behalf of Latin American independence), reported that the Spanish learned after the attack had been canceled that it had been a fortunate decision, since the English had expected such an attack. There is nothing in the British records to indicate such vigilance.[34]

The eighth of May, 1781, began like so many of the preceding days. At 6:00 A.M. the British in the Queen's Redoubt began shelling the Spanish again, and the Spanish returned the fire from two howitzers from their redoubts. Between 8:30 and 9:00 one of the shells burst just outside the open door of the magazine where the British were obtaining powder. An explosion rocked the redoubt and "in an instant reduced the body of the redoubt to a heap of rubbish." Campbell reported that "48 military [mainly Pennsylvania Loyalists], 27 seamen, and one

32. Campbell to Clinton, May 12, 1781, BHP, 9918, reel 27; "Miranda's Diary," pp. 185–88; Gálvez, "Diary," pp. 72–73. Captain Deans reported that the British lost two men killed and two wounded ("Mentor's Logg Book," May 5, 1781).
33. Campbell to Germain, May 7, 1781, quoted in Rush, *Battle of Pensacola*, p. 100; Campbell to Clinton, May 12, 1781, BHP, 9918, reel 27; Gálvez, "Diary," p. 73; "Miranda's Diary," pp. 188–89; "Robert Farmar's Journal," pp. 325–26.
34. "Miranda's Diary," pp. 189–90; Gálvez, "Diary," pp. 73–74.

Negro" were killed by the explosion and 24 others were wounded—"most of them dangerously." Captain Johnstone and the Royal Artillery repelled the first Spanish assault on the redoubt, which allowed Captain Byrd and seventy men of the Sixtieth Regiment in the Prince of Wales' Redoubt to carry off the wounded and part of the artillery. Soon Gálvez ordered a large force against the advanced redoubt, and the remaining British troops, after spiking the few pieces of artillery that remained, withdrew to the middle redoubt.[35]

The Spanish seized what was left of the Queen's Redoubt, set up batteries, and opened fire on the Prince of Wales' Redoubt. The British returned the fire, but the advanced redoubt held a commanding position, and thirty of the British defenders soon lay wounded. Realizing that he could hold out only a few more days and at the expense of many lives, at three o'clock Campbell ordered the white flag raised and proposed a truce until noon the following day.[36] Gálvez agreed to the armistice on condition of eleven "articles which must be agreed to, without which, a cessation will not be granted for a capitulation."[37] The terms were not entirely agreeable to Campbell, and he and Governor Chester worked out terms which "are nearly the same granted by the British [in the] last war to your nation at the Havana." Campbell concluded, "I trust they will not be objected to. Should they, however, be refused, contrary to my expectations, I do not consider my case desperate nor my situation past hope, and am determined to abide the chance of war, rather

35. Campbell to Clinton, May 12, 1781, BHP, 9918, reel 27; Campbell to Germain, May 12, 1781, quoted in Almon, *The Remembrancer. For the Year 1781*, part 2, p. 277; Gálvez, "Diary," p. 74. The "Diary" (p. 74) estimated the British killed at 105, while Miranda placed the figure at 108 ("Miranda's Diary," p. 192). "Robert Farmar's Journal," p. 326, stated that 85 were killed. The same author reported that the Pennsylvania Loyalists had replaced the Sixteenth Regiment inside the advanced redoubt at 6:00 P.M. on the seventh. Eelking, *Die Deutschen Hulfstruppen*, p. 19, states that a provincial deserter informed the Spanish where to fire in order to do the most damage and it was because of this guidance that the Spanish hit the magazine. There is no evidence to support this charge. See also Fred Cubberly, "Fort George (St. Michael), Pensacola," p. 228.

36. Campbell to Gálvez, May 8, 1781, C.O. 5/597 and BHP, 9922, reel 27; Campbell to Clinton, May 12, 1781, BHP, 9918, reel 27.

37. "Articles which must be agreed to . . . ," Gálvez to Campbell, May 8, 1781, BHP, 9922, reel 27 and C.O. 5/597. Hostages were also exchanged: Lieutenant Meggs of the Sixtieth Regiment went to the Spanish and Lieutenant Kenny of the Irish Brigade came to the British. "Robert Farmar's Journal," p. 327.

than comply with the terms you have been pleased to offer."
The next morning, Campbell proclaimed to Gálvez that "we are
in possession of works that would cost blood and require time
to reduce."[38] Gálvez did not agree to the terms Campbell and
Chester proposed, but both parties finally sat down and concluded acceptable articles of capitulation. The articles were
similar to others granted in West Florida: the British surrendered the entire province of West Florida, and in return they
received the full honors of war; noncombatants were protected;
slaves were restored to their rightful owners; the prisoners were
to be transported as quickly as possible to any location they
chose, except St. Augustine and Jamaica; all the soldiers kept
their own personal baggage; and so forth.[39]

The formal surrender took place at 3:00 P.M. on the afternoon
of May 10, 1781, whereby all of what was once British West
Florida became Spanish again. The troops marched out with
drums beating and colors flying and laid down their weapons to
the superior arms of Spain. The following day, the 139 men of
the Royal Navy Redoubt turned over that post to the Spanish.[40]

Considering the number of troops involved, the casualties
were light on both sides. The British had 90 killed (45 of them
Pennsylvania Loyalists), 46 wounded, and 83 deserting (22 of
whom were West Florida Royal Foresters). The Spanish, on the
other hand, had 96 killed and 202 wounded (including seamen). The Spanish reported taking 1,113 prisoners, while a
British note indicates there were only 953 total in the garrison
when it surrendered. If the 173 total killed and deserting
among the British forces are subtracted from the original 1,186 in
Pensacola, however, the total number of regulars, Waldeckers,
provincials, and seamen taken prisoner was probably 1,013. The
Spanish force captured a sizeable amount of booty. An inven-
tory made after the siege of Pensacola lists 4 mortars, 143

38. Campbell to Gálvez, May 8, 1781, BHP, 9922, reel 27; Campbell to Gálvez,
May 9, 1781, quoted in Caughey, Gálvez, p. 211.

39. Gálvez, "Diary," p. 75; Articles of Capitulation, May 9, 1781, BHP, 9916,
reel 27 and MPA,SD, 1:414–23; Gálvez, "Diary," pp. 75–83.

40. Surrender of Pensacola, May 10, 1781, Mackenzie Papers; Gálvez, "Diary,"
p. 75. The Spanish had decided not to attempt to take the Royal Navy Redoubt; it
would have been extremely difficult to take by land, and, despite its threatening
appearance, the battery caused more noise than damage (Faye, "British and
Spanish Fortifications," p. 278).

cannon, 6 howitzers, 40 swivel guns, thousands of artillery cartridges, shells, bombs, and grenades, 298 hundred-weights of gunpowder, and tens of thousands of infantry stores such as guns, bayonets, sabers, cartridges, flints, and bullets.[41]

According to Article 1 of the capitulation, the Spanish agreed to transport the prisoners to any British post they chose, except St. Augustine and Jamaica. The British embarked on Spanish transports on June 1, and left Pensacola four days later. After a fifteen-day voyage to Cuba and a ten-day layover there to take on provisions and water, the British prisoners left Havana on June 30 and arrived in New York on July 12, 1781.[42]

Just before the transports left Pensacola, Lieutenant Colonel

---

41. "Return of Killed & Wounded &c," May 10, 1781, BHP, 9917, reel 27; Gálvez, "Diary," p. 75; "Combined force of France and Spain at the reduction of Pensacola," Florida Miscellaneous, 1525–1821; "Statement of the Arms and Munitions of War," in Gálvez, "Diary," p. 84.

42. "Robert Farmar's Journal," p. 327. Campbell reported he left Pensacola June 7, arrived in Havana on June 19, and finally reached New York on July 14 (Campbell to [Germain?], Aug. 12, 1781, W.O. 34/136, University of Florida photostat). On the voyage to New York, a rebel privateer captured one of the vessels, the St. Joseph and St. Joachim, carrying Pennsylvania Loyalists, but after some delay it arrived in New York on July 25, 1781. "Report of Captain Swift . . . ," July 27, 1781, Adm. 1/491; "Report of William Woodside . . . ," July 27, 1781, ibid.; "Report of Don Gaspar de Miranda . . . ," July 27, 1781, ibid.; Gentleman's Magazine 51 (1781):485. Apparently another of the vessels, the Sally, was captured later with six prisoners on board, but the records are not clear on this matter (Ford, Journals, pp. 1009–11). Governor Chester went to Charlestown on a flag of truce directly from Pensacola (Chester to Germain, July 2, 1781, C.O. 5/596). According to the articles of capitulation, the British were "not to serve against Spain or her allies" (Articles of Capitulation, May 9, 1781, BHP, 9916, reel 27). As Spain did not have an alliance with the Americans, the British interpreted the capitulation as not prohibiting the use of the troops against the American army. Upon learning of these terms, the Americans were upset at Gálvez' apparent disregard of their interests. William Sharpe to Christian Febiger, July 19, 1781, quoted in Burnett, Letters, 6:150; Edmund Randolph to George Webb, July 23, 1781, ibid., p. 151; Virginia delegates to the Governor of Virginia [Thomas Nelson], July 24, 1781, ibid., pp. 152–53; Joseph Jones to Thomas Jefferson, July 24, 1781, ibid., pp. 153–54; Joseph Jones to John Taliaferro, July 24, 1781, ibid., pp. 154–55; Richard Potts to Samuel Hughes, July 24, 1781, ibid., pp. 155–56; James Lovell to John Jay, Aug. 15, 1781, ibid., p. 187; Samuel Huntingdon to George Washington, July 2, 1781, ibid., p. 132. Referring to this matter, Washington wrote, "I have no doubt, from General Gálvez's well-known attachment to the cause of America, that he would have refused the articles, which have been deemed exceptionable, had there not been very powerful reasons to induce his acceptance of them" (Washington to Francisco Rendon, n.d., quoted in Cubberly, "Fort George," p. 229n). Fortunately for Spanish-American relations, after the troops arrived in New York, they performed mainly common garrison duties and saw very little, if any, action.

Arturo O'Neill (whom Gálvez had appointed governor of West Florida) ordered Brigade Major James Campbell and Captain Robert Deans to remain behind as hostages. According to the articles of capitulation, the British surrendered all of West Florida to Spain. The British subjects at Natchez had rebelled against Spain, however, on orders from General Campbell. Gálvez considered this action a breach of the articles of capitulation, and, consequently, felt himself authorized to keep the entire Pensacola garrison prisoner. Realizing it was not to his benefit to keep all of the troops, and not wanting to bear the expense of maintaining them, Gálvez ordered all of the British to embark except Major Campbell and Captain Deans. This action, Gálvez explained, he took "in order to show my court that my orders were not to be disobeyed or my contracts flouted without unpleasant results."[43] Naturally, a disagreement developed between General Campbell and Gálvez over the retention of Campbell and Deans. The two commanding officers carried on a bitter correspondence, freely denouncing each other. Soon the disagreement spread beyond the two generals as other men on both sides took up the argument. Spain sent James Campbell and Robert Deans to Havana, and the dispute lasted throughout the remainder of the war. The Spanish then carried Deans to Madrid, but ordered Campbell back to Mobile. Apparently the Spanish exchanged Deans but kept Major Campbell a prisoner at least until the fall of 1783. The episode reveals a petty side of both commanding generals—a pettiness that had been generally absent in the chivalrous conduct of the siege of Pensacola.[44]

43. Gálvez to Clinton, Dec. 30, 1781, MPA,SD, 1:449–50 and BHP, 4000, reel 13; Arturo O'Neill to Campbell, June 5, 1781, C.O. 5/597; Deans to Vice Admiral Marriott Arbuthnot, June 1, 1781, C.O. 5/132; Chester to Germain, June 2, 1781, BHP, 3541, reel 12. In July 1782, Campbell replied to Gálvez that the charges were so false that "I disdain the thoughts of disavowing" them. He continued, "I glory in recollecting, that the handful of gallant and intrepid officers and men I had the happiness to command resisted a multitude of foes (in the combined forces of France and Spain) in a manner I leave to the chaste pen of a candid historian to relate, for mine I confess inadequate to the task of doing justice to their merit" (Campbell to Gálvez, July 17, 1782, BHP, 5082, reel 16). The Natchez rebellion will be discussed in chap. 9.

44. Archibald Campbell to Lt. Gen. John Campbell, May 21, 1782, BHP, 4631, reel 15; Robert Ross (Deputy Commissary General of Prisoners) to Lt. Gen. Alexander Leslie, July 15, 1782, BHP, 9996, reel 27 and C.O. 5/107; Lt. Gen. John Campbell to Sir Guy Carleton, Oct. 5, 1782, BHP, 5795, reel 18 and C.O. 5/107;

Pensacola had fallen to Spain and along with it all of British West Florida. Campbell, however, praised the conduct of all the troops under his command at West Florida, including regulars, royal artillery, Waldeckers, provincials, and seamen: "In general, my Lord [Germain], notwithstanding the mixture of corps, and the consequent incohesion and disunity of action that might have thence been apprehended, yet I have the pleasure to say, that the handful of troops, both officers and soldiers, under my command, seemed animated with vigor and spirit to the last, and eager to distinguish themselves; even the dispiriting circumstances of frequent desertions, appeared not to affect or discourage those who remained, but to excite to vengeance and resentment."[45]

Campbell feared that the home government would blame him for the fall of Pensacola. He lamented his fate at having been employed in West Florida, "but, I trust, that the calamities that have befallen West Florida will not be imputed to me."[46] The preceding statement came from Campbell's "Publick Letter" reporting the surrender of Pensacola. Nine days later, reviewing the situation of the province when he went to West Florida and the aid that the province received after his arrival, he confided to Clinton in a private letter, "What interpretation can the whole bear, but that it was considered no object of national concern, and left as a gewgaw to amuse and divert the ambition of Spain and prevent it from attending to objects of greater moment and importance." Asserting that he had done all that he possibly could to defend Pensacola against a force superior in number, "yet (satisfied that a soldier's reputation is liable to calumny and detraction) I feel the keenest and most sensible anxiety from your Excellency's approbation of my conduct."[47] The approval Campbell sought was forthcoming from Germain: "Unavoidable as the loss of that province seems to have been, under the circumstances of inequality of force to defend it, which you have represented; yet it is a consideration that gives

Archibald Campbell to Evan Nepean, Aug. 29, 1783, C.O. 5/598; Germain to Maj. Gen. John Campbell, Sept. 15, 1781, C.O. 5/244 or BHP, 3783, reel 13.

45. Campbell to Germain, May 12, 1781, quoted in Almon, *The Remembrancer. For the Year 1781*, part 2, pp. 279–80. See also Campbell to Clinton, May 12, 1781, BHP, 9918, reel 27.

46. Campbell to Clinton, May 12, 1781, BHP, 9918, reel 27.

47. Campbell to Clinton, May 21, 1781, BHP, 9919, reel 27.

great satisfaction to His Majesty, that the intrepidity and bravery of the officers and men under your conduct and example made so gallant a defense, and were able so long to resist the combined force of His enemies so superior and formidable both by land and sea. I have therefore much pleasure in signifying to you His Majesty's entire approbation of your conduct, as well as of the behavior of both officers and men on that occasion."[48]

Campbell's direction of the defense of Pensacola merited the king's approval. The general could have done more, namely, constructed an adequate battery on Santa Rosa Island and used regular troops in addition to mainly Indians and provincials in harassing the Spanish forces (particularly before the reinforcements arrived from Havana). Yet, although Campbell is not without blame, he and the men under his command rendered a remarkable defense of Pensacola. They withstood a siege of over two months' duration and even then would not have surrendered except for the unfortunate explosion in the Queen's Redoubt. After that accident, Fort George was untenable, and surrender was a necessity.

The major share of blame for the fall of Pensacola must rest with the home government. Pensacola never received adequate reinforcements, ordnance stores never arrived, and positive orders for a strong naval reinforcement from Jamaica never left Whitehall. With even two or three strong ships of war in Pensacola Bay, it is unlikely that the Spanish could have forced an entrance. Without the Spanish fleet, it would have been virtually impossible for an attack against Pensacola to succeed. It is possible troops could have disembarked elsewhere and marched overland to Pensacola, but they could not have carried the artillery, munitions, and supplies necessary for a siege through the swamps and forests surrounding Pensacola.

The Spanish siege was successful. Great Britain no longer had a foothold in West Florida. The former colony was no longer an active participant in the American Revolution or in the Anglo-Spanish war, but the fate of the British who remained in West Florida and of the province itself was still to be decided.

48. Germain to Campbell, Sept. 15, 1781, C.O. 5/244.

9

"Conquered by Its Own Force"

Pensacola surrendered in May 1781, two years before the general peace settlement. These two years in West Florida were filled with intrigue and rebellion as England, Spain, and the United States pondered the final disposition of the remote region. The most notable event of these years was the revolt in mid-1781 of the English settlers at Natchez against Spanish rule. This rebellion is primarily a chapter in Spanish history, and its main significance, as far as British West Florida is concerned, rests with the consequent exodus of some of the residents around Natchez and the detention of the leaders of the rebellion.[1] After the capitulation of Baton Rouge, which included the surrender of Natchez to Spain, some of the settlers in the Natchez district had sought aid from Campbell to attempt to regain the territory. Campbell did nothing to encourage this small group of settlers until mid-March of 1781. At that time, Christopher Marr came from Natchez once again seeking aid,

1. The "Natchez Rebellion" is covered well by John W. Caughey in chap. 13, "The Natchez Rebellion," of his biography of Gálvez. His article "The Natchez Rebellion of 1781 and Its Aftermath" is almost identical. My treatment of this subject will be sketchy and will draw much from Caughey's work. See also Wilbur H. Siebert, "The Loyalists in West Florida and the Natchez District," pp. 477–79; Stanley Faye, "The Arkansas Post of Louisiana: Spanish Domination," pp. 664–79; D. C. Corbitt, "James Colbert and the Spanish Claims to the East Bank of the Mississippi." Esteban Miró to Gálvez, June 6, 1781, and accompanying declaration of "an Englishman named Gray," MPA,SD, 1:424–34; Jack D. L. Holmes, "Juan de la Villebeuvre: Spain's Commandant of Natchez during the American Revolution," pp. 107–10.

and, since the Spanish had already begun the siege of Pensacola, Campbell felt that a diversion at Natchez might help save Pensacola. Consequently, Campbell issued five blank commissions for captains of "such volunteer inhabitants as you can procure to serve under your command, who prefer the British government to tyrannic despotism and rule, and are willing to risk their lives for the attainment thereof."[2] Marr returned to Natchez and, with John and Philip Alston and John Turner, planned skillfully and perhaps unscrupulously to seize Fort Panmure. They persuaded John Blommart, one of the most respected men in the Natchez region, to lead them. A force of about two hundred settlers and Indians began their attack against Fort Panmure on April 22. A combination of military might and deception finally led to the capitulation of the post in early May.[3]

The insurgents at Natchez soon received word that Pensacola had surrendered and that all of West Florida—except Natchez—was in the hands of Spain. Blommart realized that he could not hope to hold out against Spanish forces now that Campbell had surrendered to Gálvez. Many of the settlers fled from the region, but Blommart and a majority of the settlers remained to protect the fort and to turn it back over to the Spanish. Louisiana militiamen reoccupied Fort Panmure on June 22 and 23 and sent Blommart, William Eason, Samuel Bingamin, and William Williams to New Orleans as prisoners. The Spanish sought other leaders of the revolt, some of whom they eventually captured.

With the resurrender of Fort Panmure the Natchez rebellion ended, but the settlers were just beginning to feel the consequences of the unsuccessful revolt. More of the terrified English settlers fled the Natchez region, some escaping to live with the

2. Blank commission, Mar. 17, 1781, Voucher #8 of the claim of John Blommart, Mar. 8, 1790, A.O. 13/2 and A.O. 12/76. A copy of this commission is in Kinnaird, *Spain in the Mississippi Valley*, 1:424. Campbell to Clinton, July 17, 1781, BHP, 9925, reel 27.

3. "Summons at Fort Panmure," May 2, 1781, BHP, 9922, reel 27 and C.O. 5/597. Copies of the articles of capitulation are in the same two sources. Although it is not clear whether Blommart raised the volunteer companies before or after the initial rebellion, he raised eight companies (including one artillery company and one "troop of horse") with 448 men ("A General Muster Roll of the Natchez Volunteers . . . ," in the claim of John Blommart, Mar. 8, 1790, A.O. 13/2).

Choctaws, a larger group fleeing to the Chickasaw tribes, and a small party of about twelve families fleeing the region by marching overland to British posts in Georgia, the Carolinas, and East Florida. Generally speaking, however, the Spanish treatment was surprisingly lenient. The Spaniards included all but the leaders of the revolt in a general amnesty. Toward the leaders they were harsh; despite Campbell's commissions, which gave legal sanction to the effort as a military venture, the Spanish considered the attack a rebellion and treated the leaders as rebels guilty of treason and meriting death.

Throughout most of the remainder of the Anglo-Spanish war, British officials made efforts to obtain the release of Blommart and his cohorts from detention in New Orleans.[4] Perhaps the most effective attempt to gain their release was by James Colbert, who had lived for many years among the Chickasaws. Leading a group of white men and Chickasaws, Colbert raided Spanish vessels on the Mississippi River and sought to exchange captured Spaniards for the British prisoners. On May 2, 1782, his force captured a boat on which Madam Cruzat—the wife of the Spanish commander at St. Louis—and her four sons were passengers. Colbert soon allowed Madam Cruzat and part of the prisoners to proceed to New Orleans, where the Spanish were to release Blommart and his fellow prisoners in exchange. The Spanish, however, considered Colbert a rebel and did not honor the agreement. By allowing the prisoners to go to New Orleans on a "parole of honor," Colbert lost his best opportunity to secure the release of the Natchez leaders. He continued to raid on the Mississippi, but his chance for success was gone.[5] Finally, after England, France, and Spain had drawn up preliminary articles of peace, in April 1783, Gálvez ordered the release of the prisoners, and the matter came to an end.[6]

While the Natchez insurrection marked the end of open

4. The correspondence between Campbell and Gálvez over the Natchez revolt is in C.O. 5/597.

5. The role of Colbert in the efforts to obtain the release of the British prisoners is covered well in Caughey, *Gálvez*, pp. 228–42; Corbitt, "James Colbert"; Faye, "The Arkansas Post," pp. 670–79; Silvestre L'Abbadie to Miró, May 22, 1782, in Kinnaird, *Spain in the Mississippi Valley*, 2:15; Carlos de Grand-Pré to Miró, May 26, 1782, ibid., pp. 16–18; Martín Navarro to José de Gálvez, June 4, 1782, ibid., pp. 18–34.

6. Gálvez to Prince William, Duke of Lancaster, Apr. 6, 1783, MPA,SD, 2:1–2; William Henry [Prince William] to Gálvez, Apr. 13, 1783, ibid., p. 3.

fighting against the Spanish in what was once British West Florida, it by no means ended British intrigue in the area. Throughout the remainder of the Anglo-Spanish war and even after the conclusion of the war, many ex–West Floridians and others attempted to induce England to retake West Florida as a haven for the loyalists. The desire for land speculation, anxiety to regain lands and possessions lost when Spain captured the province, and plans eventually to unite British-held Canada and West Florida through the Ohio Valley as a check on the rebellious states all militated in favor of such a venture.

From the capitulation of Pensacola to the peace in 1783, British Indian commissaries in the Southern Department constantly reported the weak state of Spanish defenses in West Florida.[7] These reports apparently had their desired effect, for several Englishmen proposed plans for expeditions against Spanish West Florida and Louisiana. Farquhar Bethune urged Lieutenant General Alexander Leslie, senior military officer in the South, to allow him to raise "one or two troops of light horse" from among the Natchez refugees living with the Choctaws to act with the Indians against the Spanish.[8] A person living in London identified only as "A.Z." proposed the reduction of West Florida and Louisiana with "a view to provide an asylum for our unfortunate American friends, as well to promote the commercial interests of this country." Proclaiming himself "an advocate for the betrayed loyalists of America," the anonymous "A.Z." asserted that a force of 3,500 men— mainly provincials—with a few ships could take the area within three months. The author's motives went beyond love for the "betrayed loyalists," however: "The advantages that would result to this country from the possession of those extensive and fertile regions are immense. The Indian trade would be solely ours; our manufactures would find an easy vent into Mexico; to the loyalists who would immediately settle there, would soon be added . . . the crowds of emigrants from the revolted colonies, seeking, on the fertile banks of the

7. Thomas Browne to Clinton, Dec. 28, 1781, C.O. 5/82; Browne to Carleton, Feb. 23, 1783, BHP, 6953, reel 20; Browne to Thomas Townshend, Feb. 25, 1783, C.O. 5/82; Alexander McGillivray to Browne, Apr. 10, 1783, ibid., and BHP, 10085, reel 28; "Strength of the Spanish Garrisons and Outposts in West Florida and Louisiana," in John Graham's letter of Sept. 28, 1783, C.O. 5/82.

8. Bethune to Lt. Gen. Alexander Leslie, Jan. 19, 1782, C.O. 5/82.

Mississippi, refuge from oppressive government and heavy taxes. The quantities of rice, tobacco, indigo, and hemp, that might be produced in soil and climate so eminently favorable to the culture of those valuable articles, would soon compensate the loss of our southern provinces. No country in the world is better adapted for making pitch, tar, and turpentine; nor does any in America more abound in timber for shipbuilding." Indian commissary William McIntosh urged in the spring of 1783 that "God send a few frigates round and have that province [West Florida] retaken to make us easy."[9]

The most ambitious and most advanced intrigue was that of Lord John Murray, Earl of Dunmore and ex-governor of Virginia. Dunmore returned to America in December 1781, landing in Charleston in the company of Alexander Ross, late of West Florida. At the urging of Ross and others (several West Floridians were in Charleston, including Governor Chester), he began advocating an attack on West Florida to bring it back under British control. Dunmore felt such an undertaking would have several salutary effects. It would provide a home for dispossessed and fleeing loyalists, allow West Floridians to regain their homes and possessions, and, not incidentally, allow Dunmore to gain new lands for speculation to replace the four million acres he had lost in the Ohio Valley.[10]

John Cruden, "Commissioner for Forfeited Estates," proposed to Dunmore early in January 1782 that the governor could arm the 10,000 Negroes he could easily raise in South Carolina, rid the colony of rebels, and open all of South Carolina as a loyalist haven. Dunmore had used black troops earlier in Virginia, and he was not averse to using them again. He sought Clinton's approval to raise the black troops with white provincial officers ("who are swarming in the streets here perfectly idle") and noncommissioned officers, "now and then" filling the latter positions "with Black People, as their services should entitle them to it." Such a force of Negro troops along with white

9. "A.Z." to Lord Thurlow, Oct. 9, 1782, Shelburne Papers; William McIntosh to Browne, Apr. 14, 1783, C.O. 5/82. For more information on British efforts to regain West Florida, see J. Leitch Wright, Jr., "British Designs on the Old Southwest: Foreign Intrigue on the Florida Frontier, 1783–1803."

10. For a full discussion of Dunmore's intrigue, see J. Leitch Wright, Jr., "Lord Dunmore's Loyalist Asylum in the Floridas." See also Germain to Clinton, Oct. 3, 1781, C.O. 5/244.

loyalists was the only hope left for South Carolina. Seven years of war had proved that regulars could not do the job; "this country must now be conquered by its own force, or not at all."[11]

Anxious to see West Florida regained, Robert Ross described West Florida and Louisiana to Dunmore and proposed a plan of attack on the Spanish territory. In his letter of March 3, 1782, he gave Dunmore needed information.[12] Five days later, Ross sent Dunmore additional intelligence about the Natchez region and its settlers. Dunmore urged the home government to undertake the conquest of West Florida and Louisiana in order to provide an asylum for the loyalists. Five months later, Dunmore reviewed the situation and his actions, outlined the advantages to be gained from such a conquest, and recommended the expeditious implementation of his plans. He continued to urge the adoption of his proposal throughout 1782 and 1783, but the home government never fully embraced the scheme.[13]

Even after 1783, Dunmore and others continued to intrigue in an attempt to regain West Florida. Many of the local Indian agents (who were loyalists) remained in the area and continued to exert on the Indians and in the South strong influence for the British cause. Thus, Great Britain maintained a tenuous control which encouraged men like Dunmore to continue to scheme for complete domination.[14]

The 1783 Anglo-American Treaty of Paris ended the Ameri-

11. John Cruden to Dunmore, Jan. 5, 1782, C.O. 5/175; Dunmore to Clinton, Feb. 2, 1782, ibid.; Dunmore to Germain, Feb. 5, 1782, ibid.

12. Robert Ross to Dunmore, Mar. 3, 1782, ibid., and Chalmers Papers. See also "Observations on the Importance of Louisiana to Great Britain, with a state of the Force now actually in it, and some hints which may be useful should an attempt be made to reduce that colony and to annex it to his Majesty's Dominions," BHP, 5937, reel 18; Jack D. L. Holmes, "Robert Ross' Plan for an English Invasion of Louisiana in 1782."

13. Ross to Dunmore, Mar. 8, 1782, C.O. 5/175; Dunmore to Germain, Mar. 30, 1782, ibid.; Dunmore to Thomas Townshend, Aug. 24, 1782, Viscount Sydney Papers, William L. Clements Library, hereafter cited as Sydney Papers. James Bruce—late collector of customs in Pensacola—supported Dunmore's plans and, as an eighteen-year resident of West Florida, offered his observations on the state of the province (Bruce to [Shelburne?], Aug. 22, 1782, Shelburne Papers).

14. Wright, "Lord Dunmore," pp. 375–79; Wright, "British Designs," pp. 266–67. See also Wright, Britain and the American Frontier, 1783–1815, pp. 57–65.

can Revolution, and the accompanying treaties among England, France, and Spain crushed any real chance of success for British intrigue in West Florida.[15] The fate of West Florida was under consideration long before the end of the war, even before Spain entered the war. Adam Smith (author of *The Wealth of Nations*) wrote in early 1778: "If . . . we should restore Canada to France and the two Floridas to Spain; we should render our own colonies the natural enemies of those two monarchies and consequently the natural allies of Great Britain. Those splendid, but unprofitable acquisitions of the late war, left our colonies no other enemies to quarrel with but their mother country. By restoring those acquisitions to their ancient masters, we should certainly revive old enmities, and probably old friendships. Even without this restitution, tho' Canada, Nova Scotia, and the two Floridas were all given up to our rebellious colonies, or were all conquered by them, yet the similarity of language and manners would in most cases dispose the Americans to prefer our alliance to that of any other nation."[16]

A year later, the rebel William Henry Drayton reported to the Continental Congress that the Minister of France, Conrad Alexandre Gérard, had stated that Spain wished to close the navigation of the Mississippi River, to gain possession of the Floridas, and to exclude Great Britain as neighbors in the area.[17] James Chalmers, commander of the Maryland Loyalists, offered as his opinion in May 1779 that "this province [West Florida] appears necessary to Spain, who at least seems invariably attached to it; wherefore . . . I would most humbly suggest a wish that Great Britain in exchange for Puerto Rico would cede East and West Florida."[18] Thirty-six London merchants (who had been engaged

15. For a discussion of the peace negotiations and settlement, see Richard B. Morris, *The Peacemakers: The Great Powers and American Independence*, and Samuel Flagg Bemis, *The Diplomacy of the American Revolution*, pp. 228–64; Vincent T. Harlow, *The Founding of the Second British Empire, 1763–1793*, 1:279, 304–8, 338, 354–56, 358–60, 436–37.

16. Adam Smith, "Adam Smith on the American Revolution: An Unpublished Memorial," p. 718.

17. "William Henry Drayton, Memorandum of Conference with the Minister of France," Feb. 15, 1779, in Burnett, *Letters*, 4:69–70. See also Ford, *Journals*, 16:114–16.

18. James Chalmers to Lord Rawdon and [John André], May 21, 1779, Clinton Papers. Undersecretary of State for America William Knox also urged giving up West Florida in order to please Spain and perhaps lead to an alliance ("Peace or War," Oct. 14, 1779, William Knox Papers).

in trade with West Florida) and some ex-residents of the province petitioned Shelburne in late October 1782 to consider seriously the restoration of West Florida to the British Empire as a refuge for loyalists.[19]

The preliminary articles of peace which the English and American negotiators signed in Paris on November 30, 1782, contained a curious provision concerning West Florida. Article 2 called for the southern boundary of the United States to run from the Mississippi River along the thirty-first parallel to the Apalachicola River. This boundary line was the same as that set in the peace treaty ending the French and Indian War in 1763. The negotiators, however, added a "Separate Article" to the preliminary treaty: "It is hereby understood and agreed, that in case Great Britain at the conclusion of the present war, shall recover or be put in possession of West Florida, the line of north boundary between the said province and the United States, shall be a line drawn from the mouth of the River Yazoo, where it unites with the Mississippi, due east to the River Apalachicola."[20]

When the Spanish and English negotiators had concluded preliminary articles of peace between their respective countries, Spain had retained possession of West Florida. As a result, the "Separate Article" was meaningless and was not even included in the definitive Treaty of Paris signed between England and the United States on September 3, 1783.[21]

In the treaty with Spain, England did not define the boundary of West Florida. The United States interpreted the boundary to

19. Memorial to Shelburne, Oct. 31, 1782, Shelburne Papers.

20. "Separate Article," Nov. 30, 1782, British Museum, Additional MSS, 36596. A copy of the preliminary treaty, including the "Separate Article," is in Bemis, Diplomacy, pp. 259–64, and Morris, The Peacemakers, p. 552. For parliamentary debate over the preliminary articles of peace concerning West Florida, see Hansard, Parliamentary History, 23:378, 400, 414, 448–50, 467, 473. The Continental Congress discussed the "Separate Article" at least twice, but there is no record that they ever took any action (Ford, Journals, 24:193, 25:714–15; Morris, The Peacemakers, pp. 441–43). George III's ideas concerning the fate of West Florida are in Sir John William Fortescue, ed., The Correspondence of King George the Third from 1760 to December 1783, 6:167–68, 170, 182–83, 192.

21. Bemis, Diplomacy, p. 251. A copy of the treaty between England and Spain is in Francis G. Davenport and Charles O. Paullin, eds., European Treaties Bearing on the History of the United States and Its Dependencies, 4:158–61.

be the thirty-first parallel, as agreed to in the Treaty of Paris. Spain, however, chose to set the northern border at least as far north as it had been throughout the British period—from the mouth of the Yazoo River eastward. This discrepancy quickly led to friction between the United States and Spain, and a controversy developed which lasted until 1795 when the two countries agreed to the Pinckney Treaty (Treaty of San Lorenzo).[22]

At the end of the war, Britain's most pressing problem concerning West Florida was the fate of the loyalists whom the Spanish had evicted from the colony. The home government had first to identify the loyalists and then decide whether, as victims of the war with Spain rather than of the American rebellion, they should be compensated for their losses by England. Specifically, should the home government treat them the same as loyalists from the other colonies? England proved slow in providing an answer.

22. See Isaac Joslin Cox, *The West Florida Controversy, 1798–1813; A Study in American Diplomacy*, chap. 1; Samuel Flagg Bemis, *Pinckney's Treaty: America's Advantage from Europe's Distress, 1783–1800*.

10

"The Betrayed Loyalists of America" or Loyal by Default?

In recent years we have witnessed a rebirth of interest in loyalist studies as historians have attempted to explain why some men remain loyal to a cause when their neighbors are changing allegiance. In the case of West Florida, not all residents of the colony can be included under the nebulous term of "loyalist." The military and high-ranking civil officials cannot be considered tories since their positions precluded any other loyalty. The immigrants who fled to West Florida from the colonies in rebellion after 1775 are also omitted as it was the refugees' loyalty to England that had caused them to seek sanctuary in the colony. The West Florida loyalists, then, were the civilian population who had arrived in the province before 1775; it was they who were forced to confront the issue of loyalty.

The West Florida loyalists shared little with their loyal brethren in the colonies in revolt. The ideological conflicts which some writers discuss were almost totally absent. The decision to rebel or remain loyal was only once briefly forced upon them. Religion, wealth, occupation, and other factors generally used to describe a loyalist had little meaning in West Florida as there were other overriding conditions. Factors were present in the colony which set it apart from the thirteen colonies in rebellion. The province was not unique in the British Empire, for a few

225

other colonies (particularly East Florida) shared some of the distinctive characteristics of West Florida.[1]

The correspondence of the day indicates that residents of the colony felt the frontier colony was of dubious loyalty. Indian agent Robert Taitt asserted in May 1777 that "excepting the army and navy, the number of loyalists I believe is very small." A month later, John Blommart reported that he did not believe there were five men in Natchez loyal to the king. John Stuart felt there were "few persons fit to be trusted" in Pensacola. After Willing's raid down the Mississippi, William Dunbar confided to his diary that "one half of the inhabitants were in the American interest, which circumstance being well known to the loyal part of the people, was the means of tying up their hands and preventing their attempts to oppose the banditti." The most severe indictment came from General Campbell, who on more than one occasion complained, "I find the inhabitants in general, self-interested and without public spirit, whose minds

1. Robert M. Calhoon, The Loyalists in Revolutionary America, 1760–1781; Claude H. Van Tyne, "Sovereignty in the American Revolution: An Historical Study"; Max Savelle, "Nationalism and Other Loyalties in the American Revolution"; John W. Blassingame, "American Nationalism and Other Loyalties in the Southern Colonies, 1763–1775"; Leonard W. Labaree, "Nature of American Loyalism," and Conservatism in Early American History; Moses Coit Tyler, "The Party of the Loyalists in the American Revolution"; William A. Benton, Whig-Loyalism: An Aspect of Political Ideology in the American Revolutionary Era. See also Mary Beth Norton, "The Loyalist Critique of the Revolution." What was a loyalist? To answer the query in the broadest sense would require a total evaluation of loyalist backgrounds, interest, sympathies, and so forth. But in a narrower sense, the question poses the problem of a workable definition. The patriot definition of a tory was simple: "A tory is a thing whose head is in England, and its body in America, and its neck ought to be stretched" (Claude H. Van Tyne, The Loyalists in the American Revolution, p. 192). The political scientist Martin Grodzins argues persuasively that "loyalties are a part of every individual's life because they serve his basic needs and functions" (Grodzins, "Functions of Loyalty," in G. N. D. Evans, ed., Allegiance in America: The Case of the Loyalists, p. 177). What then set the loyalists of the American Revolution apart from the rebels? William Nelson writes that to define the tories simply as "people who remained attached politically" to Great Britain would "distort their outlook and . . . ignore the necessities of their case" as many of them saw the broader problem of determining the kinds of institutions America would have (Nelson, The American Tory, p. 1). Such an inclusive description may be accurate for the established colonies, but for frontier provinces such as West Florida, the argument is too sophisticated and takes into account factors which were not present. Probably the best definition for West Florida is the simplistic and perhaps naive statement, similar to the patriot definition: "Tories were simply those who remained actively or passively loyal to George III" (Brown, The King's Friends, p. 252).

are only attached to gain and their private concerns. In short nothing can be had from them . . . but at an enormous extravagant price, and personal service on general principles of national defense is too generous and exalted for their conceptions."[2]

While the indictments against the people of West Florida are predominant, the records also reveal a few letters of approbation. Early in the Revolution, Governor Chester bragged that "ever since the unhappy differences between Great Britain, and her colonies have subsisted, I have always found that the conduct of the refractory provinces has been much disapproved by His Majesty's faithful subjects of the government committed to my care, who have viewed with the utmost concern the unwarrantable proceedings, and acts of disobedience into which most of the colonies have been very unfortunately misled."[3] After the capitulation of Pensacola, Campbell had kind words about his troops, including the provincials, but it can be argued that this change of attitude was a justification of his defense. He said nothing about the civilian population. The contemporary written evidence indicates overwhelmingly that West Florida was not a "loyal" colony at all, but that, on the contrary, the civilian population was attached to the American cause. It should be remembered, however, that most of these letters are in the official correspondence and were perhaps slanted in an effort to obtain reinforcements for the colony. Also, most of these letters were written before the loyalty of the citizens was tested by the Spanish. Fortunately, the historian of British West Florida can draw on more than correspondence and diaries.

While most of the West Florida inhabitants were loyal, there is no denying that there were disloyal elements present. Willing's raid was an invasion led by a former resident of West Florida which drew strength from part of the civilian popula-

2. Taitt to Browne, May 23, 1777, C.O. 5/558; Robert McGillivray and Robert Welch to Bethune, June 4, 1777, C.O. 5/78; Stuart to Howe, Aug. 23, 1777, BHP, 649, reel 2; Rowland, William Dunbar, p. 62; Campbell to Germain, Sept. 14, 1779, C.O. 5/597.
3. Chester to Dartmouth, Aug. 5, 1775, C.O. 5/592. Harry Alexander, a loyalist who had fled from St. Vincent to the Mississippi, wrote Germain in 1777: "I believe the people of this province are remarkably well affected to His Majesty and government. . . . It is not probable the seeds of rebellion will ever be sown here; indeed, I flatter myself that is of all others a plant that will not grow here" (Harry Alexander to Germain, Apr. 25, 1777, C.O. 5/155).

tion along the way. Several other former residents of the colony became rebels, notably Bernard Romans (who had received a salary of £ 50 per year to "prosecute his discoveries in botany" in West Florida) and Thomas Hutchins (who surveyed West Florida but later became "geographer to the southern army" of the rebel colonies).[4] Chester also proposed to Germain in 1778 the cessation of all commerce to New Orleans, because it appeared certain that British merchants there were engaged in trade with the Americans.[5] There were those in West Florida who preferred the rebel cause to that of King George, but by and large the actions of the residents of the colony indicate a strong degree of loyalty to Great Britain. Throughout the Revolution and the war with Spain, the inhabitants constantly supported British arms in defense of West Florida.

The most obvious factor in the colony's loyalty to Great Britain was its isolation from the fighting and from contact with the colonies in rebellion. There was intercourse between the Americans and the Spanish by way of the Mississippi River, but few West Floridians were concerned about matters that had very little or no effect on their lives. There is little in the correspondence of the inhabitants even to indicate that a rebellion was in progress. William Dunbar made no mention of the Revolution at all until James Willing descended the river in early 1778. During Willing's excursion the problem of loyalty briefly forced itself upon the inhabitants along the Mississippi River, but soon the American threat disappeared, and the people showed more concern with the immediate problems of surviving on a newly opened frontier than with potential decisions of loyalty or rebellion. When war came again, the conflict was with Spain, and the situation changed.

West Florida was a colony of recent immigrants, people who had not had time to form a local tradition or to establish strong self-government. In 1775 the longest possible time a British settler could have been in the province was twelve years. While many of the original settlers had come from the older colonies, they were from the back country, out of the political mainstream. Once they arrived in their new home, they were too in-

4. Chester to Dartmouth, Apr. 10, 1776, C.O. 5/155; Diary of Richard Smith, Jan. 4, 1776, in Burnett, Letters, 1:295; Ford, Journals, 20:476.
5. Chester to Germain, May 30, 1778, C.O. 5/594.

volved in establishing themselves to be concerned with remote political questions.[6] Many of the settlers in West Florida were not even one generation removed from their English background. They felt a strong sense of loyalty to the mother country they had recently left and had little of the sense of American nationalism so often attributed to the other loyalists. Also, it was as easy, if not easier, to communicate with England than with the other colonies.

The strength of the loyalty of West Florida increased following Chester's proclamation of November 1775 which established West Florida as a haven for loyalist refugees. The trickle of loyalists which had been coming to West Florida to escape the colonies in rebellion became a flood. The figures for this new immigration are, of necessity, taken from the petitions for land in the minutes of the council. The only people counted as loyalists in this study were those who had stated that they had left their homes because of the rebellion. This excludes many loyalists who had arrived and simply petitioned for land without reference to their reasons for coming to West Florida. Also excluded were those whose petitions were postponed or rejected; the council was extremely liberal in granting land, sometimes on flimsy evidence, and if it postponed or rejected a petition, there must surely have been a strong reason for doing so (usually the petitioner was not in the colony, or his claims were fraudulent). Loyalists who arrived before November 1775 have not been included either. This excludes a large number of loyalists who arrived earlier, some of whom even declared that their loyalty was the reason they fled to West Florida. Chester's proclamation seemed a logical starting point, and in the years 1776, 1777, and 1778 the biggest number of grants to loyalists were made. The number of petitions declined markedly after 1778, and the number of postponements increased as the fate of the colony came into question.[7] Certainly not everyone who fled to West Florida made application for lands, and the number of loyalists counted is undoubtedly low, perhaps not including even a majority of those who came to the colony.

6. Johnson, British West Florida, p. 232. Mary Beth Norton makes passing reference to this opportunism on the part of many loyalists (The British-Americans: The Loyalist Exiles in England, 1774–1789, p. 8).

7. The petitions cease completely after January 1780.

Recognizing that some of the loyalists who received grants did not stay in the colony very long, and that it is unclear in several cases whether the petitioner's family was in the colony (reflected in the totals in the table), the statistics concerning loyalist immigration in Table 1 are partial and approximate. At best they represent only a portion of those who fled to West Florida.

TABLE 1

LOYALIST IMMIGRATION INTO WEST FLORIDA, 1775–81[8]

Colony or Area of Origin	Number of Immigrants
Cherokee Nation	3
Connecticut	48–67
Dominica	1–35
East Florida	31
Georgia	278–339
Grenada	10
Maryland	19
Massachusetts	35
New England	14
New York	168–73
North Carolina	59
Pennsylvania	166–91
Rhode Island	2–11
St. Vincent	104–87
South Carolina	262–357
Virginia	110
Not stated	2
Total	1,312–1,643

The loyalists who sought asylum in West Florida came from almost every colony in revolt, as well as from East Florida and the West Indies. Over 40 per cent of those for whom we have dependable records came from Georgia and South Carolina. The total figure of 1,312–1,643 loyalist refugees is undoubtedly low. Based on the frequency of names of people mentioned in the records who did not petition for land, on loyalists who had arrived before November 1775 or who had petitioned for land without reference to their motives for moving to West Florida, and many for whom there is no existing record, it is safe to conclude that between 2,000 and 2,500 loyalists fled to West

8. Minutes of the Council, Nov. 11, 1775–Jan. 13, 1780, C.O. 5/634 and C.O. 5/635, RSUS, reels 7, 8. The immigrants from the West Indies came to West Florida mainly because of a scarcity of provisions caused by the Revolution.

Florida during the Revolution, and perhaps many more. Various estimates in 1769 place the number of residents in West Florida at about 2,000.[9] The record of land grants through the same date indicates there were 512 families with a total of 1,265 to 1,340 members in West Florida. These figures show an average family size of 2.47–2.62—undoubtedly a low figure. Howard used an average family size of 4.0 in his analysis of population, and Greene and Harrington argue that the family size in colonial America was 5.7 to 6.0.[10] Certainly the family size in a newly established frontier colony may have been smaller than 5.7, but it is equally clear that the families were larger than the land records indicate. Taking this discrepancy into consideration as well as the number of people who did not petition for land, the approximation of a population of 2,000 in 1769 is reasonable. By 1781, the population of the colony had increased to 3,312–3,643 from loyalist immigration alone, but these figures do not reflect the true growth of the colony. Land records after 1769 show an additional 611 heads of families receiving grants. Size of family is clearly shown to be larger; there were 2,916–3,265 people in the new families, an average of 4.77 to 5.34. Again this family size is undoubtedly small. The land records indicate that the population in 1781 was between 4,916 and 5,265 (1,421 to 1,665 of whom were slaves). In addition to the land grants, other documents (such as muster rolls and petitions) reveal that during the British period there were at least 612 other heads of families in West Florida. Using the unquestionably low average family size of 4.0, these data show that at least 2,448 more people were in the frontier colony during this period. Taking into account troop reinforcements, natural increase, continued immigration, and, of course, emigration out of West Florida and deaths, a census of West Florida by the end of the British period would probably reveal about 7,000 to 8,000 inhabitants. Loyalist immigration nearly doubled the population of the province during the American Revolution.[11] The addition of such a strong contingent of loyal-

9. Johnstone to Pownal, Apr. 1, 1766, C.O. 5/574; Howard, "Early Settlers," pp. 54–55.
10. Howard, "Early Settlers," pp. 54–55; Evarts B. Greene and Virginia D. Harrington, *American Population before the Federal Census of 1790*, p. xxiii.
11. Durnford estimated 4,900 inhabitants in 1774 ("A Description of West

ists to the original loyal inhabitants was an important factor in keeping West Florida loyal to the British cause.

Van Tyne has argued that "loyalty was the normal condition, the state that *had* existed, and *did* exist; and it was the Whigs,—the Patriots, as they called themselves,—who must do the converting, the changing of men's opinions to suit a new order of things which the revolutionists believed necessary for their own and their country's welfare."[12] In other words, it was the revolutionary party and not the loyalist party that had to be created. While this statement is a simplistic way of avoiding the question of motivation in the original thirteen colonies, it seems to explain the situation in West Florida. In that colony there was never any pressure on the residents to join the rebellion; consequently, no revolutionary party was formed. Loyalty was the norm, and with the brief exception of Willing's raid—which probably strengthened opposition to the Americans—there was never any reason to question the norm. Taxation was not an issue; Parliament supported the civil government by an annual grant to the contingent fund. Consequently, the only taxes collected were to pay the small expenses of the assembly, which did not meet during the early years of the Revolution. While there was some opposition to the Stamp Act, there is little indication that Governor Johnstone was not able to enforce it. As for the Townshend Acts, there is no evidence that the West Floridians were even aware of their existence. For internal disputes the residents of West Florida had to resort to petty bickering between the civilian government and the military over such issues as whether or not the guns of the fort should be fired on St. Patrick's Day, and between the governor and assembly over representation. While there were important implications in these and similar issues in the other colonies, the disputes seldom got beyond the stage of trivial arguments in West

---

Florida with the State of Its Settlements," Jan. 15, 1774, C.O. 5/591). John H. Wynne, *A General History of the British Empire in America*, 2:349, incorrectly reported that there were 6,000 persons in West Florida. His estimate was picked up by William Darby, *Memoir on the Geography, and Natural and Civil History of Florida*, p. 50; Abiel Holmes, *The Annals of America, from the Discovery by Columbus in the Year 1492 to the Year 1826*, 2:165.

12. Van Tyne, *The Loyalists in the Revolution*, pp. 2–3. See also Norton, *The British-Americans*, p. 8. Calhoon, *The Loyalists in Revolutionary America*, p. 506, disagrees with Van Tyne's reasoning, but the basic argument appears valid for West Florida.

Florida. Overall, there was little cause for disaffection in the province, and what grievances existed did not coincide with those of the colonies in rebellion.

Governor Chester skillfully (and perhaps unscrupulously) managed the government of the colony in such a way as to stifle possible controversy. When the Continental Congress sent a letter to the Speaker of the Assembly of West Florida (Edmund Rush Wegg) in 1774, seeking to gain the support of the colony, he gave the letter to Chester. The governor never made the letter public in West Florida: "I had great reasons to apprehend from the spirit and temper of many of the inhabitants, that the calling a House of Assembly could neither promote His Majesty's Service, nor be productive of any advantage to the colony."[13] Chester also did not call the assembly together between 1772 and 1778, thus preventing it from becoming a revolutionary agency as had happened in the rebellious colonies. When he did finally call the assembly in 1778, after Willing's raid, it disputed the question of representation with Chester and failed to act on the measures for which he had called it. Chester adjourned the legislature and never summoned it again.

Several other factors were of major importance in determining the loyalty of West Florida. The first was the presence of troops. In proportion to the population, the number of troops at the strategic British posts on the Mississippi River and the Gulf of Mexico was high and had a stabilizing effect on the colony. The realization that any act of open rebellion would be met with armed retaliation by British regulars served as a strong deterrent to rebellion. Second, when the colony became involved in a war with Spain, the whole situation in West Florida changed. The choice now was loyalty to Britain or alliance with an ancient enemy. While a few inhabitants may have harbored some desire to join the Americans, the thought of siding with the troops of "His Catholic Majesty" was abhorrent. The West Floridians displayed only slight opposition to the Americans (with the lone exception of Willing's raid), but their opposition to the Spanish was vigorous. It is debatable whether those who opposed Spain were "loyalists" in the traditional sense applied to the original thirteen colonies. But in the broader context of a

13. Chester to Germain, Nov. 24, 1778, C.O. 5/595; Ford, *Journals*, 1:101–3.

global war, the inhabitants of West Florida remained loyal to Great Britain against American, Spanish, and French foes.

The composition of the loyalists is a problem of much recent study. One important factor in the thirteen "original colonies" was the number of officeholders who were dependent upon the British government for livelihood. In West Florida, however, this point must be relegated to a position of low importance. All of the colonies had influential officeholders, but not all of those colonies remained loyal. Other motivations are of much more importance.[14] While it is true that the stereotypical

TABLE 2
LOYALIST EMIGRATION[15]

Destination	Number
Bahamas	21
England	37
Jamaica	2
New York	4
Nova Scotia and New Brunswick	3
Total	67

loyalists—officeholders, Anglican clergy, landowners, and merchants—were present in the frontier colony and remained loyal, so did virtually everybody else. Personal factors were of minor importance when compared to the isolation of the colony, heavy loyalist immigration, a lack of grievances, the presence of troops, and the war with Spain. These elements all combined to determine the loyalty of the early settlers of West

14. Brown, in The King's Friends, p. 239, points out that in the eighteenth century "oaths were taken seriously" and the reluctance to break an oath of office was a definite factor in the loyalty of officeholders. Without denying the argument, it is far more likely that economic motivation maintained the loyalty of the royal officials in West Florida.

15. These meager statistics were drawn from various Audit Office and Colonial Office papers; the British Headquarters' Papers; the Shelburne Papers; Parrish, "Records of Some Southern Loyalists"; Thelma Peters, "The American Loyalists in the Bahama Islands: Who They Were"; Siebert, "Loyalists in West Florida"; Thelma Peters, "The American Loyalists and the Plantation Period in the Bahama Islands" (Ph.D. diss.); Wilbur H. Siebert, Loyalists in East Florida, 1774 to 1785, vol. 2; William Wylly, A Short Account of the Bahama Islands; "Latin America, South America, Brazil; Papers Relating to Rio Janeiro, 1794," Force Collection, Library of Congress; "Papers Relating to Havannah," ibid. I have excluded East Florida because most of those who went to that province were merely en route elsewhere. I have omitted the troops who were prisoners with the Spanish; only a few West Florida Royal Foresters can be considered West Florida loyalists, and they were not emigrating by choice.

Florida. It was easier to be a loyalist than not in West Florida; the difficult choice of loyalty to the mother country or to the American soil was never actually confronted. Not to decide was, in fact, to be a loyalist by default.

There is a dearth of information about the fate of the loyalists after the Spanish conquest. Lydia Parrish's *Records of Some Southern Loyalists* (1959), which investigates loyalists who went to the Bahamas, is an example of the type of research necessary to an understanding of emigration patterns. Table 2 shows the destinations of only sixty-seven West Florida loyalists after the conquest of Pensacola.

The problems involved in determining loyalist emigration are almost insurmountable. The records are scattered, and many of the West Florida refugees wandered to several places before they settled. For example, the Spanish carried Adam Chrystie to Havana, then to New York. He requested land in Nova Scotia but, after a brief period in England, apparently settled in the Bahamas. Dr. John Lorimer followed the same path to New York, where he served as Inspector of Military Hospitals. After the war was over he went to England.[16]

The troops captured by the Spanish at Pensacola went to Havana and from there to New York. There, on August 15, 1782, the commander-in-chief ordered the West Florida Royal Foresters disbanded, and they apparently went separate ways. The only certain information is that Chrystie went from New York to England and then to the Bahamas.[17] Certainly more than 67 people left the beleaguered province. The 67 persons for whom we have records were apparently heads of families, and consequently we can assume the number to be at least four times as many, or 268. Still, this small figure, even when added to the number of prisoners, is but a small percentage of the 7,000-

16. Peters, "American Loyalists and the Plantation Period," p. 78; memorial of Adam Chrystie, Nov. 3, 1783, C.O. 5/598; Parrish, *Records of Some Southern Loyalists*, pp. 202–11; Chrystie to Carleton, Nov. 3, 1783, BHP, 9541, reel 26; Robert R. Rea and Jack D. L. Holmes, "Dr. John Lorimer and the Natural Sciences in British West Florida," p. 369.

17. James Boyd [Clerk in the Inspector General's Office] to T. Knox, Nov. 1783, BHP, 9554, reel 26. The Maryland Loyalists received a grant of land in Nova Scotia, and seventy-six of them set sail on the transport *Martha* in September 1783. There was a shipwreck, and fifty-seven men, women, and children lost their lives. Augustine Prevost to the Adjutant General, Oct. 10, 1783, C.O. 5/111; Return of survivors, Sept. 23, 1783, ibid.

8,000 inhabitants in West Florida. Until more evidence is un-
covered, this minute and perhaps misleading figure will have
to stand as the best available.

While the records concerning those who left West Florida are
partial, it is clear that more of the inhabitants remained in West
Florida than left, most notably in the Mississippi region. Most of
the inhabitants of Pensacola left the area in order to escape close
Spanish scrutiny, but the majority of the English settlers on the
Mississippi took an oath of allegiance to Spain and remained in
possession of their property. Estevan Miró reported in 1785 that
many of the English settlers remained in their homes on the
Mississippi, and that others who had been in Mobile and Pensacola when Spanish arms captured those towns were also settling on the river.[18] A Spanish statement of production figures
for tobacco produced in the Natchez region in 1789 lists eighty-
three names recognizable as those of British loyalists who remained in the area. Once again, this figure represents heads of
families, and can safely be quadrupled. It is possible that some
of the other names on the list were also loyalists of whom there
is no record. There were also loyalists in Natchez who did not
raise tobacco.[19] A Spanish census of the Natchez region three
years later contained at least 145 names recognizable as the
heads of loyalist families. It is quite likely that more of the
English names on the census represent loyalists who remained
in the region. These statistics of the Natchez region alone are
sufficient to indicate that large numbers of loyalists did not
leave the colony, but instead took an oath of allegiance and
remained in their homes.[20]

18. Miró to Gálvez, Sept. 5, 1785, MPA,SD, 2:220–21; Gálvez to Miró,
Oct. 20, 1785, ibid., p. 167. See also Howard, "Early Settlers," p. 46; Mrs. S. J.
Gonzalez, "Pensacola: Its Early History," p. 13. In March, Miró had forwarded
to Gálvez a petition from twelve English settlers on the Mississippi requesting
that the Spanish allow them to remain in their homes on the Mississippi
(Memorial to Gálvez, Mar. 1, 1785, MPA,SD, 2:109–11).

19. Statement of tobacco grown at Natchez, 1789, Mar. 2, 1790, in Kinnaird,
Spain in the Mississippi Valley, 2:306–11.

20. Mrs. [Eron] Dunbar Rowland, "Mississippi's Colonial Population and
Land Grants," pp. 418–28. After the surrender of West Florida the lives of
loyalists who remained in the province changed very little except for their
allegiance to Spain. Letterbook of John Fitzpatrick, vol. 3. A search of the land
records in the American State Papers: Documents Legislative and Executive, of
the Congress of the United States: Public Lands, pp. xxviii–xxxi, reveals many
English names, but the difficulty in determining if the name represents a

The evidence suggests that at least a majority and perhaps as many as two-thirds of the loyalists remained in West Florida after the Spanish conquest. Indeed, throughout all the colonies, many loyalists remained at their homes, or returned to them when the opposition to their doing so was slight. Since the Spanish had little objection to the loyalists remaining, many of them did not move. Not only did many West Floridians remain in the colony, but large numbers of loyalists from other colonies (particularly East Florida) sought the protection of the Spanish government in West Florida. Governor Patrick Tonyn of East Florida reported in early 1784, for example, that 4,000 inhabitants from East Florida were moving to the "back settlements on the Mississippi."[21] Thus, the loyalist haven which Dartmouth attempted to establish in 1775 and which Dunmore planned during the last years of the war became, in part, a reality. It was not the refuge under British control which they had envisioned, but it was, nevertheless, an asylum for the loyalists of West Florida and the other ex-British colonies. West Florida became an island of semitranquillity on the western edge of an ocean of hatred, distrust, and confusion; but it was a tranquillity which would not long survive the expansionist ardor of the westward-moving Americans.

In his opening speech to Parliament on December 5, 1782, George III announced that he had ordered an inquiry into the situation of the American loyalists, "and I trust you will agree with me, that a due and generous attention ought to be shown toward those who have relinquished their properties or professions from motives of loyalty to me, or attachment to the mother country."[22] Parliament subsequently created the Commission for

---

constant resident, a new immigrant, a son, and so forth, makes these records useless for statistical purposes.

21. Quoted in Siebert, *Loyalists in East Florida*, 1:156. See also Arturo O'Neill to Gálvez, May 20, 1783, MPA,SD, 2:5–6, and Joseph B. Lockey, "The Florida Banditti, 1783," pp. 89–103.

22. Hansard, *The Parliamentary History of England*, 23:208. The history of the Loyalists' Claims Commission is treated by a member of the commission in John Eardley-Wilmot, *Historical View of the Commission for Enquiring into the Losses, Services, and Claims of the American Loyalists. . . .* The notes of another commissioner, Daniel Parker Coke, are in Hugh Edward Egerton, ed., *The Royal Commission on the Losses and Services of American Loyalists, 1783 to 1785.* Modern accounts of the commission are in Wallace Brown, *The King's Friends,* and *The Good Americans: The Loyalists in the American Revolution;* Eugene R. Fingerhut, "Uses and Abuses of the American Loyalists' Claims: A

Enquiring into the Losses, Services, and Claims of the American Loyalists, which heard the claims of the loyalists and recommended to Parliament appropriate compensation. In its first report in 1784, the commission declined to consider cases of "losses sustained in East and West Florida, or elsewhere, out of the limits of the United States. We have considered the enquiry necessarily confined to these limits; as we do not conceive Parliament to have had in its contemplation any other description of sufferers than such as have sustained losses in the revolted provinces, in consequence of their adherence to the British government."[23] Probably at the urging of loyalists from East and West Florida, a law providing for an investigation into claims in these colonies soon passed in Parliament. Thirty-eight ex–West Floridians had petitioned Lord North, asserting that they were "equally entitled to a compensation for their losses, as their other fellow sufferers on the same continent."[24] Again, in 1787, the loyalists attempted to obtain compensation for their losses to Spanish arms. In that year they printed a sixteen-page pamphlet entitled *The Case and Petition of His Majesty's Loyal Subjects, Late of West Florida*, but their efforts were in vain.[25]

Within a year and a half after the commission started meeting,

---

Critique of Quantitative Analysis." Any discussion of the loyalists of the American Revolution would be incomplete without an analysis of one of the most valuable sources of information for loyalist studies, the so-called loyalists' claims papers. They are of less importance for West Florida than for other mainland colonies, but they are still a part of the story. One historian of the loyalists asserted that "there are no individual claims for losses" for West Florida (Parrish, *Records of Some Southern Loyalists*, p. 60). There are, in fact, a few claims, but their monetary value is low.

23. Eardley-Wilmot, *Historical View*, p. 113.

24. Memorial to Lord North from "the Proprietors of Land, Planters, Merchants, and other Inhabitants late of West Florida," n.d. C.O. 5/596. See also Archibald Dalzel to his brother, London, Mar. 6, 1783, Dk.7.52/103, Edinburgh University Library. This letter was called to my attention by Professor Robin Fabel of Auburn University.

25. Before Parliament established the commission, the British had granted temporary subsistence allowances to loyalists who had fled behind British lines or to England. The records reveal that only three people from West Florida received these allowances, at a total cost to England of about £90 per year. But these allowances were temporary until the end of the war, when Parliament could appoint a committee to make a closer investigation. Lists of people on temporary allowance are in BHP, 6588, reel 19; ibid., 7258, reel 21; ibid., 8252–53, reel 23; ibid., 10330, reel 28; Shelburne Papers; A.O. 12/104; American Loyalists' Transcripts, 2:336. The three people who received the grants were Rebecca Dutton (£50), John Allen Martin (£20), and Sarah Amos (£21.5).

it began considering claims from West Florida for losses caused by the Americans. In West Florida this meant compensation for losses occasioned by Willing's raid. Many West Floridians had already petitioned the commission before this change in policy became public, and the decision of their claims simply read, "Does not come within the scope of this enquiry," or "not admitted."[26] There were at least ten West Florida loyalists who suffered losses to Willing but failed to make the distinction between losses to Spain and losses because of the American raid, and consequently the commission disallowed their claims. Only two of these loyalists re-petitioned the commission after making the necessary distinction. The commission's decision on the claim of John Allen Martin in February 1784 is perhaps the best summation of their view: "The loss of all his employments and property were occasioned by the invasion of a foreign enemy and unless we could extend the bounty which it is our province to distribute to sufferers of the war all over the globe, we cannot extend it to this gentleman. He did his duty to this country with great zeal and honor to himself but he fought against Spaniards and it is his misfortune that his losses cannot immediately be attributed to the civil commotions in America tho' ultimately they may be derived from that source."[27]

If the commissioners had granted compensation to West Floridians for their losses to Spain, England would at once have been saddled with debts arising from claims around the world because of the global conflicts in which she became involved. The decision on one West Florida claim stated that the petitioner had as little right "to expect an allowance from this board as if they had been made at Gibraltar."[28] At the same time, many West Florida loyalists suffered almost total destruction of their personal fortunes, and the failure of England to grant some kind of relief through direct compensation or an annual pension seems callous. The commission did grant small annual pensions to eight West Floridians for property lost to the Americans during Willing's raid. The pensions amounted to a total of £ 410 per year. The West Florida loyalists contin-

26. Claim of Edmund Rush Wegg, Mar. 8, 1783, A.O. 12/99; claim of Richard Seamark, Apr. 7, 1783, ibid.

27. Claim of John Allen Martin, Feb. 16, 1784, A.O. 12/100.

28. Claim of Anthony Hutchins, July 12, 1784, ibid.

ued for over thirty years to seek compensation or confirmation by the United States of their British land grants in West Florida. The efforts of the West Florida loyalists were largely in vain.[29]

29. Registers of the Land Office East of Pearl River, 1804–5, West Florida Papers, reel 5; *American State Papers, Public Lands*, pp. xxviii–xxxi; Castlereagh to the British American Commissioners, July 28, 1814, Henry Goulburn Papers, William L. Clements Library. See also the five enclosures in Castlereagh's letter cited above. A brief discussion of some of the later efforts of the loyalists to keep their lands in West Florida is in R. S. Cotterill, "The National Land System in the South, 1803–1812," pp. 495–99.

11

Conclusion

W hen West Florida became a British possession at the conclusion of the French and Indian War in 1763, Great Britain
found itself the guardian of a sparsely settled, unhealthy, and
dilapidated piece of real estate. Twenty years later, England
returned the province to Spain with larger towns, better
fortifications, and a much larger population capable of producing royal revenues through various crops. In general, Spain
received a colony of considerably more value. During the
British period, the history of West Florida encompassed growth,
internal discord, loyalty during the American Revolution, and
war with Spain. Yet for 160 years it was a colony without a
written history, as historians bypassed the brief interruption in
the history of Spanish Florida.

The story of the American Revolution and the concomitant
Anglo-Spanish war in West Florida fills almost half of the brief
history of the British possession of the colony. The province
was a frontier area, remote from the scene of the Revolution, at
peace but in fear of war. During the first three years of the
rebellion, West Florida was cognizant of the war only through
correspondence and occasional rebel excursions to New Orleans
for supplies. James Willing, a former resident of West Florida,
forcefully brought home the rebellion to the inhabitants of the
British frontier outpost. Briefly, and for the first time, the original inhabitants had to define their loyalties and determine
priorities, just as loyalists of the colonies in rebellion had.

The American Revolution in West Florida ended almost as quickly as it began—once Willing left New Orleans, the revolt was at an end. The American excursion had merely confirmed the loyalty of the West Floridians, and the Continental Congress did not want another expedition against the colony unless there was a chance of greater benefits to the American cause. The loyalists fleeing to the haven provided for them in West Florida served as a constant reminder of the plight of the loyalists in the rebellious colonies and of the possibility of further hostilities. In order to prepare for such an event, the home government ordered reinforcements to the weakly defended province.

Upon their arrival in early 1779, General John Campbell and his troops had had time to do little more than disembark and begin repairing the fortifications before Spain and England declared war upon each other. The outbreak of this Anglo-Spanish war marked the beginning of another phase of the history of British West Florida. While they were aware that a rebellion was still in progress to the north, the West Floridians faced an even greater and more direct threat from their Spanish neighbors. No longer was there any question of where their loyalty should rest. War against Spain in 1779 was no different from war with Spain in 1762; traditional loyalties became dominant as the American Revolution became more and more remote.

The Spanish followed a surprise attack on Baton Rouge with rapid advances on Mobile and Pensacola, so that within two years the entire British province was in the possession of Spain. The Treaty of Paris (1783) confirmed this possession, and British West Florida ceased to exist. Many inhabitants of the British colony did remain, however, and were important in the continued growth and expansion of the area. Those loyalists who left the province and threw themselves upon the mercy of England met with frustration and failure and, in general, apparently fared worse than those inhabitants who remained in the colony under Spanish protection.

As far as the American Revolution was concerned, West Florida played only a minor role. The only incident of any importance was Willing's raid, which did little more than strain relations between Oliver Pollock and Bernardo de Gálvez and reconfirm the loyalty of the West Floridians. Alarmed that the Americans could make such a raid with very little effective resistance, the British government reacted by sending over a thousand men to West Florida. British commanders in the rebellious colonies could ill afford the loss of these men, but the home government considered the frontier outpost of enough strategic importance to order the troops to West Florida. The retention of these men might have made a difference in British fortunes in North America. In spite of the "Separate Article" in the preliminary treaty, the Treaty of Paris indicated that Great Britain was not strongly dedicated to the retention of West Florida, and, in retrospect, the movement of vital troops to a place of such low priority appears ill considered.

The major action in West Florida during the period of the American Revolution was the war with Spain. This conflict occupied most of the military efforts of the colony in defending Baton Rouge, Mobile, and Pensacola. The battle for Pensacola involved about 10,000 troops, yet, as Cecil Johnson suggests, there is a "lack of documentary evidence showing a cause-and-effect relationship between the Spanish conquest of West Florida and its subsequent cession to Spain."[1] George III at first wished to give up Gibraltar and keep the Floridas, but after the British defense of that rock, he submitted to the relinquishment of West Florida. However, despite the lack of documentary evidence, the fact that West Florida was in the hands of Spain while the negotiations were underway was certainly influential to some extent in the peace settlement.[2] As Robert Rea points out, "The plain fact was that Spain would be as unlikely to part with conquered West Florida as Britain was to part with unconquered Gibraltar."[3]

The defense of West Florida is an important chapter in British colonial policy during the Revolution. By reinforcing the colony, the British kept the Spanish from engaging their troops against the British troops in the colonies in rebellion. It is significant that West Florida fell to Spanish arms just a few months before Yorktown, indicative of the final breakdown

1. Johnson, "West Florida Revisited," p. 130.
2. In The Peacemakers, Morris discusses the adamant unwillingness of Spain to give up West Florida. See also J. Leitch Wright, Jr., Anglo-Spanish Rivalry in North America, pp. 132–33.
3. Rea, "British West Florida: Stepchild of Diplomacy," pp. 61, 76. The Spanish conquest of West Florida also had an important effect on the British decision to give East Florida to Spain in 1784.

of British fortunes in America. Historians have strongly documented the fact that Spain's ownership of West Florida facilitated American acquisition of the area later. The loyalists who settled in West Florida are an important part of the history of the American loyalists of the Revolution. Perhaps more important, however, is the fact that they proved the fertility of the soil on the Mississippi and consequently encouraged the expansion into the Old Southwest. If England had retained West Florida, she would have been an obstacle to American expansion. Under the weak control of Spain and with the presence of large numbers of loyalists who in time became pro-American, however, the new nation began achieving its manifest destiny long before John L. O'Sullivan even coined the phrase.

Appendix: Note on Loyalist Historiography

Recently there has been a renewal of interest in loyalist studies. Unfortunately, these studies have been limited in their scope to the original thirteen colonies. The most recent survey, Robert M. Calhoon's *The Loyalists in Revolutionary America* (1973), and the somewhat older but still valuable *The American Tory* by William H. Nelson (1961), neglect to include West Florida at all. Calhoon's oversight of the "loyal" colonies is clearly shown when he asserts that the American Revolution "was a struggle in which the pro-British partisans were, at best, politically, numerically, and militarily inferior to those of the rebel government." Paul Smith's excellent *Loyalists and Redcoats: A Study of British Revolutionary Policy* (1964) mentions West Florida only in passing and argues that provincial troops that "were recruited outside the thirteen colonies . . . or had arrived in America only shortly before the rebellion . . . ought not to be classified as loyalists."[1] Wallace Brown's analytical study *The King's Friends* (1965) includes only the colonies that

1. Paul H. Smith, "The American Loyalists: Notes on Their Organization and Numerical Strength," p. 263; Calhoon, *The Loyalists in Revolutionary America*, p. 506. Smith does include statistics on the West Florida Royal Foresters in the article cited here. The problem in omitting the "loyal" colonies is demonstrated in unfortunate statements such as that of Norton in her otherwise excellent study *The British-Americans:* "for southern loyalists in particular there were few avenues of escape until Savannah fell to royal forces late in 1778. Before that time the loyal residents of the South were completely at the mercy of the rebel provincial governments" (p. 34). Such generalizations fail to take into account the few thousand loyalists who fled to East and West Florida prior to 1778.

became the United States.[2] These four books indicate the problem inherent in all the loyalist studies: an emphasis on the thirteen colonies in rebellion, to the exclusion of all others.

While these authors may argue—perhaps persuasively— that West Florida was outside the limits of their discussion, the omission of West Florida and other loyal colonies weakens their arguments. Syntheses such as those of Calhoon and Nelson are incomplete when their generalizations are not applicable in the main to a "loyal" colony such as West Florida. "A study in British revolutionary policy" which neglects an entire colony, dominated by a military force in part dependent on loyal residents and Indians, must be judged a partial study of the policies of the military. A quantitative analysis which attempts to draw conclusions about loyalists without examining the claims of colonies in which loyalists were predominant is at best incomplete and at worst of questionable validity. In this analysis of recent loyalist literature I am not attempting to degrade the value of these four books. Calhoon, Nelson, Smith, and Brown have written four of the most informative and thought-provoking works available at present. The point of such an evaluation is to endeavor to illustrate the necessity of including the tories of the "loyal" colonies with those of the "rebel" colonies if an accurate appraisal is to be made.

Concluding that a precise evaluation of loyalism in the American Revolution requires the inclusion of the story of the "loyal" colonies, it must appear obvious that historians must first analyze these provinces. One of the purposes of this study is to appraise the loyalists of West Florida without retracing the Revolution. The materials necessary for such an investigation are scattered, buried, or even nonexistent, and many of the conclusions are of necessity reasoned conjecture on the basis of voluminous material only peripherally related to the loyalists.

2. Fingerhut's "Uses and Abuses of the American Loyalists' Claims: A Critique of Quantitative Analysis" should be used in connection with Brown's study.

Bibliography

KEY TO ABBREVIATIONS

AHQ	*Alabama Historical Quarterly*
AHR	*American Historical Review*
AR	*Alabama Review*
BHP	British Headquarters' Papers
FHQ	*Florida Historical Quarterly*
HAHR	*Hispanic American Historical Review*
JMH	*Journal of Mississippi History*
JSH	*Journal of Southern History*
LH	*Louisiana History*
LHQ	*Louisiana Historical Quarterly*
MPA,SD	Mississippi Provincial Archives, Spanish Dominion
MVHR	*Mississippi Valley Historical Review*
PMHS	*Publications of the Mississippi Historical Society*
RSUS	Records of the States of the United States of America
Wm. and Mary Qtly.	*William and Mary Quarterly*

Unless otherwise noted, all Public Record Office and British Museum references are to Library of Congress transcripts and photostatic copies.

I. MANUSCRIPTS

Alabama Department of Archives and History, Montgomery
    Peter J. Hamilton Papers
    Robert Farmar Papers, 1768–1834
    West Florida Transcripts
British Museum, London
    Additional Manuscripts
    15485   (Accounts of the exports and imports of British North American
                Colonies, 5 Jan. 1768–5 Jan. 1769)
    21631–21660 (Henry Bouquet Papers, 1754–65)
    21661–21892 (Frederick Haldimand Papers)

Colonial Williamsburg, Inc., Williamsburg, Virginia
    British Headquarters' Papers (Carleton Papers or Lord Dorchester Papers;
        microfilm located at The Florida State University)
Diocese of Mobile, Archives
    Records, 1763–90
Huntington Library, San Marino, California
    Miscellaneous items containing muster roll of provincials at Pensacola, De-
        cember 24, 1780 (microfilm located at the P. K. Yonge Library)
John C. Pace Library, University of West Florida, Pensacola
    "Mentor's Logg Book Commencing 9th March 1780"
Library of Congress, Washington, D.C.
    Documentos y Relaciones Para la Historia de la Florida y la Luisiana, 1493–
        1780
    Florida Miscellaneous, 1525–1821
    Force Collection. "Latin America, South America, Brazil; Papers Relating to
        Rio Janeiro, 1794" and "Papers Relating to Havannah"
    George Morgan Papers, 1775–1822
    Louisiana. Miscellaneous Papers Relating to Louisiana, 1731–1806 and
        1740–1928
    Louisiana. Virginia Letters, 1776–78
    Records of the States of the United States of America (microfilm located at The
        Florida State University)
    West Florida Papers (microfilm located at The Florida State University)
Mississippi Department of Archives and History, Jackson
    Correspondence of Bernardo de Gálvez, 1779–81 (transcripts)
    Mississippi Provincial Archives, English Dominion (transcripts)
    Mississippi Provincial Archives, Spanish Dominion (transcripts)
    William Dunbar Papers, 1776–1880
National Archives, Washington, D.C.
    Record Group 45, Naval Records Collection of the Office of Naval Records and
        Library
    Record Group 59, General Records of the Department of State. Territorial Pa-
        pers: Territory Southwest of the River Ohio, 1790–95
    Record Group 267, Supreme Court. The Revolutionary War Prize Cases:
        Records of the Court of Appeals in Cases of Capture, 1776–87
New York Public Library, New York City
    Chalmers Collection of Documents Relating to West Florida, 1763–82
    Letterbook of John Fitzpatrick, 1768–90
    Letters and Documents of Philip Livingston and His Son, Peter Van Brugh
        Livingston, 1541–1859 (photostats)
    Loyalist Commissioners. Calendar of the Original Memorials, Vouchers, and
        Other Papers Deposited with the Commission of Enquiry into the Losses
        and Services of the American Loyalists
    Loyalist Commissioners. Proceedings, and Testimony of American Loyalists
        (notes of Daniel Parker Coke)
    Papers Relating to the Settlement in the Mississippi Valley of South Carolina
        and Virginia Loyalists
    "Petitions etc. of Former Officers of the British Army and Navy, to Governor
        Peter Chester, of West Florida, for Lands Now Lying in Mississippi and
        Louisiana"
    Transcripts of the Manuscript Books and Papers of the Commission of
        Enquiry into the Losses and Services of the American Loyalists . . .
        1783–90 (American Loyalists transcripts)

Transcripts of Various Papers Relating to the Losses, Services, and Support of the American Loyalists and His Majesty's Provincial Forces During the War of American Independence . . . 1777–83 (transcripts)
P. K. Yonge Library of Florida History, University of Florida, Gainesville
    Elizabeth H. West Papers
    General Manuscripts, Boxes 4, 11, 27, 30, 32, 45
    Joseph Lockey Collection, 1606–1832
Public Archives of Canada, Ottawa
    Amos Botsford Papers, 1762–1839 (MG 23)
    British Military and Naval Records, Record Group 8 (C Series)
    Earl of Shelburne Papers, 1663–1782 (MG 23)
    Edward Winslow Papers, 1695–1877 (MG 23 D2)
    Frederick Haldimand Papers, 1779–91 (MG 23)
    Frederick Mackenzie Papers, 1755–91 (MG 23 K34)
    Henry Hamilton Papers, 1778–92 (MG 23)
    King's Manuscripts, vols. 208–9 (1753–84), 213 (1764–65) (MG 21)
    Johnson Family Papers, 1763–1807 (MG 19 F2)
    Joseph Frederick Wallet Desbarres Papers (MG 23 F1)
    Nova Scotia: List of Loyalists Embarked for, 1783 (MG 23)
    St. John, New Brunswick, Loyalists of (MG 23)
    Thomas Carleton Papers, 1784, 1796–99, 1810 (MG 23)
    Viscount Sydney Papers, 1750–98 (MG 23)
    Ward Chipman Papers, 1751–1844 (MG 23 D1)
Public Record Office, London
    Admiralty Office 1
    Audit Office 1
    Audit Office 12
    Audit Office 13
    Board of Trade. Journal of the Commissioners for Trade and Plantations
    Colonial Office 5: Volumes 2–8, 66–111, 114–17, 119–32, 138–58, 161–73, 175, 182–84, 201–3, 218, 225, 227–29, 233–40, 244–45, 263, 280–82, 540, 542, 548–59, 563, 574–635
    House of Lords. Copy of His Majesty's Instructions to the Governors of Nova Scotia, New Hampshire, New York, Virginia, No. Carolina, South Carolina, Georgia, East Florida, & West Florida, Respecting the Granting of Lands in Those Provinces. February 3, 1774
    War Office 1
    War Office 10
    War Office 34
Royal Engineer Corps Library, Chatham, England
    T. W. J. Conally Manuscripts
Sheffield City Library, Sheffield, England
    Rockingham MSS, Wentworth Woodhouse Collection
William L. Clements Library, Ann Arbor, Michigan
    Sir Jeffery Amherst Papers
    Sir Henry Clinton Papers
    Sir Thomas Gage Papers
    Henry Goulburn Papers
    William Knox Papers
    Frederick Mackenzie Papers
    Sackville-Germain Papers
    Earl of Shelburne Papers
    Viscount Sydney Papers

Alexander Wedderburn Papers

II. NEWSPAPERS AND CONTEMPORARY PERIODICALS

Almon, John, ed. *The Remembrancer; or, Impartial Repository of Public Events*. London, 1780–81.
British Magazine: or, Monthly Repository for Gentlemen and Ladies. London, 1760–67.
Gentleman's Magazine. London, 1765–83.
The Court, City, and County Magazine. London, 1761–65.
The London Chronicle. London, June–September 1765.
The Times. London, 1785–88.

III. PRINTED BOOKS AND PAMPHLETS

Alden, John Richard. *John Stuart and the Southern Colonial Frontier; A Study of Indian Relations, War, Trade, and Land Problems in the Southern Wilderness, 1754–1775*. Ann Arbor: University of Michigan Press, 1944.
———. *The South in the Revolution, 1763–1789*. Baton Rouge: Louisiana State University Press, 1959.
Allen, Joseph. *Memoir of the Life and Services of Admiral Sir William Hargood*. Greenwich: Henry S. Richardson, 1841.
Alvord, Clarence Walworth. *The Mississippi Valley in British Politics*. 2 vols. New York: Russell and Russell, Inc., 1959.
American State Papers: Documents, Legislative and Executive, of the Congress of the United States: Public Lands. 8 vols. Washington: Gales and Seaton, 1832–61.
An Appeal to the Public, in Behalf of George Johnstone, Esq., Governor of West Florida. London: C. Moran, 1763.
Annals of Congress.
Bartram, William. *Travels Through North and South Carolina, Georgia, East & West Florida*. Edited by Francis Harper. Naturalist's edition. Reprint of 1791 ed. New Haven: Yale University Press, 1958.
Bemis, Samuel Flagg. *The Diplomacy of the American Revolution*. Bloomington: Indiana University Press, 1957.
———. *Pinckney's Treaty: America's Advantage from Europe's Distress, 1783–1800*. New Haven, 1960.
Benton, William Allen. *Whig Loyalism: An Aspect of Political Ideology in the American Revolutionary Era*. Cranbury, N.J.: Fairleigh Dickinson University Press, 1968.
Boatner, Mark Mayo III. *Encyclopedia of the American Revolution*. New York: David McKay Co., 1966.
Borden, Morton, and Borden, Penn, eds. *The American Tory*. Englewood Cliffs, N.J.: Prentice-Hall, 1972.
Born, John D. *Governor Johnstone and Trade in British West Florida, 1764–1767*. Wichita: Wichita State University Press, 1968.
Brown, Wallace. *The Good Americans: The Loyalists in the American Revolution*. New York: William Morrow and Co., 1969.
———. *The King's Friends: The Composition and Motives of the American Loyalist Claimants*. Providence, R.I.: Brown University Press, 1965.
Burnett, Edmund C., ed. *Letters of Members of the Continental Congress*. 8 vols. Washington: Carnegie Institution of Washington, 1921–36.
Calhoon, Robert McCluer. *The Loyalists in Revolutionary America, 1760–1781*. New York: Harcourt Brace Jovanovich, Inc., 1973.
Callahan, North. *Flight from the Republic: The Tories of the American Revolution*. Indianapolis: Bobbs-Merrill, 1967.

————. *Royal Raiders: The Tories of the American Revolution*. Indianapolis: Bobbs-Merrill, 1963.

Campbell, Richard. *Historical Sketches of Colonial Florida*. Cleveland: Williams Publishing Co., 1892.

The Case and Petition of His Majesty's Loyal Subjects, Late of West Florida. N.p., 1787.

Case of the Florida Claimants [for Losses Occasioned in the War with America by British Merchants on Neutral Ground]. London: J. Cunningham [1830].

Caughey, John Walton. *Bernardo de Gálvez in Louisiana, 1776–1783*. Berkeley: University of California Press, 1934.

————, ed. *McGillivray of the Creeks*. Norman: University of Oklahoma Press, 1938.

Clark, John G. *New Orleans, 1718–1812: An Economic History*. Baton Rouge: Louisiana State University Press, 1970.

Clowes, William Laird, et al. *The Royal Navy*. 7 vols. London: Samson Low, Marston and Co., 1897–1903.

Cluny, Alexander. *The American Traveller: Containing Observations on the Present State, Culture and Commerce of the British Colonies in America. . . .* Reprint ed. Tarrytown, N.Y.: William Abbatt, 1930.

Coleman, Kenneth. *The American Revolution in Georgia, 1763–1789*. Athens: University of Georgia Press, 1958.

Cox, Isaac Joslin. *The West Florida Controversy, 1798–1813; A Study in American Diplomacy*. Reprint ed. Gloucester, Mass.: Peter Smith, 1968.

Darby, William. *Memoir on the Geography, and Natural and Civil History of Florida*. Philadelphia: T. H. Palmer, 1821.

Davenport, Francis Gardiner, and Paullin, Charles Oscar, eds. *European Treaties Bearing on the History of the United States and Its Dependencies*. 4 vols. Washington: Carnegie Institution, 1917–39.

Dibble, Ernest F., and Newton, Earle W. *In Search of Gulf Coast Colonial History*. Pensacola: Historic Pensacola Preservation Board, 1970.

Durnford, Mary. *Family Recollections of Lieut. General Elias Walker Durnford*. Montreal: John Lovell, 1863.

Eardley-Wilmot, John. *Historical View of the Commission for Enquiring into the Losses, Services, and Claims, of the American Loyalists at the Close of the War Between Great Britain and Her Colonies in 1783: with an Account of the Compensation Granted to Them by Parliament in 1785 and 1788*. London: J. Nichols, Son, and Bentley, 1815.

Eelking, Max Von. *Die Deutschen Hulfstruppen im Nordamerikanischen Befreiungskrieg, 1776 bis 1783*. Translated by Henry McLellan, Louis Krupp, and Mary Lou Robson. Pensacola: Pensacola Historical Museum, 1938.

————. *The German Allied Troops in the North American War of Independence, 1776–1783*. Translated by J. G. Rosengarten. Albany, N.Y.: Joel Munsell's Sons, 1893.

Egerton, Hugh Edward. *The Causes and Character of the American Revolution*. Oxford: Clarendon Press, 1923.

————, ed. *The Royal Commission on the Losses and Services of American Loyalists, 1783 to 1785*. Oxford: The Roxburghe Club, 1915.

Einstein, Lewis. *Divided Loyalties: Americans in England During the War of Independence*. London: Cobden-Sanderson, 1933.

Ellicott, Andrew. *The Journal of Andrew Ellicott. . . .* Reprint ed. Chicago: Quadrangle Books, 1962.

Evans, G. N. D., ed. *Allegiance in America: The Case of the Loyalists*. Reading, Mass.: Addison-Wesley Publishing Co., 1969.

Ford, Worthington Chauncey. *British Officers Serving in America, 1754–1774.* Boston: David Clapp and Son, 1894.

Ford, Worthington C., et al., eds. *Journals of the Continental Congress, 1774–1789.* 34 vols. Washington: Government Printing Office, 1904–37.

Fortescue, Sir John William, ed. *The Correspondence of King George the Third from 1760 to December 1783.* 6 vols. Reprint ed. London: Frank Cass & Co., Ltd., 1967.

———. *A History of the British Army.* 13 vols. London: Macmillan and Co., 1899–1930.

French, Benjamin Franklin, ed. *Historical Collections of Louisiana and Florida, Including Translations of Original Manuscripts Relating to Their Discovery and Settlement.* 7 vols. New York; Sabin, 1846–75.

Gayarré, Charles. *The History of Louisiana.* 4 vols. 4th ed. New Orleans: F. F. Hansell and Brother, 1903.

Gillis, Norman E. *Early Inhabitants of the Natchez District.* Copyright by the author, 1963.

Gipson, Lawrence Henry. *The British Empire before the American Revolution.* 15 vols. New York: Alfred A. Knopf, 1936–70.

———. *The Coming of the Revolution, 1763–1775.* New York: Harper and Row, 1962.

Gold, Robert L. *Borderland Empires in Transition: The Triple-Nation Transfer of Florida.* Carbondale: University of Illinois Press, 1969.

Great Britain. Historical Manuscripts Commission. *Report on American Manuscripts in the Royal Institution of Great Britain.* 4 vols. London: Mackie & Co., Ltd., 1904–9.

Greene, Evarts B., and Harrington, Virginia D. *American Population before the Federal Census of 1790.* New York: Columbia University Press, 1932.

Greene, Jack P. *The Quest for Power: The Lower Houses of Assembly in the Southern Royal Colonies, 1689–1776.* New York: W. W. Norton, Inc., 1972.

Gruber, Ira D. *The Howe Brothers and the American Revolution.* New York: W. W. Norton and Co., 1975.

Hamilton, Peter Joseph. *Colonial Mobile; an Historical Study Largely from Original Sources, of the Alabama-Tombigbee Basin and the Old South West, from the Discovery of the Spiritu Santo in 1519 until the Demolition of Fort Charlotte in 1821.* Reprint of 1910 ed. Mobile: First National Bank of Mobile, 1952.

Hansard, Thomas C. *The Parliamentary History of England from the Earliest Period to the Year 1803.* 36 vols. London: Longman, Hurst, Rees, et al., 1806–20.

Harlow, Vincent T. *The Founding of the Second British Empire, 1763–1793.* 2 vols. London: Longmans, Green and Co., 1952–64.

Harris, Michael H., comp. *Florida History: A Bibliography.* Metuchen, N.J.: The Scarecrow Press, 1972.

Haynes, Robert V. *The Natchez District and the American Revolution.* Jackson: University Press of Mississippi, 1976.

Higginbotham, Don. *The War of American Independence: Military Attitudes, Policies, and Practice, 1763–1789.* New York: Macmillan Co., 1971.

Holmes, Abiel. *The Annals of America, from the Discovery by Columbus in the Year 1492 to the Year 1826.* 2 vols. Cambridge, Mass.: Hilliard and Brown, 1829.

Holmes, Jack D. L. *The 1779 Marcha de Gálvez: Louisiana's Giant Step Forward in the American Revolution.* Baton Rouge: Baton Rouge Bicentennial Commission, 1974.

Howard, Clinton Newton. *The British Development of West Florida, 1763–1769*. Berkeley: University of California Press, 1947.

Hutchins, Thomas. *An Historical Narrative and Topographical Description of Louisiana and West Florida*. Facsimile of 1784 ed. Gainesville: University of Florida Press, 1968.

James, Dorris Clayton. *Antebellum Natchez*. Baton Rouge: Louisiana State University Press, 1968.

James, James Alton. *The Life of George Rogers Clark*. Chicago: University of Chicago Press, 1928.

———. *Oliver Pollock: The Life and Times of an Unknown Patriot*. New York: Appleton-Century Co., 1937.

Jensen, Merrill. *The Founding of a Nation*. New York: Oxford University Press, 1968.

Johnson, Cecil S. *British West Florida, 1763–1783*. New Haven: Yale University Press, 1943.

King, J. Estelle Stewart, comp. *Mississippi Court Records, 1799–1835*. Baltimore: Genealogical Publishing Co., 1969.

Kinnaird, Lawrence, ed. *Spain in the Mississippi Valley, 1765–1794*. 3 vols. In the Annual Report of the American Historical Association for the year 1945. Washington: Government Printing Office, 1949.

Kurtz, Stephen G., and Hutson, James H., eds. *Essays on the American Revolution*. New York: W. W. Norton and Co., 1973.

Labaree, Leonard W. *Conservatism in Early American History*. New York: New York University Press, 1948.

Learned, Marion Dexter. *Philipp Waldeck's Diary of the American Revolution*. Translated by Angelika Hyrnda Bores. Philadelphia: Americana Germanica Press, 1907.

Lowell, Edward J. *The Hessians and the Other German Auxiliaries of Great Britain in the Revolutionary War*. Reprint ed. Williamstown, Mass.: Corner House Publishers, 1970.

McBee, May Wilson. *The Natchez Court Records, 1767–1805*. 2 vols. Ann Arbor, Mich.: Edwards Brothers, Inc., 1953.

Mackesy, Piers. *The War for America, 1775–1783*. Cambridge: Harvard University Press, 1965.

Maier, Pauline. *From Resistance to Revolution: Colonial Radicals and the Development of American Opposition to Britain, 1765–1776*. New York: Vintage, 1972.

Marshall, Douglas W., and Peckham, Howard H. *Campaigns of the American Revolution: An Atlas of Manuscript Maps*. Ann Arbor: University of Michigan Press, 1976.

Meng, John J. *Despatches and Instructions of Conrad Alexandre Gerard, 1778–1780*. Paris: Librairie E. Droz, 1939.

Mereness, Newton D., ed. *Travels in the American Colonies*. New York: Macmillan Co., 1916.

Miller, Nathan. *Sea of Glory: The Continental Navy Fights for Independence, 1775–1783*. New York: David McKay Co., Inc., 1974.

Morgan, Edmund S., and Morgan, Helen M. *The Stamp Act Crisis: Prologue to Revolution*. Rev. ed. New York: Collier Books, 1967.

Morris, Richard B. *The Peacemakers: The Great Powers and American Independence*. New York: Harper and Row, 1965.

Mowat, Charles Loch. *East Florida as a British Province, 1763–1784*. Berkeley: University of California Press, 1943.

Nelson, William H. *The American Tory*. Oxford: Clarendon Press, 1961.

Norton, Mary Beth. *The British-Americans: The Loyalist Exiles in England, 1774–1789.* Boston: Little, Brown and Co., 1972.

O'Donnell, James H. III. *Southern Indians in the American Revolution.* Knoxville: University of Tennessee Press, 1973.

Ontario Bureau of Archives, Second Report, 1904. 2 vols. Toronto: L. K. Cameron, 1905.

Pettcngill, Ray Waldron, trans. *Letters from America 1776–1779; Being Letters of Brunswick, Hessian, and Waldeck Officers with the British Armies during the Revolution.* Reprint ed. Port Washington, N.Y.: Kennikat Press, 1964.

Phelps, Matthew. *Memoirs and Adventures of Captain Matthew Phelps.* Edited by Anthony Haswell. Bennington, Vt.: Press of Anthony Haswell, 1802.

Phillips, Richard. *The Present State of the British Empire in Europe, America, Africa and Asia.* London: W. Griffin, J. Johnson, W. Nicoll, and Richardson and Urquhart, 1768.

Pittman, Capt. Philip. *The Present State of the European Settlements of the Missisippi* [sic]. Edited by Frank Heywood Hodder. Facsimile reprint ed. Cleveland: Arthur H. Clark Co., 1906.

———. *The Present State of the European Settlements on the Missisippi* [sic]. Facsimile of 1770 ed. with introduction by Robert R. Rea. Gainesville: University of Florida Press, 1973.

Romans, Bernard. *A Concise Natural History of East and West Florida.* Facsimile of 1775 ed. Gainesville: University of Florida Press, 1962.

Rowland, Eron Dunbar, ed. *Life, Letters and Papers of William Dunbar.* Jackson: Press of the Mississippi Historical Society, 1930.

Rush, N. Orwin. *The Battle of Pensacola.* Tallahassee: Florida State University Press, 1966.

Sabine, Lorenzo. *Biographical Sketches of the Loyalists of the American Revolution, with an Historical Essay.* Boston: Little, Brown and Co., 1864.

Savelle, Max. *George Morgan: Colony Builder.* New York: AMS Press, 1967.

Serrano y Sanz, Manuel, ed. *Documentos historicos de la Florida y la Luisiana siglos XVI al XVIII.* Madrid: Librería General de Victoriano Suárez, 1912.

Shaw, Helen Louise. *British Administration of the Southern Indians, 1756–1783.* Lancaster, Pa.: Lancaster Press, 1931.

Shortt, Adam, and Doughty, Arthur G., eds. *Documents Relating to the Constitutional History of Canada, 1759–1791.* 2 vols. 2d ed. Ottawa: Canadian Archives, 1918.

Shy, John. *Toward Lexington: The Role of the British Army in the Coming of the American Revolution.* Princeton: Princeton University Press, 1965.

Siebert, Wilbur Henry. *Loyalists in East Florida, 1774 to 1785.* 2 vols. Deland: Florida State Historical Society, 1929.

Smelser, Marshall. *The Winning of Independence.* New York: New Viewpoints, 1973.

Smith, Paul Hubert. *Loyalists and Redcoats: A Study in British Revolutionary Policy.* Chapel Hill, N.C.: Institute of Early American History and Culture, 1964.

Sosin, Jack M. *The Revolutionary Frontier, 1763–1783.* New York: Holt, Rinehart and Winston, 1967.

Stevens, Benjamin Franklin, ed. *Facsimiles of Manuscripts in European Archives Relating to America, 1773–1783.* 25 vols. London: Malby and Sons, 1889–98.

Sullivan, James. *The Papers of Sir William Johnson.* 14 vols. Albany: The University of the State of New York, 1921–65.

Thwaites, Reuben Gold, and Kellogg, Louise Phelps, eds. *Frontier Defense on the Upper Ohio, 1777–1778.* Madison: Wisconsin Historical Society, 1912.

Upton, Leslie F. S., ed. *Revolutionary Versus Loyalist: The First American Civil War, 1774–1784*. Waltham, Mass.: Blaisdell Publishing Co., 1968.

Van Tyne, Claude Halstead. *The Loyalists in the American Revolution*. Reprint ed. New York: Peter Smith, 1929.

Whitaker, Arthur Preston. *The Spanish-American Frontier, 1783–1795*. Reprint ed. Gloucester, Mass.: Peter Smith, 1962.

Wilkinson, James. *Memoirs of My Own Times*. 3 vols. Philadelphia: Abraham Small, 1816.

Wright, J. Leitch, Jr. *Anglo-Spanish Rivalry in North America*. Athens: University of Georgia Press, 1971.

———. *Britain and the American Frontier, 1783–1815*. Athens: University of Georgia Press, 1975.

———. *Florida in the American Revolution*. Gainesville: University Presses of Florida, 1975.

———. *William Augustus Bowles, Director General of the Creek Nation*. Athens: University of Georgia Press, 1967.

Wylly, William. *A Short Account of the Bahama Islands*. London: n.p., 1789.

Wynne, John Huddlestone. *A General History of the British Empire in America*. 2 vols. London: W. Richardson and L. Urquhart, 1770.

IV. ARTICLES

Abbey, Kathryn T. "Efforts of Spain to Maintain Sources of Information in the British Colonies before 1779." *MVHR* 15 (1928):56–68.

———. "Intrigue of a British Refugee against the Willing Raid, 1778." *Wm. and Mary Qtly.*, 3d ser. 1 (1944):397–404.

———. "Peter Chester's Defense of the Mississippi after the Willing Raid." *MVHR* 22 (1935):17–32.

———. "Spanish Projects for the Reoccupation of the Floridas during the American Revolution." *HAHR* 9 (1929):265–85.

Abercrombie, Lelia. "Early Churches of Pensacola." *FHQ* 37 (1959):446–62.

Aiton, Arthur S. "The Diplomacy of the Louisiana Cession." *AHR* 36 (1931):701–20.

Albrecht, Andrew C. "The Origin and Early Settlement of Baton Rouge, Louisiana." *LHQ* 28 (1945):5–68.

Anderson, John Q., ed. "The Narrative of John Hutchins." *JMH* 20 (1958):1–29.

Beer, William, ed. "The Capture of Fort Charlotte, Mobile." *Publications of the Louisiana Historical Society* 1, part 3 (1896):31–34.

———. "The Surrender of Fort Charlotte, Mobile, 1780." *AHR* 1 (1896):696–99.

Blassingame, John W. "American Nationalism and Other Loyalties in the Southern Colonies, 1763–1775." *JSH* 34 (1968):50–75.

Born, John D., Jr. "Charles Strachan in Mobile: The Frontier Ordeal of a Scottish Factor, 1764–1768." *AHQ* 27 (1965):23–42.

Boyd, Mark F., and Latorre, José Navarro. "Spanish Interest in British Florida, and in the Progress of the American Revolution." *FHQ* 32 (1953):92–130.

Brannon, Peter A. "The Coosa River Crossing of British Refugees, 1781." *AHQ* 19 (1957):149–55.

Brown, Douglas Stewart. "The Iberville Canal Project: Its Relation to Anglo-French Commercial Rivalry in the Mississippi Valley, 1763–1775." *MVHR* 32 (1946):491–516.

Butler, Louise. "West Feliciana—A Glimpse of Its History." *LHQ* 7 (1924): 90–120.

"By the King, A Proclamation. George, R." *FHQ* 3 (1925):36–42.

Calhoon, Robert M. "Civil, Revolutionary, or Partisan: The Loyalists and the Nature of the War for Independence." Proceedings of the Sixth Air Force Academy Symposium on Military History (1974). Forthcoming from the Government Printing Office.

———. "The Floridas, the Western Frontier, and Vermont: Thoughts on the Hinterland Loyalists." In Eighteenth-Century Florida: Life on the Frontier, edited by Samuel Proctor, pp. 1–15. Gainesville: University Presses of Florida, 1976.

Campbell, John. "Account of the Surrender of Pensacola, 1781." Westminster Magazine 9 (1781):551–53.

Carter, Clarence E. "The Beginnings of British West Florida." MVHR 4 (1917):314–41.

———. "British Policy towards the American Indians in the South, 1763–1768." English Historical Review 33 (1918):37–56.

———. "Some Aspects of British Administration in West Florida." MVHR 1 (1914):364–75.

Caughey, John Walton. "Bernardo de Gálvez and the English Smugglers on the Mississippi, 1777." HAHR 12 (1932):46–58.

———. "The Natchez Rebellion of 1781 and Its Aftermath." LHQ 16 (1933):57–83.

———. "The Panis Mission to Pensacola, 1778." HAHR 10 (1930):480–89.

———. "Willing's Expedition down the Mississippi, 1778." LHQ 15 (1932):5–36.

Conover, Bettie Jones. "British West Florida's Mississippi Frontier Posts, 1763–1779." AR 29 (1976):177–207.

Corbitt, D. C. "James Colbert and the Spanish Claims to the East Bank of the Mississippi." MVHR 24 (1938):457–72.

Cotterill, R. S. "The National Land System in the South, 1803–1812." MVHR 16 (1930):495–506.

Cubberly, Fred. "Fort George (St. Michael), Pensacola." FHQ 6 (1928):220–34.

Dart, Henry P., ed. "The British Proclamation of October 7, 1763, Creating the Government of West Florida." LHQ 13 (1930):610–16.

———. "West Florida—The Capture of Baton Rouge by Gálvez, September 21, 1779, from Reports of the English Officers." LHQ 12 (1929):255–65.

———. "West Florida—Documents Covering a Royal Land Grant and Other Land Transactions on the Mississippi and Amite Rivers during the English Rule." LHQ 12 (1929):630–44.

DeRosier, Arthur H., Jr. "William Dunbar, Explorer." JMH 25 (1963):165–85.

———. "William Dunbar: A Product of the Eighteenth-Century Scottish Renaissance." JMH 28 (1966):185–227.

Drake, W. M. "A Note on the Jersey Settlers of Adams County." JMH 15 (1953):274–75.

Dungan, James R. " 'Sir' William Dunbar of Natchez, Planter, Explorer, and Scientist, 1792–1810." JMH 23 (1961):211–28.

Everett, Donald E. "Free Persons of Color in Colonial Louisiana." LH 7 (1966):21–50.

Fabel, Robin F. A. "George Johnstone and the 'Thoughts Concerning Florida'—A Case of Lobbying?" AR 29 (1976):164–76.

———. "Governor George Johnstone of British West Florida." FHQ 54 (1976):497–511.

Fabel, Robin F. A., and Rea, Robert R. "Lieutenant Thomas Campbell's Sojourn among the Creeks." AHQ 36 (1974):97–111.

Farmar, Robert. "Bernardo de Gálvez's Siege of Pensacola in 1781 (as Related in Robert Farmar's Journal)." Edited by James A. Padgett. LHQ 26 (1943):311–29.

Favrot, J. St. Clair. "Baton Rouge, the Historic Capital of Louisiana." LHQ 12 (1929):611–29.

Favrot, Mortimer H. "Colonial Forts of Louisiana." LHQ 26 (1943):722–54.

Faye, Stanley. "The Arkansas Post of Louisiana: Spanish Domination." LHQ 27 (1944):630–716.

———. "British and Spanish Fortifications of Pensacola, 1781–1821." FHQ 20 (1942):277–92.

———. "The Forked River." LHQ 25 (1942):917–42.

Fingerhut, Eugene R. "Uses and Abuses of the American Loyalists' Claims: A Critique of Quantitative Analysis." Wm. and Mary Qtly., 3d ser. 25 (1968): 245–58.

Gálvez, Bernardo de. "Diary of the Operations against Pensacola." Translated by Gaspar Cusachs. LHQ 1 (1917):44–84.

———. "A Journal of Don Bernardo de Gálvez . . . against Pensacola and Mobile . . . March 20, 1780." The Remembrancer, 1780 (Part 2):90–101.

Gauld, Charles A. "A Scottish View of West Florida in 1769." Tequesta 29 (1969):61–66.

Gold, Robert L. "Governor Bernardo de Gálvez and Spanish Espionage in Pensacola, 1777." In The Spanish in the Mississippi Valley, 1762–1804, edited by John Francis McDermott, pp. 87–99. Urbana: University of Illinois Press, 1974.

———. "Politics and Property during the Transfer of Florida from Spanish to English Rule, 1763–1764." FHQ 42 (1963):16–34.

———. "The Settlement of the Pensacola Indians in New Spain, 1763–1770." HAHR 45 (1965):567–76.

Gonzalez, Mrs. S. J. "Pensacola: Its Early History." FHQ 2 (1909):9–25.

Griffen, William B. "Spanish Pensacola, 1700–1763." FHQ 37 (1959):242–62.

Haarmann, Albert W. "The Siege of Pensacola: An Order of Battle." FHQ 44 (1966):193–99.

———. "The Spanish Conquest of British West Florida, 1779–1781." FHQ 39 (1960):107–34.

———. "The 3rd Waldeck Regiment in British Service, 1776–1783." Society for Army Historical Research, Journal 48 (1970):182–85.

Haldimand, Frederick. "Private Diary of Gen. Haldimand, 1785–1790." In Report on Canadian Archives, 1889, by Douglas Brymner, pp. 123–299. Ottawa, 1890.

Hamer, Philip M. "John Stuart's Indian Policy during the Early Months of the American Revolution." MVHR 17 (1930):351–66.

Hamilton, Peter J. "Acts of the Assembly of British West Florida." Gulf States Historical Magazine 2 (1904):273–79.

———. "British West Florida." PMHS 7 (1903):399–426.

Harrell, Laura D. S. "Colonial Medical Practice in British West Florida, 1763–1781." Bulletin of the History of Medicine 41 (1967):539–58.

Haynes, Robert V. "James Willing and the Planters of Natchez: The American Revolution Comes to the Southwest." JMH 37 (1975):1–40.

"Historical Research." Year Book of the Louisiana Society Sons of the American Revolution for 1919–1920 (1920), pp. 64–90.

Holmes, Jack D. L. "Alabama's Bloodiest Day of the American Revolution: Counterattack at The Village, January 7, 1781." AR 29 (1976):208–19.

———. "José de Evia and His Activities in Mobile, 1780–1784." *AHQ* 34 (1972):105–12.

———. "Juan de la Villebeuvre: Spain's Commandant of Natchez during the American Revolution." *JMH* 37 (1975):97–129.

———. "Law and Order in Spanish Natchez, 1781–1798." *JMH* 25 (1963):186–201.

———. "Medical Practice in the Lower Mississippi Valley During the Spanish Period, 1769–1803." *Alabama Journal of Medical Science* 1 (1964):332–38.

———. "Robert Ross' Plan for an English Invasion of Louisiana in 1782." *LH* 5 (1964):161–77.

———. "A Spanish Province, 1779–1798." In *A History of Mississippi*, edited by Richard Aubrey McLemore, 2 vols., 1:158–73. Jackson: University and College Press of Mississippi, 1973.

Howard, Clinton Newton. "Alleged Spanish Grants in British West Florida." *FHQ* 22 (1943):74–85.

———. "Colonial Natchez: The Early British Period." *JMH* 7 (1945):156–70.

———. "Colonial Pensacola: The British Period." *FHQ* 19 (1940–41):109–27, 246–69, 368–401.

———. "Early Settlers in British West Florida." *FHQ* 24 (1945):45–55.

———. "Governor Johnstone in West Florida." *FHQ* 17 (1939):281–303.

———. "The Interval of Military Government in West Florida." *LHQ* 22 (1939):18–30.

———. "The Military Occupation of British West Florida, 1763." *FHQ* 17 (1939):181–99.

———. "Some Economic Aspects of British West Florida, 1763–1768." *JSH* 6 (1940):201–21.

James, James Alton. "Oliver Pollock, Financier of the Revolution in the West." *MVHR* 16 (1929):67–80.

———. "Oliver Pollock and the Free Navigation of the Mississippi River." *MVHR* 19 (1932):331–47.

———. "Spanish Influence in the West during the American Revolution." *MVHR* 4 (1917):193–208.

Jenkins, William H. "Alabama Forts, 1700–1838." *AR* 12 (1959):163–79.

Johnson, Cecil S. "The Distribution of Land in British West Florida." *LHQ* 16 (1933):535–53.

———. "Expansion in West Florida, 1770–1779." *MVHR* 20 (1934):481–96.

———. "A Note on Absenteeism and Pluralism in British West Florida." *LHQ* 19 (1936):196–98.

———. "Pensacola in the British Period: Summary and Significance." *FHQ* 37 (1959):263–80.

———. "West Florida Revisited." *JMH* 28 (1966):121–32.

Kammen, Michael G. "The Unique and the Universal in the History of New World Colonization." In *Eighteenth-Century Florida and Its Borderlands*, edited by Samuel Proctor, pp. 48–60. Gainesville: University Presses of Florida, 1975.

Katcher, P. R. N. "The First Pennsylvania Loyalist Battalion, 1777–1783." Society for Army Historical Research, *Journal* 48 (1970):250–51.

Kerr, Wilfred B. "The Stamp Act in the Floridas, 1765–1766." *MVHR* 21 (1935):463–70.

Kinnaird, Lawrence, ed. "Clark-Leyba Papers." *AHR* 41 (1935):92–112.

Kynerd, Byrle A. "British West Florida." In *A History of Mississippi*, edited by Richard Aubrey McLemore, 2 vols., 1:134–57. Jackson: University and College Press of Mississippi, 1973.

Labaree, Leonard W. "Nature of American Loyalism." American Antiquarian Society, *Proceedings* 54 (1944):15–58.

Lewis, Anna, trans. and ed. "Fort Panmure, 1779, as Related by Jean Delavillebeuvre to Bernardo de Gálvez." *MVHR* 18 (1932):541–48.

Lockey, Joseph B. "The Florida Banditti, 1783." *FHQ* 24 (1945):87–107.

Miranda, Francisco de. "Miranda's Diary of the Siege of Pensacola, 1781." Translated by Donald E. Worchester. *FHQ* 29 (1951):163–96.

Moore, John Preston. "Anglo-Spanish Rivalry on the Louisiana Frontier, 1763–68." In *The Spanish in the Mississippi Valley, 1762–1804*, edited by John Francis McDermott, pp. 72–86. Urbana: University of Illinois Press, 1974.

Morgan, Madel Jacobs. "Sarah Truly: A Mississippi Tory." *JMH* 37 (1975):87–95.

Morris, Richard B. "The Treaty of Paris of 1783." In Library of Congress, Symposia on the American Revolution, 2d, 1973, *Fundamental Testaments of the American Revolution*, pp. 83–106. Washington: Library of Congress, 1973.

Moses, Alfred G. "A History of the Jews of Mobile." *Publications of the American Jewish Historical Society* 12 (1904):113–25.

Mowat, Charles L. "The First Campaign of Publicity for Florida." *MVHR* 30 (1943):359–76.

———. "The Southern Brigade: A Sidelight on the British Military Establishment in America, 1763–1775." *JSH* 10 (1944):59–77.

Murphy, W. S. "The Irish Brigade of Spain at the Capture of Pensacola, 1781." *FHQ* 38 (1960):216–25.

Nachbin, Jac, ed. "Spain's Report of the War with the British in Louisiana." *LHQ* 15 (1932):468–81.

Neeley, Mary Ann Oglesby. "Lachlan McGillivray: A Scot on the Alabama Frontier." *AHQ* 36 (1974):5–14.

Norton, Mary Beth. "The Loyalist Critique of the Revolution." In Library of Congress, Symposia on the American Revolution, 1st, 1972, *The Development of a Revolutionary Mentality*, pp. 127–48. Washington: Library of Congress, 1972.

Nunemaker, J. Horace. "Louisiana Anticipates Spain's Recognition of the Independence of the United States." *LHQ* 26 (1943):755–69.

Ogden, Jonathan. "Pensacola in 1770." Edited by Charles C. Cumberland. *Rutgers University Library Journal* 13 (1949):7–13.

Osborn, George C. "Major-General John Campbell in British West Florida." *FHQ* 27 (1949):317–39.

———. "Relations with the Indians in West Florida during the Administration of Governor Peter Chester, 1770–1781." *FHQ* 31 (1953):239–72.

Padgett, James A., ed. "Commission, Orders and Instructions Issued to George Johnstone, British Governor of West Florida, 1763–1767." *LHQ* 21 (1938):1021–68.

———. "Governor Peter Chester's Observations on the Boundaries of British West Florida about 1775." *LHQ* 26 (1943):5–11.

———. "Minutes of the Assembly of West Florida (Sessions: February 23–June 6, 1767; December 15, 1767–January 11, 1768)." *LHQ* 22 (1939):943–1011.

———. "Minutes of the Council of West Florida, April 3–July 22, 1769." *LHQ* 23 (1940):353–404.

———. "Minutes of the First Session of the Assembly of West Florida (November 3, 1766–January 3, 1777)." *LHQ* 22 (1939):311–84.

———. "Minutes of the West Florida Assembly (Sessions: August 23–October 21, 1768; January 25–February 2, 1769; May 22–June 29, 1769)." *LHQ* 23 (1940):5–77.

————. "The Reply of Peter Chester, Governor of West Florida, to Complaints Made against His Administration." *LHQ* 22 (1939):31–46.

Pease, Theodore. "The Mississippi Boundary of 1763." *AHR* 40 (1935):278–86.

Peters, Thelma. "The American Loyalists in the Bahama Islands: Who They Were." *FHQ* 40 (1962):226–40.

Rea, Robert R. "Belles-Lettres in British West Florida." *AR* 13 (1960):145–49.

————. "Brigadier Frederick Haldimand—The Florida Years." *FHQ* 54 (1976):512–31.

————. "British West Florida: Stepchild of Diplomacy." In *Eighteenth-Century Florida and Its Borderlands*, edited by Samuel Proctor, pp. 61–77. Gainesville: University Presses of Florida, 1975.

————. " 'Graveyard for Britons,' West Florida, 1763–1781." *FHQ* 47 (1969): 345–64.

————. "The King's Agent for British West Florida." *AR* 16 (1963):141–53.

————. "Lieutenant Colonel James Robertson's Mission to the Floridas, 1763." *FHQ* 52 (1974):33–48.

————. "Military Deserters from British West Florida." *LH* 9 (1968):123–37.

————. "A Naval Visitor in British West Florida." *FHQ* 40 (1961):142–53.

————. "Outpost of Empire: David Wedderburn at Mobile." *AR* 7 (1954):217–32.

————. "Pensacola under the British (1763–1781)." In *Colonial Pensacola*, edited by James R. McGovern, pp. 56–87. Pensacola: Pensacola-Escambia County Development Commission, 1972.

————. "Planters and Plantations in British West Florida." *AR* 29 (1976):220–35.

————. "Redcoats and Redskins on the Lower Mississippi, 1763–1776: The Career of Lt. John Thomas." *LH* 11 (1970):5–35.

————. "1763—The Forgotten Bicentennial: An Historiographic Commentary." *AHQ* 25 (1963):287–93.

————. "The Trouble at Tombeckby." *AR* 21 (1968):21–39.

————, ed. "Henry Hamilton and West Florida." *Indiana Magazine of History* 54 (1958):49–56.

————, ed. "A New Letter from Mobile, 1763." *AR* 22 (1969):230–37.

Rea, Robert R., and Holmes, Jack D. L. "Dr. John Lorimer and the Natural Sciences in British West Florida." *Southern Humanities Review* 4 (1970): 363–72.

Riley, Franklin L. "Sir William Dunbar—The Pioneer Scientist of Mississippi." *PMHS* 2 (1899):85–111.

Robertson, James A., ed. "Spanish Correspondence Concerning the American Revolution." *HAHR* 1 (1918):299–316.

Rowland, Eron Dunbar. "Mississippi's Colonial Population and Land Grants." *PMHS* 1 (Centenary Series, 1916):405–28.

————, ed. "Peter Chester, Third Governor of the Province of West Florida under British Dominion, 1770–1781." *PMHS* 5 (Centenary Series, 1925): 1–183.

Savelle, Max. "Nationalism and Other Loyalties in the American Revolution." *AHR* 67 (1962):901–23.

Scott, Kenneth, ed. "Britain Loses Natchez, 1779: An Unpublished Letter." *JMH* 26 (1964):45–46.

Scramuzza, V. M. "Gálveztown—A Spanish Settlement of Colonial Louisiana." *LHQ* 13 (1930):553–609.

Shepherd, W. R. "The Cession of Louisiana to Spain." *Political Science Quarterly* 19 (1904):439–58.

Siebert, Wilbur H. "How the Spaniards Evacuated Pensacola in 1763." *FHQ* 11 (1932):48–57.

———. "The Loyalists in West Florida and the Natchez District." *MVHR* 2 (1916):465–83.

Smith, Adam. "Adam Smith on the American Revolution: An Unpublished Memorial." Edited by George H. Guttridge. *AHR* 38 (1933):714–20.

Smith, Paul H. "The American Loyalists: Notes on Their Organization and Numerical Strength." *Wm. and Mary Qtly.*, 3d ser. 25 (1968):259–77.

Starr, J. Barton. "Campbell Town: French Huguenots in British West Florida." *FHQ* 54 (1976):532–47.

———. " 'The Spirit of What Is There Called Liberty': The Stamp Act in British West Florida." *AR* 29 (1976):261–72.

Sturdivant, Laura D. S. "One Carbine and a Little Flour and Corn in a Sack: The American Pioneer." *JMH* 37 (1975):43–65.

Taylor, Garland. "Colonial Settlement and Early Revolutionary Activity in West Florida up to 1779." *MVHR* 22 (1935):351–60.

Thomas, Daniel H. "Fort Toulouse: The French Outpost at the Alibamos on the Coosa." *AHQ* 22 (1960):135–230.

Tregle, Joseph G., Jr. "British Spy along the Mississippi: Thomas Hutchins and the Defenses of New Orleans, 1773." *LH* 8 (1967):313–27.

Trexler, Scott A. II, and Walck, Lee A. "Rebel and Tory Colonel, Lieutenant Colonel William Allen, Jr." *Proceedings of the Lehigh County Historical Society* 26 (1966):13–84.

Turner, Frederick Jackson, ed. "George Rogers Clark and the Kaskaskia Campaign, 1777–1778." *AHR* 8 (1903):491–506.

Tyler, Moses Coit. "The Party of the Loyalists in the American Revolution." *AHR* 1 (1895):24–45.

Van Tyne, Claude Halstead. "Sovereignty in the American Revolution: An Historical Study." *AHR* 12 (1907):529–45.

Wells, Gordon M., comp. "British Land Grants—William Wilton Map, 1774." *JMH* 28 (1966):152–60.

Wright, J. Leitch, Jr. "British Designs on the Old Southwest: Foreign Intrigue on the Florida Frontier, 1783–1803." *FHQ* 44 (1966):265–84.

———. "Lord Dunmore's Loyalist Asylum in the Floridas." *FHQ* 49 (1971): 370–79.

V. Unpublished Papers, Theses, and Dissertations

Abbey, Kathryn T. "Florida as an Issue during the American Revolution." Ph.D. dissertation, Northwestern University, 1926.

Anderson, Robert L. "A History and Study of the Pensacola Forts." Master's thesis, Auburn University, 1969.

Begnaud, Allen Eustis. "British Operations in the Caribbean and the American Revolution." Ph.D. dissertation, Tulane University, 1966.

Born, John Dewey, Jr. "British Trade in West Florida, 1763–1783." Ph.D. dissertation, University of New Mexico, 1963.

Brewster, Lawrence F. "The Later History of British West Florida, 1770–1781. Governor Peter Chester and the Heyday of the Province." Master's thesis, Columbia University, 1932.

Calhoon Robert M. " 'Filled with Anxiety': Recent Scholarship on Loyalist Personality and Intellect." Paper presented at Conference on American Loyalists, St. Augustine, Florida, 1975.

Chambers, Moreau B. C. "History of Fort Panmure at Natchez, 1763–1785." Master's thesis, Duke University, 1942.

Conover, Elizabeth May Jones. "British West Florida's Mississippi Frontier during the American Revolution." Master's thesis, Auburn University, 1972.

De Coste, Fredrik. "Loyalists in Florida during the American Revolution." Manuscript, P. K. Yonge Library, University of Florida, Gainesville.

"Despatches of Spanish Governors of Louisiana, 1766–1798." Typescript. Baton Rouge: Sponsored by Louisiana State University, 1937–41.

Fabel, Robin Francis Abbot. "Governor George Johnstone, 1730–1787." Ph.D. dissertation, Auburn University, 1974.

Gray, Robert Edward. "Elias Durnford, 1739–1794: Engineer, Soldier, Administrator." Master's thesis, Auburn University, 1971.

Hamilton, William Baskerville. "American Beginnings in the Old Southwest: The Mississippi Phase." Ph.D. dissertation, Duke University, 1937.

Holt, Sara Baker. "Christ Church, Pensacola, Florida, 1763–1950." Manuscript, P. K. Yonge Library, University of Florida, Gainesville.

Inglis, Gordon Douglas. "Anthony Hutchins: Early Natchez Planter." Master's thesis, University of Southern Mississippi, 1973.

Ingram, Earl Glynn. "A Critical Study of the British West Florida Legislative Assembly." Master's thesis, Auburn University, 1969.

Jova, Joseph John. "Hispanic Support to the United States War of Independence." Paper presented at the Conference of the Center for Latin American Studies, Gainesville, Florida, 1976.

Long, Jeanette M. "Immigration to British West Florida, 1763–1781." Master's thesis, University of Kansas, 1969.

McMillan, Lucy M. "Natchez, 1763–1779." Master's thesis, University of Virginia, 1938.

Miller, Wilbert James. "The Spanish Commandant of Baton Rouge, 1779–1795." Master's thesis, Louisiana State University, 1965.

Parrish, Lydia. "Records of Some Southern Loyalists: being a Collection of Manuscripts about Some 80 Families, Most of Whom Immigrated to the Bahamas during and after the American Revolution." Manuscript, Harvard College Library, Cambridge, 1959.

Peters, Thelma. "The American Loyalists and the Plantation Period in the Bahama Islands." Ph.D. dissertation, University of Florida, 1960.

Quattrocchi, Anna Margaret. "Thomas Hutchins, 1730–1789." Ph.D. dissertation, University of Pittsburgh, 1944.

Rutherford, Robert Erwin. "Spain's Immigration Policy for the Floridas, 1780–1806." Master's thesis, University of Florida, 1952.

Spindel, Donna J. "The Stamp Act Riots." Ph.D. dissertation, Duke University, 1975.

Starr, J. Barton. "A Case for the 'Loyal' Colonies: The West Florida Loyalists." Paper presented at the Conference on American Loyalists, St. Augustine, Florida, 1975.

————. " 'Left as a Gewgaw': The Impact of the American Revolution on British West Florida." Paper presented at the Florida Bicentennial Symposium, Pensacola, Florida, 1976.

————. "Spanish Louisiana and West Florida Loyalists." Paper presented at the Conference of the Center for Latin American Studies, Gainesville, Florida, 1976.

Topping, Aileen Moore. "Spanish Agents at the Continental Congress and Spanish-American Plans for the Conquest of East Florida." Paper presented at the Conference of the Center for Latin American Studies, Gainesville, Florida, 1976.

Index

Active, 114, 115, 116
Admiralty, 51
Alabama Indians, 177
Alabama River, 32
Alberti, Capt., 200n
Alexander, George, 90n
Alexander, Harry, 90n, 227n
Alexander, William, 90n
Allen, Lt. Col. William, 162
Alston, John, 217
Alston, Philip, 217
Amite River: settlement on, 33; and
    British offensive against Willing,
    104; British posts on captured, 152;
    mentioned, 49, 90
Amity and Commerce, Treaty of, 123
Amos, Sarah, 238n
Anderson, John, 157n
Ann and Elizabeth, 188
Apalachicola River, 3, 223
Arbuthnot, Adm. Marriott, 144
Army. *See* British Army
Arnold, Benedict, 81
Assembly: description, 4; Gov.
    Johnstone's instructions on, 11;
    1766 session, 11–12; 1767 session,
    18–19; 1768 session, 24–25;
    relations with Gov. Chester, 28,
    162, 180, 233; 1778 session, 113,
    122–28; evaluation of, in West
    Florida, 128
Atalanta: undermanned, 57; in New
    Orleans, 67, 68; in Pensacola, 106;
    mentioned, 68n, 95

"A.Z.," 219–20

Bahamas, 234–35
Balise, 94
Bard, Lt., 200n
Barker, Capt. William, 114n, 153n
Barry, Capt., 69
Bartram, William, 50, 165
Baton Rouge: surrender of, 147–48,
    155–56; Gálvez prepares to attack,
    148; Spanish campaign against,
    151–57; and Mobile articles of
    capitulation compared, 173;
    mentioned, 77, 137, 171, 242, 243
Bay, Elihu Hall, 55
Beaufort, S.C., 50
Bethune, Farquhar: Hutchins requests
    reinforcements from, 111; force
    arrives at White Cliffs, 112;
    arrested, 151; ordered to defense of
    Mobile, 177; urges action against
    the Spanish, 219
Bingamin, Samuel, 217
"Black Prince." *See* Durnford, Elias
Blackwell, Jacob, 36, 39
Blommart, John: financial losses, 92n;
    and 1781 Natchez rebellion,
    217–18; on West Florida Loyalists,
    226
Board of Commissioners for Executing
    the Office of Indian Affairs, 134–35
Board of Trade, 3
Board of War, 81, 82
Boquet, Col. Henry, 15n

Boston, Mass., 75
Bouligny, Col. Francisco, 169–70
Boundaries (of West Florida), 2–4
Bowles, William Augustus, 134n, 184n
Bradley, John, 25, 124
Brettell, John, 39
British Army: Royal American Regiment of Foot, Third Battalion, 4; as standing army, 4n; brigadier general, 15; troops withdrawn, 24–25; West Florida troop returns, 43, 57, 140n, 154, 190; at Fort Pitt and Wheeling, 63; reinforcements sent to West Florida, 120–21; Campbell on provincial troops, 134; health of, 144; Royal Artillery, 203, 210; presence in West Florida, 233. See also Desertion
—Sixteenth Regiment: ordered to West Florida, 26; Campbell on, 133; replacements for, 140; surrenders colors, 156; takes position in Queen's Redoubt, 202; replaced by Pennsylvania Loyalists, 210n; mentioned, 190
—Twenty-first Regiment, 7
—Twenty-second Regiment, 5
—Thirty-first Regiment, 7
—Thirty-fourth Regiment, 5
—Sixtieth Regiment: first battalion at Jamaica to assist West Florida, 51; inexperience of, 54; Chester on, 54n; ordered to Pensacola, 114; Campbell on, 133; to be reinforced, 140; attacks Village of Mobile, 183–84; Battle of Pensacola, 202, 203, 206–7, 210; mentioned, 190
British King, 23
British Navy. See Navy; Admiralty; names of specific ships
Brown, Wallace, 245–46
Browne, Lt. Gov. Montfort: dispute with Gov. Johnstone, 15; ordered to stop hostilities against the Indians, 17; takes over government, 17–18; allied with enemies of Gov. Johnstone, 18; arrival in West Florida, 18; relations with the assembly, 18–19, 24; requests investigation of his accounts, 19; petitions against, 20; resumes control of government (upon Eliot's

death), 20, 21; supported, 20–21; recalled, 21–22; dispute with Durnford, 22–23; duel with Evan Jones, 23; imprisoned, 23; leaves West Florida, 23; on troop withdrawal, 24; on O'Reilly, 26, 43; initiates petition for Johnstone's removal, 40; and Stamp Act, 41; orders concerning Massachusetts Circular Letter, 45; mentioned, 27, 42, 122
Browne, Col. Thomas, 138, 138n
Brownhall, 168
Bruce, James: on Campbell Town, 18n; on trade, 66n; losses, 92n; observations on West Florida, 221n
Buenos Aires, Argentina, 43
Burdon, Lt. George: commands West Florida, 67; complaint against, 80; on Spanish detention of West Florida, 100–101; reinforcements for, 103, 108, 108n; mentioned, 113
Bute, Earl of, 9n
Bute, Fort: troops withdrawn, 24; dismantled, 25; support of, 153n; mentioned, 135
Byrd, Capt., 203, 206–7, 210

Cagigal, Field Marshall Juan Manuel de, 205, 206
Calbo, José. See Irozabal, José Calbo de
Calhoon, Robert M., 245–46
Calvert, Joseph, 68n, 89
Cambel, John, 20
Cameron, Alexander: and Loyal Refugees, 58n, 107; appointed Indian superintendent, 138; believes Mobile will be attacked first, 164; on Indians and defense of Pensacola, 177; on Campbell's Indian policy, 177; proposes to raise force, 179n; reprimands Choctaws, 182n; on confusion at Village of Mobile, 183; leads Indians against Spanish camp, 203; mentioned, 76, 182
Campbell, James: as Gen. Campbell's secretary, 145n; possible author of "Robert Farmar's Journal," 190n; detained as hostage, 213
Campbell, John, 99n, 109

Campbell, General John: surrenders, 1;
ordered to West Florida, 130;
voyage to West Florida, 130–32;
views on West Florida, 131, 133,
137; on smallpox among Maryland
Loyalists, 131n; evaluates troops,
133–34, 159, 192, 227; and
provincial forces, 134, 135, 161,
174n, 179n, 191; orders to him
concerning defense of West Florida,
135; request for Negroes, 135n;
informs Gálvez of his arrival and
asks for cooperation, 136;
difficulties in constructing post at
Manchac, 136–37; recommends
William Ogilvie as Indian
superintendent, 138; complains of
his situation in West Florida.
138–39, 140; requests reinforcements, 140; notified of war
with Spain, 144, 148n; and attack
on New Orleans, 144–145, 147–48,
163; orders Dickson to prepare
defenses of Manchac, 145; seized
all vessels capable of carrying
troops, 145; and embargo, 145,
146n, 163; requests Chester declare
martial law, 146; on distribution of
gunpowder, 146n; and militia,
146–47, 147n; on West Florida
Loyalists, 147, 147n, 226–27; sends
Waldeckers to Manchac, 149;
response to Baton Rouge defeat,
158–60; and Pennsylvania and
Maryland Loyalists, 162; urges
Chester to call assembly, 162; on
security of Pensacola, 164, 175,
193n; and Battle of Mobile, 165,
171–74; describes Mobile, 167;
orders strengthening of Fort
Charlotte, 167; and Spanish
campaign against Pensacola,
175–80, 183–87, 191, 199–215;
Indian policy, 177–79, 182n;
dispute with Chester, 180–81;
opinion of civil government in
West Florida, 181–82; refuses
request for stockade, 182; sends
force after Indian raiding party,
182; possible author of "Robert
Farmar's Journal," 190n; issued
blank commissions for captains,
217; mentioned, 29, 141, 151, 242

Campbell Town, 11, 18, 18n
Canada, 3, 51
Canary Islands, 151
Carlos, King (of Spain), 65
Carolinas, 143, 218
Carteret: detained, 145–46; brings
news of Spanish War, 148n; leaves
Pensacola, 163; causes hardship,
163n
Case and Petition of His Majesty's
Loyal Subjects, Late of West
Florida, The, 238
Castang Bayou, 49
Caughey, John Walton, 115
Chalmers, Lt. Col. James, 131, 222
Chambequin, 195
Chance, 115
Charleston, S.C., 50, 220
Charlotte, Fort: Fort Conde renamed,
5; possessed by British, 5; repairs
recommended, 54; condition of,
133; description of, 165–67; troops
in, 167–68; and defense of Mobile,
169–73; arsenal of, 173n; men-
tioned, 79
Charlotte County, 125–26
Cherokee: Indians, 57, 74, 142;
Nation, 230 (table)
Chester, Gov. Peter: relations with
Haldimand, 15, 28–29; arrival in
West Florida, 27; provides
continuity, 27; Indian policy, 28,
76n, 137–38; relations with
assembly, 28, 122–28, 162–63, 180;
on troops on the Mississippi,
28–29, 53, 159n; instructions
concerning land grants, 30–32;
evaluates condition of Pensacola,
43; recommends silence on letter
from Continental Congress, 46; and
West Florida as loyalist haven,
47–48, 229; on privateers, 50;
reports on rumored American
invasions, 53–54, 55, 56, 57; on
Sixtieth Regiment, 54n; and
embargo, 54–55, 145, 163;
evaluated as a leader, 57–58; on
Gibson's mission, 62, 64; on illegal
American commerce in Louisiana,
64; strengthens defenses, 78; and
Panis mission, 79–80; and Willing's
expedition, 87, 101–8, 110, 113–14,
115; orders the Hound to the

Mississippi, 98; on captured American property, 119; informed of Spanish war, 145, 145n; detains *Carteret*, 145–46; on martial law, 146, 146n; dispute with Campbell, 159, 180–81; complaints against, 180n; on indispensability of navy to defense of Pensacola, 187–88; requested merchantmen be ready to join war ships, 188–89; and parole of Spanish prisoners, 201, 204; and safety of women and children, 201, 202–3, 204; and Articles of Capitulation, 210–11; in Charleston, 212n, 220; on West Florida loyalists, 227, 233; on British trade in New Orleans, 228; mentioned, 27n, 45, 51, 60, 65, 76, 84, 86, 92, 97, 117, 118, 134, 163n

Chickasaw Indians: communications with, 54; loyalty questionable, 174; in Pensacola, 177; Natchez settlers flee to live among, 217–18; mentioned, 142

Chief justice, West Florida, 4

Childers, 189

Choctaw Indians: communications with, 54; stand guard at Walnut Hills, 84; loyalty questionable, 147, 174; divide the colony, 159; attempt to improve relations with, 162; ordered to defense of Mobile, 177; in Pensacola, 177; sent after Indian raiding party, 182; murdered Spaniards, 182n; Natchez settlers flee to live among, 217–18; mentioned, 16, 142, 219

Christianna, 115, 116

Chrystie, Adam: immigration effort, 33; financial losses of, 92n; accompanies Loyal Refugees to the Mississippi, 103; and offensive against Willing's party, 104–5, 105n, 124; elected Speaker of the House of Assembly, 123; as a loyalist, 147n; in command of West Florida Royal Foresters, 161, 190n; on Strachan's surrender, 174n; dispute with Chester, 180; migration, 235; mentioned, 118

Cincinnati, 73

Civil establishment, 48

Clark, Daniel, 18

Clark, George Rogers, 73, 120

Clarke, Col. John, 33

Clifton, William: suspended, 14; refuses bail for Montfort Browne, 23; Johnstone's opponent, 39, 40; opinion of embargo, 55

Clinton, Gen. Henry: and reinforcements, 78, 129–30, 140; allows Willing parole, 117; request for Negroes, 135; fails to support Campbell, 137; appoints Cameron as Indian superintendent, 138; orders to Cornwallis, 144; on security of West Florida, 144n, 187; orders separation of United Corps of Pennsylvania and Maryland Loyalists, 162; and use of black troops, 220; mentioned, 122, 135n, 139, 140, 143, 146, 179, 191, 192, 214

Coercive Acts, 36

Colbert, James, 218

Collins, Maj. Luke, 86

Collins, Robert, 40–41

Columbus, 69, 70n

Comite River, 33, 49

Commerce. *See* Trade

Commerce Committee, 82–83

Commission for Enquiring into the Losses, Services, and Claims of the American Loyalists, 237–40

Company of Military Adventurers, 33

Conde, Fort, *See* Charlotte, Fort

Congress, 50

Connally, Col. John, 118n

Connecticut, 50, 230

Continental Association, 46

Continental Congress: West Florida representation, 45–46; orders expedition, 51n; plans attack on West Florida, 57; Spanish agent to, 72n; appoints Indian superintendents, 74; and Willing's raid, 81–83; seeks resignation of Johnstone, 123n; Drayton reports to, 222; and "Separate Article," 223n; seeks support of West Florida, 233; mentioned, 242

Contraband trade. *See* Smuggling

Cornwallis, Earl of, 144, 179, 180

Council: and war against Creeks, 16; and defenses of West Florida, 16, 54–55, 181–82; agrees to allow

Montfort Browne to leave West Florida, 23; prepares memorials, 24–25; thanks Hillsborough, 27; and land grants, 31, 48–50; and Stamp Act, 36; and charges against William Struthers, 55–56; on impressment, 57; sends members to New Orleans to investigate seizures, 69; and Willing's raid, 92, 98, 103–8, 113–14, 115; on captured American property, 119; recommends calling assembly, 122; and embargo, 145, 163; and martial law, 146; and militia, 146, 147, 147n; on loyalty of West Floridians, 182; mentioned, 4

Coupée, Point, 88

Cox, John, 88

Crawford, 130

Creek Indians: and Gov. Johnstone, 16; American invasion of their land, 55; desire for neutrality, 75; in Pensacola, 177–78; McGillivray ordered to march Creeks to Pensacola, 178; mentioned, 74

Cruden, John, 220

Cruzat, Madam, 218

Cuba, 1. See also Havana

Cumberland River, 53

Currency Act, 36

Cushing, Thomas, 46

Dallas, Dr. James, 147n

Dalling, Gov. John: reinforcements for West Florida, 114, 115n, 163; informed of outbreak of war, 143

D'Almadavar, Marquis, 142

Dartmouth, Earl of: on land grants, 31; and West Florida as loyalist haven, 47–48, 237; becomes secretary of state, 48n; mentioned, 32

Davey, Capt. Thomas, 55

David Ross and Company, 89

Dawes, Joseph, 87

Deans, Capt. Robert: lifted embargo, 189; ordered Mentor inland, 204; on casualties, 209n; detained as hostage, 213; mentioned, 196n

Declaration of Independence, 62

DeHorn, Lt. Col. Albrecht, 208

Desertion: among Waldeckers, 193n; during Battle of Pensacola, 204, 211; mentioned, 134, 144, 180, 180n

D'Estaing, Comte, 145n

Dickinson, John, 46

Dickson, Col. Alexander: on probable American invasion, 51–52, 53; on defenses of West Florida, 53; investigates ship seizures, 69; requested to obtain reinforcements, 105; prepares defenses of Manchac, 145; surrenders, 147–48; orders destruction of British ship, 152; and Baton Rouge campaign, 152–58; anecdote about, 155n; returns to England, 158n; burns houses at Baton Rouge, 171; bears message to Gálvez, 200; on parole, 200n; mentioned, 149, 159

Diligence, 188

Diseases, 7

Dispatch, 89

Dog River, 169

Dolony, Francis, 119n

Dominica, 50, 230

Drayton, William Henry, 222

Dry Tortugas, 51

Dunbar, William: on Spanish war, 70; describes Willing, 82; on West Florida loyalists, 118, 226; on Willing's raid, 120; arrested, 151; on Anglo-Spanish alliance, 151–52n; on the American Revolution, 228

Dunmore, Earl of (Lord John Murray), 220–21, 237

Durnford, Elias: goes to England, 21; returns to Pensacola, 22; appointed lieutenant governor, 22, 22n; anecdote about, 22n; dispute with Montfort Browne, 22–23; acting governor, 23, 27; immigration effort, 33; warns Hiorn of possible expedition, 149; proposes the dismantling of Fort Charlotte, 165–67; and defense of Mobile, 167, 168–74; mentioned, 160

Dutton, Rebecca, 238n

Dutton, William, 92n

Dutton, 189–90

Earl of Bathurst, 163, 188

Earnest, Henry, 85

Earnest, John, 85

Eason, William, 217

East Florida: and non-exportation, 46; loyalists from, 50, 237; fears

American attack, 56; Natchez settlers flee to, 218; immigration from, 230; and loyalist claims, 238; mentioned, 3, 45, 226

Eelking, Max von, 132

Eglington, Earl of, 30

El Cayman, 150n

Eliot, James, 118n

Eliot, Gov. John, 18, 19, 19n

Ellis, Richard, 86

Embargo: on American trade to West Florida, 46; on trade to Americans, 47; of 1776, 54–55; of 1778, 108, 114; of 1779, 145, 163; of 1780, 188

England: Spain declares war on, 141, 142; and loyalist emigration, 234; Chrystie in, 235; Lorimer in, 235; and war with Spain, 242, 243

Escambia River, 55

Espionage: British, 59–60; Spanish, 60, 78–80

Ezpeleta, José de: in command at Mobile, 176; receives orders to march to Pensacola, 196; arrives from Mobile, 201; takes command while Gálvez recovers, 205; reinforces Pine Hill, 208

Falkland Islands: dispute over, 43, 44; mentioned, 26n

"Family right," 29, 31, 48–49

Farmar, Maj. Robert: ordered to occupy Mobile, 5; opinion of Mobile, 6; dispute with Johnstone, 14; Johnstone's opponent, 40; and "Robert Farmar's Journal," 189–90n

Fergusson, Capt. John: ordered to the Mississippi, 92; and Willing's raid, 92–101; thanked by assembly, 124; mentioned, 103

Figuerola, Pablo, 208

Finances, in West Florida, 4

Fish River, 115

Florida: to transport Loyal Refugees, 103; transfer of officers, 108n; ordered to West Florida, 114, 115; attempts to oppose Americans near Mobile, 115; reinforced, 116; mentioned, 108

Floridas, Spanish possession of both, 59, 71

Flowers, Samuel, 153, 153n, 171

Forbes, Maj. William, 6

Ford, Lt. Thomas, 5

Forster, Capt. Anthony, 157

Fortescue, John, 148n

Francis, Mr., 118n

French, 1, 8, 10

French and Indian War, 223, 241

Gage, Gen. Thomas: on military-civil relations, 14; appoints brigadier general for West Florida, 15; orders withdrawal of troops, 24; and reinforcements for West Florida, 26; on O'Reilly's force, 26n; orders Haldimand not to move troops to western posts, 29; on leave of absence, 29; on Stamp Act in West Florida, 39; on attack on New Orleans, 43, 44; on offensive use of Indians, 75–76; on British posts on the Mississippi, 153; on support of Natchez and Fort Bute, 153n; mentioned, 13, 15n, 16, 25

Gage Hill: fortifications to be constructed on, 184–85; Spanish entrenchments on, 207

Galphin, George, 74

Gálvez, Gen. Bernardo de: accepts surrender at Pensacola, 1; sends spies to West Florida, 60, 78–79; on admission of Americans to Spanish ports, 64; becomes governor, 65; experiences before becoming governor, 65; English evaluation of, 65; age, 65n; and smuggling, 65–68, 69; seizes British ships in Louisiana, 66; sends flour to Pensacola, 69; and American shipping on Mississippi River, 69–70; ordered to encourage the Americans, 70–71; correspondence with George Morgan, 70–71, 82; correspondence with Patrick Henry, 71–73; and Panis mission, 79–80, 79n; and Willing's raid, 83, 89–102, 109, 112, 116–17; informed of Campbell's arrival in West Florida, 136; agrees to allow British to purchase vessels in New Orleans, 136; Dickson surrenders to, 147–48; learns of outbreak of war, 148–49; suspicious of British activities, 149; campaign against Baton Rouge, 150–58; threatens all of West Florida, 160; placed at head of

expedition against West Florida,
164–65; wants attack on Mobile
first, 164–65; and Battle of Mobile,
168–74; and Pensacola campaign,
175–77, 183, 193–213; and use of
Indians, 177; builds Village of
Mobile, 183; orders release of
Blommart and others, 218;
mentioned, 77, 114n, 242

Gálvez, José de: orders expedition
against British West Florida,
149–50; mentioned, 65, 72n, 79

Gálvez, 168

Gálveztown, 198–99

Gálveztown, La., 90, 152

Garnier, Capt. William, 92, 103, 105

Gayton, Adm. Clark, 51

George III, King (of England): and
Proclamation of 1763, 2; appoints
George Johnstone as governor, 9;
and American loyalists, 237; and
the Floridas, 243; mentioned, 228

George, Lt. Robert, 117

George, Fort: constructed on Gage
Hill, 185, 186n; cannon from
removed to Royal Navy Redoubt,
186; Pensacola to be defended
from, 200; Spanish move closer to,
203; Spanish reconnaissance near,
204; abortive Spanish diversionary
attack on, 209; untenable, 215

Georgia: and non-exportation, 46;
loyalists from, 49, 50; Natchez
settlers flee to, 218; immigration
from, 230; mentioned, 81, 143

Gérard, Conrad Alexandre, 120n, 222

Germain, Lord George: prohibits trade
with rebellious colonies, 47; orders
ships to West Florida, 51; on
security of West Florida, 51, 55;
accepts Stuart's proposal for raising
rangers, 53; refuses 1777 request for
a general officer in West Florida,
58; criticizes Indian Department,
84; orders Chester to avoid war
with Spain, 102; on British
offensive against Willing's party,
105; on captured American
property, 119; on defenses of West
Florida, 129, 135, 161; orders
concerning Loyal Refugees, 135;
approves Campbell's request for
Negroes, 135n; appoints Cameron

and Browne as Indian superintendents, 138; on war with
Spain, 142–43, 145n, 148n; on
Baton Rouge defeat, 159; on calling
the assembly, 162–63, 163n;
denounces captain of the Carteret,
163; requests assistance for West
Florida, 163; informed of plans for
new fortifications in Pensacola,
184; orders Jamaica to support
West Florida, 187; approves
Campbell's conduct at Battle of
Pensacola, 214–15; mentioned, 50,
128, 136, 141, 144n, 175, 181, 228

Gibraltar, 239, 243

Gibson, Capt. George: mission to New
Orleans, 61–63; carries gunpowder,
63n; mentioned, 64

Girty, Simon, 73

Glover, John, 49–50

Gordon, Hugh Mackay: sickness
among Maryland Loyalists, 131n;
on West Florida, 132–33; bears
message to Gálvez, 200; gives
Campbell sketch of Spanish lines,
206

Gordon, Lt. James, 183, 184

Government, structure in West
Florida, 4

Grampus, 9, 10n

Grand jury, 40

Grand Pré, Col. Carlos, 152

Grant, Dr., 200n

Grant, Gov. James, 36

Gray, James, 7

Graydon, Alexander, 109

Greene, Evarts B., 231

Grenada, 50, 230

Gulf of Mexico, 3, 43, 50, 233

Haldimand, Gen. Frederick: appointed
brigadier for West Florida, 15;
relationship with Chester, 15,
28–29; withdraws troops, 24, 25;
ordered to Pensacola, 26; on
sending troops to the Mississippi
River, 28–29; directs construction
of fortifications, 29; leaves West
Florida, 29; preparations for attack
on New Orleans, 43, 44; evaluates
Spanish troop strength, 44

Hamilton, Peter J., 7

Hand, Gen. Edward: to command
expedition against West Florida,

81; to assist Willing, 82, 84; mentioned, 83

Harrington, Virginia D., 231

Harrison, Reuben: land grant, 111n; and expedition to Natchez, 111–12; joins Willing, 118n; mentioned, 118

Harrison, Richard, 118n

Havana: O'Reilly returns to, 43; Unzaga to obtain supplies from, 63–64; British prisoners at, 109, 158, 212, 213, 235; news of war received, 148; reinforcements from, 175–76, 205; Spanish troops return to, from Mobile, 176; Gálvez visits to obtain support, 193–95; Chrystie in, 235; mentioned, 78, 164, 210

"Headright." See Family right

Health conditions, 6–8

Helms, David, 138n, 182n

Henry, Gov. Patrick: requests Spanish aid, 71–73; on conquering West Florida, 72n; orders G. R. Clark to meet Col. Rogers on return trip, 73

Herrera, Miguel de, 196

Hillsborough, Lord: recalls Browne, 21–22; receives memorials and petitions about troop withdrawal, 24–25; on troop withdrawal, 26; orders troops to West Florida, 26, 27; on probability of war with Spain, 44, 45; and Massachusetts Circular Letter, 45

Hillsborough, 103

Hiorn, William, 86, 111n, 149

Hodges, David, 92n

Holstein, 178

Holston River, 56

Hound: on the Mississippi River, 98, 101, 106, 114; to remain in West Florida, 114; in Pensacola, 176, 188; escorted merchant vessels to England, 189; chased by Spanish fleet, 195

Howard, Clinton, 35, 231

Howe, Gen. William: on fortifications in West Florida, 52; on security of Pensacola, 52; warns of attack on West Florida, 52; and Stuart, 52, 58, 73; on quality of leadership in West Florida, 57–58; on Mobile, 167; mentioned, 53

Huay, Daniel, 33

Huguenots, 18, 18n

Hurricane, 124–25, 150

Hutchins, Anthony: and Willing's raid, 85–87, 108–12; financial losses, 92n; thanked for services, 112n, 124; on captured American property, 119; and establishment of militia, 124; mentioned, 118

Hutchins, Lt. Thomas: ordered not to spend money on fortifications, 57; spy mission to New Orleans, 60; becomes a rebel, 228

Iberville River: clearing of, 8–9; settlement on, 33; construction of post on, 135; inadequacy of, 136; mentioned, 90, 104

Immigration, 32–34, 228–31

Imperialists, 2

Indentured servants, 29, 49

Indians: and Proclamation of 1763, 2; leave Pensacola, 5; British policy toward, 8, 9, 73–77, 177–79; and Gov. Johnstone, 16; peace made, 17; law for regulation of Indian trade, 23; relations during Chester's administration, 28; loyalty, 52, 74, 161, 174; communications with, 54; as source of Anglo-Spanish friction, 59; at Fort Pitt and Wheeling, 63; attacked Col. Rogers, 73; Alexander McGillivray on, 74; British relations with, 74–77, 162; as an ally, 77, 102, 107; attacking Spanish boats on Mississippi, 79; for defense of Natchez, 111; suffering from excessive rum, 113; as scouts near Mobile, 115; and calling of 1778 assembly, 122; commission appointed upon Stuart's death, 137–38; to be used in expedition against New Orleans, 143; presents for, 168; on relief expedition to Mobile, 171; expense in maintaining, 178n; and West Florida Royal Foresters, 182; attack Village of Mobile, 183–84; at Battle of Pensacola, 190, 199, 202, 203, 204–5, 206, 207; assisted in 1781 Natchez rebellion, 217; mentioned, 16, 32, 55, 64, 72, 106, 110, 142, 144, 159, 164. See also individual tribes

Irozabal, Capt. José Calbo de: refused
to enter harbor, 198, 199; sails for
Havana, 199n; sends ships to ferry
troops across the Perdido River,
201; ships under his command,
206n

Jackson, Capt. Michael, 111, 112
Jamaica: reinforced, 123, 144; reinforcements from, 129, 131–32,
175, 176, 178, 189; *Unicorno*
carried to, by *Ulysses*, 206; British
prisoners forbidden to go there,
211; and loyalist migration, 234;
mentioned, 44, 50, 80, 89, 108n,
114, 140, 143, 161, 205, 212, 215
Jamaica squadron, 51
Jane, 188
John and Peter, 116
Johnson, Cecil, 126, 243
Johnson, Isaac, 86, 157n
Johnstone, Capt., 203–4, 210
Johnstone, Gov. George: and
boundaries of West Florida, 3;
details governmental structure, 4;
appointed governor, 9; leaves
England, 9; opinions of, 9, 17;
arrives in West Florida, 10;
evaluates West Florida, 10; initial
actions in West Florida, 10–11;
relations with assembly, 11–12;
disputes with military, 12–15, 15n;
suspends Chief Justice William
Clifton, 14; suspends Attorney
General E. R. Wegg, 14; dispute
with Lt. Gov. Montfort Browne, 15;
relations with the Indians, 16–17;
leaves West Florida, 17; recalled,
17, 17n; later career, 17n; and
"Scotch Party," 18; and land
grants, 29–30; on settlement on the
Mississippi River, 33; and Stamp
Act, 36–42, 232; and Carlisle Peace
Commission, 123, 123n; on attack
against New Orleans, 143n;
mentioned, 8, 122
Johnstone, Isaac, 156–57, 157n
Johnstone, William, 149
Jones, Evan, 23, 23n
Jones, John Paul, 51n

Kaulican, 168
Kennedy, Capt. Patrick, 203

Kenny, Lt., 210n
Keppel, Gen. William, 5
Key, Capt. Philip B., 183
Kingston, Jamaica, 130
Knox, William, 222n

Land: policy, 29–32, 32n; speculation,
30–31, 30n; grants to loyalists,
48–49
Laurens, Henry, 81–82
Lee, Gen. Charles, 61–62
Lee, Richard Henry, 46
Leeward Islands, 161
Legislature of West Florida, 4. *See*
Assembly
Le Montais, Capt., 145n
Leslie, Gen. Alexander, 219
Lewis, Francis, 55
Linn, Lt. William, 62–63
Liverpool, England, 25
Livingston, Philip, Jr.: as Chester's
secretary, 27n; on settlement of the
Mississippi, 33n; opinion on
embargo, 55; mentioned, 127
Lloyd, Capt. Thomas: and im-
pressment, 57; stopped and
searched *Margarita* and *Marie*, 67;
protests Gálvez' ship seizures,
67–68; requested by British
merchants to leave New Orleans,
68; and Gálvez' warning, 70n;
requested to remain in Pensacola,
106; mentioned, 95, 96
London, England, 25
Long Island, 56, 178
Lords Commissioners for Trade and
Plantation. *See* Board of Trade
Lorimer, Dr. John, 235
Love and Unity's Increase, 188
Lowe, Quartermaster, 200n
Loyalist historiography, 245–46
Loyalists: West Florida as a haven for,
vi, vii, 32, 34, 47–50, 219–20;
required affidavit, 48; immigration
to West Florida, 48–50, 242;
condition of refugees, 49–50; fate
of, 224; in West Florida, 225–40,
244; definition of, 226n; factors in
maintaining loyalty in West
Florida, 228–35; emigration from
West Florida, 234–37; claims,
237–40; mentioned, 81, 110
Loyal Refugees: organized, 58; troop

returns, 58n, 112; as defense
against Willing, 103; offense against
Willing's party, 104–5, 104n; sent
to Mobile, 107; new company
established, 114; requested to man
Christianna, 116; on service in
Indian department, 110, mentioned,
108, 110, 111, 179n
Loyalty: oath of, required, 105–6,
173n; of British settlers on
Mississippi River, 118–19;
increased as result of Willing's
raid, 120; mentioned, 77
Lyman, Gen. Phineas, 33

McCraight, James, 89
McDonald, Maj. John, 208
McGillivray, Alexander, 74, 178
McGillivray, John: offer to raise force
to defend Mobile, 55; raises
provincial corps to oppose Willing,
107–8; arrived at Natchez, 112;
ordered to reinforce Manchac, 114;
thanked by assembly, 128n;
mentioned, 153n
McGillivray and Struthers, 56
McIntosh, Alexander, 106, 107
McIntosh, John, 55
McIntosh, William: treatment of, by
Willing, 87; ordered to reinforce
Manchac, 114; his Loyal Refugees
as crew for *Christianna*, 116; urges
retaking of West Florida, 220
McIntyre, John, 33
McIntyre, Lt. Thomas: arrival at
Walnut Hills, 85; arrival at
Manchac, 88; insults Fergusson, 94;
reward for capture of, 109; men-
tioned, 87
Mackinen, Capt. Robert, 14
McNamara, Capt. James, 188
Macullagh, Alexander, 138n
Madrid, Spain, 62, 213
Manchac: J. Willing received town lot,
82; and Willing's raid, 88, 98,
104–5; representation in assembly,
113, 122; establishment of post at,
113, 137, 139, 140, 145; Gálvez
prepares to attack, 148; Spanish
campaign against, 151–54; men-
tioned, 93, 97, 110, 126, 143
Margarita, 67
Marie, 67

Marine Committee, 51n
Marr, Christopher, 216–17
Marshall, John Richmond, 85
Martha, 235n
Martin, John Allen, 238n, 239
Maryland, 50, 230
Maryland Loyalists: at Jamaica, 130,
131; smallpox among, 131n;
Campbell on, 134; combined with
Pennsylvania Loyalists, 161–62;
attack Village of Mobile, 183–84;
troop return, 190; forced to
abandon post, 203; attack on Pine
Hill, 208; migrate to Nova Scotia,
235n; mentioned, 191, 222
Massachusetts Bay, 45, 50, 230
Massachusetts Circular Letter, 45
Maurepas, Lake: boundary of West
Florida, 3; naval protection, 51; as
invasion route, 54; Spanish
prevented from fishing on, 80; *West
Florida* on, 100; *Florida* ordered to,
115; Gálvez wants control of, 152;
mentioned, 103
Maxent, Capt. Maximiliano, 196
Medicine, 62
Meggs, Lt., 203, 210n
Mentor: in Pensacola, 176, 188, 189;
to aid in attack on Village of
Mobile, 183; captures Spanish
vessels, 188n; description of, 189n;
crew augmented garrisons, 191;
warned of Spanish arrival, 196;
fired on Spanish, 196; captures
Gálvez' baggage, 196n; forced to
withdraw, 198, 198n; abandoned
and burned, 204
Mercantilism, 2
Mexico, 62, 151
Middleton, Arthur, 81
Militia: request for establishment of,
123; bill for creation of, 124–25;
proclamation for enrollment of,
146–47; inhabitants request
permission to form, 147; placed
under Campbell, 147n
Miller, Capt. Francis, 134, 200n
Miller, John, 124
Miralles, Juan de, 72n
Miranda, Francisco de, 206n, 209,
210n
Miró, Estevan, 236
Misdale, John, 36

Mississippi River: navigation of, vi, 59; settlements on, 3, 50; boundary of West Florida, 3, 223; migration on, 32, 49; effort to establish lands along as a separate colony, 34; as invasion route, 51, 53, 54, 56; Jones' naval expedition to, 51n; British espionage on, 59–60; Gibson's journey down, to New Orleans, 61; Linn's journey on, 62–63; trade on, 65–69, 113, 120, 228; climate on, 81; Willing's expedition on, 83–102, 117; Spanish goods for Americans on, 109; Col. Rogers' expedition on, 116; and loyalists, 118–19, 236; construction of post on, 135, 136–37; refugees from, 191; British troops on, 233; fertility of, 244; mentioned, 72, 144, 148, 154, 226

Mitchell, John, 103, 138n

"Mitchell's Map of North America," 3

Mobile: occupied by British, 5; population, 5; condition of, 6, 133, 137; poor health conditions in, 6–8; and the assembly, 11, 113, 122, 125–27, 180; troops in, 24, 43, 57; schooners from captured, 50; proposed attack against, 52, 56, 70, 81, 148, 161, 164; possible consequences of loss of, 54; McGillivray's offer to raise defense force for, 55; and Panis mission, 79, 80; and Willing's raid, 102–3, 115, 117; residents requested reinforcements, 105; loyalty oath in, 106, 108; Loyal Refugees sent to, 107; defenses of, 140, 165–67; embargo in, 145; battle of, 161–74; Indian Council at, 162; safety of, 163; map of, 166; reinforcements to sail for, 175; road from, to Pensacola, 176; refugees from, 191; and loyalist emigration, 236; mentioned, 3, 32, 63, 77, 152, 159, 160, 182n, 242, 243

Mobile Bay, 115, 165, 168

Mobile River, 165, 171

Montelle, Marquis de, 205

Moore, Alexander, 23

Moore's Lagoon, 203

Morgan, Col. George: requests Spanish aid, 70–71; plan for attack on West Florida, 81; and correspondence with Gálvez, 82; mentioned, 86

Morris, Robert, 63, 117n

Morris, 117, 117n, 152

Mortar, The, leader of Upper Creeks, 16

Murray, Lord John. *See* Dunmore, Earl of

Natchez: troops withdrawn, 24; post taken over by John Bradley, 25; migration to, 32; Willing received land grant, 82; and Willing's raid, 85–88, 109–12, 118; request for reinforcements, 106, 107; McIntosh to raise troops in, 107; representation in assembly, 113, 122; dispute over command of, 116; loyalists in, 118, 226; Gálvez prepares to attack, 148; support of, 153n; included in Baton Rouge capitulation, 156–57; garrison of, 157n; 1781 rebellion, 213, 216–18; tobacco production in, 236; Spanish census of, 236; mentioned, 80, 97, 99, 126, 149, 154

Nautilus, 10n

Navarro, Diego Josef: forwards news of war to Gálvez, 148; receives instructions concerning expeditions against West Florida, 149; wants naval attack against Pensacola, 164; stopped reinforcements from leaving Cuba, 175; refuses reinforcements for Gálvez, 193

Navy: British, 67–68; American, 83

Negroes, 135. *See also* Slaves

Neil, Arthur, 12, 39–40

Neil's Meadows, 203

Nelson, William H., 245–46

Neptune, 89

Neutrality, 99

New Brunswick, 234

New England, 230

Newfoundland, 46

New Orleans: proposed attack against, 43, 44, 142–43, 143n, 144–45, 147–48, 163; British want it to be part of West Florida, 59; British espionage in, 59–60; as American depot, 60–64, 70–73; defenses, 63, 150; Morgan desires vessels from,

70; Panis returns to, 80; George
Morgan to be sent to, 81; and
Willing's raid, 83, 85, 88, 89,
90–94, 97, 98–100, 108–12, 117;
one of delegates to go to, 87; news
of war arrived, 149; hurricane hits,
150; secured by Baton Rouge
victory, 157; Natchez garrison
arrives at, 157n; prison for English,
158; Spanish troops return to, from
Mobile, 176; reinforcements arrive
from, 201–2; British trade in, 228;
mentioned, 69, 78, 82, 115, 116,
120, 136, 154, 168
New Spain, 65
New York: loyalists from, 49–50, 230;
Willing imprisoned, 117; British
prisoners taken to, 212, 212n, 235;
and loyalist emigration, 234;
Chrystie in, 235; Lorimer in, 235;
mentioned, 26, 27n, 130, 133
Nitalbanie River, 103, 104
Noble, James, 40
Non-exportation agreement, 46
Noopock, Michael, 85n
North, Frederick Lord, 238
North Carolina, 50, 230
Norton, 68n
Nova Scotia: and non-exportation, 46;
and loyalist emigration, 234, 235n;
Chrystie in, 235
Nuestra Señora del Carmen, 158n
Nunn, Capt. Joseph: and Willing's
raid, 98–101; requested to sail to
the Mississippi, 106; on reinforcing
Burdon, 108n; complaints to,
concerning Hutchins' activities,
112; thanked by assembly, 124

Oaths of Allegiance, 8
Odell, Major, 189
Ogden, Nicholas, 117
Ogilvie, William, 92n, 138, 175
Ohio country, 178
Ohio River: as invasion route, 51,
53–54; Gibson's journey on, 61;
proposed post at mouth of, 71, 72;
Willing's expedition on, 83–85
"Old Spanish Cowpen," 55
O'Neill, Arturo, 213
Ord, Capt. George, 63
O'Reilly, Gov. Alexandro: arrived in
Louisiana, 26, 43; size of his force,
26n; raises militia in Louisiana, 44;

evaluates Louisiana, 44; and Oliver
Pollock, 61

Pallas, 50
Panis, Jacinto: spy mission to West
Florida, 60, 79–80, 79n; on
Mobile's reaction to Willing's raid,
102–3; describes Mobile, 167; plan
of attack, 196n; mentioned, 84
Panmure, Fort, 112, 156–57, 217
Parilla, Gov. Diego Ortiz, 4–5
Paris, Treaty of: 1763, 4; 1783,
221–24, 242, 243
Parker, Adm. Sir Peter: and
reinforcements for West Florida,
114–15, 143, 145n, 163, 189–90;
mentioned, 187
Parkman, Francis, 12
Parliament: annual grant to West
Florida, 4, 232; appropriates funds
to assist loyalists, 48; and loyalist
claims, 237–40
Parrish, Lydia, 235
Parry, Adm. William, 25–26
Pearis, Lt. [George?], 104
Pearis, Richard: and Loyal Refugees,
58n; and counteroffensive against
Willing, 103, 104–5, 105n; mentioned, 118
Pennsylvania, 50, 230
Pennsylvania Loyalists: at Jamaica,
130; Campbell on, 134; combined
with Maryland Loyalists, 161–62;
attack Village of Mobile, 183–84;
troop return, 190; at battle of
Pensacola, 208, 209–10, 210n, 211;
vessel carrying, captured, 212n
Pensacola: observations on, 5–6, 23;
health conditions in, 6–7, 7n, 69;
representation in assembly, 11, 113,
122; headquarters for brigadier
general, 15; troops in, 24, 43, 192;
as object of attack, 51, 51n, 52, 70,
81, 115, 148, 161, 164; reinforcements for, 51, 129–32;
Spanish espionage in, 78–80;
Watkins leaves for, 85; and
Willing's raid, 97–98, 102–3;
Hound and Sylph arrive, 101; naval
defense of, 105; loyalty oath in,
105–6, 108; and 1778 hurricane,
124–25; condition of its fortifications, 132–33, 137, 139–40; and
Cornwallis' expedition, 144;

security of, 144n, 163; embargo in, 145; confusion in, following Baton Rouge expedition, 158; necessity of cultivating lands around, 162; West Florida reduced to, 163n; its preparations for Spanish attack, 175–77, 182–92; Indians in, 177; battle of, 196–215; map of battle of, 197; loyalty of inhabitants, 226; and loyalist emigration, 236; mentioned, 1, 26, 32, 39, 49, 54, 60, 63, 64, 77, 83, 104, 107, 113, 114, 116, 126, 135, 136, 152, 159, 160, 171, 182n, 227, 235, 242, 243

Pensacola Bay, map of, 194

Pentzell, Maj. Friedrich, 186

Percy, Charles, 86

Perdido River, 168, 171–72

Perry, Hardy, 84

Philadelphia, Pa.: Linn sails for, 63; Willing paroled to, 117; mentioned, 25, 57, 81, 82

Phoenix, 188

Pickett, Albert James, 7

Pickles, Capt. William, 68n, 152

Pinckney Treaty, 224

Pine Hill, 207, 208–9

Pinhorn, Lt. Joseph, 204

Pitchlin, Mr., 182

Pitt, Fort: possible attack on, 52; American troops assembled at, 57; Gibson's force at, 61; Linn arrives at, 63; and Willing's raid, 83, 84; mentioned, 70

Pittman, Capt. Philip, 6

Point Coupée, 88

Pollock, Oliver: influence over Unzaga, 61; considers himself an American, 61n; on Unzaga and Gibson, 62; offers services to Robert Morris, 63; as agent for Congress, 72–73; sends goods to Virginia, 73; partner of Willing, 82; and Willing's raid, 83, 90, 92, 116–17; reward for capture of, 109; outfitted the Morris, 117n; credit destroyed, 120; on Manchac campaign, 151; and Natchez surrender, 157n; mentioned, 88, 242

Pollock, Thomas, 88

Polly and Nancy, 50

Pontchartrain, Lake: boundary of West Florida, 3; settlement on, 33; naval protection, 51; as invasion route,

54; Spanish vessels on seized, 67; Spanish prevented from fishing on, 80; West Florida on, 100; Florida ordered to, 115; Gálvez wants control of, 152; mentioned, 49, 91, 103, 108

Pontiac's Rebellion, 2, 8

Population of West Florida, 230–31

Port Royal: arrived in Pensacola, 176, 188; remains in Pensacola, 188, 189; crew augmented garrisons, 191; men from captured, 196; fired on Spanish, 196; forced to withdraw, 198; abandoned, 204

Portugal, 65

Prevost, Gen. Augustine: takes possession of Pensacola, 4–5; opinion of Pensacola, 5–6; disparages rumor of American attack on West Florida, 56; on possibility of American attack on East Florida, 56; ordered to place Indian management under Stuart's control, 73; and reinforcements for West Florida, 114; on loyalty of West Floridians, 118

Prince of Wales' Redoubt, 185, 210

Privateers, 50–51, 68

Privy Council, 19

Proclamation of 1763: issued, 2–4; encourages settlement, 12; and land grants, 29, 29n, 31

Provincial troops. See Loyal Refugees; Maryland Loyalists; Pennsylvania Loyalists; Royal Volunteers; West Florida Royal Foresters

Puerto Rico, 222

Quebec, 45, 46

Queen's Redoubt: constructed, 185; and Battle of Pensacola, 205n, 206, 207, 209–10; mentioned, 215

Quit rents, 47

Rainsford, Andrew, 138n

Rapicaut, M., 92n

Rattletrap, 84

Rea, Robert, 243

Rebecca, 88, 92, 152

Red Cliffs, 57, 185–86, 198, 201

Rees, Huberd, 170

Reid, William, 119n

Resource, 189–90

Rhode Island, 135, 230

"Robert Farmar's Journal." See
 Farmar, Maj. Robert
Roberts, Charles, 57, 116
Robinson, Lt. Col. John, 49
Rogers, British officer exchanged for
 Willing, 117
Rogers, Col. David, 72–73, 116
Romans, Bernard, 228
Ross, Alexander, 90, 102n, 220
Ross, Robert, 99n, 109, 221
Routh, Jeremiah, 118n
Royal Navy Redoubt: constructed,
 185–86; surrender of, 186n, 211;
 sailors at, 191; fired on Spanish,
 196, 199, 201, 202, 206; in-
 effectiveness of, 199n; British
 retired to, 200; Spanish decision
 not to attack, 211n
Royal Volunteers, 191

St. Augustine: troops transported to,
 24–25; troops leave for West
 Florida, 26; Stuart arrives at, 75;
 reinforcements for, 129–30; Spanish
 plans to attack, 148n; British
 prisoners forbidden to go there,
 211; mentioned, 15, 23, 49, 114,
 212
St. Catharine's Creek, 33
St. John, 75
St. John, Bayou, 151
St. Joseph and St. Joachim, 212n
St. Kitts, 51n
St. Louis, Missouri, 73, 120
St. Patrick's Day, 12, 232
St. Vincent, 50, 230
Sally, 212n
San Juan, Bayou de, 100
San Lorenzo, Treaty of. See Pinckney
 Treaty
San Pio, 195, 201
San Ramón, 195, 198, 199
Santa Cecilia, 195
Santa Clara, 195
Santa Rosa Island: fortifications on,
 186–87; Spanish land on, 196;
 Spaniards left to defend, 202;
 mentioned, 199, 215
Savannah, Ga., 50, 74–75
"Scotch Party," 18
Second Creek, 33
"Separate Article," 223
Shakespear, Stephen, 92n, 99n
Shelburne, Earl of: on inexpediency of

an Indian war, 16; recalls Gov.
 Johnstone, 17; instructions to
 Browne, 17; comments on
 Johnstone's administration, 17;
 petitioned by London merchants,
 222–23
Ship Island, 115, 116
Siguenza Point, 196, 199n
Simpson, Capt. Andrew, 14
Slaves: and land grants, 29; belonging
 to loyalists, 49; proposal for
 exchange of runaways, 80; and
 Willing's raid, 87, 88, 97; at Fort
 Charlotte, 167; in Galvez' force
 against Mobile, 168; at Battle of
 Pensacola, 190–91, 202, 202n;
 population, 231; mentioned, 89, 90
Smallpox, 131, 131n
Smith, Adam, 222
Smith, Paul H., 143, 245–46
Smuggling, 47, 65–69
Solano, Josef (Chief-of-Squadron),
 205, 206n
Southampton, 92, 103, 105
South Carolina: loyalists from, 49, 50;
 John Stuart flees, 74; as a loyalist
 haven, 220–21; immigration from,
 230; mentioned, 81
South Carolina Royalists, 49
Spain: aid to Americans, vi, vii; cedes
 Florida, 1; evacuates Pensacola, 5;
 threat to West Florida, 26, 27;
 dispute over Falkland Islands, 43;
 relations with British, 43, 57, 59;
 assistance to Americans, 59, 60–64,
 70–73; efforts to alienate British
 Indians, 74; espionage, 78–80;
 rights as a neutral, 79; and
 Willing's raid, 89–102; declares war
 on England, 141, 142, 142n; West
 Florida's lack of loyalty, 233–34;
 and war with England, 242, 243
Spanish Fort. See Village of Mobile
Stamp Act, 36–42, 232
Steady Friend, 68n
Stephenson, John: investigates ship
 seizures, 69; on Panis' mission, 80;
 on possibility of Spanish war,
 102n; messenger from Chester to
 Gálvez, 202–3, 204
Sterling, Lt., 183, 184
Stevens, Capt. [Alexander ?], 199
Stiell, Lt. Col. William: requested to
 assist in construction of for-

tifications, 54; evaluates troops in West Florida, 54, 58; Indian policy, 76n; sends troops to the *West Florida*, 103; on reinforcements for Mobile, 105; requested to reinforce troops on Lake Pontchartrain, 106–7; and reinforcements for Natchez, 107; orders troops to Manchac, 113; reinforcments requested of, 116; on 1778 hurricane, 125

Stork, 114–15, 188

Strachan, Charles, 9

Strachan, Patrick, 172n, 174, 174n

Strothers, Arthur, 124

Struthers, William, 55–56

Stuart, Charles, 138, 177

Stuart, Henry, 87, 90, 90n

Stuart, John: loses authority, 28; warned of attack on West Florida, 52; and Loyal Refugees, 52–53, 58, 103, 105n, 107, 114, 135; opinion on American invasion, 53–54; southern Indians under his direction, 73–74; forced to flee South Carolina and Georgia, 74–75; Indian policy of, 74–77; wife escapes, 75n; orders guard at Walnut Hills, 84; criticized by Germain, 84; sends Bethune to Natchez, 111; requested to send out scouts, 115; on use of the *Christianna*, 115–16; death, 137; on West Florida loyalists, 226; mentioned, 56, 79, 107, 108, 134

Suffrage, 11

Sugar Act, 36

Sutton's Lagoon, 203, 204

Swayze, Rev. Samuel, 33

Sylph: ordered to the Mississippi, 92; British inhabitants refuse to board, 97; leaves Mississippi, 101; ordered to Manchac, 114; to remain in West Florida, 114; survives 1778 hurricane, 124; mentioned, 93, 94, 95, 98, 103

Tacon, Capt. Andrés, 208

Taitt, David, 53, 138n

Taitt, Robert, 226

Tally, John, 111

Tartar Point, 185, 186, 200

Taxation, 232

Tayler, Col. William: appointed acting brigadier, 15; disgust with Johnstone, 15n; requested to erect fortifications, 16; conciliates Indians, 17

Tennessee, 56

Tensa, 171, 172

Tensa River, 171

Thistle, 50, 57

Thomas, John, 28, 92n

Thompson, Joseph, 86

Thompson, Primrose, 41

Thompson's Creek, 152

Tombeckby, Fort, 5

Tombigbee River: migration on, 32, 33; as invasion route, 56; settlers on seek permission to form a militia, 147; mentioned, 5

Tonyn, Gov. Patrick, 56, 237

Tories. *See* Loyalists

Toulouse, Fort, 5

Townshend Acts, 36, 45, 232

Trade: West Florida as center for trade with the Spanish, 2; Gov. Johnstone on, 10; prohibited to West Florida, 46; prohibited with rebellious colonies, 47; Anglo-Spanish rivalry, 59; New Orleans as American depot, 60–64; British trade in New Orleans, 64, 228; Anglo-Spanish, 65–69; Franco-Spanish, 66; Anglo-Franco-Spanish, 66n; Indian, 74, 80; petitions of British merchants on the Mississippi, 113; interrupted by Willing's raid, 119; closed on Mississippi, 120; protection of, 135

Treasury, Lords Commissioners of, 143

Treaty of Paris. *See* Paris, Treaty of

Turner, John, 217

Ulysses, 189–90, 205–6

Unicorno, 205–6

United Corps of Pennsylvania and Maryland Loyalists, 162

Unzaga y Amezaga, Gov. Luis de: and Falkland Islands dispute, 44; receives and meets with Gibson, 61–63; replies to Lee's request for aid, 62; ordered to assist the Americans, 63–64; Chester protests his cordiality toward Gibson, 64; ignored smuggling, 65

Valenzuela, 168, 169, 198
Van Tyne, Claude H., 232
Vera Cruz, Mexico, 43, 158
Vicksburg. *See* Walnut Hills
Village of Mobile, 183–84
Virginia: loyalists from, 50, 230; planning attack on West Florida, 57; Committee of Safety, 61; goods for, 73; use of black troops in, 220; mentioned, 72
Volante, 168
Von Hanxleden, Col. Johann Ludwig Wilhelm, 183–84

Waldeck, Chaplain Philipp: on West Florida, 132; describes confusion in Pensacola following Baton Rouge expedition, 158; on flight of *Carteret*, 163n; on high cost of living, 178n; on construction of Fort George, 186n
Waldeck, Third Regiment of: at Jamaica, 130; reaction to West Florida, 130, 132; Campbell on, 133; sent to Manchac, 149; fifty-five captured, 152; prisoners in New Orleans, 158; desertion among, 180n, 193n; attacks Village of Mobile, 183–84; troop return, 190; attack on Pine Hill, 208; mentioned, 121, 157
Walker, Capt. Charles, 170
Walnut Hills (present-day Vicksburg), 61, 84, 85
Walsh, Lt. Col. Ralph, 12, 14, 40, 41
Washington, George, 57, 212n
Watauga, 178
Watkins, John, 85–86
Watts, Stephen, 40, 153, 153n, 171
Wealth of Nations, 222
Wedderburn, Col. David, 9
Wegg, Edmund Rush: suspended, 14; on Stamp Act, 38, 40; Gov. Johnstone's opponent, 39; and letter from Continental Congress, 46, 233; opinion on embargo, 55; on committee to establish a militia, 124; mentioned, 42

Wells, Samuel, 86
Welsh, Robert, 84, 85, 87n
West Florida: retained in Pensacola, 54; seized Spanish vessels engaged in contraband trade, 67; detained on Bayou de San Juan, 100; troops sent to reinforce, 103; captured, 152; mentioned, 80, 113
West Florida Royal Foresters: at Mobile, 170, 174; as part of relief force, 172n; attacked by Indians, 182; attacked Spanish near Mobile, 182; attack Village of Mobile, 183–84; troop return, 190; skirmish against Spanish lines, 204–5; desertion among, 211; disbanded, 235; mentioned, 161n, 179n, 234n
West Indies: West Florida as source of supplies for, 47; loyalists from, 49, 50, 230; mentioned, 62
Wheeling, West Virginia, 63
Whissel, William, 200n
White Cliffs, 111–12
Williams, Capt., 115, 116
Williams, William, 217
Willing, James: efforts to obtain backing, 81–83; background, 82; leads raid, 84–91; released Welsh, 87n; losses caused by raid, 92n, 239; reward for capture of, 109; extended stay in New Orleans, 116–17; leaves New Orleans, 117; captured, 117; analysis of raid, 118–21; impact of raid, 129; captured *Rebecca* at Manchac, 152; joined by West Floridians, 227–28; raid and loyalty of West Florida, 232; mentioned, 27, 29, 58, 59, 70, 73, 77, 78, 80, 105n, 111, 128n, 153n, 156, 180, 226, 233, 241, 242
Willing, Thomas, 82
Willing and Morris, 82

Yamasee Indians, 5
Yazoo River, 3, 84, 223, 224
York, Fort. *See* Tombeckby, Fort
Yorktown, battle of, 243